THIRTY-FIVE YEARS OF
NEWSPAPER WORK

Thirty-five Years of Newspaper Work

A Memoir by

H. L. MENCKEN

Edited by
FRED HOBSON
VINCENT FITZPATRICK
BRADFORD JACOBS

The Johns Hopkins University Press

Baltimore and London

Frontispiece: H. L. Mencken at forty-two. 1922. E. O. Hoppé.

© 1994 The Johns Hopkins University Press
All rights reserved
Printed in the United States of America on acid-free paper

03   02   01   00   99   98   97   96   95   94   5   4   3   2   1

The Johns Hopkins University Press
2715 North Charles Street
Baltimore, Maryland 21218-4319
The Johns Hopkins Press Ltd., London

ISBN 0-8018-4791-5

Library of Congress Cataloging-in-Publication Data
will be found at the end of this book.

A catalog record of this book is available from the British Library.

In Memoriam

Carl Bode, 1911–1993

CONTENTS

Contents

INTRODUCTION

When, on my father's death, as I was eighteen, I was free at last to choose my trade in the world, I chose newspaper work without any hesitation whatever, and, save when the scent of a passing garbage-cart has revived my chemical libido, I have never regretted my choice. More than once I have slipped out of daily journalism to dally in its meretricious suburbs, but I have always returned repentant and relieved, like a blackamoor coming back in Autumn to a warm and sociable jail. It was the printing press that left its mark, not only upon my hands, face and clothing, but also on my psyche.

    —Henry Louis Mencken
      Happy Days (New York: Alfred A. Knopf, 1940), p. 212

Rather flatly, as if he were tallying the contents of one more cigar box, H. L. Mencken labeled this book "Thirty-five Years of Newspaper Work." By that time (1941–42), true, he had written for newspapers for thirty-five years. It is also true that he was superb at it—Alistair Cooke calls Mencken "the master craftsman of daily journalism in the twentieth century"[1]—and that these pages give a detailed account of high spots and low. What that cigar-box label conceals, however, is something more vibrant, something close to personal passion.

To be sure, Mencken was a confusing bundle of enthusiasms. He wrote thirty books and contributed to twenty more—the output of several lifetimes for ordinary people. For a famous spell he delighted in literary criticism. While he and George Jean Nathan edited the monthly *Smart Set* from 1914 to 1923, Mencken applauded the literary rebels who spurned the Genteel Tradition. Because of his efforts, American writers gained more freedom to discuss the subjects of their choice in the language that best suited their ends. With the *American Mercury*, which he helped to establish in 1924 and ran with consummate skill from 1925 to 1933, this iconoclast became, to his embarrassment, an icon himself. William Manchester has called Mencken "the last of the great cultural editors."[2]

In another mood, Mencken discovered that politics set before him a huge array of delightful horrors; his flamboyant coverage of presidential nominating conventions still piques the envy of today's reporters. Hypochondriacal, he was fascinated by medicine. Music was his first love and provided lifelong solace. Words themselves proved an endless curiosity; *The American Language* ran to four editions and two supplements. Mencken concluded, quite incorrectly, that he would be remembered best for his philology.[3]

These were sideshows. Nothing enthralled him as much as the sweaty, contentious world of daily journalism that he inhabited, with two interruptions, for nearly fifty years. By his own account he was a journalist first of all.[4] From Baltimore he wrote—at different times—for the New York *Evening Mail*, the *Chicago Sunday Tribune*, and the New York *American*. His columns occasionally appeared through syndication in other parts of the country. Early on, he served as the American correspondent for newspapers in Japan, China, and Ceylon. But he was most taken with the world alleged to have revolved around the Baltimore *Sunpapers*. He could have gone elsewhere, many times, for a higher salary, but money was never what motivated him. In his preface to this volume, he makes a confession: "The attempt to make a great newspaper of *The Sun* was an adventure that I enjoyed thoroughly, and there were times when it almost took on to me the proportions, considering my generally unsentimental view of things, of a great romance."

He could have gone further. He could have added without exaggeration that the *Sunpapers* filled a void in his own family life and that, for the *Evening Sun* in particular, he cheerfully strode forward as journalistic father, mentor, bully-in-chief. With all its quirky contrariness, the *Evening Sun* replaced the one exasperating joy that Mencken on rare occasions desired but never had: a child of his own.

If together the two newspapers furnished the lifeline of his adult years, it was a union scarcely more serene than any other romance. Here burned a relationship at once loving and tempestuous, as slyly scheming as it was steadfastly loyal. Over the years, inspiration wrestled with near calamity. Personal spats left serious bruises. Journalistic styles collided. Tempers blazed, sizzled, and died morosely, but sturdy friendships grew as well. During Mencken's years, a once humdrum newspaper became a highly creative enterprise and a swelling audience looked on as prizes brightened the *Sun*'s ascent. Its ultimate decline, if that is indeed what it was, Mencken attributed to failings widespread across the American scene.

———

Mencken was by long odds the paper's most visible figure; for a number of readers, "Mencken" and the *"Sunpapers"* were all but synonymous. He played many roles: writer and editor, talent scout and in-house evaluator, and, in later years, member of the board of directors and chief negotiator with the Newspaper Guild. To our present age of specialization, the range of his columns seems even more staggering. He wrote about books and music, politics and religion, food and fashion, sports and philology. John Owens, the papers' editor-in-chief, assessed Mencken at forty-nine as "incomparably the most brilliant man engaged in journalism in America."[5] Yet it is putting Mencken too high to suggest that the *Sunpapers'* glory years would have gone unachieved without him. The principal point—and everyone on the newspaper knew it—was that Mencken commanded center stage: restless with those less quick than he, impatient with conventional moralisms, always pushing for vigorous style and genuine quality.

Characteristically, he refused to equivocate. The paper, he insisted, must resist all outside pressures to shape its ideas. His belief in the need for a fierce independence permeates this volume. It is perhaps most cogent in Mencken's lengthy account of the 1934 dispute with the Baltimore *Catholic Review,* an uproar generated by an ill-advised comparison that led to a boycott by Baltimore's Catholic community. Mencken also proclaimed that the *Sunpapers* must serve as part of America's adversary culture by providing lively and unceasing opposition to the incumbent political party. "[W]hen a scoundrel is on the block," Mencken insisted, "he ought to be denounced in plain terms, and without any judicial tenderness. So with fools. So with fool ideas."[6] With huge delight he pummeled the Prohibitionists and celebrated home-brew. He relished the bizarre and the indelicate and gloried in the farcical proceedings in Dayton, Tennessee— the trial of the "infidel Scopes"—where the attorney for the prosecution, a man nominated three times for the presidency of the United States, thundered that man is not a mammal. If little proved sacred, then it was for the simple reason, as Mencken saw things, that very little deserved to be.

How entertaining it is, in our current technological age, to picture Mencken pecking away with two fingers at his old and battered Corona, chewed cigar in mouth and spittoon alongside, rising regularly to wash his hands, as if some of his subjects were somehow unclean, and quickly producing glorious copy that required little revision. He saved many of his typescripts; to read them is humbling. His expertise seems almost unfair.

At the outset, when shaping his own obstreperous style, Mencken had turned to George Bernard Shaw. Shaw's wit, a deceptively soft weapon for driving home a hard lesson, taught one how to tickle a reader into at least tentative acceptance of an otherwise spiky idea. Mark Twain did the same for Mencken, adding a rich overlay of Americanism—and this in newspapers. So did Finley Peter Dunne, "Mr. Dooley," and Will Rogers, Mencken's contemporary and friend. Wit and humor, sometimes at the cost of reasoned judgment, were their hallmarks.

Mencken's words leaped and sparkled. He injected them into the paper's news columns and editorial pages. In "The Free Lance," which ran daily from 1911 to 1915, Mencken jabbed at local politicians and visionaries, at homeopaths and antivivisectionists, and at moralists, whom he dubbed, with his flair for neologism, "snouters" and "virtuosi of virtue."[7] Baltimoreans had never seen such a column before, and they never would again. His "Monday Article," which ran weekly from 1920 to 1938, generally proved even more rousing. He entitled his first column, about the presidential aspirants, "A Carnival of Buncombe." The House of Representatives became "The Asses' Carnival," and America's overcrowded schools were lampooned as "Educational Rolling Mills." President Harding's oratory, which Mencken was forced to endure in Washington in early 1921, was scorned as "Gamalielese," a spoof on the chief executive's middle name. His inaugural address reminded Mencken of "a string of wet sponges," "tattered washing on the line," and "dogs barking idiotically through endless nights."[8]

Working to infuse his own vitality throughout the paper, Mencken tried to influence the entire staff. From his huge range of contacts in the literary world, wider by far than that of any of his colleagues, he recruited bright young journalists. With Harry Black in 1919 he wrote the "White Paper" that set forth the parameters for what a great newspaper must do—and must not. Not everyone could, or would, obey instantly, and Mencken grew angry. He treated even Paul Patterson, the paper's president, with only tentative respect. Mencken was so bellicose that he admitted that Patterson had every right to fire him.[9] But, because of his eminence outside the *Sun,* the sense and urgency of his expostulations inside, and Patterson's wise tolerance, Mencken managed to exert wide influence although he held no formal authority at all.

Mencken's dualism, one of his personal oddities, plainly emerges in this volume. Many pages seethe with caustic commentary upon his *Sun* colleagues. How curious it is to read on and find a placid account of a lunch, a dinner, an after-hours drink (often proposed by Mencken) happily shared with the man denounced on the previous page. But maybe this was not so odd after all. Philip Wagner, himself alternately praised and disdained, believes that Mencken reserved his irritation primarily for ideas contrary to his own but could still cherish the man who disagreed.[10]

This quirk followed Mencken beyond the newspaper. Dr. Howard Kelly, a distinguished Baltimore physician of fiercely Christian principle, was subjected publicly to Mencken's ridicule. Personally, however, Mencken found the venerable doctor, one of Johns Hopkins Hospital's "Big Four," rather admirable. Another victim was Gerald L. K. Smith, publicly denounced as a reactionary zealot but privately regarded by Mencken as entertaining. Although Mencken mocked Bishop Cannon and his Anti-Saloon League of America, the two men enjoyed each other's company. Curiously, Mencken the agnostic accomplished something that has eluded many conventionally religious people: he could look past the sin and embrace the sinner.

By the early 1940s, when he was composing this volume, Mencken had learned far more about human frailty and imperfection than he might have preferred. His marriage of five years had been immensely happy—"a beautiful adventure," he had called it—but Sara Haardt Mencken had been dead since 1935. "Now I feel completely dashed and dismayed," the usually stoical Mencken had then lamented. "What a cruel and idiotic world we live in!"[11] His best friend, Dr. Raymond Pearl, had died in 1940. Many other friends were ill. His own health was failing; throat, heart, and blood pressure proved troubling. He did hospital time and was warned, unsuccessfully, to slow down.

Some of the events outside hardly made Mencken more sanguine. At odds with the *Sun,* he no longer wrote for the paper. Long before December 7, 1941, World War II had rumbled in the distance. In Mencken's view, wily England was once again conning America into a war not its own. Germany, Mencken's ancestral home, suffered sizable loss of life at Soviet hands. About much of this Mencken said little.

There was also, however, a brighter light coloring these memoirs. Mencken in his early sixties had attained a literary and journalistic pinnacle, and he knew it. The treacherous years of the 1930s, when one newspaper spoke acidly of "the late H. L. Mencken," were behind him.[12] His career had been reinvigorated by the considerable success of the first two volumes of the *Days* trilogy, one of the most delightful autobiographies ever produced in America. The observations in the present volume are acute, the manner confident. His ability to tell a story remains unimpaired, as even the most cautious new reader must admit.

A relaxed Mencken tells his story as if he were reminiscing over evening drinks in front of the fire with his faithful brother August. Events run more or less chronologically. To a considerable extent, the language is stripped of Menckenian glitter. Masterful with analogy, he offers here relatively few of those extended metaphors and similes that he loved to concoct when he was writing at the top of his lungs. But Mencken was one of America's finest humorists, perhaps its greatest after Mark Twain, and his wit, as expected, graces this volume. He laughs at the grotesquely humorous efforts of men and women to deal with one another, pokes fun at the Socialist Robert Rives La Monte living in regal splendor, and ridicules the American South as a "Pellagra Belt." He gratefully recalls, from his salad days, a colorful hymn proclaiming "There Are No Flies on Jesus." For the most part, though, the humor tends to be restrained, eliciting a chuckle rather than a guffaw. Characteristically, this volume shows him as an observer of himself as well as others, sparing nobody.

It also proves revealing of Mencken's ideas. He was a derivative thinker and never tried to hide the major influences upon his thought: Charles Darwin, Herbert Spencer, Thomas Henry Huxley, and Friedrich Nietzsche. Like the rest of Mencken's canon, "Thirty-five Years" displays a skeptical individualist who endorsed common sense, extolled competence in all fields, and believed that life's fundamental problems are essentially insoluble. He distrusted democracy—"the art and science," he snorted, "of running the circus from the monkey cage"—and scoffed at the supposed virtues of the average American.[13] For him, the typical economic victim in America was not one of life's unfortunates but rather that individual who acquired competence at a trade, paid the bills, and refused to yell for help during bad times.

Not surprisingly, Mencken excoriated President Franklin Roosevelt's New Deal, which he saw as a profanation of the traditional American work ethic. Mencken was hardly alone in his reservations; other prominent journalists such as Walter Lippmann and Dorothy Thompson questioned the policies of this man whom the great majority of Americans celebrated as the country's savior from the Depression. Yet Mencken's fury was so pronounced and his attack so prolonged that he surprised even a number of his friends. Along with Woodrow Wilson and William Jennings Bryan, Roosevelt descended into Mencken's triumvirate of shame; in his eyes they were, respectively, liar, fool, and thief. Deal the cards anew, again and again, was always the gist of Mencken's rejoinder to Roosevelt's scheme. But if the game naturally runs its course, the competent player will invariably leave the table with more money than he brought, and the incompetent player will inevitably go home a loser. You may mean well, Mencken said, in essence, but you are misguided and dangerous. You cannot restructure American society because you cannot change the nature of man.

Hardly in vogue during Mencken's time, such thinking has become even less fashionable during our own fiercely egalitarian age. America changed greatly between 1906 and 1941; Mencken's fundamental convictions remained the same. By his own admission, he was an unsentimental person, and this volume details, both literally and metaphorically, his unsentimental journey from young adulthood to his sixty-first year.

Portions of this memoir amount to a travel diary, recording in detail several trips to Europe, particularly Germany. One section describes Mencken's stint, a brief one, as war correspondent, in Berlin and on Germany's Eastern Front in January and February 1917. He recalls his adventures with great relish, and he records them exactly twenty-five years later, just as another war is raging in Germany. He notes with good humor the hardships of a seventeen-day, mid-winter voyage on the Danish *Oscar II,* a virtual ship of fools with Danes, Norwegians, Swedes, Germans, and a walrus-like Russian general on board. At the front he nearly freezes in temperatures plunging to forty degrees below zero, and then, back in Berlin, he manages to be the first journalist out—at a time when foreign correspondents were forbidden to leave for eight weeks after returning from the front. On his way home, sailing into Havana, he runs into a week-long revolution in Cuba and stays around to cover that. This account clearly reveals Mencken's immense gusto for his work, as well as the resourcefulness and industry that helped to make it so distinguished.

Even more revealing are the narratives detailing the trips to Germany in 1922 and 1938. Mencken confronts here both his own spiritual alliance with Germany and, particularly in 1938, the country's dark side: anti-Semitism. When he had first traveled to both England and Germany in 1908, it was in England that he felt most at home—a product of his early apprenticeship in English literature and history. However, World War I had changed all that. Like many other German-Americans, Mencken suffered considerably because of his heritage. His mail was opened, and he feared for the safety of his mother and sister in the face of mob violence. Jingoists masquerading as literary critics assaulted him repeatedly, and during the war he was denied the opportunity to defend himself. The bitterness developed then never left him. Understandably, he approaches the home of the Menckens in 1922 with more German self-consciousness than ever before. He arrives in Munich during Oktoberfest, stays with a German friend who had been detained in America during the war, and reports a "grand time." Outwardly, all is serene. Mencken hears nothing of Hitler, who was in Munich at the same time, but is aware of skirmishes between Communists and Bavarian soldiers. He notes that "every intelligent man looks for a catastrophe. If it comes, then there will be a colossal massacre of Jews."

When he returns during the summer of 1938, this massacre is, of course, well under way. On November 9, *Kristallnacht* would disgrace Germany. However, in the section of "Thirty-five Years" given to this six-week stay, he betrays little sense of alarm. One might contrast Mencken here with another American Germanophile, Thomas Wolfe, who had visited Germany two years earlier and returned to the United States with a rage to explain the horrors of the Hitler regime. Employing the device of third-party commentary, Mencken makes note of the persecution of Jews and reports that "every German" he encounters "looked upon the war as inevitable," but he is curiously calm about it all. It is clear that he has traveled to Germany not to write about German politics— he does not even send back dispatches to the *Sunpapers*—but rather to revisit an earlier Germany, the land of his fathers, for what he feels (correctly, as it turns out) will be the final time.

His disinclination to write publicly about this 1938 trip, as well as his virtual silence (except in letters to friends) about Germany's treatment of the Jews throughout the 1930s, leads inevitably to that subject which seems to arise nearly every time Mencken's name has been

xvi

mentioned since publication of his diary in 1989: his own alleged anti-Semitism. This has become by long odds the most controversial, and problematic, issue pertaining to Mencken's life and work. Both sides can be argued with equal effectiveness. In truth, a hundred of Mencken's statements over the years, both in print and in his correspondence, could be cited to "prove" him anti-Semitic, and a hundred other statements and actions could be marshaled to "prove" that he was not.

From the time of his *Treatise on the Gods* in 1930 until the posthumous publication of the diary, Mencken certainly seemed at times to vilify the Jews. In the diary he sometimes referred to Jews as "kikes," and in letters he spoke of "professional Jews" and "hysterical Jews" and expressed a belief that "the Jews probably deserve their problems." He also insisted that in Germany Jews should be "kept within bounds."[14] Nonetheless, not only some but many (for a time, *most*) of his best friends and closest professional acquaintances—Alfred A. Knopf, George Jean Nathan, Philip Goodman and Louis Cheslock among them—were Jewish. In the early days of World War II Mencken invested a great deal of time and effort and assumed considerable financial risk in helping a number of Jews escape from Europe to the United States. In a 1938 column entitled "Help for the Jews," Mencken attacked President Roosevelt's refusal to relax the immigration laws: "he is sorry for the Jews, but unwilling to do anything about it that might cause him political inconvenience at home." Mencken proceeded to argue that "there is only one way to help the fugitives, and that is to find places for them in a country in which they can really live. Why shouldn't the United States take in a couple of hundred thousand of them, or even all of them?"[15] In brief, this issue is more complicated than some of Mencken's detractors have made it seem.

What Mencken writes of Jews in "Thirty-five Years" casts more light on this complicated subject. On the one hand, from the mid-1930s on, Mencken had some sympathy for those German friends who believed that the Jews brought on some of their own troubles. However, it is also clear—in this volume and elsewhere—that he detested Hitler and his regime for a number of reasons. As a libertarian, Mencken despised all totalitarian governments with their contempt for human rights. In his eyes, Hitler resembled the worst sort of political demagogue found in the American South. As a royalist, Mencken wanted a restoration of the German monarchy—and Hitler he saw as the ranting evidence of a democracy gone mad. As partisanly German as he was, Mencken refused to join the Friends of Germany and other American pro-German groups. Quite significantly, this memoir also makes it clear *why* he refused to condemn Hitler publicly throughout the 1930s. With American Jews demanding that he use the *Evening Sun* to denounce Hitler "categorically and at once," his response was typical: "In the face of their attempt to browbeat me I could only refuse to write a line."

In matters of race as well as ethnicity, the Mencken of "Thirty-five Years" is largely consistent with the Mencken of the other published works. Conditioned by his family and his German-American Baltimore childhood, he held certain stereotypes about Jews, just as he held stereotypes about Russians and Poles, Italians and Greeks, southern poor whites (on whom he was the roughest) and African-Americans. He loved the vernacular, and his impulse to use colorful language helped to generate such painful racial references as "blackamoors" and "niggeros" and "darkies." Unfortunately, sound sometimes mattered more to Mencken than sense did, comic intent more than sensitivity.

And yet, Mencken could prove far more enlightened. His most representative statement about race combines common sense with common decency: "Personally, I hate to think of any man as of a definite race, creed, or color; so few men are really worth knowing that it seems a shameful waste to let an anthropoid prejudice stand in the way of free association with one who is."[16] He numbered blacks among his friends and had them to his home for dinner—a situation far more unusual during the 1930s than it is today, especially for a white man who considered himself a Southerner. During the 1920s, he did more than any other editor to help African-American writers, and Countee Cullen praised "the intrepid Mr. Mencken."[17] As "Thirty-five Years" points out, he used the *Evening Sun* to attack lynchings on Maryland's Eastern Shore, an area that he viewed as shamefully un-Reconstructed. His attacks caused the paper financial risk, and there were threats that Mencken would be wise not to cross the Chesapeake Bay. Here, as elsewhere, he was never afraid. Finally, in matters of race and ethnicity, Mencken was, like the rest of us, imperfect. Yet he was also a staunch defender of civil liberty for all people regardless of heritage, color, gender, or social class.

Mencken's account of this remarkable career may well generate speculation about its relevance today. Anniversaries invite reassessment, and we are approaching the centennial of Mencken's first newspaper piece in February 1899. An equally significant landmark is the impending fiftieth anniversary of his final column in November 1948. It is worth pointing out that, when Mencken was born, the Linotype had not yet been invented—that when he began his career some small newspapers were still setting type by hand. When he signed on with the Baltimore *Herald,* the paper had no morgue (a subject file of published stories) and only two telephones. All of this now seems a long time ago indeed. Do we read his columns in the same way that an archaeologist examines cuneiform? Would Mencken, were he alive today, find employment in the profession that he graced as so few American journalists have?

His lack of formal education would definitely hinder him in our specialized age with its proliferation of baccalaureate and advanced degrees. He graduated, first in his class, from the Baltimore Polytechnic Institute at age fifteen and was then spared, he remarked caustically, "the intellectual humiliations of a college education."[18] One learns to write by writing, Mencken believed, not by sitting in a classroom and talking about writing. Russell Baker asserts that "Mencken would be unemployed in today's journalism world, for he had no use for journalism schools, which now control access to newspaper jobs."[19] He would certainly not be hired by today's metropolitan daily with the credentials that he presented in 1899: a high-school education and no experience. But let us conjecture, for the sake of argument, that he would persevere and find a job on a rural weekly and then become so highly skilled— certainly a reasonable assumption—that his clippings would convince a city paper to take him on.

Once employed, could he write now as he wrote then? It has been said that a sizable portion of Mencken's copy would be killed today. He would be too combative and irreverent, the argument goes, to be trusted in today's highly litigious age, where a hyperbolic sentence, indeed an unrestrained adjective, can generate huge monetary judgments. Mencken was libeled repeatedly, yet he never sued. That was not his way; he found it unsporting. Instead, working within the limits of the law, he took the opportunity to thrash his opponents at the typewriter. Many came to wish that they had left him alone. "Mencken was a supreme rhetorician," Philip Wagner has observed. Far from being scientific, his use of words was aesthetic. He used them as an artist uses color and a musician the arrangement of notes in clusters—to play upon the senses and emotions of his readers, to make them laugh, sigh, weep, go along with him, grind their teeth in fury, and to put across his point whether it was intrinsically worth making or just a piece of wayward mischief."[20] Were he writing today, he would abhor the greater restraints, but he certainly would produce copy that would be legally unassailable.

A close observer of his trade, keenly aware of the fluidity of the journalistic world, he could make the other necessary adjustments as well. He would perhaps write shorter columns now, about seven or eight hundred words instead of the fifteen hundred in which he loved to cavort. His paragraphs and sentences might diminish in length by fiat of television-influenced editors; and, because he would be addressing a less literate audience, the diction would grow more colloquial. Many of the foreign terms that he scattered throughout his prose would have to be translated, if not dispensed with entirely. There is little doubt that he would hone his style until it reached out and caught today's readers with the same power that fetched them yesterday.

And what editor, hungry as ever for circulation, would dare say no? If anything, contemporary newspapers move toward Menckenesque commentary rather than away from it. Op-Ed pages bristle everywhere, the product of only the last few decades. To fill them up, editors now buy written commentary bundled up in syndicated packages; no longer can they afford to grow their own. The result is that the great observers of the American scene—the likes of Ben Franklin, Tom Paine, that breed to which Mencken gave an especially zestful character—now emerge as national, not local, figures.

If Mencken were alive today, he would not lack material. He would continue to lampoon all visionaries and castigate the thought police, be they on the political Right or Left. Mencken believed that the great masses of the plain people would never grow discriminating and that a glut of quacks would always compete garishly for attention. Our age has not proven him wrong. He would howl at tearful televangelists and air-conditioned doghouses, at tabloid sightings of Elvis Presley's face on yet another lucky person's back screen door, at congressional perks and a debate in which a presidential candidate's most memorable line was "Where's the beef?" Mencken hated moralists and loved a well-turned phrase. How he would roar at the grotesque euphemisms concocted in the name of political correctness. Mencken viewed life in his native land, which he laughingly labeled a "glorious commonwealth of morons," as far more comic than tragic.[21] Many things have changed in this country since Mencken's time. Fortunately however, America's gargantuan potential for the absurd has not diminished. Mencken's commentary would continue to prove both trenchant and salubrious.

NOTES

1. Alistair Cooke, ed., *The Vintage Mencken* (New York: Vintage Books, 1990), v.
2. William Manchester, *Disturber of the Peace: the Life of H. L. Mencken* (New York: Harper & Bros., 1950), 216.
3. See Mencken, "Autobiographical Notes, 1941" (Enoch Pratt Free Library).
4. Mencken, "Henry Louis Mencken," in *Portraits and Self-Portraits,* collected and illustrated by Georges Schreiber (Boston: Houghton, 1936), 106.
5. Quoted by Mencken, "Thirty-five Years of Newspaper Work," manuscript p. 565 (Enoch Pratt Free Library).
6. Mencken to Paul Patterson, July 21, [1928], in *The New Mencken Letters,* ed. Carl Bode (New York: Dial Press, 1977), 223.
7. Mencken, "The Free Lance," Baltimore *Evening Sun,* July 8, 1911.
8. These columns appeared in the Baltimore *Evening Sun* on February 9, 1920; January 31, 1921; April 16, 1923; and March 7, 1921.
9. Mencken, "Thirty-five Years of Newspaper Work," manuscript p. 491 (Enoch Pratt Free Library).
10. Philip Wagner to Bradford McE. Jacobs, July 29, 1992, letter in possession of Jacobs.
11. Mencken to Ellery Sedgwick, June 7, [1935], in *Letters of H. L. Mencken,* ed. Guy Forgue (New York: Knopf, 1961), 392.
12. Elrick B. Davis, Cleveland *Press,* July 20, 1935; quoted by Carl Bode, *Mencken* (Carbondale: Southern Illinois University Press), 313.
13. Mencken, *A Mencken Chrestomathy* (New York: Knopf, 1949), 622.
14. Mencken, *The Diary of H. L. Mencken,* ed. Charles A. Fecher (New York: Knopf, 1989); Mencken to Tom R. Hutton, August 20, 1937 (New York Public Library); Mencken to James Cain, August 19, 1940 (NYPL); Mencken to Benjamin de Casseres, August 3, 1935 (NYPL); Mencken to Anna Mencken, April 13, 1935 (Enoch Pratt Free Library).
15. Mencken, "Help for the Jews," Baltimore *Evening Sun,* November 27, 1938.
16. Mencken, "The Library," *American Mercury* 23 (May 1931): 125.
17. Floyd Calvin, "Interview with Countee Cullen," *Pittsburgh Courier,* June 18, 1927. Quoted by Charles Scruggs, *The Sage in Harlem: H. L. Mencken and the Black Writers of the 1920s* (Baltimore: Johns Hopkins University Press, 1984), 26. This volume offers an insightful, thoroughly documented discussion of Mencken's dealings, as editor and critic, with African-American writers. See also Fenwick Anderson, "Black Perspectives in Mencken's *Mercury,*" *Menckeniana* 70 (Summer 1979): 2–6.
18. Mencken, "Under the Elms," Trenton (N.J.) *Sunday Times,* April 3, 1927; in *A Mencken Chrestomathy,* 132–33.
19. Russell Baker to Bradford McE. Jacobs, September 16, 1992, in possession of Jacobs.
20. Philip Wagner, *H. L. Mencken* (Minneapolis: University of Minnesota Press, 1966), 30–31.
21. Mencken, "On Being an American," in *Prejudices: Third Series* (New York: Knopf, 1922), 18.

NOTE ON THE MANUSCRIPT
AND EDITORIAL METHOD

Mencken had a healthy contempt for chaos and was ever mindful of posterity. In 1930, the year of his fiftieth birthday, he began his diary, the first of the multivolume projects eventually consigned to time-lock at the Enoch Pratt Free Library in Baltimore. (To forestall its loss in the event of local disaster, Mencken sent some of this same material to the New York Public Library and the Dartmouth College library.) Covering 1930 to 1948, the diary became public on January 29, 1981, twenty-five years after Mencken's death. Edited by Charles A. Fecher and published eight years later, *The Diary of H. L. Mencken* (New York: Alfred A. Knopf, 1989) generated considerable controversy. On the same day the library broke the seal to the diary it made two other manuscripts available to scholars: four volumes entitled "Letters and Documents Relating to the Baltimore *Sunpapers*" and three volumes called "Notes and Additions to the *Days* Books." Neither has been published.

In January 1991, thirty-five years after Mencken's death, the library adhered to the terms of the gift and opened two more of his projects: "My Life as Author and Editor" in four volumes, which Jonathan Yardley edited and Alfred A. Knopf published, and three volumes entitled "Thirty-five Years of Newspaper Work." These two sets of memoirs make up the final papers that Mencken consigned to prosperity. He managed his career from the grave with much the same skill he exhibited while alive.

As Mencken notes in his own preface, he began "Thirty-five Years" in 1941. He wrote quickly (sometimes as many as 3,000 words per day), finished his narrative in March 1942, and completed revisions in May of that year. He thus composed this memoir at the same time that he worked on the diary and collected the documents that went into his volumes on the *Sunpapers*. In places these projects employed the same material and overlapped.

Once Mencken completed revision of this manuscript, his secretary, Mrs. Rosalind C. Lohrfinck, typed the fair copy that Mencken placed in time-lock. We may deduce this part of the story from the neatness of the pages: Mencken's typing usually contained more errors, words struck over, and idiosyncratic spacing. Too, one finds in the time-lock copy few of his usual upper-case letters situated between lines and relatively few corrections in Mencken's hand. The author apparently did not save his first draft, for, after all, he wanted to ensure the manuscript's security.

The editors have followed the general rule of maintaining the integrity of the time-lock text, preserving, for example, journalistic usages that differ from preferred style in our own day. Misspelled proper names have been silently emended; the editors have corrected obvious typographical errors.

More important, they have pruned a massive original manuscript in order to make it publishable in a single volume. Mencken's narrative text runs to 1,391 typescript pages broken into ninety-eight untitled chapters. Thirty appendixes, differing widely in subject matter and length, run to another 257 typescript pages. Mencken (who estimated that the total approached 520,000 words) heavily annotated the text, identifying persons and making asides with great frequency and sometimes with manifest delight. He interleaved these notes on the same pages as the matters to which they refer.

To aid readers in appreciating Mencken's strong feelings about the rightful role of newspapers in American life and his objections to the rise of the liberal state in the 1930s, the editors have chosen to print two of Mencken's appendixes. Out of the narrative portion of the memoir, the editors have selected some 650 full or partial pages—about 45 percent of Mencken's text. Most of the cuts involve whole paragraphs. In a few instances the editors have deleted sentences within paragraphs or introduced paragraph breaks. For the sake of simplicity and readability, this printed text omits ellipses—the usual trappings of editorial excision—except where the editors have shortened material that Mencken quoted at length in the original manuscript. Chapter beginnings and endings occasionally coincide with Mencken's own beginnings and endings; where they do not (or where chapters are missing), extra space in the text marks the end of one chapter and the beginning of another in the original. In a few places the editors have chosen to publish Mencken's annotation (in whole or in part); in those cases it appears within curled brackets at or as near as possible to the point where Mencken marked its placement. Square brackets enclose editorial explanation. Fuller comment and a few factual corrections appear in notes at the bottoms of appropriate pages. The editors' Dramatis Personae identifies the principal figures whom Mencken mentions in the published text.

In "Thirty-five Years," Mencken comments on local, national, and international issues. In selecting material for publication, the editors have tried to do justice to Mencken's immense variety of interests, and thus this book should appeal broadly. It provides a cache of Americana and demonstrates Mencken's sense of consternation as well as delight as he looks upon his world.

These selections present Mencken abridged but not bowdlerized. In view of the uproar generated by the publication of the *Diary*, it should be said here that the editors have made no effort to remove controversial material or ungenerous references. Given Mencken's long and ardent defense of free speech, such censorship would have been unconscionable. Much to his credit, Mencken feared no one, never courted public approval—"I don't give a damn," he once snorted to Theodore Dreiser, "what any American thinks of me"—and wrote exactly what he thought. All of these attitudes are obvious, as they should be, in the edited version of "Thirty-five Years." Most probably, this volume will continue a tradition begun many decades ago: Mencken will enthrall some and outrage others.

The complete typescript of "Thirty-five Years of Newspaper Work" is of course available to serious researchers at the Enoch Pratt Free Library, Baltimore, Maryland.

The images we have selected to illustrate this volume belong to the Pratt Library's H. L. Mencken Collection and are used with the library's permission.

CHRONOLOGY

1880   Born in Baltimore (September 12) at 811 W. Lexington Street.

1883   Family moves to 1524 Hollins Street.

1896   Graduates at age 15 from the Baltimore Polytechnic Institute, a high school (end of formal education).

1899   Death of August Mencken, Sr., January 13; Mencken begins journalism career as reporter for Baltimore *Morning Herald;* first story runs on February 24.

1900   Takes first trip (for his health) outside the United States, to Jamaica.

1901   Becomes drama critic of *Herald,* September; becomes editor of *Sunday Herald,* October (continues until October 1903).

1903   Becomes city editor of *Morning Herald,* October (continues until August 1904); *Ventures into Verse* is published.

1904   *Herald* printed in Washington and Philadephia after Baltimore's Great Fire, February; covers Republican National Convention, Chicago, June 19–24; covers Democratic National Convention, St. Louis, July 5–11; becomes city editor of *Evening Herald,* August 25; Saturday Night Club is established.

1905   Becomes managing editor of *Herald;* publication of *George Bernard Shaw: His Plays.*

1906   *Herald* folds, June 17; serves as news editor, Baltimore *Evening News,* June–July; accepts job on Baltimore *Sunday Sun,* July 25 (continues until April 18, 1910).

1908 First trip to Europe, March; assumes additional duties as editorial writer for the *Sunpapers;* begins monthly book review article
for the *Smart Set* magazine, November (continues until December 1923); publication of *The Philosophy of Friedrich Nietzsche.*

1909 Edits and also writes introductions and notes to Henrik Ibsen's
A Doll's House and *Little Eyolf.*

1910 Charles Grasty purchases *Sunpapers* from Abell family, March;
Baltimore *Evening Sun* established, April 18, with Mencken
as one of the editors (continues until December 1916); ghost-
writes Leonard Hirshberg's *What You Ought To Know About
Your Baby;* publication of *The Gist of Nietzsche,* arranged by
Mencken, and *Men Versus the Man,* an epistolary debate with
Robert Rives La Monte.

1911 Begins "The Free Lance" column in the Baltimore *Evening Sun,*
May 8.

1912 Trip to England, France, Switzerland and Germany, April; publication of *The Artist: A Drama Without Words.*

1913 First meets Alfred A. Knopf.

1914 H. Crawford Black syndicate purchases A. S. Abell Company;
trip to Europe with George Jean Nathan and Willard H. Wright,
April; publication of *Europe After 8:15,* with Nathan and
Wright; Charles Grasty resigns from the Baltimore *Sunpapers,*
September; Mencken and Nathan become co-editors of *Smart
Set,* October.

1915 Cessation of "The Free Lance" column, October 23.

1916 Sails to England, December 28; proceeds to Germany to report
on World War I; publication of *A Book of Burlesques* and *A Little Book in C Major.*

1917 Returns to United States, March; begins to write for *New York
Evening Mail,* June 18 (continues until July 8, 1918); "The Sahara of the Bozart," an indictment of the cultural sterility of the
American South, published on November 13; "A Neglected Anniversary," Mencken's facetious "history" of the bathtub, appears on December 28; publication of *A Book of Prefaces* (the
first of Mencken's books issued by Alfred A. Knopf) and *Pistols*

for Two, written with George Jean Nathan under the pseudonym "Owen Hatteras."

1918   Publication of *Damn! A Book of Calumny* and *In Defense of Women.*

1919   Paul Patterson becomes president of the A. S. Abell Company; publication of *The American Language* (First Edition) and *Prejudices: First Series.*

1920   Begins "Monday Articles" for Baltimore *Evening Sun,* February 9 (continues until January 31, 1938); covers Republican National Convention, Chicago, June 7–13; covers Democratic National Convention, San Francisco, June 26–July 7; "divorce" between Baltimore *Sun* and *Evening Sun,* October; publication of *Prejudices: Second Series, The American Credo,* written with George Jean Nathan, and *Heliogabalus,* written with George Jean Nathan; publication of *The Anti-Christ* by Friedrich Nietzsche, translated and with an introduction by Mencken.

1921   Covers the Disarmament Conference in Washington, D.C., November–December (a final column appears on January 9, 1922); publication of *The American Language* (Second Edition).

1922   Trip to England and Germany, August–October; publication of *Prejudices: Third Series.*

1923   Meets Sara Powell Haardt of Alabama and Goucher College, his wife-to-be, May; Mencken and Nathan resign as co-editors of the *Smart Set,* December (magazine continues publication until 1930); publication of *The American Language* (Third Edition).

1924   First issue of the *American Mercury* magazine, with Mencken and Nathan as co-editors, January; covers Republican National Convention, Cleveland, June 9–13; covers Democratic National Convention, New York City, June 23–29; first column appears in the *Chicago Tribune,* November 9 (columns continue until January 29, 1928); publication of *Prejudices: Fourth Series.*

1925   Nathan withdraws as co-editor of the *American Mercury,* February; covers the trial of John Scopes in Dayton, Tennessee, July; death of his mother, Anna Abhau Mencken, December 13; publication of *Americana, 1925;* appearance of the first two books devoted entirely to Mencken: Ernest Boyd's *H. L. Mencken* and Isaac Goldberg's *The Man Mencken: A Biographical and Critical Survey.*

1926 In the most famous censorship case of his career, Mencken challenges the Boston Watch and Ward Society after the *American Mercury* is banned because of a story entitled "Hatrack," April; begins train journey through the American South and ends in California, October; publication of *Notes on Democracy, Prejudices: Fifth Series,* and *Americana, 1926.*

1927 Publication of *Prejudices: Sixth Series* and *Selected Prejudices.*

1928 Covers Pan American Conference, Havana, January; covers Republican National Convention, Kansas City, June 11–16; covers Democratic National Convention, Houston, June 23–30; covers Al Smith campaign tour, October 12–30; publication of *Menckeniana: A Schimpflexikon* (a collection of abuse heaped upon Mencken); *American Mercury*'s circulation reaches 84,000, its zenith under Mencken's editorship.

1930 Covers London Naval Conference, January–February, and travels in Germany; sails for home on February 13; marries Sara Powell Haardt in Baltimore, August 27 and travels to Canada on honeymoon; publication of *Treatise on the Gods;* begins diary (published as *The Diary of H. L. Mencken,* 1989).

1931 Uproar on Maryland's Eastern Shore after Mencken publishes "Monday Articles" attacking lynchings there, December.

1932 Trip to West Indies with Sara, January; covers Republican National Convention, Chicago, June 13–18; covers Democratic National Convention, Chicago, June 26–July 2; publication of *Making a President.*

1933 Further uproar on Maryland's Eastern Shore after Mencken attacks second lynching, October; Mencken resigns as editor of the *American Mercury,* December (Knopf sells magazine in 1934; magazine continues publication until 1980).

1934 Trip to the Mediterranean with Sara, February–April; writes first column for the New York *American,* July 9 (last column appears on April 22, 1936); joins the board of directors of the A. S.

Abell Company, October 15; delivers speech to the Gridiron Club in Washington, D.C., December 8; publication of *Treatise on Right and Wrong.*

1935 Death of Sara Haardt Mencken from tubercular meningitis, May 31; Mencken and his brother August sail for England, June 15.

1936 Leaves the apartment at 704 Cathedral Street that he had shared with Sara and returns to 1524 Hollins Street, March; *New Yorker* publishes the first of the character sketches later used in the *Days* trilogy, April 11; covers Republican National Convention, Cleveland, June 8–13; covers Democratic National Convention, Philadelphia, June 22–28; covers Townsend Convention, Cleveland, July 14–20; covers Coughlin Convention, Cleveland, August 13–18; covers Landon campaign tour, August–October; publication of *The American Language* (Fourth Edition).

1937 Edits *The Charlatanry of the Learned* by Johann Burkhard Mencke; publication of *The Sunpapers of Baltimore,* written with Frank R. Kent, Gerald W. Johnson, and Hamilton Owens.

1938 Serves as temporary editor of Baltimore *Evening Sun,* January 24–May 9; begins "Sunday Articles" for *Sun,* May 16 (continues until February 2, 1941); travels in Germany, June–July; appointed Chairman of the *Sunpapers'* committee negotiating with the Newspaper Guild, summer.

1939 "The Baltimore *Sun* Goes Down" is published in *The Nation,* February 4; suffers minor stroke, "generalized arteriosclerosis," July.

1940 Covers Republican National Convention, Philadelphia, June 22–29; covers Democratic National Convention, Chicago, July 13–19; covers Willkie campaign tour, August–November; death of Dr. Raymond Pearl, Mencken's closest friend, November; publication of *Happy Days.*

1941 Stops writing for the *Sunpapers* because of disagreement with the policy concerning President Roosevelt and World War II, February 2; travels to Havana, April; publication of *Newspaper Days.*

1942 Begins *My Life as Author and Editor;* publication of *A New Dictionary of Quotations.*

1943   Publication of *Heathen Days.*

1944   Refuses an offer from the *Sunpapers* to attend the presidential conventions as a spectator.

1945   Publication of *The American Language: Supplement I.*

1946   Publication of *Christmas Story.*

1947   Suffers minor stroke, August; publication of *The Days of H. L. Mencken* (one-volume edition of the trilogy).

1948   Rejoins staff of *Sunpapers;* covers Republican National Convention, Philadelphia, June 19–22; covers Democratic National Convention, Philadelphia, July 10–15; covers Progressive Party Convention, Philadelphia, July 23–26; writes 16 articles for the *Sun,* the last an attack upon segregation, August 1–November 9; suffers massive stroke which robs him of the ability to read and write, November 23; publication of *The American Language: Supplement II.*

1949   Publication of *A Mencken Chrestomathy.*

1955   Publication of *The Vintage Mencken,* edited by Alistair Cooke.

1956   Dies in his sleep of a coronary occlusion, January 29; posthumous publication of *Minority Report: H. L. Mencken's Notebooks.*

DRAMATIS PERSONAE

The year 1920 marked the beginning of a remarkable confluence of talents at the Baltimore *Sun*, something Mencken called "a great romance . . . almost." A short cast of the leading characters:

Walter W. Abell (1872–1941). Grandson of the ink-stained founder of the Baltimore *Sun* (established in 1837), Arunah S. Abell (1806–1888), son of Edwin F. Abell (1840–1904), Walter served as president of the A. S. Abell Company from 1904 to 1909 and thereafter remained highly visible in *Sunpapers* affairs.

Francis F. Beirne (1890–1972). Earlier a *Sun* reporter, he began in 1931 writing "The Rolling Road" column of light, miscellaneous pieces that irked Mencken.

Van Lear Black (1875–1930). Elder son of H. Crawford Black, who made a fortune in Western Maryland coal before investing heavily in the *Sun*, this Black became chairman in 1914 and reorganized the paper's finances. Mencken admired him, partially; Black liked business and loved fun, and he could afford it.

Harry C. Black (1887–1956). Van Lear's younger brother followed him as chairman of the A. S. Abell Company and served until his death. A man of grace, charm, and money; backing Mencken and Patterson, he elevated the *Sunpapers* to their finest years so far, beginning in 1920.

James Bone (1872–1962). London editor of the *Manchester Guardian* between 1912 and 1945, he was an informal guardian of the *Sun*'s London correspondents. Mencken distrusted him.

Edmund Duffy (1899–1962). *Sun* cartoonist with a stark, powerful style. Three times a Pulitzer Prize winner during his years at the *Sun*, 1924–1948, he was sometimes more liberal than the paper.

J. Fred Essary (1881–1942). As a cub reporter and stringer for the *Sun* in 1903, he broke the story of the Wright brothers' flight at Kitty Hawk. Essary later served as *Sun* Washington bureau chief for most of the years between 1912 and 1941. A gentleman of the old school, he dug for news in Washington wearing a homburg and carrying a walking stick.

Vincent dePaul Fitzpatrick (1885–1953). Worked for Baltimore *News* before joining *Sunpapers*, which in 1920 he left to become managing editor of the Baltimore *Catholic Review*.

Charles H. Grasty (1863–1924). Charming, aggressive, some said arrogant new publisher of the *Sun* in 1910, he hired Mencken as Sunday editor and later founded the *Evening Sun*. He resigned in 1914 amid financial troubles.

R. P. Harriss (1903–1989). A North Carolina-born reporter who joined the *Evening Sun* news staff in 1927 and then made his mark writing editorials.

Gerald W. Johnson (1890–1980). Another North Carolinian, he joined the *Evening Sun* staff in 1926 and between 1939 and 1943 contributed to the *Sun*. He wrote more than forty books. An office rebel and liberal, office Southerner and stylist, Johnson could approach Mencken's stature but never equal it. Mencken despised him for, among other things, being Southern and soft on the New Deal.

Frank R. Kent (1877–1958). A *Sun* and *Evening Sun* managing editor and rival of Paul Patterson, he was best known between 1923 and 1958 for writing the nationally syndicated column (for many years the only syndicated *Sun* column) "The Great Game of Politics."

Folger McKinsey (1866–1950). After working for Baltimore *News* and Washington *Post*, he joined the *Sun* in July 1906 and became locally famous for his daily column of verse and light commentary under his pseudonym, The Bentztown Bard.

J. Edwin Murphy (1876–1943). Legendary managing editor of *Evening Sun*, 1920–39, he was a demanding editor who "ruled the premises with thunder and lightning."

Hamilton Owens (1888–1967). Editor of *Evening Sun,* 1922–38; editor of *Sun,* 1938–43; and editor-in-chief of *Sunpapers,* 1943–56. Less fixed philosophically than his distant cousin John, more flexible on office policy than the defiant Mencken, Owens was a debonair writer. His *Evening Sun* editorials were saucy, fey, disorderly—delightful to all but those he needled. To Mencken's annoyance, he temporarily embraced the New Deal.

John W. Owens (1884–1968). Appointed editor of the *Sun* in 1927, he received a Pulitzer Prize for distinguished editorial writing in 1937 and then served as *Sunpapers* editor-in-chief from 1938 to 1943. Owens believed that facts were sacred, opinion free. A man of intellectual balance and old-fashioned liberalism, he ruled the opinion pages after 1938. His forceful morality intimidated Patterson and drove Mencken into spasms of anger.

Paul Patterson (1878–1952). *Sunpapers* president, 1919–51. Less talented than Mencken, less graceful than Harry Black, less ideological than John Owens, Patterson (known to staff members below decks as *PP*) had a quality denied the others—a leader's patience, specifically a knack for harmonizing the discordant voices of willful, opinionated men. He recognized Mencken's promise as a writer and let it bloom.

William F. Schmick, Sr. (1883–1963). Vice president of A. S. Abell Company, 1924; executive vice president, 1934; president, 1951–60. Possessed of a superb businessman's mind, he was indispensable in keeping the paper clear of fiscal hazards.

Neil H. Swanson (1896–1983). Executive editor, *Sunpapers,* 1941–54. Flamboyant, dictatorial, maybe cruel, Swanson was perhaps the most highly professional newsman either the *Sun* or the *Evening Sun* ever produced. Mencken believed so, but since Swanson worked in news rather than editorials, he appears in these pages more as an icon than as a participant.

Philip M. Wagner (1904–   ). Editor, *Evening Sun* editorial page, 1938–43, and editor, *Sun* editorial page, 1943–63. More professor than what-the-hell journalist, he asked for style, fairness, and depth—for research and documentation, not just the rhetoric of the past. Mencken seemed never to figure him out.

Richard Q. Yardley (1903–1979). Joined the *Evening Sun* in 1923 and in the 1930s began drawing cartoons that whimsically borrowed from styles as disparate as Early Ming, Bayeux Tapestry, Persian rug, and prehistoric cave dweller. He filled "maps" of Baltimore and Maryland with characters and details reflecting his puckish sense of humor.

THIRTY-FIVE YEARS OF
NEWSPAPER WORK

Preface

This record was born of my experience while at work on "Happy Days" and "Newspaper Days." I found then that it was a dreadful nuisance, in the midst of a flowing narrative, to have to stop every now and then to verify a name or a date: worse, I found that my recollection, when thus put to the test, often turned out to be inaccurate, and sometimes grossly so. The first of those books covered the period from my birth to 1892 and the second that from 1899 to 1906. When "Newspaper Days" was finished and proof-read, in July, 1941, I determined to draw up a documented schedule of the rest of my life, with all names and dates checked, on the chance that I might want to do another volume or two later on. This schedule, it appeared at once, would have to be divided into two roughly equal parts, as my life had been—the one dealing with my activities as a newspaper man, and the other with my doings as a writer for magazines, an editor thereof, and an author of books. It is the first, or newspaper part that here follows. I assumed, at the start, that it would run to no more than 50,000 words, but once I had got into it I turned up so many documents and recalled so many things forgotten that it soon became a really formidable record. I decided, however, to let it run on, feeling that, in such a log-book, it would be better to put in too much than too little. Also, I added reflections from time to time, for they flowed out of the story quite naturally, and often seemed an integral part of it. A great deal of the material that finally got itself on paper will never be of any use for the sort of writing I had in

A portrait of the journalist as a young man, about 1903. John Siegel.

mind, but there was no telling as I went along what would be useful and what not.

I have tried to ascertain the exact truth in all matters of the slightest significance, and to set it forth without equivocation. In autobiography, of course, that is really not quite possible. The best any man can do, in such a work, is to record events and estimate men as they appeared to *him*, with a large allowance for prejudice, false judgment and every other sort of human fallibility. Naturally enough, I have laid chief stress upon events in which I had a direct hand, and men with whom I was in close contact. Many things went on in the *Sun* office between 1906 and 1941 in which I had no part, and of which I heard only vaguely, if at all. But it is fair to say, I think, that I was usually in a position to see the inner workings of the machine, and that I had a share of some influence in operating it, at least until toward the end of the 30's. At that time, to my considerable distress, I began to suspect that it would be eternally impossible to make a really first-rate newspaper of the *Sun,* and so my interest in it gradually lessened. But to this day (1942) I remain a director in the publishing corporation, visit the office an average of three times a week, and am usually informed in advance of all important projects. My connection with the paper may terminate in unpleasantness at any moment, for I continue to dissent from and protest against its present editorial course, but meanwhile I continue on reasonably good terms with all the brethren, and do not afflict them with too much back-seat driving. It may be that they are right, and I am wrong. I can only describe the flow of events as my own eye saw them, and my own peculiar principles interpreted them.

As I have said, this record was undertaken for my own use only, but as it grew and grew I began to realize that it was probably too late in life for me to utilize it according to my original plan. As the years had accumulated my strength had declined, so that I could no longer work as steadily and as diligently as aforetime; moreover, there had appeared signs of disease which warned me that my remaining days in this vale might not be long. But I was still able to go on, and it soon occurred to me that much of the material I was putting together had some interest of its own, and maybe even some importance, as a contribution toward the history of American journalism in my time, and even toward the general history of the country. Now that the job is done at last, I can only lay the manuscript on the shelf, for large parts of it are not printable as they stand, at least at present. Later on, when time has released all confidences and the grave has closed over all tender feelings, my narrative may be useful and even instructive to persons coming after, and so I have arranged for its preservation. By that dim tomorrow most of what follows will have become moot, and there will be no harm in plain-speaking. I have laid on blame when it seemed to me to be due, but I hope I have avoided the crasser sorts of malice, and I am sure that no grievance has animated me. My whole disposition, in truth, is against the cherishing of grievances, for I am too much of a determinist to see anything resembling tort in human folly. All my life long I have managed to keep at peace with men who have differed from me most violently, though I hold to my ideas more tenaciously than most, and can't recall any of the slightest importance that I have ever abandoned. The attempt to make a great newspaper of the *Sun* was an adventure that I enjoyed thoroughly, and there were times when it almost took on to me the proportions, considering my generally unsentimental view of things, of a great romance. That it failed is no argument, by my philosophy, against the men who, as I think, were responsible for that failure. Within the limits of their capacities and their imagination they did their level damndest, and angels could have done no more. If, from time to time, I deal with this or that one harshly, I want it to be understood that I remained completely convinced, save for a few exceptions, of their good faith. All such exceptions are noted explicitly.

That I was always right and the other fellow always wrong I do not argue or believe. There were, in fact, plenty of occasions when the other fellow was right and I was wrong, and I have not tried to conceal those occasions. But this, after all, is *my* story, and so I do not apologize for its pervasive subjectivity. I believe that my influence on the *Sun,* taking one day with another, was for the good, and left some marks, however faint. Certainly it was always thrown upon the side of every honest enterprise, and against every sort of cheapness and false pretense. I advocated telling the truth under all circumstances, no matter how high the cost of unearthing it or how serious the risk in publishing it. I was opposed to the *Sun* having any truck, open or covert, with any professional politician, reformer or other rogue with fish to fry, whether domestic or foreign. In the field of administration I was in favor of paying all members of the editorial staff, however humble, the highest possible wages, and of making them secure in their jobs against everything save their own hopeless incompetence or deliberate malfeasance. I advocated, both as a director and before I joined the board, longer vacations, full salaries in sickness, generous care of the superannuated, and help whenever needed by the families of the dead. I don't recall ever supporting any move that would

4

have diminished in the slightest the security or dignity of any good newspaper man or woman of the staff. My lifelong prejudices against fraud in all its forms set me against the fakes who occasionally turned up, and I did my best to put them down, but I don't think I ever attempted an injury to any competent person, though some of them I disliked. In matters of policy, as opposed to personnel, I argued first and last, in season and out of season, for making the *Sun* a really independent, courageous and forthright newspaper, with no predisposition save for the truth and making no compromise with imposture in any form. It was, of course, a program that constantly collided with human weakness and the nature of things, and so it was necessary, from time to time, to effect compromises, but when they were made with my consent they were surely not made with my approval.

My advantage, during all the years of my connection with the *Sun*, lay in my unusual disinterestedness. Unlike almost every other man in the place, I was not dependent upon the paper for my livelihood; moreover, I had no desire for executive office, and everyone knew it. Thus I could speak freely when others had to keep silent, and more than once, I fear, my doing so made me unpopular. But I don't think that that unpopularity was ever general, and certainly it was never prolonged. I had another advantage, and sometimes it counted heavily: I was the only member of the staff, over long years, who had what might be called a definite position outside. I was known to many more people than anyone else in the office, and I knew many more people, and many more kinds of them. Thus, if it was to my interest, as it was to my pleasure, to continue as a *Sun* man for many years, it was also to the interest of the *Sun*, during most of those years, to have me do so. I gained thereby a kind of authority that gave me more freedom than most of my colleagues had, and I could fight for ideas and causes that would have been otherwise forlorn. More than once, I fear, I was stimulated to such battles by a mere love of combat—a weakness that has got me into trouble off and on since my earliest days. But on the whole, I believe, I kept the good of the paper in mind, and when a war was lost I forgot it as soon as possible.

The period covered by my story was an extraordinarily interesting and fateful one for American journalism. News enterprise advanced very rapidly in my time, and though the old authority of editorial writers diminished and finally vanished almost altogether, there was a compensatory rise of what came to be known as columnists, and I was myself one of them. Simultaneously, newspapers became more prosperous than they had ever been before, and with their growing solvency there came a

5

growing honesty. Unhappily, that growth in solvency also brought with it a change in the point of view of newspaper proprietors, and it was for the bad. Once they had been interested primarily in propagating opinions, but now they devoted themselves almost exclusively to merchandising, and it often became difficult, if not downright impossible, to distinguish them from other merchants. There was less of that commercial spirit on the *Sun* than on most other papers, but nevertheless it showed itself, and my narrative will show how it influenced men who, at the start, held it in vast contempt. As I write, there is another turning of the tide, and the American journalism of the next generation seems likely to face serious and maybe even insuperable difficulties. I'll be gone by the time its test comes, but my narrative, I hope, shows the way the shadows are already falling. Newspapers, in truth, are always either rising or falling. It is rare for them to remain static, and it is rare for one of them to survive as long as the *Sun*, whether up or down. Publishing them, though it has become big business, can never become really sound business. Its hazards are many and ineradicable, and soon or late they will fetch every present adventurer, even if they do not fetch the company of adventurers as a whole.

The principal figure in the narrative following is Paul Patterson, my close associate for thirty years, and my almost daily intimate until we began to differ so radically over the current war (1942) that we took a little distance to avoid useless quarrelling. My narrative points out some of his defects as a publisher. He has, in fact, some bad ones, most of them originating in his somewhat bleak background. But I believe that he is nevertheless an extraordinarily competent man, and that such progress as the *Sun* has made since 1914 is due more to him than to any other, or indeed than to all others put together. I am moved to say this, without doubt, largely because he and I have usually agreed, but I want it to stand for times when we have not. I think he has failed to make the *Sun* the really great newspaper that it might have been, but he has certainly taken it some distance along the road. As it stands today, it has some shocking deficiencies, but also some striking merits. For those merits he is to be given credit. He stopped short before his job was done, but while he was under way he was always shrewd, bold and resourceful, and sometimes he was magnificent.

H. L. Mencken

I

Young Editor Out of a Job

1906–1910

When the Baltimore *Evening Herald* suspended publication on June 17, 1906, and I found myself a young editor out of a job, the first offer of employment that reached me came from Charles H. Grasty, publisher of the *Evening News*. My acquaintance with Grasty, at that time, was rather slight, though I had met him more than once. Back in 1901 or thereabout his managing editor, Folger McKinsey (The Bentztown Bard) had offered me a place on his reportorial staff, and during the years following Grasty himself had twice done the same. I refused every time, but on one of these occasions I had a considerable palaver with Grasty, and heard him expound his philosophy of journalism. It appeared to be grounded on a relentless and mainly unfriendly scrutiny of public affairs, and especially of local affairs. He gave me to understand that he regarded all professional politicians as suspicious characters *ex officio,* and that he believed it was the duty of a newspaper to assume the worst about them at all times, and never to have any truck with them. Inasmuch as this attitude, as he presented it, seemed to be devoid of moral indignation, and was thus sharply differentiated from that of the reformers who were then beginning to afflict the United States, I saw nothing in it to cavil at. It had led Grasty, in the years before 1895, to carry the *News* into an attack upon the reigning powers of Maryland that resulted in a political revolution of the profoundest sort, and his fame, in 1906, filled Baltimore. Indeed, he had brought the *News* to such a position that it was challenging the ancient hegemony of the *Sun.* So when he now asked me to become his news editor I accepted at once, and went to work at once, without the loss of a single day. To be sure, he offered me only $40 a week, which was certainly not princely, but it was $5 more than I had been getting on the *Herald*; moreover, my *Herald* salary, for months past, had been paid only in part, and, toward the end, not at all. I was to succeed Stuart Olivier, who became managing editor. Within the week Grasty left Baltimore for a trip abroad, leaving Olivier in command. I got on very well with Olivier, and in fact remain on friendly terms with him to this day (1942), but I had no sooner begun work on the *News* than I discovered that the method of its operation was such as to give much uneasiness to a news editor of any enterprise. Grasty himself, as I was later to discover, was but little interested in ordinary news, and, so long as the crusades he carried on were properly attended to, gave hardly any attention to the daily panorama of events. The *News* was making rapid gains in advertising, and the setting of ads pretty well occupied its composing-room all morning; in fact, there were days on which all those that flowed in could not be set. As a result there was but little room on the linotypes for editorial copy, and especially for news copy. Before the dispatches of the Associated Press began to run—in those days this was along toward ten o'clock—Charles W. Bump, the telegraph editor, would filch fifteen or twenty columns of matter out of the New York, Philadelphia and Washington morning papers, provide it with minute heads that the *News* affected, and send it to the composing-room. There it would occupy the machines until advertising copy began to displace it. Sometimes all of it would be set, and sometimes only a part of it. But when real news began to arrive from the Associated Press the linotypes were too busy to take it on, and in consequence the paper often came out with its so-called news columns given over mainly to the fruits of Bump's grape-vine. If a story of really capital importance came along it would be jammed through, of course, as a special job, but all ordinary news had to wait until the advertising copy of the day had been worked off, and sometimes it was still waiting when the first edition closed at 2.30.

This maniacal system of handling news naturally upset me, and so did the *News*'s old-fashioned and irrational make-up. The obvious remedy was to put in more linotypes, but Grasty was still so much surprised by his new prosperity that he feared it would not last, so nothing was done until he sold the paper to Frank A. Munsey, in 1908, two years after my own departure. I made a few small improvements in make-up, and quickened the flow of copy from the city-room, but that was as far as I could go. There were also difficulties about the editorial page, which was in charge of Dr. Fabian Franklin. It was supposed to close at noon, but Franklin was a shiftless fellow, and usually began work so late that it was not until after closing time that his last copy reached the composing-room. He would follow on its heels, demanding proofs instantly and otherwise harassing the printers. On the average day the editorial page was half an hour late, and on not a few days it was even later. Who the other editorial writers were I don't recall, though I do remember that they were less dilatory than Franklin. After I had been in the *News* office about a month he asked me to write some editorials myself, and the first of them, on the death of Alfred Beit, who died on July 16, 1906, appeared the next day. My records indicate that I wrote relatively few, first and last, but I also did editorial paragraphs, and undertook an occasional column headed "Mere Opinion" and signed M. My last two editorials were printed on July 30, the day I began work on the Baltimore *Sun,* and two of my "Mere Opinion" columns, delayed by Franklin's dilatoriness, appeared during the week following. Despite my brief service on his staff, my editorials seem to have made some impression on him, for many years afterward he was still talking about them, and hinting idiotically that he had taught me how to write. The *News* composing-room in 1906, though it was inadequately equipped, was competently managed by an old-time tobacco-chewing foreman named Bill Johnson, and I got on with the printers very well, but it was simply impossible to produce a presentable newspaper. My vain efforts to do so greatly augmented that distaste for executive work which had been growing in me since my days as city editor of the *Herald,* and I was thus in a receptive mood when I was invited to join the *Sun* as its Sunday editor, for a Sunday editor's staff is small, he has plenty of opportunity to write himself, and he is given all week to get out his paper.

I recall very few of my associates on the staff of the *News,* and can fetch up nothing about even the city editor save the fact that his name was Darby. Some of the reporters I knew from my own reportorial days, but as news editor I had little contact with them. The functionary I remember most clearly was Virginia Woodward Cloud, the literary editor. She was a prim old maid who had printed several volumes of verse, and was regarded in Baltimore as a literary figure of importance. It was hot weather during the brief term of my servitude, and most of the printers in the composing-room worked in their undershirts. Indeed, I always took off my own shirt when the business of make-up got seriously under way. This display of the male form was shocking to La Cloud, and when she had occasion to come to the composing-room she always stopped at the door, and sent in an office-boy to request my presence. I was thus forced to put on my shirt every time she appeared, which was usually at the busiest hour of the morning. The printers got a great deal of fun out of her prudery, and paraded near the door, with their undershirts open to show their hairy chests, whenever she was waiting for me there. Every time they did so she turned her eyes decorously away. Another ornament of the *News* in those days was Major Walter E. McCann, the dramatic critic. He was a courtly Irishman in an elegant brown toupée and always wore a dinner-coat when he went to the theatre. His ideas about the drama were almost as archaic as those of William Winter, of the New York *Tribune,* but he was the possessor of an extraordinarily lucid and luscious style. I had met him when I became dramatic editor of the *Herald* in 1903, and was to see much of him between 1906 and 1910, when I did theatre notices for the *Sun.* I always marvelled that a man of such preposterous notions should be able to put them into such graceful and colorful English. Of all the newspaper men I knew in those days, he was probably the best writer.

The fact that I was not offered the Sunday editorship of the *Sun* immediately after the *Herald* suspended was due solely to the slow tempo of all *Sun* operations in those twilight years of the Abell management. The paper had been looking for a Sunday editor for some time, and when it became apparent that the *Herald* was not long for this life the city editor, Allen S. Will, recommended to Walter W. Abell, president of the publishing company, that I be asked to take the post. But hiring a new editor, or even a new reporter, was not Walter's prerogative: he had to get authority from the board of directors, and it was not until July 16 that the board acted. It then authorized him to offer me the job at $40 a week, and at another meeting on July 25 he reported that I had accepted. All I recall of my negotiations with him is that I demanded $45, and he held out resolutely for $40, though promising me a raise to $43 at the first chance. He mentioned, as a makeweight, the fact that no member of the *Sun* staff was ever discharged save for the grossest sort of dereliction, and that salaries went on in sickness as in health, for better or for worse. This was a fact, and it remained a fact so long as the Abells were in control of the paper. No *Sun* reporter had been fired, to my knowledge, since 1902 or thereabout, when the star of the local staff, Dorsey Guy by name, was let out for excessive and incessant drunkenness, to the vast amazement of all Baltimore newspaperdom. Ordinary boozing, even when it ran to occasional helplessness, carried no penalty worse than reproachful looks, and among the men who were most esteemed by the Abells in my time were some who drank heavily. The $40 that Walter offered me was precisely what I was getting on the *News,* but I'd have accepted even if it had been less, for the *News* job had become intolerable, and I was eager for more peace of mind and more time to do outside writing. I was by now, in fact, altogether out of humor with executive work in the news department, and determined to see as little of it as possible in future. The *Sun* records show that I went on the payroll on July 30, 1906.

Getting rid of my *News* job, of course, was not easy, for Grasty had given it to me, and he was now abroad and out of reach. I knew that he had been hunting a news editor for some time past, and that he had left Baltimore confident that his troubles in that line were now laid, and I didn't want to let him down, especially in his absence. But the *Sun* was in a hurry, and I had already made up my mind to ask for some other assignment on Grasty's return, so it seemed best to have the business over at once. I put all the facts before Olivier, and found him understanding and sympathetic, and it was with his consent that I resigned. While all this was going on General Felix Agnus, publisher of the Baltimore *American,* sent for me and offered me a post of an undisclosed nature on his staff. The general was full of blarney, and upbraided me for not giving him a chance at my services before going on the *News,* but I disposed of him by reminding him that Grasty had spoken first. Only dire need could ever have induced me, or any other Baltimore newspaper man of any dignity, to work for him, for the *American* was atrociously written and he himself was not beyond suspicion of selling its editorial opinion and even its news columns. I was, of course, in no such dire need. My income for outside writing was already appreciable, and I knew that if I had more free time I could increase it. From 1908 onward it approximated my newspaper salary, and after 1914 it was always materially larger.

There were then three Abells in the office, all of them grandsons of the Founder. First there was Walter W., who was president of the company; then came his brother, Arunah S., II, who was treasurer; and finally, there was their cousin, Charles S., who was secretary, and devoted himself mainly to the mechanical departments. Walter and Charlie were already at loggerheads, and in the end their disputes were to lose the Abell family control of the paper, but during my first year or two in the office they kept their disagreements well under cover, and the staff, save for a few men at the top, was hardly aware of them. My own dealings were mainly with Walter, who was, in 1906, but 34 years old. He was a slim, smooth-shaven, dark-haired and singularly handsome fellow, and all the office gossips marvelled that he had never fallen into the jaws of holy matrimony, for in addition to his agreeable person he had a great deal of money. The Abell family had got on socially by this time, and he was a member of the Bachelors' Cotillon, the most fashionable of all Baltimore social clubs. That there were plenty of Baltimore damsels willing to love, honor and obey him was scarcely a secret, but he managed somehow to resist both their sex appeal and the machinations of their mothers. When he married at last, which was some years later, he chose a red-haired grass-widow with a couple of growing daughters. She had good looks and was a charming woman, but marrying a divorcée got him into trouble with the Catholic Church, of which he and all the other Abells were faithful members. I did not know it at the time, but years later Walter's nephew, Edwin F. A. Morgan, told me that this was a great grief to him. Though he was debarred from the sacraments he attended mass every Sunday morning, and was a liberal contributor to all Catholic charities. In the course of time his wife's first husband, one Zell, died, and the two were remarried by bell and book, immensely to Walter's relief.

As I have said, Walter Abell harassed me very little in my job of Sunday editor. It was rare, indeed, for him to suggest a story for the paper, and almost as rare for him to object to one that I had printed. This last, however, did happen occasionally. Once it followed the publication of an article on the great steel plant of the Maryland Steel Company (now the Bethlehem) at Sparrows Point, Md., with a beautiful eight-column pen drawing by James Doyle, one of my free-lance artists. This was on September 30, 1906. The story mentioned casually that Sparrows Point, which was surrounded by swamps, was plagued by malaria. This brought forth a dreadful bellow from an old fellow named Wood, the president of the steel company, and Walter warned me politely to be more watchful. Another time I got into trouble over an article by Sterling Heilig, who sent me a weekly illustrated contribution from Paris, and had lived there so long that he was dead to American pruderies. I usually read his copy carefully, but one day I slipped, and so did the proofroom, and the result was the appearance the next Sunday of an article describing the indelicate behavior of some prehistoric animals alleged to have been discovered in the interior of Alaska. It told how those of one species pursued those of another species, and how the pursued tried to throw off the pursuers by letting blasts *a posteriori*. This device was described in weasel words, but nevertheless it was described, and on Monday morning Walter's mail was full of gloats from the wicked and protests from the pure in heart. I got a few myself, so I knew what was afoot when he sent for me. Entering his office, I said: "I am not up for trial, but for sentence." Walter was very grave, but also very polite. Not a word of upbraiding came out of him. Instead, he delivered himself of a long and murky lecture on the duties and responsibilities of a copy-reader, laying heavy stress on carefulness. Inasmuch as I had done a hundred times as much copy-reading as he had, I needed no such instruction, but I received it as politely as it was given, and we parted on the best of terms. The matter was never mentioned again.

My days on the *Sun* under the Abells were placid and happy ones, and I had plenty of time for other enterprises, both inside the office and out. My first business was to improve the archaic make-up of the Second Section, and this I quickly effected, using type that was already in the composing-room. The Second Section consisted of ten (later twelve) pages, but its first page was given over to news from the Maryland and Virginia counties, so my Sunday stuff did not begin until page 2. I made active efforts to collar page 1, and to introduce large layouts, but it was not until 1908 that I succeeded. As quickly as possible I got rid of the old-fashioned features that Baldwin had been using, but there were three that had firm roots, and resisted elimination. One was a column of Maryland genealogy, another was a column of Virginia genealogy, and the third was a series of travel articles by William Jennings Bryan, who was then touring Northern Europe. I shed Bryan when he returned home, but the two genealogy columns were tougher, and the best I could do for a long while was to amalgamate them and reduce their joint space. [J.S.M.] Hammond and La Kerchner, [Helen Forman Kirchner, who later married J. Fred Essary] were diligent youngsters, and I got a great deal of work out of them. Hammond began with a series on the various foreign colonies of Baltimore, and then proceeded to other such projects, always producing excellent copy. In the spring of 1907 he fell in with a pioneer Maryland motorist named Howard Gill, and Gill undertook to take him on a motor-trip every week, hoping thus to demonstrate to the readers of the *Sunday Sun* that motoring had become a feasible recreation, despite the bad Maryland roads. I joined the two on several such trips, and recall how violently I was bounced by Gill's primitive car. It had no cover, and the back seat in which Hammond and I rode was at least five feet above the road. Gill's enthusiasm in promoting the new sport of motoring was not entirely disinterested, for he had a share in a firm that sold cars. He was a tall, slim, rather good-looking young fellow who came of an old Maryland family, and was hot for all the more adventurous sports, of which motoring was then one. When airships came in he took to them instantly, and was presently killed in one of the first smashes. He was reputed, in 1907, to be in love with La Kerchner, and it is possible that she had something to do with arranging Hammond's motor trips, though she never joined him in any of them. Most of them were very short—to Towson, to Westminster, to Sparrows Point and so on. One of the longest, recorded by Hammond on August 25, 1907, was to Havre de Grace. The thirteenth [story], printed on November 10, 1907, described a trip to Middle River—only ten miles from the Baltimore City Hall!

On May 17, 1906, during the last days of the *Evening Herald,* I had printed in it an editorial on the *Sun*'s acquirement of a staff poet, the Bentztown Bard (Folger McKinsey), and this had brought forth a friendly reply in the *Sun* by Baldwin. When I entered the *Sun* office on July 30 Baldwin suggested at once that I write an occasional editorial for him, and my first appeared on August 1. Thereafter I did a couple every week—mainly of the so-called light sort. My principal subjects at the start were the joys of eating and the delights of the bachelor life, but in the course of time I gradually worked my way into other themes, and presently I was engineering controversies with the editors of other newspapers, notably Henry Watterson [of the Louisville *Courier-Journal*] and John Temple Graves [of the New York *American*]. My editorials had some success in the office, and one day at the end of 1908 I was surprised to find a notice on the bulletin-board that I had been promoted to the austere rank of editorial writer. How that notice came to be posted I do not know, for the Abells were so secretive that they seldom made any announcements to or about the staff. Simultaneously, my salary was increased $3 a week. But my promotion was really only a brevet one, for I continued as Sunday editor, and had to write editorials in my spare time. My records show that I did 48 in 1908 and 146 in 1909. In the latter year Baldwin was ill off and on, and his place was taken by Thomas J. C. Williams. Williams, a solemn fellow, put me to discussing more serious themes, and was a good deal harder to please than the amiable Baldwin. When the *Evening Sun* was launched, in April, 1910, I transferred to it, but I seem to have kept on writing editorials for the *Sun* for a little while after the first issue of the evening edition on April 18, for I find among my clippings an obituary tribute to Mark Twain, who died on April 21. But maybe this was written in advance, for old Mark had been dying for months. Altogether, I wrote 106 editorials for the *Sun* during the first four months of 1910.

As Sunday editor I commonly came to work at 9 A.M. and was the only commissioned officer in the office until noon, when the city editor and managing editor began work. Thus, when a big news story broke in the morning I usually made some effort to get the hang of it, if only by telephone, and now and then I actually went out on it. I also had to receive such editorial-room visitors as couldn't be got rid of by the single office-boy on duty. Save for this office-boy and an ancient retired bookkeeper named Heindl I had the office to myself of a morning. Heindl was a Pennsylvania German who had been retired on a pension in 1904, but he continued to come to the office at seven o'clock every morning and remained there until 4 P.M., diligently reading the *Sun,* including especially the want ads. He kept on his overcoat all Winter, indoors and out, and inasmuch as he was not a believer in bathing the aroma that he radiated was often pretty strong. I always greeted him as I came in, and he grunted in reply. One morning in the late Spring of 1907, observing that he had laid off his overcoat, I ventured upon some banal pleasantry about the weather being warm enough to affect even him. He took it as an insult, and refused to speak to me for three years. When the Abells retired from the *Sun,* in 1910, he was so upset that he stopped coming to the office—to the immense relief of all the reporters whose desks were near his chair. He died in 1916, aged 88. He took his free copy of the *Sun* home every day, and it was believed in the office that he had tons of back numbers stored in the cellar of his house in a decayed downtown street, given to him by the original Arunah S. Abell nearly half a century before.

My work as Sunday editor naturally brought me into contact with many interesting persons, for fully a half of the contents of the Sunday supplement came from volunteers, and they were constantly streaming through the office. One of the most unusual was a young Italian named Enrico Casalegno, a cook by profession. He was working at the time as second chef at the Maryland Club, and came in one day to propose an article on Maryland terrapin. I told him to go ahead and he produced a piece of copy done in very fair English, and later on he wrote other articles. In 1910 or thereabout this Casalegno went to New York, changed his name to Henry Woodhouse (a translation of the Italian original), and began to interest himself in aviation. In a little while he was launched on a career which included editing three or four aeronautical magazines, advising Peary, Amundson, Bartlett, Shackelton and other arctic explorers on aeronautical matters, testifying as an expert before various congressional committees, organizing and directing international aeronautical congresses, and accumulating a considerable fortune. In some way or other he acquired the concessions that had been given to Rear Admiral Colby M. Chester, U.S.N., by the Turkish government, and organized a company to work them. The company built 2700 miles of railroad in Eastern Anatolia, operated ports on the Black Sea and the Mediterranean, drilled for oil at Mosul, and had a hand in planning and building the new Turkish capital, Ankara. By 1924–25 Woodhouse's autobiography in Who's Who in America ran to nearly 75 lines, and was almost as long as that of Nicholas Murray Butler. I used to hear from him frequently in his early days in New York, but after 1914 I lost contact with him. Another curious member of my extramural staff was Samuel C. Oliphant, a Johns Hopkins philologian. Oliphant was a slight, shy fellow with a waterfall moustache like Walter Pater's. His specialty was Lithuanian, and he had only one student at the Johns Hopkins. He did a long series for *Sunday Sun* on Maryland surnames, and it was a big success. In 1910 he became professor of Greek at Grove City College, a small institution in Pennsylvania, and there became famous as teacher of the largest undergraduate classes in Greek in America.

A third figure of some strangeness was a woman who came in one day to propose writing a series of articles on the care of children. She was of an almost unbelievable homeliness, and I remember wondering how anyone so obviously cut off from connubial bliss could know anything about the young. She staggered me by telling me that she had three children of her own. I never met her husband: he must have been either a blind man or one of the world's great unknown heroes. Yet another who interested me, though chiefly as a bore, was James Ryder Randall, the author of "Maryland, My Maryland." When he began to infest the *Sun* office, in 1907, he was 68 years old, but somehow seemed much older. He had been living in New Orleans for years, but had now come back to Baltimore, and let it be known that he believed the people of Maryland should be glad to assume the support of the author of their State anthem, doggerel though it was. So far as I could find out, the only Baltimorean who agreed with him was William Pinckney Whyte, former Mayor of Baltimore, Governor of Maryland and United States Senator, and then 83 years old. I gathered from Randall that Whyte slipped him an occasional $20 bill. As for me, I commissioned him to write his reminiscences for the *Sunday Sun,* and he presently came in with a hand-written manuscript. It was dull stuff indeed, and apparently made no impression on the readers of the paper. I sent the manuscript to the composing-room as I had received it, and it was chopped up and lost by the printers. It was not until a long while afterward that it occurred to me that the Pratt Library or the Maryland Historical Society would have been glad to receive it. Randall died on January 14, 1908, greatly to the relief of all the Baltimoreans he had been importuning.

My outside writing increased steadily during my first four years on the *Sun*. After the publication of my book on George Bernard Shaw, in 1905, the publisher, Harrison Hale Schaff of Boston, had suggested that I do a book on F. W. Nietzsche, whose name was then being heard for the first time in America. I knew nothing about Nietzsche, but I found that the Enoch Pratt Library had a few of his books in German, and one or two small English commentaries on him, so I set to work. It turned out to be a hard job, and in the end I had to go to the Library of Congress for more material, but I stuck to it doggedly all through 1906 and 1907, and in 1908 Schaff brought out "The Philosophy of Friedrich Nietzsche" in a stately maroon volume of 325 pages, and during the same year it was published in London by T. Fisher Unwin. It was vealy and superficial stuff, but there was nothing better in English at the time, so it got good notices and was a considerable success. I remember being somewhat uneasy, in the days before it came out, about the possible reaction of the Abells, who, as Catholics, might be offended by my acquiescent account of Nietzsche's headlong attack on Christianity. But the Abells, so far as I could learn, never read the book, nor even heard of it; indeed, it is highly probable that they never read *any* book. In the spring of 1908, when I was making ready for my first trip abroad, Walter summoned me to his office and handed me a check for $100, which was to go, he said, toward my expenses. He explained that it was not a gift, but compensation for the extra work that I had been doing.

It was also in 1908 that I began to write a monthly article on books for the *Smart Set,* and in a little while it was getting me some notice. Even in the office I began to pass as a literary man, and by the end of the Abell régime I was the principal literary man of the staff, for by that time I had three books behind me, not to mention my youthful "Ventures Into Verse," and was beginning to be known as a contributor to the magazines. In many newspaper offices this outside activity might have damaged my stock, but the Abells were tolerant in such matters; moreover, they had once produced a literary man of their own, to wit, Walter R. (*d.* 1891), who was a poet. From Baltimore in general I began to receive some attention, and my first invitations to make speeches reached me.

I refused them all, and have refused to speak in Baltimore to this day, though on a few occasions I have broken that rule. Even so far back as 1904 I had been invited to join a dinner club made up partly of writers, and at one of its meetings in that year I read several chapters of my book on Shaw, then still in manuscript. The club's principal member was George Bronson Howard, a curious Baltimorean who had some sort of relation to the Maryland Howards. He was then a bachelor and lived with two younger sisters in an apartment in North avenue. He was a writer of popular fiction and an extraordinarily diligent fellow: for a long while he wrote, under various pseudonyms, nearly the whole contents of the *Popular Magazine,* which then had a large circulation.

The club was not at all pedantic or arty; on the contrary, its dinners were very wet and gay, and after one of them Flood leaped out of the second-story of a Baltimore hotel. It was called the Vagabonds, probably at the suggestion of Howard, and there still exists a pamphlet in which its members are listed and described. Howard's main contribution to its more intellectual proceedings was a mock hymn beginning "There are no flies on Jesus."

At about the same period my interest in music, which had been growing in my teens but had succumbed by my hard work as a reporter for the *Herald* after 1899, was revived by my acquaintance with W. G. Owst, the *Herald*'s music critic, and Joseph H. Callahan, a copy-reader on the paper and after 1903 my assistant as city editor. Callahan introduced me to Albert Hildebrandt, a professional violin-maker and amateur cellist who was destined to become one of my intimates. In 1903 or thereabout Hildebrandt and I and Emanuel Daniel, assistant sporting editor of the *Herald,* began to play trios in Hildebrandt's store in Howard street, and out of that playing arose a little club—the Saturday Night Club—which still exists.* Callahan died in 1917, Hildebrandt in 1932 and Daniel soon afterward, and I am now (1942) the only original member left. At one time or another the club has included as many as twelve members, and some of them have been first-rate professionals, though most of the members have always been amateurs. When it was formed the average age of the members was less than 30 years; now it is beyond

---

* The Saturday Night Club began unofficially in 1902. By 1904 a foursome played regularly—Mencken on the piano joined by two fiddles and a cello. It was Mencken's wish that the club continue after his stroke in 1948; it lasted until December 1950, when it formally disbanded and donated its extensive music collection to the Enoch Pratt Free Library.

60, and four of them—Adolf Torovsky, W. Edwin Moffett, Frank Purdum and Theodor Hemberger—are more than 70. Through Callahan I also met Frederick H. Gottlieb, a rich brewer who brewed intolerably bad beer—it was called Goldbrau—and played the flute for pleasure. Across an alley from his brewery (the Globe) in Hanover street, he had built a three-story building which was ostensibly his office, but was largely given over to the kinds of mirth he affected. There was a large music-room on the top floor, and under it a billiard-room, and hidden about were also a couple of bedrooms. Gottlieb liked to give parties which began with music, proceeded to eating and drinking, and ended in venery. On many a night Al Hildebrandt and I, after playing for and toasting the female guests, entertained them in a more confidential manner in the bedrooms. They ranged all the way from ladies belonging to the first social circles of Baltimore to the kept women of police captains. One night we were presented to two amiable creatures who turned out to be sisters-in-law, and for a year or more thereafter we met them regularly, both at the brewery and elsewhere. Each, of course, knew what the other was doing, but though one was the sister of the other's husband they appeared to be on the best of terms. In the end, however, they had a sisterly spat, and each threatened to betray the other, so we had to offer them our adieux. The Saturday Night Club played at Hildebrandt's violin store—first in Howard street, then in Saratoga street, and then in Charles street—and proceeded after the music to some convenient drinking-place for a couple of hours of feasting and song. For years we had a private room at the Rennert Hotel, and for years more we met at Adam Obst's old-time beer-house in Lexington street, opposite the market. When the murrain of Prohibition came down, in 1920, we took to meeting at the homes of the members, all of whom became amateur brewers. When Prohibition blew up, in 1933, we returned to a room above the Hildebrandt store—now at 619 St. Paul street—as the guests of one of our non-playing members, H. E. Buchholz, who owned the building. When, in 1939 or 1940, he rented the room we moved to another of his buildings, this time at 10 east Center street. There we still play today (1942), but the deaths of two members—Raymond Pearl in 1940 and Max Broedel in 1941—and the advancing age of the surviving members have reduced the club to a low state, and its inevitable end begins to approach. It has lasted nearly forty years.

In 1910 my circle of musical intimates was widened by the organization of the Florestan Club. It had a clubhouse in Charles street near Center, and I was one of the charter members. Half a dozen of us formed a

19

dinner club within the club, and that dinner club kept on meeting every second Sunday long after the club itself blew up. Some of the members of the former were the McDannald, Flood, Hemberger, Moffett and Hildebrandt who have been mentioned, William W. Woollcott (a brother to Alexander), John Ruhräh (a Baltimore pediatrician, and an acquaintance of mine since early reportorial days), an elderly Norwegian named Lie (pronounced Lee), and Howell Fisher. The dinners of the club, so long as they were given at the Florestan Club, were wild and woolly affairs. The standard *aperitif,* invented by Flood, came to be known as the Florestan cocktail. It consisted of two-thirds gin, one-sixth Italian vermouth and one-sixth French vermouth, mixed in a pitcher without ice. A large glass of this concoction was served, along with a glass of beer. We first drank half the cocktail, then all the beer, and then the rest of the cocktail. I have seen one round knock out a sturdy and unsuspecting guest. We always served two and sometimes three. {When the Florestan Club blew up the dinner club took to dining alternately at the homes of two members, Woollcott and Flood, both of whom had pleasant places at Catonsville, near Baltimore. It was at one of these dinners in his own house that Woollcott wrote his song, "I Am a 100 Percent. American, Goddamn!" He hummed the tune to me, and I took it down at the piano. Later it was harmonized by another member, Hemberger. I printed it in the *American Mercury* and then circulated a reprint as a broadside.} The Florestan Club was made up of about 130 musicians and music-lovers. There was an unspoken rule barring singers as members and even as guests, but it was waived in favor of a young fellow named John Charles Thomas, then a church-choir singer in Baltimore and later a star of the Metropolitan Opera and the concert-rooms. Various other Baltimore musicians, noted for their quarrelsomeness, were also barred—among them, Joseph Pache, conductor of the Baltimore Oratorio Society. The club got along pretty well until 1914, when the animosities engendered by the war began to show themselves. Thereafter it went downhill and in 1917 it closed its doors.

As I have said, I made my first trip abroad in 1908. I had been to Jamaica three times, and had also journeyed up and down the American coast, but this was my first crossing of the Atlantic. I traveled alone, and visited London, Leipzig, Munich and Paris. In London I met George Fawcett, former manager of the stock company at the Lyceum Theatre, Baltimore, and he showed me the sights of the City region and bought me my first dinner at Simpson's in the Strand. I well recall how impressed I was when he took me into the Temple garden at twilight and pointed to the graves of Thackeray and Goldsmith. Fawcett was then playing at a West End theatre, and I was astonished to find that he was a matinée idol, for he was already past his youth, had stooped shoulders and a burly figure, and was surely no beauty. At Leipzig I sought out the Menckestrasse in Gohlis, named after my ancestor, Dr. Lüder Mencke, and made some photographs of it for the family album. In 1912 I made another trip abroad, this time in company with the before-mentioned McDannald, and in 1914 McDannald and I went back with W. Edwin Moffett. The three of us sailed from New York for Naples, and thereafter worked our way through Italy to Switzerland, to South Germany and to Paris, where we met George Jean Nathan and Willard H. Wright (later to be known as S. S. Van Dine) and put in a riotous week. In Rome we had an audience with the Pope—a tale I plan to tell in another place.* We got home just in time to escape the outbreak of World War I.

During 1909 my magazine writings brought me into contact with a parlor Socialist named Robert Rives La Monte, then serving as book reviewer of the Baltimore *News* in succession to La Cloud. He took to bombarding me with letters in favor of Socialism, and I replied with arguments against it. Finally he suggested that we make a book of this exchange, and volunteered to find a publisher for it. The result was "Men vs. the Man," published by Henry Holt and Company in 1910. It was a complete failure. Before the manuscript was ready for the printer La Monte moved to New Canaan, Conn., and when the time came for the final revision he proposed that we meet at his father's house in Bound Brook, N.J., as equidistant from New Canaan and Baltimore. It turned out that his father was a man of wealth, and we were entertained in a house that was, in size at least, almost a palace. As the representative of capital in our debate I arrived at Bound Brook in a day-coach, and La Monte, as the representative of the lowly, met me with an elegant carriage driven by a colored coachman with a gilt sunburst on the side of his plug hat. At the outbreak of the war in 1914 La Monte threw overboard his Socialism, and joined the Connecticut home-guard. Later on he became a judge. I have not heard from him for many years. He is now (1942) nearly 75 years old.

When I joined the *Sun* in 1906 it had a dramatic critic whose name I forget. His health failing, he went to the Southwest, and Allen S. Will, the city editor, asked me to do the principal theatrical notice every Monday night. I was not eager for this service, for my four years as a reviewer

---

* "A Roman Holiday," *Heathen Days*, 128–29.

for the *Herald* had pretty well wearied me of the theatre, but Will was insistent and so I succumbed. My first review appeared in the *Sun* of September 10, 1906: the play I covered was "Man and His Angel," by Stanley Dark, with Holbrook Blinn as the principal actor. Thereafter, for nearly four seasons, I continued the chore, with increasing unwillingness. The drama of the day was in a low state and most of my notices had to deal with balderdash by such playwrights as Charles Klein, Channing Pollock, Theodore Burt Sayre, Sydney Rosenfeld, Edward Peple, William C. DeMille, Jules Eckert Goodman and the French Jews who wrote for Charles Frohman and David Belasco, for example, Henri Bernstein. It was a happy Monday night when I encountered Forbes Robertson in Shaw's "Caesar and Cleopatra," or William Faversham in Stephen Phillips's "Herod" for the actors I had to write about were usually almost as bad as the plays. I leaned as far as possible toward the side of generosity, but it was seldom that I could do a notice without getting some acid into it, and so I became very unpopular among the Baltimore theatrical managers. One of them, Charles E. Ford, of Ford's Opera House, finally filed a bitter complaint with Walter Abell. My notices, he said, were injuring his business and doing him a serious injustice, for he had to take whatever plays the Theatrical Trust—which is to say, Klaw and Erlanger—sent him. This was true, and I sympathized with him, but I could not be expected to print favorable reviews of such trash as Clyde Fitch's "Toodles" and William Anthony McGuire's "The Heights," so I kept away from Ford's as much as possible, and I was glad, in 1910, when the birth of the *Evening Sun* relieved me of regular dramatic criticism. I did a few reviews for it after I transferred to it, but only a few. There is a legend in Baltimore that I resigned my job on the *Sun* publicly, and even took paid advertising space to explain why, but that is only a legend. The touch of truth in it is the fact that Ford filed his protest, that I sympathized with him, and that I asked to be relieved a number of times before the *Evening Sun* finally delivered me.

At the time I joined the *Sun* the older members of the staff must have known that there were serious differences among the Abells, but they kept the matter quiet, and I was not aware of those differences myself until shortly before Walter was ousted as president, on April 19, 1909. The quarrels within the Abell family, in all probability, were more damaging to the property than any other influence. The Abells were now in the third generation, and the inevitable clashes of will and interest were showing. Walter and Arunah, as the sons of Edwin F., represented one faction; Charlie, as the only son of George W., represented the second; and the heirs of Walter R., who left no sons, represented the third. The agent of the last-named, since 1904, had been Nelligan. He was responsible, as I have indicated, for the ousting of Walter in 1908, but he soon found that Charlie was quite as bad as Walter, and in many ways much worse, and he saw that some sort of catastrophe was inevitable soon or late. He was thus in a receptive frame of mind when Charles H. Grasty called on him one day toward the end of 1909 with an offer for the paper. Grasty had been unhappy since he sold the *News* to Frank A. Munsey in 1908, and was eager to return to Baltimore. He knew all about the situation of the *Sun*, and had got together a small syndicate of wealthy Baltimoreans to back him in his effort to buy it. He was a good trader, and knew that he stood his best chance with Nelligan, who was a business man pure and simple, and not with the Abells themselves, who had a vast pride in the paper, and would have been outraged by his proposal. He worked on Nelligan by making it plain that he was determined to come back to Baltimore willy nilly, and by hinting that if he couldn't get the *Sun* he would try to buy back the *News* from Munsey, or buy the *World,* a small evening paper that had been struggling along since 1890, or the *Star,* which had been set up as an evening edition of the *American* in 1908, or start a wholly new paper, probably with both morning and evening editions. This dark talk alarmed Nelligan, and he decided that it was his duty as agent of the Walter R. Abell heirs to accept Grasty's offer. Once his mind was made up he was a man of vigorous and even violent action, and in a little while he had beaten Charlie Abell into line.

I shall never forget the next two days, for they were days of acute suffering to many decent fellows, some of whom I held in genuine affection. I took it as a matter of course that Grasty would fire me, for I assumed that he remembered and resented my quick walk-out from the *News* office in 1906, but I didn't care, for I had two books behind me and a third nearly done, I had been doing my monthly book article for the *Smart Set* for two years, and my income from other outside writing was growing steadily. If this was to be the end of my career on newspapers, then let it *be* the end, and be damned to it. But the situation of some of the others, especially of the older moiety, was much more serious. Some of them had been on the *Sun* since the early 80's, and were too old to look for jobs elsewhere; not a few, indeed, had spent their whole professional lives on the paper. Moreover, the new boss who loomed before them was not merely a stranger, but also an enemy. They had seen how

Grasty with his *News* had gradually encroached upon the old monopoly of the *Sun,* and they had resented it as contumacious, immoral and against God. From 1895 or thereabout to the beginning of 1908, when he sold the *News* to Munsey, he had been Antichrist in the *Sun* office, and now he had come back to Baltimore to launch a crowning infamy. It may sound a shade ridiculous after all these years, but the agony of those old-timers was cruelly bitter while it lasted. The Abells who had had their undeviating and lifelong devotion were selling them out—and to the very man they hated most fiercely as a cardinal article of their Abell loyalty. They were not only being sold down the river; they were being sold to the heathen, to the Turks, to Beelzebub himself.

The Abells never faced it out with these worst victims of their own disaster, and I don't blame them. Walter was still in Egypt, and Charlie and Peruna [Arunah] simply took to the woods. On the second night after the news got out my telephone-bell rang at home, and the voice at the other end of the wire announced that it belonged to Grasty. Not having heard it for nearly four years I did not recognize it, and was inclined at first to believe that some strangely sportive *Sun* man was trying to have fun with me. But I was quickly assured that my caller was Grasty himself, and he asked me to come to see him at the Belvedere Hotel at once. When I got there he was very cordial, and told me without being asked that he did not blame me for leaving the *News* for the *Sun.* I replied politely that, if it came to being sold down the river, I'd prefer being sold to Grasty to being sold to Munsey, and we were presently on excellent terms. Grasty asked me to stand by the ship at least until he could get his bearings, and went on to explain that though he had no intention of firing any of the old-time *Sun* men he'd feel safer if they were leavened with a sufficiency of men trained on other papers. I told him frankly that I was not eager for executive work, and was in fact thinking of leaving daily journalism altogether, but I promised to make no move until he had had a chance to reorganize the office. I then brought up the matter of the old-timers. "You have told *me,*" I said, "that you are not going to fire them, but you have not told *them,* and they are now full of horrible fears, and suffering beyond all reason. Why not let me go down to the office at once, and tell them, as coming from you, that they are safe?" To this Grasty demurred on the ground that his contract for the purchase of the paper was still unsigned. He hoped, he said, to sign it the next day, but though the Abells seemed willing at that moment there was no telling whether they would stay put. I then proposed that he let me tell the old-timers that they would be safe *if* the contract were signed, and reminded him that they had nothing to fear if it were not. He agreed to this, and I made off for the *Sun* office at once.

I found all the oldsters, at least of commissioned rank, gathered in a huddle in the big room that housed the editorial writers and the library. Baldwin was there, and Will, and all three editorial writers—John Pleasants, Dr. Ammen and Tom Williams—beside one or two other men that I forget. Their heads were close together and their faces were drawn with care. When I walked in on them there was a sudden silence, for, after all, I had been on the *Sun* but little more than three years and was thus still, by *Sun* standards, a kind of stranger. I wasted no time on preliminaries. "Gentlemen," I said, "I have just come from Mr. Grasty, and he asks me to give your a message. He wants to say that if he gets control of the *Sun,* which he hopes to do tomorrow, the job of every man in the editorial department will be safe. He says he has a high opinion of the *Sun* staff, and wants to maintain it intact. He may bring in a few new men, but no old man will be fired." That was all, but it was enough. The oldsters leaped to their feet to a man, and all their careworn faces broke into wide smiles. They had, of course, many questions to ask, and I answered them as best I could, but the main fact was what interested them most. An immense load was off their minds, and they rejoiced almost like schoolboys. Never in this life have I ever felt more like a Boy Scout with a Class A good deed to his credit. They all shook hands with me, and some of them even slapped my back. In a few minutes the news was spread through the office, and the prevailing glooms vanished. Every typewriter began to bang at a gay rate, and every copy-reader was busy with pencil and paste-brush. By eleven o'clock I was in a nearby saloon with half a dozen reporters, and we were drinking to the health and prosperity of Grasty. One bold and revolutionary fellow even proposed drinking to the damnation of the Abells.

2

Prime Minister without Portfolio

1910–1914

When Grasty made his entry into the *Sun* office he came in quietly. One morning he was seen in Walter Abell's old office—and that was all. He knew relatively few members of the staff, and I had the job of introducing him. He had long palavers with Baldwin, Will and other of the older men, and what he told them must have been comforting, for they were all in reasonably good humor. A few days later John Haslup Adams appeared, but for the moment he did not displace Baldwin as chief editor of the paper. No one knew it at the time, but Grasty was keeping him in reserve for the new afternoon edition that was in mind. Adams, though a fierce doctrinaire in his professional ideas, was a very amiable fellow personally, and he therefore got on very well with the old *Sun* crowd. It was inevitable that he and Baldwin, who was an even fiercer doctrinaire, should come into conflict soon or late, but they did not actually clash until some time afterward, and then the cards were obviously stacked against poor Baldwin.

The arrangements that Grasty had made with his backers are described in full in Chapter XVI of "The *Sunpapers* of Baltimore." I wrote that chapter myself, and it is reasonably accurate. Grasty's main aim was to keep the money men from harassing him, especially in editorial matters. He devised such a stock set-up that they could not oust him save by a legal process comparable to the explosion of a volcano. I saw him daily in those early days, and knew, of course, that all his attention and energies were concentrated on the projected evening edition. It hardly, in fact, needed telling, for he was notoriously (and correctly) convinced that destiny was on the side of evening papers, and in that doctrine nearly all the other more reflective newspaper men of the time agreed with him. It soon became plain that he thought of the *Sun* as no more than a convenient springboard—or maybe even only falseface—for an *Evening Sun*. All his experience had been with afternoon papers, and he knew almost nothing about the operation of a morning paper.

Though the stockholders were kept in the dark, plans for the new evening paper were under way in the office from the day of Grasty's entrance, and many members of the staff knew about them. It was understood that John Haslup Adams, who had been Grasty's chief of staff on the *News,* was to be the editor, and at an early stage of the preparations he offered me the post of first assistant to him, with no title and no executive duties. Just what I was to be called remained uncertain in the office until I suggested myself that it might be reasonable to call me "prime minister without portfolio," As a matter of fact, I was forced, in the first days, to take a hand in many executive matters, though I disliked such work and was determined to steer clear of it for the rest of my life. It was at my suggestion that my old friend, Richard D. Steuart, was made city editor of the new paper, and Steuart, Adams and I organized the first local staff. When Monday, April 18 came at last I made up the first issue of the *Evening Sun.* It reached the streets at 4 P.M., for Grasty was still opposed to early editions. But the *Evening News,* now under Munsey and Olivier, was already issuing them, and in a little while the *Evening Sun* had to follow suit. The first number was surely no great shakes. It ran to twelve pages and carried about forty columns of advertising, four of them on the first page. The body type was somewhat larger than that of the *Sun,* but headings were the small ones that Grasty had used in his time on the *News:* they had been borrowed originally from the Kansas City *Star,* whose publisher, William R. Nelson, was his mentor and almost god. There were two display heads on the first page—one announcing the arrival of a band of suffragettes in Washington, and the other reporting that the steamship Minnehaha had gone on the rocks of the Scilly Islands. All the principal local news was on the last page—a Baltimore custom that is still maintained by both *Sunpapers.*

Neither Adams nor I knew it at the time, but Grasty, during the Spring of 1910, was making hard efforts to induce Woodrow Wilson, then president of Princeton, to take the post of editor-in-chief of both *Sunpapers.* He and Wilson both came from the Valley of Virginia and both were the sons of Presbyterian preachers; moreover, Grasty had a weakness for college dons, as had been shown by his appointment of

Fabian Franklin to the titular editorship of the *News*. Wilson, it turned out later, was considerably tempted, for he was making heavy weather of it at Princeton and yearned for wider and less troubled fields. Unfortunately, Col. George B. M. Harvey and others were already proposing him for Governor of New Jersey, and he had begun to suspect (and hope) that his destiny lay in political endeavor. His nomination followed in September, 1910, and his election in November, and after that he had his eye on the White House, and was no longer to be allured by the chance to edit a great Democratic organ. {Ten years later, in 1920, Van Lear Black toyed with the idea of offering the editorship to Herbert Hoover, who had just got back from Europe and was generally supposed to be a Democrat. Black sent Paul Patterson to Washington to feel out Hoover. Unhappily, Patterson could only report that he was too stodgy a fellow to make an editor, and so no formal offer to him was made.} Grasty, as I have said, was but little interested in the handling of actual news: he centered his whole attention upon the editorial page, with frequent sallies into crusading in the news columns. The editorial page of the first issue of the *Evening Sun* showed two columns of editorials, one of them a salutatory written by Grasty and Adams jointly, and the rest concocted by Adams and me. Save for Adams, I was the only regular editorial writer. I also had a column of my own next to the editorials, and on the first day it was given over to an article entitled "Good Old Baltimore" and signed M. The subjects I dealt with reflected my interests at the time. There were a number on the drama, for I was still more or less interested in plays, though not in the theatre—"William Shakespeare" on April 23, "The One Hundred Best Plays" on April 27, "A Great Norwegian" on April 28, "The Winter's Tale" on May 10, and so on. There were also two articles on Socialism, on April 20 and April 30, both of them by-products of the book that I was writing with Robert Rives La Monte. On April 25 I had an article on Robert Koch [a German and the Nobel Prize winner for medicine in 1905], on April 26 one on Joseph Conrad, and on April 29 a denunciation of psychotherapy, then newly fashionable in America. On May 4 I had a short one headed "The Charity Bill," calling attention to the mounting costs of public relief and hinting that much of the money spent was wasted. It was so short that I must have written it as an editorial: no doubt Adams thought it went further than he cared to commit the paper, but had no objection to printing it over the signature of M. That signature, at the start, was sometimes omitted altogether, but by April 26 it was expanded to H.L.M. and in this form it remained.

After I moved to the last column of the editorial page, and thus broke my cheek-by-jowl contact with the editorials, I became more sportive, and my first piece in the new spot was entitled "The Pestiferous Fly." But even in the old place I had sometimes indulged in a mild jocosity, and I well recall my struggles with a burlesque of Henry James, headed "The Wedding Season," printed on May 16, 1910, just before my shift. I was doing so much typewriting at the time that I became intolerably tired of the machine, and came down to the office the night before to write the piece by hand. Between April 18, 1910, and May 9, 1911, when I began my Free Lance column, I did more than 200 such articles for the editorial page of the *Evening Sun*. The subjects I discussed ranged all the way from marriage to hanging, and from poverty to bald heads. I did critical pieces on Shakespeare, Mark Twain, Nietzsche, Shaw, Strindberg, Ibsen, J. M. Synge, Tolstoi and many another. I denounced such current quackeries as psychotherapy, Christian Science, Prohibition, Comstockery and the New Thought. I had my say about music, cookery, medical fees, whiskers and profanity. During March of 1911 I printed a series of seven articles on what was then known as the Oregon Plan, and during January of the same year three on Lizette Woodworth Reese, the Baltimore poetess. On June 4, 1910, my subject was the possibility that one or two copies of the First Folio Shakespeare might be hidden in the ancient country-houses of Maryland. I recall that it brought me a hot summons from a Baltimore schoolma'm who believed that she had discovered one, but she turned out to be an idiot and the book a trade edition of 1830 or thereabout. During October, 1910, I did five articles that were the remote progenitors of "The American Language." Three of them included my first attempts to write a grammar of the American vulgate. On April 28, 1911, I followed with an article on honorifics, and especially "the Hon.," which also provided materials, years afterward, for "The American Language." In February, March and April, 1911, I likewise laid the foundations for another book of the days to come—the "New Dictionary of Quotations" of 1942. One day early in June, 1910, the managing editor of the *Sun*, Baldwin, asked me to do an article for the news columns on Roosevelt I, who was then on his way home from Africa and making powerful medicine along the road. The result was a brobdingnagian treatise which filled nearly six columns on June 17. Like my articles for the *Evening Sun* editorial page it was signed H.L.M.

Adams made every effort to do his fair share of the editorials, but the arthritis that was to kill him in 1927 was already troubling him, and sometimes he was out of service. There were days during the first six months when I wrote all of them. Some time in 1910 Adams told me that he believed that aviation was coming in, and asked me to investigate the subject, so that I might write about it. I agreed with him as to the first part, but told him that my distaste for mechanical matters, and my incapacity to understand them—though I was an honor graduate of the Baltimore Polytechnic—were such that I could never hope to qualify. Nevertheless, I was put to the job, and wrote a number of bad editorials on aerial themes before I finally begged off.

Early in 1911 there appeared in the editorial rooms two new men who were destined to have a large influence upon the future of the two *Sunpapers,* and scarcely less upon my own fortunes. They were Harry C. Black and Paul Patterson. Black was a son of H. Crawford Black, the richest of Grasty's backers. He was then a youngster of twenty-four, and had but lately returned from London, where he had gone, on graduating from Princeton, to work for the Fidelity and Deposit Company, a bonding company in which his father was a large stockholder. During his year and a half there he acquired an English wife and a very marked English accent, both of which he retains to this day (1942). When he first appeared in the office that accent aroused the derision of the old-timers, and he came to be called Penelope. But those who got to know him discovered quickly that there was nothing effeminate about him; on the contrary, he turned out to be a very hard-headed young fellow, with a lot of new and interesting ideas. Grasty's scheme to keep his backers off his board of directors had by this time begun to break down, and Harry Black was elected to the board on February 8, 1911. He told me some time ago that his first job for the *Sun* was to go to his father's safe-deposit box every few weeks, take out a handful of bonds, pledge them at a bank for a loan, and pay in the money to meet the paper's constant deficits. But his main interest was always in the editorial department, not in the business office, and when he began to appear regularly he was gradually accepted, not as the mere son of his father, but as an interesting fellow on his own account. In the early Spring of 1911, as I was to learn later, he suggested to Grasty that I was being wasted on my editorial-page column, with its daily change of theme—that it would be more effective if it were made more personal, and I were free to ride some of my hobbies, for example, my detestation of messiahs. What put this notion into his mind, as he told me long afterward, was his delight in the English

During his seventh year with the Baltimore *Sunpapers,* Mencken poses with eight colleagues. 1913. *Left to right:* Robert B. Ennis, Clark Fitzpatrick, J. H. Adams, Robert B. Vale, H.L.M., Frank R. Kent, John E. Cullen, Paul Patterson, Charles H. Grasty.

weekly called *John Bull,* then a great success under the celebrated Horatio Bottomley, later jailed for financial malpractise. Grasty thought it might be a good idea, and presently revealed it to me as his own. The result was the Free Lance, a column that began on May 9, 1911, and continued until the end of October, 1915.

It started out under a two-column head, with the matter set in two-column measure, but on May 12 it was reduced to a single column, and so it continued to the end, though now and then there was a sort of annex in the column adjoining. {The first Free Lance led off with a list of American synonyms for *whiskers* and ended with a brief vocabulary of German beer slang.} Its place was the last column of the editorial page. It began somewhat gingerly, with buffoonery predominating, but in a little while I was touching up some of the more conspicuous and well-esteemed frauds and charlatans of Baltimore, and by the end of May I was after them full tilt. In so far as they were politicos this assault was precisely to Grasty's taste, and he gave me eager encouragement, but when I began to bulge into other fields he showed a certain nervousness. In theory, at least, he read copy on me every day, for Adams had washed his hands of the Free Lance from the start, but in reality he seldom saw my stuff until it reached him in proof, for he was usually busy when the copy was ready for the composing-room. One day he rushed into my office holding up a galley of proof, and with his face showing a considerable alarm. What had scared him, it appeared, was a paragraph denouncing the Methodist clergy of the town, then engaged in promoting a vice crusade. "That is one thing," he declared, "that you simply *can't* do. It would ruin us if we got into a row with the preachers. We are trying to sell the *Evening Sun* to the town as a home paper, and we must have the pulpit on our side. I want you to promise me that you will never print a line against a clergyman unless I have seen it first and O.K.'d it. Sometimes I am too busy to read your proofs, and sometimes I am away from the office." {It was my invariable rule, during all my connection with the *Sunpapers,* to submit to editorial authority without protest, either open or covert. Between 1921 and 1936, when I was writing for the *Evening Sun* once a week, it was not unusual for J. Edwin Murphy, the managing editor, to strike what he regarded as dangerous sentiments from my copy, and more than once he killed an article altogether. I never made any complaint against this, for I was a firm believer in order and discipline. A part of my doctrine was insistence on editorial responsibility for whatever got into the paper. If there was a slip in one of my articles—it didn't happen often—I put the blame on whoever had read the copy. It was impossible, I argued, for any man to read his own.}

I made the promise readily enough, for Grasty, after all, was the boss, but it didn't hamper me very long. Only a little while later the Ministerial Union of the town, which was dominated by Methodists, Presbyterians and Baptists, passed resolutions denouncing me as a friend of saloonkeepers, gamblers, whores, cops and other sinners. It was printed in the *Evening Sun* and I went to Grasty and asked him if, under the rules he had set for the paper, I didn't have the right to reply. He admitted that I did—and after that the fat was in the fire. During the rest of my four years or more I gave constant attention to the evangelical pastors, and often treated them very roughly. I also belabored the Anti-Saloon League, which was then just getting on its legs. The politicians, of course, were my constant marks, and I gave special attention to the city government. The Mayor of Baltimore, during the whole life of the Free Lance, was a berserkeran but very vain and sensitive fellow named J. Harry Preston, of whom much more anon. I had at him for depositing city money in a bank of which he was a director, for appointing all sorts of political hacks to office, and for neglecting the city's health. In those days the water supply of Baltimore was dubious, and there was an epidemic of typhoid fever every Summer. I printed frequent tables, derived from the *Public Health Reports*, showing how Baltimore's death-rate from typhoid compared to those of other American cities, and almost every week it was the highest. I also subscribed to the *Monatsbericht* of the city of Munich, and was thus able, on the basis of its mortality returns, to compare Baltimore's record with that of a German city of approximately the same size. In this comparison, of course, Baltimore came off very badly, for typhoid was almost as rare in Munich as leprosy or Asiatic cholera.

My Free Lance job was the pleasantest that I had ever had on a newspaper, at least since my early reportorial days, and I enjoyed it immensely. Once the column had really got under way, and its success was apparent, Grasty seldom undertook to curb me, and I therefore laid about me in a lusty manner. I derided all the rich bankers and industrialists of the town, I denounced both the uplifters and the boomers, and I invented opprobrious nicknames for most of the politicians. My belief is that running the column was very beneficial to me, professionally speaking, for it not only rid me of the last vestiges of executive work, but also served to clarify and organize my ideas. Before it had gone on a year I knew precisely what I was about and where I was heading. In it I worked out much of the material that was later to enter into my books, and to color the editorial policy of the *American Mercury*. After a few months the correspondence it attracted and the visitors it brought left me no time to write any editorials for the *Evening Sun*, so I was relieved of that drudgery. Thereafter my only duty, beside writing the column six days a week, was to edit the letters-to-the-editor on the editorial page. That job I also enjoyed, and in it I set up rules that still prevail on the *Evening Sun*, though sometimes they are forgotten—for example, the rule forbidding any correspondent to attack a living person without signing his own name. My Free Lance, of course, was signed in full, and thereafter I never printed anything anywhere that was not readily identifiable as mine.

Despite the general violence of my invective I always managed to keep on friendly personal terms with my chief antagonists, including even the J. Harry Preston aforesaid. One of them, William H. Anderson, superintendent of the Anti-Saloon League of Maryland, I saw frequently, and more than once we planned a bout head-to-head before launching it. When the news got about town that we were often lunching together some of Anderson's Methodist backers were outraged, but he was a bold and independent fellow and bade them mind their own business. Once I had some fun with him by bombarding him with a mass of statistics credited to official sources in Norway and Switzerland, purporting to show that the use of alcohol in moderation greatly increased the strength and endurance of military conscripts. I had, of course, invented these figures myself, but my ascriptions seemed plausible, and it took Anderson a lot of time to prove that they were bogus. When a bit later, he made an effort to pay me off in my own coin, I exposed the falseness of his own home-made statistics with a great show of moral indignation, and professed thereafter to regard *all* of his figures as fraudulent.

Another reformer with whom I had amicable relations was Dr. Howard A. Kelly [one of the original four doctors] of the Johns Hopkins Medical School. {The others were William Osler, William S. Halsted and William H. Welch. Halsted was the least known to the public, but he was the greatest man, and by far. His innovations in surgery were revolutionary. In his early days he became a cocaine addict, and the legend was that he had cured himself by shipping on a sailing vessel bound 'round the Horn. But in all probability he pursued the habit more or less to the end of his days. Greatly to my regret, I never met him, though my friend Max Broedel, professor of art as applied to anatomy at the Johns Hopkins, often offered to take me to see him. Osler I saw often in my reportorial days. He was a charming fellow, but always more the popular physician than the scientist. Welch I knew quite well in his later years. He was a medical politician and money-raiser rather than a scientist. He brought in more money to the Hopkins than all its other collectors put together, but he did very little original work after the age of thirty. In his last two decades he was hardly more than a museum piece.} Despite the fact that Kelly was one of the Big Four of the Hopkins Medical School and a gynecologist of international fame, he was what he himself called a Bible Christian and spent a large part of his time and even more of his money promoting all sorts of Pecksniffian causes— Prohibition, vice crusading, Sabbath observance, and so on. When I began to maul such things in the Free Lance he came down to the office, remonstrated earnestly, and told me that he proposed to pray for me, and hoped to bring me up to grace. I bade him do his damndest, but predicted that he would never fetch me. Thereafter, for many years, he called on me regularly and bombarded me in the intervals with pious letters. When I took to denouncing the various varieties of medical quackery that then flourished—for example, chiropractic, anti-vaccination, anti-vivisection and Christian Science—he had to allow that I was not altogether evil, but nevertheless he kept on protesting against my animosity to Christian endeavor.

Kelly was a highly competent operative surgeon, but his scientific attainments were much more modest. His staff pathologist, a Hungarian named Nicholas M. Alter, once told me that he knew next to nothing about pathology, and could not distinguish between normal and cancerous tissue under the microscope. He ran a private hospital in Eutaw place, and was notorious for his extravagant fees. He invented the system of charging a husband a month's income for an operation on his wife. If the husband protested he would say, "Well, then, tell me how much saving your wife's life is worth to you, and I'll take it." His hospital was expensive otherwise, and in consequence nine-tenths of his patients were the wives of wealthy men. It was reported that he not infrequently demanded and got a fee of $10,000. He had married a German woman, and owed much of his early success to German teaching and example, but when World War I broke out in 1914 he denounced the Germans violently, though I should add that he never went as far as his Philadelphia colleague, Dr. W. W. Keen, who actually gave out a statement, in 1915, denying that any German had ever made a useful contribution to medicine.

Kelly was the easiest mark that the wowsers of Baltimore had ever encountered. He was good for a substantial contribution to any pseudomoral cause, and the brethren milked him constantly. For many years he was the sole support of a frowsy and picturesque fraud named the Rev. Dr. W. W. Davis, state superintendent of the Lord's Day Alliance. I was friendly with Davis also, and in his later years he often called on me or telephoned to me, saying that he was praying for me, and inviting me to dinner at his house. I never went.

Indeed, the only do-gooder I recall unpleasantly was a Quaker homeopath named O. Edward Janney. A slim, stooping, pale, furtive-looking fellow, he was fascinated by whores, and devoted himself to vice crusading. One day he came to the office and objected bitterly to a line of argument that I was pursuing, and I offered to abandon it if he in turn would give up some enterprise that he had under way. I forget what the argument and the enterprise were, but I remember clearly that Janney agreed—and then broke his word. After that I forbade him the office, and never had anything further to do with him. My disagreeable contact with him gave me a distrust of Quakers, and it was reinforced in the years to come by A. Mitchell Palmer and Herbert Hoover. He died in

1930. As a homeopath, he was necessarily a quack in Kelly's eyes—as, indeed, he was in fact—but in his capacity of wowser he had to be tolerated, and the two were partners in many moral undertakings, all having to do with prostitutes. Whenever I argued with Kelly that Janney was a swine he always changed the subject. Another of his dubious allies was a Methodist clergyman named Kenneth D. Murray, who pastored a church in West Fayette street, only a block from one of Baltimore's red-light districts. Murray was a sexual pervert, though no one knew it when he began operations. His greatest stroke for God and virtue was delivered by reading from his pulpit a full list of the bawdy-houses in his neighborhood, giving streets and numbers. He announced this reading in advance, and as a result his church packed—chiefly by young fellows looking for reliable information. He and Kelly greatly harassed the police, for they had much influence with a young Methodist lawyer named Morris A. Soper, who was police commissioner in 1912 and 1913. {Later on he became chief judge of the Supreme Bench of Baltimore and began to acquire some worldly wisdom. In 1923 he was made the United States district judge at Baltimore, and in 1931 he was promoted to a circuit judgeship. I should say in fairness that he made excellent records in all these offices.} The cops rid themselves of Murray by a characteristic device. Getting wind of his perversion from the whores, they sneaked a spy into the Central Y.M.C.A. building, which he often visited, and after a patient and not too long wait took him one night in homosexual *flagrante* with one of his young parishioners. The district attorney, William F. Broening, on being summoned in haste, told them to their horror and indignation that what the pastor had been doing was not forbidden by the excessively liberal laws of Maryland {The maximum punishment for adultery, in those days, was $10 fine, and fornication was not punishable at all, nor were any of its fancy varieties} but they got rid of that difficulty by concealing the fact from their prisoner. Instead, they offered to let him go if he would agree to clear out of town at once, and this he did with loud hosannahs, not waiting for daylight and leaving a wife and five children behind him. He was never seen or heard of again. Years later I asked Kelly if he had ever had any word from the fugitive, and he answered no. Some time afterward the cops also polished off a colleague who had committed the unforgivable offense of aiding Kelly and Murray in their crusading. This was a sergeant named Morris Pease. The charge laid to him was that he had connived at the burglary of a warehouse, and taken a share of the swag. Whether or not this was true

I do not know, but the evidence brought forward by the cops convinced a judge and jury, and Pease was sent to the Penitentiary.

I made no reference to the Murray case in the *Evening Sun*. The whole town knew about it, and magnanimity seemed to be the proper prescription. Nor did I print anything when the cops caught one Samuel J. Pentz, chief agent of the Society for the Suppression of Vice, with a girl under age, and forced him to resign. And when a committee of the grand jury came to me with evidence against Kelly himself I not only refused to print anything about it, but persuaded the jury to abandon its plan to indict him. He was, in fact, quite innocent in intent. When the bawdy-houses in one of the red-light districts were closed I made a hypocritical uproar about the probable starvation of the girls who were turned into the street, and Kelly set up a refuge for them in an old house near his hospital, with one of the late madams in charge. The girls, of course, soon let their clients know where they were, and in a little while the place was operating as a bawdy-house of a new and improved model, for there was no rent to pay. The grand jury, informed of this by the cops, proposed to indict Kelly for maintaining a house of ill-fame. It was a grand joke, but I was in fear that if he were indicted a ribald petit jury might convict him, and I knew that in any case the scandal would do him grave damage professionally and cost him a great deal of money, so I argued the grand jurymen into finding no bill. The cops then told Kelly, and he was so upset that he rushed off to his camp in Canada and remained away from Baltimore for months. He never learned of the part I played in the affair.

Kelly had a large family of children, all of whom turned out badly. In fact, he was still supporting them at the age of 80, when senile feebleness at last forced him to retire from practise. Only one of his seven or eight sons, Edmund by name, followed him into medicine. Edmund, an amiable, baldhead fellow with none of his father's piety, was well spoken of as a surgeon, but did not like the trade, and in 1939 or thereabout he gave it up, and took to cruising in Southern waters in a small yacht. His various shipwrecks and other misfortunes provided plenty of picturesque material for the Baltimore newspapers.

Kelly's wealth enabled him to obtain the first supply of radium ever seen in America. He announced publicly that its discovery was but one more proof of the fatherly beneficence of God, but took good care that his possession of it got plenty of publicity. As a result his hospital was packed, with a long waiting list. But Alter told me that he never learned how to use radium, and that, of his first patients, a great many were burned to death.

Kelly amassed a large medical library, but I doubt that he did much reading in it. The only book he habitually patronized, in fact, was the Bible, a copy of which he always carried in his pocket. He pretended to be able to read the New Testament in Greek, but there were those who refused to believe it. In 1940, apparently becoming short of money, he began to sell off his library. Every now and then he would embrace some new scientific or pseudo-scientific fad, and pretend to a profound knowledge of its subject. For a while he collected snakes—always getting publicity when he nabbed another one in Florida or elsewhere—and at another time he started a collection of mushrooms. To make this last known he employed a German anatomical artist named Krieger to make a series of illustrations of the specimens in it. Krieger's pictures were superb, and Kelly basked in their reflected glory. At other times other collections were assembled in the headquarters beside the hospital in Eutaw place, and the newspapers gave them liberal space. It was generally believed in Baltimore that Kelly was a hypocrite, but my own dealings with him convinced me that he was sincere enough. What animated him was simply a quaking fear of Hell—the product, I daresay, of his Northern Irish ancestry. He was ostensibly an Episcopalian, but actually trained with the Methodists, and most of his moral enterprises had their support and were launched from their churches. My palavers with him gave me an excellent insight into the Wesleyan demonology, and what I learned was of constant use to me later on. He always spoke of Jahveh, rather sugarishly, as "our Heavenly Father," but it was plain that the Deity he actually visualized was a brutal and vengeful fellow, with no trace whatsoever of paternal lovingkindness. He was convinced, it appeared, that the only way he could escape the *Schrecklichkeit* [dreadfulness] of this anthropomorphous gunman *post-mortem* was to give over his days to harassing sinners on this earth. His arguments in favor of the faith that afflicted him were as hollow as those of a backwoods evangelist: in fact, it was hard to distinguish his puerile gabble from that of such a boob-bumper as, say, the Rev. Billy Sunday—whom, by the way, he vastly admired. From him I learned the useful lesson that a man may be really distinguished in a difficult field of human endeavor, and yet remain, in all other respects, a complete jackass. The Johns Hopkins bore him patiently but not joyfully, as a cross laid on it by inimical and far from all-wise Powers. Whenever he broke into the papers in his character of a jitney John Baptist all his colleagues shuddered. So far as I am aware, he

38

never made a single convert among them. Even his closest associates—for example, Burnham—refused to have anything to do with his barbaric and idiotic theology.

My denunciations of quackery, and especially of the efforts made by anti-vivisectionists to induce the Legislature of Maryland to pass laws strictly regulating animal experimentation, got me favorable notice from the Johns Hopkins brethren, and I made some friendships among them that continue to this day. But I reserved the right to criticize the Johns Hopkins itself—especially the undergraduate department—and did so freely from time to time. The university was already showing signs of decadence. During its first quarter century it was unquestionably the chief American institution of the higher learning, but with the resignation of its first president, Daniel Coit Gilman, in 1901, it began to go downhill, and no subsequent effort to rehabilitate it has ever succeeded. The Medical School, which has its own funds, has maintained its old position, but not the department of arts. As the stars of the first faculty died or dropped out they were replaced with inferior men, and the student body deteriorated along with the staff. Frank J. Goodnow, who became president in 1914, was cocksure but incompetent, and the university continued to decline during his fifteen years in office. I seldom met him and did not like him. By the time he retired fully a third of the undergraduates were Jews, and most of them were Jews of the kike moiety. In 1925 he announced grandly that the university was preparing to abandon its undergraduate department and concentrate all its energies upon graduate studies, as had been the case in its first days under Gilman. This Goodnow Plan, as it was called, was discussed at enormous length and with great heat, but nothing came of it in the end. Joseph S. Ames, who succeeded him in 1929, was not much better. He was an expansive and indeed garrulous old fellow, and he made gallant efforts, first, to raise money to meet the constant deficits of the university, and second, to get rid of the stupid old-time Baltimoreans who cluttered up his self-perpetuating board of trustees, but despite his hard sweating he failed miserably in both directions.

My daily column, in truth, was very carefully put together, and sometimes the preparation of it required a long and hard investigation. During the four and a half years it continued I was never caught in an error of any consequence, though it was constantly under the scrutiny of very hostile persons, and there was never even the threat of a libel suit.

The only time I ever backed water on a statement made therein was shortly after the outbreak of World War I in 1914. Ernest A. Boyd, the Irish writer, had just been appointed British vice-consul in Baltimore, and he and I were already on good terms and seeing each other regularly. He believed in England's crusade to save civilization no more than I did, but as a British official in war time it was his duty to challenge any hostile publication that was open to refutation, and this he did on some matter so unimportant that I forget what it was. In order to help him in the consular service, where he was already an object of suspicion, I admitted that I had been in error and apologized somewhat fulsomely. He and I, then and later, had many a pleasant laugh over this episode.

Boyd had read something or other of mine before he came to America, and I was the first American he foregathered with on reaching Baltimore. We used to meet two or three times a week in Charles Schneider's old beer-house in Fayette street near Liberty, now (1942) Miller's restaurant. There, until the supply ran out, we drank Pilsner beer, and laughed at the gaudy blather of the English propagandists in America, and the easy credulity of their Anglomaniacal dupes. I introduced him to my circle of Baltimore friends, most of them musicians, and he was very well received, though he was ignorant of music. I also introduced him to various literati in New York. He was a slim, slightly stooped young man with thinning brown hair and a round, brown beard, and had a singularly deep and resonant bass voice. His wife, Madeleine Reynier, was a Frenchwoman of considerable bulk, and of a somewhat fiery disposition. She followed him to Baltimore late in 1914, and they took an apartment far up St. Paul street. It was comfortable enough, but in the Summer of 1915 Madeleine found the heat in it unendurable, and made frequent protests. She was also unable to get used to their colored maid, whom she always spoke of as "my cannibal." One evening in 1915 I essayed to take the two of them to Bayshore, a trolley park on the shore of the Chesapeake, twelve miles below Baltimore, in my newly acquired automobile. We traveled by the old North Point road, which was still unpaved and very rough. Madeleine, sitting on the back seat, bounced around in a dreadful manner and made loud outcry. Boyd, sitting with me on the front seat, took no notice of her yells until we got to Bayshore. Then he turned round for a casual glance at her and said calmly: "Thank God, she ain't pregnant." {Boyd was transferred to Barcelona in 1915 and then to Copenhagen. Before the end of the war he was ordered home to Dublin, and remained there under suspicion until 1920, when he resigned from the British consular service and immigrated to New York.

His first job there was that of an editorial writer on the New York *Evening Post*. He soon lost it, and in 1922 I induced Alfred A. Knopf, my publisher, to employ him as foreign adviser at $100 a week. But his advice was usually bad, and after a while he so greatly neglected his work that Knopf fired him. Thereafter he held various jobs, but none of them long. For some years he lived by collecting advance royalties from publishers on books that he never wrote, and when that played out he took to living on his friends, for example, Herman Oelrichs. He borrowed often from me and from Harry C. Black, to whom I had introduced him. When, in March, 1928, Madeleine needed a surgical operation and came to Baltimore to have it, I lent her $250 to pay for it. The money was never returned. I finally shut down on Boyd, and he took to spreading hostile reports about me in New York. He and Madeleine finally separated in 1935 or thereabout. He was a man of some talent, but he drank so much after 1918 that it was impossible for him to do any sustained work. Madeleine once told me that his dipsomania was an inheritance from his mother. She herself was still borrowing money from me in 1940.}

When Grasty entered the *Sun* office in 1910 he found the paper engaged in a combat that should have been to his taste—in fact, it was a sort of imitation of him. It was a row with the Consolidated Gas, Electric Light and Power Company over its proposal to bring natural gas to Baltimore. The *Sun* opposed the plan on the ground that the supply of gas would be uncertain, and the quality inferior. The fight was in full blast when Grasty took over in January, with Baldwin writing diatribes against the company and demands that the Legislature (then in session) curb it with legislation, but Grasty showed little interest in the matter. Unlike his mentor, William R. Nelson, he was not much of a corporation fighter; he greatly preferred to assault politicians. During the rest of 1910 nothing in his line offered, and he was so busy trying to get the *Evening Sun* on its legs that he had no energy left for his usual enterprises. With the beginning of 1911 an opportunity to his taste offered, and he soon had both *Sunpapers* in action. His victim was the J. Harry Preston aforesaid, who had always trained with what remained of the Gorman-Rasin ring, which had been badly battered by Grasty and his *News* (with some help from the *Sun*) in 1895. Preston was now a candidate for Mayor of Baltimore, and the *Sunpapers* opposed him violently, mainly on the ground of his associations. He was a tall, stout and somewhat pompous fellow, and so full of vanity that it was easy to set him to bellowing. This he now did so loudly that his clamour deafened the town. What is more, he bawled to some effect, for he was elected Mayor for a four years' term in May, though by only a small majority. Once in office, he struck back by taking all the city advertising out of the *Sunpapers*—a serious blow to the *Evening Sun,* which needed the money badly. It remained out until the end of his second term in 1919, though by that time Grasty had been gone from Baltimore for nearly five years.

I took a hand, in my Free Lance column, in the attack on Preston, and had a grand time baiting him. I invented all sorts of opprobrious nicknames for himself and his friends, printed the official figures showing his large deposits of city money in his own bank, and gave special attention to the public health situation in Baltimore, with constant hints that the high death-rate was due to politics in the Health Department. Preston had some retainers who were easy to ridicule, and I did not neglect them. One was an old fellow named Jacob Hook, who owned a small bank in Old Town and had the job of city collector. When, in 1912 or 1913, he made a trip abroad, he had cards printed showing the insignia of all the fraternal orders he belonged to, and giving, of course, his military title, which was purely honorary. I printed bogus dispatches from various German towns alleging that the German authorities, taking his title for genuine and mistaking the fraternal order insignia for the badges of military orders, had turned out the guard for him. These dispatches helped to make old Jake a comic character in the town, but when he got home it turned out that in several German cities the local commandants had actually done what I alleged. Another of my favorite butts was a fifth-rate doctor John Turner, Jr., by name, who had the post of surgeon to the city waterworks. I pumped him up into a famous authority on all sorts of quackeries, and inasmuch as he was very bellicose and fought back vigorously, I had a lot of fun with him. There were plenty of other easy victims in the Preston menagerie, and I gave special attention to Harry's old newspaper backer, the Baltimore *American.* Ostensibly Republican in politics, it supported him fulsomely and even oleaginously, and was suitably rewarded with city advertising and other favors. I gave it the name of the Hot Towel—an oblique reference to the legend that General Felix Agnus, its publisher, came to the United States from his native France as a barber—and constantly derided and burlesqued its praises of its hero. The author of most of those encomiums was its political reporter, a young Jew named E. Milton Altfeld. He afterward studied law and served a couple of terms in the Maryland Legislature.

He never lacked confidence—H.L.M. at thirty-three, the year before World
War I began. 1913. Henderson (*Sun* photographer).

But though Preston took the city advertising away from the *Sun-papers* immediately after he got into the City Hall, the row with him did not reach real fury until the Autumn campaign of 1911. He was not himself a candidate in that campaign, but he was an active backer of Gorman, the Democratic candidate for Governor of Maryland. Gorman was a son of that Arthur Pue Gorman (*d.* 1906) who had been the head and forefront of the Gorman-Rasin ring, smashed by Grasty in 1895. He was a personally honest and well-meaning man, with no vice save drunkenness, and the *Sunpapers* gave him mild support, but they opposed nearly all his running-mates. When he was defeated at the November election they argued that he had been beaten by the unpopularity of Preston, who had, of course, supported him vigorously. This accusation sent Preston into a frantic rage, and he retaliated by taking advertising space in the *News* to assail Grasty. He charged, first, that Grasty aspired to become the political dictator of the Democratic party and the state of Maryland, and second, that he was a man of dubious private character, and had left Kansas City under a cloud. It was easy to dispose of the first charge, for Grasty actually had no political ambitions and every Baltimorean of any sense knew it, but the second was more difficult to deal with, for there was some truth in it. The exact facts I never learned, but it was well known in the *Sun* office that Mrs. Grasty—her maiden name was Leota Tootle—had had a husband before Grasty, Perrin by name, {They were married May 29, 1889, when Grasty was 26 years old. He described her in Who's Who in America, down to the 1914–15 volume, as Mrs. Otie T. Perrin of St. Joseph, Mo.; after that she became Leota Tootle Perrin. At the time of their marriage Grasty was managing editor of the Kansas City *Times,* owned by his hero, Nelson. He apparently left Kansas City immediately afterward.} and that this husband made a pother when she made off with Grasty. Grasty was thus somewhat nervous under Preston's attack, and his nervousness became panic when Preston demanded space in the *Sunpaper* to print further advertisements, and hinted broadly that he was about to reveal all the details of the scandal, whatever it was.

When the copy for the first Preston advertisement came in Grasty sent for me, and without showing it to me told me that he was resolved to refuse it. I argued that this would be a fatal mistake, and urged him to print it boldly, no matter how embarrassing it might be. That was the only way, I believed, to dispose of Preston, for one of his complaints had been that the *Sunpaper* always refused him any chance to state his case, and I was convinced that after he had printed one or two more advertisements at $1 a line his thrifty soul would dissuade him from going any further. But Grasty said that Adams believed, as he did, that the advertisement should be refused, and told me that his mind was irrevocably made up. I thereupon tackled Adams, and in a little while convinced him that it would be dangerous to bar Preston out of the paper, especially since the *News* and the *American* were open to him. Adams and I then called in various other functionaries, including Frank R. Kent, who had lately been made managing editor, and we ganged [up] on poor Grasty and forced him to change his decision. That night he went to dinner in the Green Spring Valley, and at 11 P.M. called up Kent, told him that he had gone back to his first position, and ordered him to kill the Preston advertisement. But automobiles were few in those days and the Green Spring Valley was remote, so Kent told Grasty that the advertisement was already in the forms of the first edition, and refused flatly to take it out. "If you want to kill it," he said, "you will have to come down to the office and do it yourself." This defiance flabbergasted Grasty, and he made no further move. The next morning, when he discovered that the effect of the advertisement had been slight (for nearly everyone of any importance in Baltimore already knew something about the Kansas City matter, if only vaguely), he was very polite to Kent, and within a week he was boasting that he had ordered the advertisement printed himself, and didn't care a damn for Preston's libels. The whole episode, I must say, left a bad taste in my mouth, and confirmed my growing suspicion that Grasty the "man of affairs" was not the old Grasty of the *News* in its heyday. When Preston discovered that no one cared much how Leota-Otie had been acquired he quickly abandoned that line of attack. During the three years following he occasionally resumed it, but never with any approach to his original enthusiasm.

During the second year of this gory and relentless war with Preston, there was another with Frank A. Munsey, to whom Grasty had sold the *News.* The presidential campaign of 1912 was then taking shape and Munsey was supporting Theodore Roosevelt. One day Grasty printed an editorial in the *Evening Sun,* probably written by himself, in which Munsey was denounced violently as a stand-pat Republican in a false-face, and following came others to the same effect, written by Adams. Munsey replied with a two-column signed article in the *News,* very violent in tone. He charged in it that when he bought the *News* it was on the understanding that Grasty would never set up a newspaper in Baltimore in competition with it, and that he (Grasty) had come back to town hoping that he could scare him (Munsey) into selling back the *News* at a bargain price. There were many other allegations, some of them very unpleasant, but these were the main ones. Grasty came into my office with the Munsey blast and was obviously much upset. He knew that he had to make some sort of reply to it, but it was obvious that he had no stomach for the job. After beating about the bush for a while he proposed that I write the reply and print it in my Free Lance column, signed. I, of course, objected to this scheme, and refused to carry it out. I was perfectly willing to belabor Preston, for he was the enemy of the paper, but I saw no reason why I should tackle Munsey, for his difference with Grasty was purely personal. I should add in candor that I thought he had an excellent case, for though it may have been true, as Grasty alleged, that he has signed no contract to keep out of the Baltimore field, it was plain that a tacit promise to do so must have been part of his bargain with Munsey. Certainly it was impossible to imagine even so monumental an ass as Munsey paying $1,500,000 for a paper on the understanding that its late editor would be free to set up a rival to it. Grasty, with the help of Adams, finally drew up a reply to Munsey himself. It was extremely feeble. Its main argument was that Grasty had not established any new paper at all—that the *Sun* was 73 years old when he acquired it, and that the *Evening Sun* was simply the old *World,* founded in 1890, under a new name. This reply made a poor impression in Baltimore, and certainly evoked no cheers in the *Sun* office. All the more thoughtful men of the staff, in fact, were ashamed of it, and confidence in Grasty continued to decline.

When he decided to support Woodrow Wilson for the Democratic presidential nomination in 1912 I do not know. The *Sunpapers* did not come out for Wilson during the early campaign, and in fact reserved their fire until almost the last instant. Meanwhile, their editorials were devoted to denouncing Taft and the Republicans, to hinting that Roosevelt's backers were highly dubious characters, and to sniping at the Democratic aspirants who were running against Wilson. The majority of Maryland Democrats, at the start, were apparently in favor of Judge Judson Harmon of Ohio, but J. Harry Preston induced the Democratic city machine in Baltimore to back Champ Clark of Missouri. The state convention was to be held in Baltimore at the end of June, 1912, and Preston was in a favorable position, as Mayor of the host city, to give effective aid to his candidate. (The party machine of the host city always provides most of the doorkeepers and assistant sergeants-at-arms of a national convention, and is thus able to pack the galleries. Also, a great many tickets go to the local committee which raises the money to pay for the convention. In 1912 the Democratic National Committee refused to hold the convention in Baltimore unless a fund of $100,000 were raised. This fund was mainly underwritten by Preston, who had a rich wife, and by Robert H. Crain, a Baltimore lawyer who was national counsel of the United States Brewers' Association, and wanted to make sure that the galleries would be safely wet.}

By the time the convention met Harmon was out of the running, and a majority of the county delegates, led by the State boss, John Walter Smith, were inclined to jump to Wilson. But though Preston controlled but 28 of the 129 votes in the convention, he managed to dragoon it into endorsing Clark by threatening to turn the city machine, at the 1913 session of the Legislature, against any county politician who resisted. This threat alarmed even Smith, and he made no fight in the convention for Wilson. Preston, by this time, was seething with an itch for second place on the ticket. He had been proposed for it in the *American* on January 11, 1912, by his dutiful Jenkins, General Felix Agnus, and had already, it appeared, come to an arrangement with the Clark managers. If, by the efforts of the Baltimore gallery or by any other device, he could insure Clark's nomination he was to have the vice-presidency for his pains. His dreams, of course, were not secret; everyone in Baltimore knew of them, and the *Sunpapers* discussed them constantly. In my Free Lance column I derided and belabored him daily, and drove him almost wild. {Preston sweated horribly under this attack, and essayed to strike back in both paid advertisements and statements for the new columns.} He was a man of great energy and some ability, and his eight years in the Baltimore City Hall saw the repaving of the town and the construction of its first adequate sewerage system, but it was hard to imagine so choleric and imprudent a fellow in the White House, where he might conceivably land if Clark were nominated and elected, for Clark was a heavy boozer and did not look to be long for this world. So I had at poor Preston with a light heart, and was probably at least partly responsible for the grotesque catastrophe that overtook him in the end.

It was not until July 1, the next to the last day of the national convention, that the *Sun* began to advocate Wilson by name, though it had been whooping against his opponents for weeks, and Grasty had been doing some hard work for him behind the door, with the aid, chiefly, of Clarence W. Watson, a rich West Virginia coal magnate who was then one of the senators from that state. Clark, at the start, had a majority of the votes, but under the rules then prevailing he needed two-thirds, and he never got them. After the tenth ballot his votes began to drift away, and on the thirtieth ballot Wilson was ahead of him. On the forty-sixth, on July 2, Wilson got the necessary two-thirds and was nominated. Preston and his local goons sweated valiantly to stem this tide, but they failed miserably—mainly, I suspect, because they got no useful help from their candidate. Quarters for Clark had been engaged at the Belvedere Hotel, and he was supposed to come to Baltimore and manage his campaign in person, but instead he took on an overdose of Bourbon and had to be put to bed in Washington. Not only the Baltimore Democratic machines, but also most of the other big city machines were for him, including Tammany, and he had the support of nearly all the Wall Street Democrats, who distrusted Wilson as a reformer and visionary. His chief opponent on the floor was William Jennings Bryan. Bryan really hoped that he might get the nomination himself, but when that turned out to be impossible he took out his rage in howling against the Money Power and arguing for Wilson. Grasty helped him, on the day the convention opened, by printing a three-column portrait of Thomas Fortune Ryan on the first page of the *Sun*—the first portrait ever printed there. The lines under it described Ryan as a Money King, and hinted that he was Wall Street's fugleman in a nefarious effort to nominate Clark. This adroit propaganda probably influenced not a few of the delegates. Ryan protested that he was present as a simple delegate from Virginia, which was his legal residence, and had no commission from Wall Street, but that disclaimer accomplished nothing. As I have said, it was not until just before the end of the convention that the *Sun* began to advocate Wilson openly. But on the day after the nomination Wilson sent the paper a telegram thanking it for its "splendid support."

With these high matters, fortunately enough, I had no direct concern, for I was no longer writing any editorials, and my Free Lance column paid more attention to Preston than to Wilson and Clark. Preston's campaign for the vice-presidential nomination was now nearing its unhappy climax, and I blasted him daily with extravagant ridicule. For the rest I contented myself with sniffing at the convention itself, which was an extremely uncomfortable affair, held in savagely hot weather in the Fifth Regiment Armory, remote from all the Baltimore hotels. I was not assigned to see and write about the show. Instead, I was told off to take charge of the *Evening Sun* side of the *Sunpapers'* news bureau, which was set up in an old house opposite the armory and there I put in long hours of hard copy-reading. It was not until the convention began balloting, on June 27, that I got into the hall at all. The session of that evening lasted until 7 o'clock the next morning, and I wrote a long account of it for the *Evening Sun* of June 28. Thereafter I returned to my copy-reading, for though there were other evening sessions I had to put in my time after dinner writing my Free Lance column for the next day. My recollection is that I missed seeing Wilson nominated on the afternoon of July 2, but I was in the press-stand that night, when the nomination of a candidate for vice-president followed. The heat was infernal, and I recall that a necessary visit to the filthy toilet under the stand left me with a case of *pediculus pubis* [pubic lice]. The session lasted until 5 A.M., and was full of the obscene buffooneries that always mark the choice of a vice-president. Poor Preston, though Clark was now done for, insisted upon having his own name presented to the convention. All the more dignified orators in the Maryland delegation begged off from the job, and he was reduced to entrusting it to a third-rate Eastern Shore politician named Alonzo J. Miles. Miles prepared for the unpleasant duty by getting drunk, and when he appeared on the platform and began to speak in a thick voice, with many slips in pronunciation, the delegates and alternates began to guffaw, and presently they were joined by the gallery. There were, of course, many Preston supporters in the gallery, but there were also many of his enemies, and one large delegation of the latter was headed by William H. Anderson, superintendent of the Maryland Anti-Saloon League. These enemies were soon trying to howl Miles down, and in a little while they succeeded. He was driven from the platform with half his speech unspoken, and the Preston boom vanished in low comedy then and there. It was a spectacle still remembered in Baltimore, and though Preston was reëlected Mayor in 1915 he never quite lived it down. I confess that the uproar gave me a certain malicious pleasure. While poor Miles was being hooted down, I stood on my desk in the press-stand with A. H. McDannald, and the two of us rocked and bellowed with mirth.

The story was too late for the *Sun*, but I wrote it for the *Evening Sun* of the next day, June 28. Some one else had been assigned to the night session, but when I got to the office in the early morning, and described the scene to Paul Patterson, then managing editor, he insisted that I sit down at once and get it on paper. I was not overly eager to do so, for I had been planning to use my notes for my Free Lance column, but Patterson appealed to me as a newspaper man, and I went to work. "Take all the space you want," he said. "If it needs a page, take a page." Years later he was fond of telling gaping young reporters that I actually filled the page, but in reality my story ran to less than three columns. When it was finished, at about 8 o'clock, I proceeded to write my Free Lance column. In it I poured mockery upon poor Preston under the guise of sympathizing with him. Who was responsible for my assignment to the *Evening Sun* bureau, with its dull copy-reading, I don't know. It was certainly not Patterson, and in all probability it was Grasty himself. I was, in those days, a better reporter than any of those told off to work under me, but Grasty, as I have said more than once, had little interest in news, and was a bad judge of its handling. He had, in his prime, many good editorial ideas, but they were always ideas for launching crusades, not for covering news. I doubt that, while the convention was going on, he ever read with any attention a report of it in his own news columns.

Toward the end of May, more than a month before the convention met, he concocted a scheme that, if it had worked, might have ruined Preston out of hand and made a first-rate sensation, at least in Maryland. The state law, at that time, provided that the name of every candidate for president or vice-president had to be filed with the Secretary of State, along with a fee of $270. It was Grasty's plan to file my own name at the very last moment, when it would be too late for Preston to come in. I would thus be the only legitimate candidate, and Grasty believed that he could induce his friends among the high-toned lawyers of Baltimore to discover such pains and penalties for violating the law that the state convention would be intimidated into naming me. I was about to go abroad with McDannald at the time he thought of his device to baffle and craze Preston, but we prepared between us a letter of acceptance over my signature, and it was arranged that I was to be notified by wireless if the scheme went through, and that my acceptance was to be published in the *Sun.* Unhappily for the success of the joke, Preston got warning that his nomination might be invalidated if he did not file and pay up, and so he appeared with his $270 at the very last moment, just as Grasty's agents were preparing to make the deposit in my name. Grasty and I often speculated, in the two years following, as to what would have happened if the plan had been a success. All the lawyers he consulted agreed that the state convention, lacking any other lawful candidate, would have been forced to choose me—a choice probably not at all unpalatable to many, and perhaps even a majority of the delegates, for though they were surely not for me, they were secretly against Preston. Moreover, the lawyers agreed that, once I had been chosen, the state delegation would have been compelled to present my name to the national convention, and Grasty insisted that, if that had happened, he would have been able to get me a good many votes, at least on the first ballot, from the friendly bosses of other delegations. Indeed, it was conceivable (though stupendously improbable) that, by one of those grotesque paranoias which so often glorify national conventions, especially when a candidate for second place is being chosen, I might have got the nomination, and gone before an astonished country as the immortal Wilson's running-mate, *vice* [instead of] Tom Marshall, dead *in utero*. It was not until years later that I recalled the fact that I was ineligible, for Article II, Section 2, of the Constitution provides that a candidate for the presidency, and *pari passu* for the vice-presidency, must be 35 years old. In 1912 I was but 32.

3

Minority of One

1914–1919

The outbreak of war in 1914 was destined to interrupt my work for the *Sun*, but I didn't know it at the time. As I have said, I had been doing a monthly article on books for the *Smart Set* since 1908, but this did not burden me, though by 1914 it had already got me a good deal of notice. The magazine had been bought by a pretentious but hollow fellow named John Adams Thayer in 1911, and he had made various efforts to induce me to do more writing for it. In 1912 he offered me the editorship, but I was determined not to live in New York, and so refused. To get rid of him I suggested that he give the post to Willard Huntington Wright, and this he did, but Wright turned out to be a very extravagant editor, and early in 1914 Thayer fired him.

The magazine, meanwhile, had begun to run deficits, and when the war broke out Thayer got into a panic, and made it over to his paper man, Eugene F. Crowe. The story of what followed belongs to the history of my adventures with magazines; suffice it to say here that Crowe offered the editorship to George Jean Nathan, the *Smart Set*'s dramatic critic, that Nathan refused to take it unless I would agree to share it with him, and that we took over on those terms in September, 1914. This venture naturally required me to make frequent trips to New York, and for six months or so I managed to make them without interfering seriously with my work for the *Evening Sun*. Sometimes I would leave Baltimore at noon, after making up my Free Lance column for the day, put in the late afternoon and evening with Nathan, and then return by sleeper that night; at other times I would go to New York for the week-end. All manuscripts that came in were shipped to me in Baltimore, and I would read them there. But after the beginning of 1915 this arrangement became increasingly onerous, for the *Smart Set* needed more and more attention, and in addition Nathan and I had decided to help out its meager income by launching a couple of pulp magazines, in association with Eltinge F. Warner, its publisher, and Crowe the paper man, its backer. By the middle of 1914 I was so hard beset that giving proper care and labor to my Free Lance column became impossible, and I notified Frank Kent, who was then managing editor of both *Sunpapers,* that I'd have to abandon it in the Autumn. He naturally protested, for it had a considerable following in Baltimore and was thus very useful to the *Evening Sun.* But I could see no other way out, and it appeared for the last time on October 23, 1915. As a solatium to Kent I agreed to write an occasional signed article for the *Evening Sun* editorial page, and the first of these articles was printed on October 25. They ran on thereafter until December 6, 1916, and there were 65 of them altogether. I was paid $15 apiece for them—an extremely low price, but I was eager to keep up some sort of connection with the *Sunpapers* and knew that they were very hard up. At the end of 1916 I went abroad to see something of the war. When I returned early in 1917 my observations were printed in the *Evening Sun,* but soon after the United States entered the war it became obvious that free speech was suspended, and I decided to write no more. Thereafter I did no regular writing for the *Sunpapers* until the beginning of 1920. But I still owned the stock that Grasty had given me, and I kept up my interest in the property, seeing Patterson constantly and Harry Black as constantly save for the period when he was in the Navy. I thus heard in detail all of Patterson's plans for pulling the paper out of the mud. His main job, down to the end of the war, was to second Van Lear Black in the effort to restore them to simple solvency, but after 1918 he also gave some thought to editorial matters, as did Harry Black, and I sat in on many of their palavers.

In my Free Lance column I had taken an anti-English line from the start of the war, and I have already described how my denunciations of the sweating Motherland produced an amicable clash with Ernest A. Boyd, the British vice-consul in Baltimore. I was convinced then, and I am still convinced, that the war was caused by English contriving far more than by German purpose, and I said so daily, and in plain language.

In those early days of the war the *Sunpapers,* like all the other American newspapers, were full of dispatches from Paris and London announcing vast and incredible French, Belgian and Russian victories. I had at them by going back to the files of the *Sun* for 1870, reprinting the reports of French victories that it printed then, and contrasting them with the facts that came out later. It was obvious from the start that American opinion was being influenced by the enormous propaganda flowing out of England, and that American officialdom, under the leadership of the Anglomaniacal Woodrow Wilson, was going the same way. By the end of 1914 it was already apparent to the judicious that Wilson would try to horn into the war soon or late, at least if it appeared to be going against England, and after the sinking of the *Lusitania* on May 7, 1915, his bitter partisanship was undisguised. Adams, as always, followed him docilely, and there was but little pretense to neutrality in the *Sun*'s editorials after the first few weeks of the war. In my Free Lance column I not only denounced Wilson, but also ridiculed the *Sun*. This course naturally brought down upon me the dudgeon of all the Anglomaniacs in Baltimore, and their protests and objurgations filled the letter column of the *Evening Sun*. Also, I received a great many indignant letters myself, most of them anonymous and not a few of them threatening me with violence. The threats were new but the indignation was not, for I had been in a minority of one very often during the past three years, and so I kept on to the end. In fact, I rather enjoyed the onslaught, for in those days things were still going very badly for the Allies, and I had plenty of material for effective ripostes.

What really incommoded me was the gratitude of the Baltimore Germans. Most of them were ignoramuses of the petty trading class, and, like my father and my grandfather before me, I had always kept away from them. But now, surrounded by hostile neighbors, they turned to me as one of them, and insisted upon regarding me as a German patriot. I was, of course, no more a German patriot than I was an American patriot, but it was impossible to make them understand and believe it, so I had to suffer their attentions from August 2, 1914, to October 23, 1915, often to my acute discomfort. They sent delegations to the office to suggest new and worse attacks upon England, they elected me an honorary member of all their singing societies, and they invited me to many of their parties. Not infrequently I received presents of chocolate cakes and other such delicacies from appreciative German housewives. It was hard to be impolite to these simple-minded and much-troubled people, but their attentions often amounted to a nuisance. The more civilized Germans of Baltimore were easier to endure, but they were few in numbers and most of them were elderly. I got well acquainted with some that I had known only vaguely before the war, or not at all, and found them

pleasant enough. They had a club called the Germania which had been
organized in 1840, and was the oldest first-rate club of the town. It had
had a luxurious clubhouse in Fayette street, west of Eutaw, for many
years, but had now moved to a fine old house in Charles street, almost
directly opposite the Maryland Club. I was elected a member in 1915 or
1916, but never made any use of the clubhouse, for it was monopolized
by a small group of the oldest members, some of whom I disliked. On my
return from Europe in 1917 I gave an account of my observations of the
war at a general meeting on a Sunday afternoon, with ladies present.
There was a turnout that packed the whole downstairs. After the United
States got into the war the club began to be harassed by spy hunters, and
finally closed its house and suspended. The excellent wine-cellar was put
up at an auction sale open to members only, but no notices of it were sent
out, and in consequence the wine was collared by a few of the old-timers,
all of them assiduous boozers. I was also invited, in 1915 and 1916, to join
all the charitable and cultural organizations of the Baltimore Germans,
and had to submit. They included the General German Orphan Asylum
(*Waisenhaus*), the General German Aged People's Home (*Greisenheim*),
the German Society of Maryland, and the Society for the History of the
Germans in Maryland, to which was later added the Goethe Society.
{When the *Greisenheim* was incorporated in 1881 virtually all the wealth-
ier Jews of Baltimore were either immigrants from Germany or the children of such immigrants, so they joined the German Catholics and
Protestants in founding the home. There were as yet very few distinc-
tively Jewish charities: they had to wait until the great immigration of
Eastern Jews began. To this day, despite Hitler, the list of "members of
the corporation," printed in the annual report of the *Greisenheim*, shows
such names as Friedenwald, Greif, Hamburger, Hecht, Hochschild, Hut-
zler, Kann, Katz, Kohn, Macht, Oppenheimer and Straus, all eminent in
Baltimore Jewry. I always appear in the list, not as H.L., or Henry L., but
as Hy. L. Mencken. In my boyhood the *Greisenheim*'s home was in West
Baltimore street, at the edge of the Steuart's Hill described in "Happy
Days." Now it is at Irvington, on the Frederick road.} I have never been
to a meeting of any of them, but I continue my membership, and contribute dues of $5 a year to the funds of each. My father and grandfather
belonged to none of them.

When two German raiders, the *Kronprinz Wilhelm* and the *Prinz
Eitel Friedrich* (both Norddeutscher-Lloyd liners in times of peace), were
forced to put into Norfolk in the late Autumn of 1914 by the exhaustion
of their coal, some of their officers came to Baltimore on visits, and I thus

Jousting with "The Free Lance." Baltimoreans had never seen such a column before, and haven't since. November, 1915. W. F. Pensch.

became acquainted with them. Among them were Captain Thierfelder, commander of the *Wilhelm;* Dr. Wilhelm Sohler, its surgeon; Count Alfred Niezychowski, one of its junior officers; and Captain Max V. Thierichens, commander of the *Eitel Friedrich.* The United States was still officially neutral in the war, and so these officers, though their ships were interned, had a considerable freedom of movement. I became especially friendly with Sohler, a gigantic and extremely amiable fellow with a superb voice: in fact, he had vacillated in his youth between studying medicine and trying for opera. The two ships were in charge of Admiral Walter McLean, U.S.N., commandant of the Norfolk Navy Yard, who was Paul Patterson's father-in-law. On New Year's Eve, 1914–15, there was a gaudy party aboard the *Wilhelm,* and Patterson, his wife Elsie and I were invited. It was an extremely wet affair, and of it I recall only a few minor incidents. One is that Thierichens, on noting that Elsie was pregnant, offered a toast to her and the newcomer, greatly to her delight. Another was that Niezychowski, who was officer of the deck, cut off the supply of beer to the North German Lloyd's sailors for an hour, beginning at 2 A.M., alleging that they lacked the drinking capacity of the Navy sailors aboard, and needed the time for recuperation. The third was that when I left Norfolk the next morning for Cape Charles, and there boarded a train for New York, I was so much used up that I slept all the way to Wilmington. Mrs. McLean took a great interest in Niezychowski, who was a youngster of charming manners, and when the United States got into the war her well-meaning effort to make him and his shipmates comfortable brought trouble to her husband. Complaints that he had been unduly friendly with the Germans were lodged in Washington by professional spy-hunters, and he was presently retired on the specious ground that he had "lost initiative." Van Lear Black, who was acquainted with Franklin D. Roosevelt, then assistant secretary of the Navy, tried through him to induce his chief, Josephus Daniels, to rescind the order of retirement, but Josephus refused to do so. Being forced out of the service in war time was naturally a severe blow to the admiral, and he moped dismally until his death in 1930.

I kept diligently away from German agents during the whole course of the war, and met the German ambassador at Washington, Count Bernstorff, only once: when I applied for a German visa at the end of 1916. When the unarmed submarine, the *Deutschland,* arrived in Baltimore on July 10, 1916, I refused to have anything to do with the welcome arranged for it. That welcome was in charge of Paul Hilken, son of old Henry G. Hilken, for many years the Baltimore agent of the North

German Lloyd. I was well acquainted with his father, and had a high esteem for him, but the son always seemed to me a suspicious character. I met the commander of the *Deutschland,* Captain Paul König, at a German *Volksfest* that I tried in vain to escape, but saw him only a few times. One day Paul Hilken came to me with a proposal that I return to Germany on the submarine. The New York *Tribune,* he said, was willing to pay $50,000 for the privilege of putting a correspondent aboard, but he was against it because of the *Tribune*'s violent support of England. If I would consent to make the trip back to Bremen I could have the exclusive right free of charge, and would be free to sell my reports to the highest bidder, excluding the *Tribune.* There seemed to be something fishy about this, and I refused at once. Indeed, I'd have refused if there had *not* been anything fishy, for I knew that a large British fleet was waiting for the *Deutschland,* outside the Chesapeake capes, and the chances of its getting through seemed very slim. König escaped that fleet, in fact, only because he got some unexpected help from friendly American naval officers, many of whom disliked the British. They marked on a chart a little-used course up the Maryland coast that enabled him to elude the waiting fleet, and he reached Bremen safely. Another unarmed German submarine, the *Bremen,* set off for America soon afterward, carrying the same cargo of drugs and dyes that the *Deutschland* had brought and planning to take home the same rubber and nickel, but it was never heard from again. König, however, made a second successful trip toward the end of 1916. When he arrived at New London, Conn., on November 1 I went there to visit him, and after the war I met him in Bremen and on his several visits to the United States. He was a tough mariner, but a very quiet and unassuming man. On his departure from New London an effort was made by English agents to ram his ship, but he baffled it and got away. After the war it turned out that my suspicions of Paul Hilken were well justified. In the course of some legal proceedings at Baltimore he went on the stand and confessed that he had had a hand in some of the principal acts of sabotage of the war years, including the Black Tom explosion.* He had left Baltimore some time before this, but was brought back to testify, which he apparently did very willingly. His father never mentioned him in my presence after the war, and it was understood that he was not to be mentioned by anyone else where the old man could hear. I gathered from various talks with König that he had never heard of

* On July 30, 1916, a massive explosion damaged the National Storage Company piers on Black Tom Island in New York harbor.

Paul Hilken's proposal that I return on the *Deutschland* in the Summer of 1916.

During the continuance of the Free Lance the Blacks never interfered with my freedom in the slightest. They were, of course, pro-English, and Harry Black, as I have said, was married to an Englishwoman and affected an extreme form of the Oxford accent, but my relation with him and also with his wife remained friendly throughout the war. He served in it as supple officer of a collier running between Cardiff and the French ports. His wife's sister, an extraordinarily tall young woman, had come out from England to bear her company, and I often had dinner with the two of them. They knew my sentiments, of course, but we got on very well. Van Lear Black I saw only seldom, and he had, in any case, very little interest in what was printed in the paper. But it amazed some of his friends that he did not get rid of me, or at least try to persuade me to let up on the English, and there were a number of wondering references to the matter in other newspapers. But he never opened his mouth on the subject, and when I gave up the Free Lance in October, 1915, it was on my own motion entirely. I was moved by various considerations. The principal one I have mentioned: the increasing extent and exigence of my interests in New York. Another was my growing conviction that Wilson would horn into the war soon or late, and that when he did so I would be forced to retire, for I could not imagine myself either going over to the English side or ceasing, while I had a signed column, to denounce its fraudulence. There was yet a third reason, and that was a feeling that I had probably been on the staff of the *Sun* long enough, and needed a change of pasture. It was now nearly ten years since I had come to the paper—and I have always, by a sort of instinct, divided my life into ten-year periods. I was co-editor of the *Smart Set* for just that long, and then followed ten years as editor of the *American Mercury*. There have been some breaks in my practise, but in the main I have stuck to it, and when I have failed to do so I have regretted it. I had an uneasy fear, without doubt well grounded, that if I kept on with the Free Lance I would become a mere columnist, bound down to a routine job and with no energy left for better things; worse, that I would degenerate into a town celebrity, a local worthy—something that I have always tried most diligently to avoid. The Free Lance is now forgotten by all save a few ancient Baltimoreans, but it did a lot for me while it lasted, if only in the way of clarifying my ideas, and I believe that it was also useful to the *Evening Sun*, for during the years between 1912 and 1915 it was the only thing in the paper that showed any sense. When I told Frank Kent, then managing editor of both *Sunpapers,* that I had made up my mind to abandon it, he protested on the sound ground that the *Evening Sun* needed it badly, but he agreed with me that its usefulness would disappear if, when and as the United States entered the war. As a sort of compromise I agreed to write some occasional signed articles for the *Evening Sun* editorial page, but I was under no obligation to do any fixed number of them. My opening article was an onslaught on Puritanism, and the next seven dealt with the war. There followed five on the report of a commission that had been appointed a year before to investigate prostitution and its attendant arts and mysteries in Baltimore. The chairman thereof was Dr. George Walker, a curious South Carolinian who practised urology in Baltimore, and he was the author of the report, which ran to five large volumes. Only one of them was ever printed; the rest existed only in manuscript, and I suspect that I was the only person, not excluding the other members of the commission, who ever read them.

When a Baltimore Symphony Orchestra was set up toward the end of 1915 I would sometimes give it a lift before a concert by printing an article on the symphony to be played. This I did mainly because the official program notes, written by a donkey named S. Broughton Tall, were stupid and inadequate. When, in March, 1916, a committee of rich and pious Baltimoreans brought the Rev. Billy Sunday, the evangelist, to town, I attended his orgies and wrote three articles upon them. I also did occasional literary articles—four on the American best-seller in May, 1916, one on James Huneker in April, four on Joseph Conrad in June and July, three on Theodore Dreiser in July and August, and a review of Ernest A. Boyd's "Ireland's Literary Renaissance" in November. But mainly I stuck to what were my two favorite themes at that time—the pernicious influence of Puritanism upon all phases of American life, and the pervasive dishonesty of Woodrow Wilson's course in the war.

I had hoped to go to Germany in the Summer of 1916 to see something of the war for myself, but it was impossible then for me to get rid of my obligations in New York. The *Smart Set* offered no difficulty, for Nathan could do the editorial work alone during my absence, but our two pulp magazines* needed a lot of attention, and it was not until October 24, 1916 that we managed to sell our shares in them to our two associates, Crow and Warner. I well recall my relief and rejoicing when

---

* *Parisienne,* founded in 1915, and *Saucy Stories,* established the following year.

the sale was effected, for I was now not only free again but had more money in hand than I had ever touched before. The very next day I began making my arrangements, and on December 28 I sailed from New York for Copenhagen in the Danish ship *Oscar II,* which took seventeen days to get there. A record of my trip, which was cut short when Wilson broke off diplomatic relations with Germany on February 1, 1917, is to be found in a volume in the Mencken collection at the Pratt Library, Baltimore, entitled "Germany–1917." I went as the representative of the *Sun,* though without salary, and it advanced $1000 toward my expenses. On my return home at the end of February in the Spanish steamship *Alfonso XIII,* sailing from La Coruña, Spain, to Havana, I received a wireless asking me to stop over in Cuba to cover a revolution then in progress. I was by this time running short of money, so the *Sun* sent me $100 more, making $1100 in all. When I got home at last I found that my total expenses, including losses on exchange, had run to $922.15, so I returned $177.85 to the cashier. The articles I wrote about my adventures in Germany, and my later observations in Cuba, were offered to various other papers by John N. Wheeler, of the Bell Syndicate in New York. I received 60% of the total receipts from Wheeler, or $534, and turned over $422.15 of it to the *Sun* as its share, leaving $111.85 for myself. This was my total cash return for a journey of 12,000 miles in ten countries, ten weeks of hard work, and probably 75,000 words of copy. The total cost to the *Sun,* setting aside a few small cable tolls, was $500 even: how I arrived at that amount I forget. Whatever the process, I did not care, for I had done well in 1915 and 1916, and at the end of the latter year had an automobile (my first, and last), nearly $2500 in cash in bank, and bonds worth, at par, more than $15,000. Several relatively lean years followed, but then my fortunes began to boom, and in 1921 I had a gross income of almost $30,000.

The record just mentioned, "Germany–1917," is accurate so far as it goes, but there are some gaps in it, for it is based on a diary I started in Berlin, and I had to be cautious about what I set down. The Germans, as it turned out, never molested me, but when Wilson broke off relations with Germany and I started home, on February 9, 1917, by way of Switzerland, France and Spain, I had to run a gauntlet of censors. At Berne I came under suspicion by consorting with Dr. Oscar Levy, editor of the English translation of Nietzsche, a German subject living in Geneva with a Frenchwoman. Levy came up to Berne to see me, and went with me to the French consulate when I applied for a visa. I well recall the sensation made by his appearance there. The place was full of detectives, and they plainly knew him and regarded him as a suspicious person. When I got back to my hotel I found that my baggage had been tumbled, apparently by prying secret agents, but nothing was missing. A few days later, when I came to the French-Spanish border, I encountered a more serious difficulty. The French customs inspector there was a woman, and when she opened my bags and saw a packet of manuscript, and, what is worse, a couple of dozen German pamphlets, she loosed a squawk, and a male inspector came running up. Inasmuch as I could not speak French I was in some alarm, but to my immense relief and delight he tackled me in English, and in fact in Cockney. It turned out that he was a French waiter who had gone to London as a young man, and there spent years of service in the "old English" chophouses of Fleet street. Summoned to the colors with the French army when the war began, he had been badly wounded, and was now relieved of military duty. I quickly came to terms with him, and he passed all my papers.

The *Sun* was too poor in those days to pay heavy cable tolls, so my instructions were to confine myself to mail stuff as much as possible. Unfortunately, it had to pass through the English blockade, and as a result very little of it got through. But I managed to keep carbons of it, and thus I was able to get it to the *Sun* after reaching Cuba. One of the best stories I sent home was mailed in duplicate from Christiania (now Oslo) and Berlin, and neither copy was ever delivered. It had to do with an episode to which I was a witness when the *Oscar II* was taken into Kirkwall by the English, and its passengers searched. One of them was a one-eyed young man named Glenn Stewart, second secretary in the American diplomatic service, who was proceeding to his post in Vienna. When the English boarding party undertook to search his baggage he claimed diplomatic immunity, and refused to give up the keys. The commander of the party, a lieutenant, thereupon went ashore for instructions. When he came back he reported that Walter Hines Page, the excessively Anglomaniacal American ambassador in London, had given the English a blanket permit to search all Americans, including all diplomats under the rank of minister. But Stewart refused to be bound by that permit, and announced that he would resist it by force. Sending a steward for me and for Ambrose Lambert, a former New York *Sun* reporter, he asked us to be witnesses of what followed as American newspaper men, and the only ones aboard. He then produced a pistol, laid it on his trunk in his cabin, and said to the lieutenant: "I know you are only doing your duty, and I do not blame you. But I can't consent to any invasion of the inalienable rights under international law of a diplomatic officer of the United

States. Page has no right to waive them. If you touch my trunk I shall be obliged to shoot you." The lieutenant there upon departed again. The next morning the captain of the port, a British admiral, came out in his barge and apologized to Stewart.

The affair had a grotesque sequel. There was a German woman aboard, coming home from Mexico, who had a large number of letters written by other Germans there. Just before we got into Kirkwall she sewed them up in a sofa cushion in her room, and then sneaked into Stewart's room, which was next door, and exchanged her cushion for his. They were identical and he did not notice the change. When we left Kirkwall she sneaked into Stewart's room again, and got her cushion back. The success of the trick was so great that she could not refrain from boasting about it. When this boasting reached the English agents aboard—they were mainly Norwegians and Danes—we were already half way across the North Sea, but they wirelessed back to Kirkwall for a destroyer, and presently it was reported to be in pursuit. But before it heaved in sight we were inside the Christiania Fjord, and if it was actually following us it did not follow us in. Stewart only laughed, but the pro-British Scandinavians were very indignant. The German woman told me that the letters were quite harmless—simply personal messages from exiled Germans to the folks back home. But she was afraid that the English would collar them, and figured shrewdly, and better than she knew, that they would not search Stewart. I wrote the story of his defiance as we sailed up the fjord and mailed it in Christiania, and a week later I mailed a carbon from Berlin, but as I have said neither copy ever reached the *Sun*. Unhappily, I had made no second carbon, and thus did not bring out a copy with my other papers.

The voyage in the *Oscar II* was long and tedious, but full of humors. The route chosen by the captain took us so far North that we came close to Greenland. The weather, of course, was cold, and going on deck was impossible, but there was plenty doing inside. On New Year's Eve there was a party that lasted all night. The captain, in order to keep the peace, issued orders that the little orchestra in the smoking-room should play no national anthems, not even the Danish, but some joker induced the bull-fiddle player, who was also the leader, to put on a potpourri of presumably innocuous German songs beginning with "Die Lorelei," and the band blazed into it, with the bull-fiddler forgetting that it ended with "Die Wacht am Rhein." When the sounds of the latter burst forth there was an uproar in the smoke-room, and all the other nationalities demanded that their anthems be played too. When the captain was sent for he ordered that this be done, and so they were solemnly played one by one. But the Swedish anthem was omitted, whereupon the three or four Swedes aboard protested bitterly. The captain, who, like most Danes, viewed all Swedes with an envious and bilious eye, argued that they *had* no anthem. They then got their heads together and proceeded to prove that this was a libel by singing it. The other passengers, far gone in liquor by now, hooted the performance, and for a little while a riot appeared to be in the making. But when the Swedes finished their horrible singing everyone had another drink, and by dawn peace and amity were restored. Only a few invalids ate breakfast or lunch the next day. The rest of the ship's company snored. Nearly all the stewards were as tight as the passengers, and even the officers showed signs of damage.

The *Oscar II* was a small and old-fashioned ship and the passengers were seated in the dining-room at four or five long tables. At the head of mine sat the ship's doctor and at the other end a Russian general with huge moustaches. Both were gigantic eaters. One day I saw the doctor eat the whole of a cabbage stuffed with sausage-meat, and at all meals the general stuffed down immense quantities of everything on the table, including especially the Danish pastry. It was brought in on large trays, each filled with ten or twelve different kinds, and the stewards boasted that the same kind was never repeated during a voyage. The general grabbed two pieces of every kind at lunch and dinner, and by the time he finished his bristling moustache was gummy with the creams and jellies that constituted the fillings. He was naturally called the Walrus, and inasmuch as he professed to know no English, though he had been in the United States buying munitions, we often spoke of him by that nickname in his presence. In Copenhagen, at the end of the voyage, he took one of the Americans aside, and told him in excellent English that he was well aware of what we had been calling him, but had decided in the interests of international comity to make no protest. I often wonder what became of the old man after he got back to Russia. The Germans, by that time, had punished the Russian army cruelly, and before the end of 1917 it was ready to collapse. In all probability, the Bolsheviki butchered him when they came into power.

From Copenhagen I proceeded to Gjedser, on the Danish coast of the Baltic, and there crossed to the little German port of Warnemünde, whence I went on to Berlin by train. My experiences in Germany in war time were extremely interesting, and some day I may do an account of them. Suffice it to say here that I was received politely at the Military Bureau of the Foreign Office, where a cavalry captain named Plettenberg was in charge, and at the Foreign Office itself, where *Legationsrat* [embassy advisor] Roediger looked after press relations, and that I soon met all of the other American correspondents in Berlin. They were, in the main, an indifferent lot, and I was somewhat upset by my first contact with the unhappy fact that American newspapers are sometimes represented abroad by men who would hardly qualify as competent police reporters at home. Of those that I recall, the best was James O'Donnell Bennett, of the Chicago *Tribune*. He held himself aloof from the rest, and seldom joined in their continuous boozing in the bar of the Adlon Hotel. Others were Oswald F. Schütte, of the Chicago *Daily News;* Raymond Swing, who was also with the *Daily News;* William Bayard Hale, who represented Hearst; Seymour Conger, head of the Associated Press Bureau; Carl W. Ackerman, head of the United Press Bureau; Guido Enderes and Philip Powers, both of the Associated Press; Oscar King Davis and Cyril Brown, of the New York *Times*. There were yet others, but I forget them. Hale lived in great state in a large apartment at the Adlon, and devoted himself mainly to drink. Brown was also given to the bottle, and so were several of the lesser lights. Ackerman, a mediocre reporter of extremely unpleasant personality, has been dean of the Columbia University School of Journalism since 1931. Conger, Davis and Bennett are dead (1942). Swing, since 1939, has been a successful radio crooner. When I met Bennett he suggested that I ask the Germans for permission to join the Turks: no correspondent, he said, had ever been to the Turkish front, and it promised a first-rate show. I put in my application, but it had to be referred to Constantinople, and while I was waiting the Germans offered to send me to their own East front. I accepted with alacrity, and was presently on my way to Königsberg, whence I proceeded to the German line along the Dvina river. My stay there was short, but I saw plenty, and greatly enjoyed the trip. I was one of a party of three in charge of Captain von Vignau of the General Staff, the other two being a Jewish journalist from Rotterdam named Blankenstein and a Swiss colonel serving as a military observer. The Bismarck centenary in 1915 had produced a great deal of discussion of Bismarck's genealogy, and most educated Germans had picked up the fact that his mother was a member of a learned Leipzig family named Mencken. Thus my name got me extra politeness, and at all division dinners behind the front I was seated beside the ranking general. Swing had warned me before I left Berlin that it would be very cold in the Baltic country, and had pressed upon me the loan of an extra overcoat and a pair of heavy shoes. I was very grateful for this thoughtfulness when I reached the field, for the temperature there was always below zero, and more than once it got down to 40 degrees below. I slept several nights on the stoves in peasant houses, always expecting to be cremated before morning but never getting beyond being pleasantly warm.

I was still at the front when Wilson gave Bernstorff his passports. When I got back to Berlin, half frozen, I found that James W. Gerard, the American ambassador, was in a great state of alarm, and full of predictions that the Germans would send all American correspondents to Ruhleben, the internment-camp for civilians. The Germans laughed at these glooms, and assured all of us that we were quite safe. When Gerard prepared to leave Berlin I decided to go with him, for my commission was for mail stuff, not for cables; moreover, my money was running low, and it would probably be impossible to get any more from home. Unhappily, I soon learned that there was a rule of the General Staff forbidding any foreign correspondent to leave the country within eight weeks of his return from the front: its aim was to prevent any leakage of military information, which might be dropped accidently as well as deliberately. My only concern at this news was about money, for I was not eager to travel with Gerard, who was a blatant and very offensive ass. But Schütte, who had plenty of cash in hand and planned to stay a while longer, urged me to go at once, for I was the only American correspondent who could be trusted, on reaching home, to refrain from libelling the Germans with bogus "revelations." Unhappily, no one in Berlin had authority to waive the General Staff's rule; only Ludendorff could do it, and Ludendorff was in the field. But Schütte managed to get word to him through the Foreign Office, and less than ten hours before the Gerard train was scheduled to leave there arrived from him a telegram giving me permission to leave. So I went out with Gerard despite myself. In Paris, however, I leaped ahead of him, and had been in Cuba a week before he arrived. Schütte told various persons after the war that Gerard had tried to induce the Germans to withhold my exit visa, even after Ludendorff had approved it, but this I doubt. For one thing, the Germans would have paid no attention to him, and he knew it. For another thing, he made no effort to hold me up at the French border, which he might have done very easily. When I met him in Cuba he was polite but somewhat distant, but that was probably due to his resentment of my arrival there a week ahead of him.

I managed to do so by the simplest of devices. When we got to Paris we found that it was impracticable to telegraph to Madrid for steamship reservations, for all telegrams across the Spanish border, even diplomatic telegrams, were held up for three days each way. Gerard told me himself, the morning of our arrival, that he could neither wire nor telephone to his colleague, Joseph E. Willard, American ambassador at Madrid. But I determined to get my Spanish visa at once, and to that end consulted the portier at the Continental Hotel, a Jew. He not only got it for me within an hour, but also hinted that, if I were willing to pay a fair price, he could get me a ticket for Madrid on the express leaving that very night. I asked him how much it would cost, and he said $20 for the proper officials and $20 for himself. I handed him two American gold notes, and in an hour he was back with my ticket. The whole transaction seemed so incredible that I went to the station that night half expecting to be barred from the train. But my ticket was received without question, and after two nights in a very comfortable wagon-lit I was in Madrid. There Willard got me passage on the *Alfonso XIII,* and on February 21 I sailed from La Coruña. Gerard and his party were still stuck in Paris, and it was a week before they got to Spain and boarded a ship for Cuba and home.

The *Alfonso XIII* was an ancient and decrepit American craft that had been bought by the Spaniards and renamed, but I greatly enjoyed my ten days voyage, for it was through summery seas. On the way from Madrid to La Coruña I had met three agreeable Americans on the train—Dr. Herman M. Biggs, then health commissioner of the State of New York; Dr. A. Raymond Dochez, of the Rockefeller Institute; and a young student of Romance languages named Geoffroy Atkinson. They had been in France as members of a commission appointed to investigate tuberculosis in the French Army. Dochez had taken his M.D. degree at the Johns Hopkins, so we had many friends in common, and on the ship the four of us ate together. Every morning after breakfast I would go to the smokeroom and write 2500 words of my expansion of my Berlin diary, and every afternoon I would return to do 2500 more, with the re-sult that I had 50,000 words on paper by the time we reached Cuba. At the same time Atkinson would sit opposite me banging out the inter-minable report of his commission, which had largely to do, so I gathered from his profane interjections, with the paucity of sanitary latrines at the French front. In the evenings Dochez, Atkinson and I would drink in the smokeroom. Biggs, who was frail and in bad health, always went to bed. Atkinson was then but 23 years old, but he sported a large blond beard, and soon afterward became a professor of French. The voyage was somewhat rough, and the lower deck where I lodged was mainly inhabi-ted by Spaniards who were seasick all night, and groaned dismally. There were some American women aboard—department-store buyers fleeing

Mencken visits the German Eastern front on January 30, 1917. *Left to right:* Riggenbach, Lieutenant Nietschmann, H.L.M., Lieutenant Urbach, Blankenstein (journalist from Rotterdam), and Captain von Vignau.

from Paris—and almost every night one or another of them was awakened by scampering rats, and set up a caterwauling.

On March 4, as the *Alfonso XIII* labored through the Bahamas, I got a wireless from the *Sun* saying that there was a story to cover in Cuba, and asking me to report on my arrival. I recalled at once that I had an acquaintance in Havana—Captain Asmus Leonhard, of the Munson Steamship Line: I had met him on a German ship crossing the Atlantic in 1912. So I wired in to him, and presently I had a reply saying that his launch would meet me. The story turned out to be a revolution against President Mario G. Menocal, led by one José Miguel Gomez, who had himself been President from 1909 to 1913. Captain Leonhard, who knew everyone in Cuba worth knowing, introduced me to some of Gomez's chief backers, and I was astonished to discover that they were carrying on the revolution from an office in a Havana office-building. Through Biggs I was likewise introduced to Menocal's supporters, and within 24 hours I had all the material I needed. The other correspondents that I met were roaring against a cable censorship that made it quite impossible to send any real news to the United States. I got round it by going down to

the dock every morning, and intrusting my copy to the first likely looking American I found on the dock of the daily ship to Key West. Some of
it was telegraphed from Key West and the rest went north by mail and all
of it got through promptly and safely. On March 9, at a battle near Caji-
gal in Camaguey province, the rebellion was crushed and José Miguel
Gomez was captured. We correspondents received advance notices of the
battle from both Julio de la Torre, a lawyer who was at the head of the
revolutionary *junta* in Havana, and Eusebio S. Azpiazu, who was Menocal's private secretary, and we prepared to go to Camaguey to see it, but
before we could start news came in that it was over. Gomez was brought
to Havana, tried by court-martial and sentenced to be shot, and we
arranged with the military to see his execution. But his sentence was
quickly reduced to life imprisonment, and then to ten years confinement
in a fortress, and then to exile, and finally to the confiscation of his property, which included a yacht. Captain Leonhard was immensely amiable.
He not only introduced me to the revolutionists; he also put me up at the
Pasaje Hotel as his guest, and gave me a ticket in the Cuban lottery. If it
had won the capital prize I'd have had $20,000, but it didn't.

I lingered long enough to see the arrival of Gerard and his party, and
on the trip to Key West had a considerable palaver with him. His talk
was almost idiotic. He insisted that the Germans had planned to intern
all the American correspondents in Berlin, and that it was only his truculent objection that made them change their minds. I knew, of course, that
this was buncombe. As we neared Washington by train Gerard let it be
known that he would be met at the station by Secretary of State Robert
Lansing and wafted at once to the White House. Instead he was met by a
very minor official, and Wilson refused to see him, not only then but afterward. I also met Grasty, who had come back from Europe with Gerard. He was then ostensibly a correspondent for the New York *Times,*
but he told me that he had actually been acting as a confidential agent for
Wilson. His talk was vague and highfalutin, and he seemed almost a burlesque of his former smart and humorous self. I listened to him for a
while in Havana, but avoided him in the ship to Key West and the train
to the north. When the Treaty of Versailles was made public he approved
it heartily, and when Wilson tried to force the United States into the
League of Nations he applauded. My last sight of him was in Union Station, Baltimore. I got off there, but he continued to New York. We shook
hands with only a polite word or two, and so he vanished from my ken.

I got home with all my German notes and souvenirs intact, including
an *Entlausungsschein* [certificate of delousing] acquired on the Russian

front. The *Sun* printed most of my Berlin diary, expanded from memory on the way home with the aid of German newspaper clippings, but on April 6 Wilson declared war on Germany and after that I could print no more. Soon after I reached Baltimore I was asked by Ellery Sedgwick, editor of the *Atlantic Monthly,* to do an article for him on Ludendorff: it was published in the *Atlantic* for June, 1917. After that, until the war was over and some measure of free speech began to be restored, I devoted myself to my magazine work and to books. But on June 18, 1917, at the request of John E. Cullen, managing editor of the New York *Evening Mail,* I began a series of innocuous articles for that paper. By this time it was impossible to write about the war save in terms of the prevailing blather, which I naturally refused to do, but I managed to get in a few licks for free speech. The *Evening Mail,* under suspicion for its pro-German leanings earlier in the war, was very hard up, and Cullen paid me but $15 an article. The only one of the series worth remembering was my fictitious history of the bathtub in America, printed on December 28, 1917.* At the end of November an old friend, Dr. George A. Stewart of Baltimore, who was at the Rockefeller Institute in New York investigating the new Carrel-Dakin treatment for wounds, suggested that I drop in on him there and meet Dr. Alexis Carrel. Always interested in medical matters, I did so gladly, and spent a couple of hours with him. I came away with the impression that he was at least half quack, and that impression was confirmed eighteen years later, when he came out for religion in his book, "Man the Unknown." I did two articles for the *Mail* on the Carrel-Dakin treatment, and they were published on December 4 and 6, 1917. I quit the paper in 1918.

In 1916, along with Willard H. Wright and George Jean Nathan I brought out a book called "Europe After 8:15," made up of articles written by the three of us for the *Smart Set.* The war killed it a-bornin'. In 1917 Alfred A. Knopf published my "Book of Prefaces," and in 1918 Philip Goodman published "In Defense of Women" and "Damn! A Book of Calumny." In 1919 came the first volume of "Prejudices" and the first edition of "The American Language," and in 1920 my translation of Nietzsche's "The Antichrist" and the play, "Heliogabalus," written with Nathan. The war years were naturally unpleasant to me, for I was convinced that the course of the United States was not only dishonest and dishonorable but also foolish, and I have never changed that view. My

---

* Mencken might have mentioned the equally memorable "The Sahara of the Bozart," which appeared in the *New York Evening Mail* November 13, 1917.

denunciations of England in the Free Lance down to the end of 1915 were remembered afterward by many professional patriots, and at the height of the spy scare, in 1918, I received a great many threatening letters. More than once tips reached me that my house was to be searched, but it was never done; moreover, I didn't care, save for the alarm it would have caused my mother, for all my more embarrassing papers were buried in a glass enclosed box in the backyard, with a brick pavement over it. I dug them up in 1919 and found they had survived their entombment. On various occasions attempts were made to lure me into compromising statements or positions, but I always eluded them. Once in 1918 a plausible looking young man came to the house and asked me to take charge of what he said was the manuscript of a book on Nietzsche, allegedly of his composition. He said that he was going to the war, and feared that his poor old mother might read it, and, since she was a pious woman, destroy it. I ordered him out of the house at once. As he left with his package under his arm he said: "You act as if you thought I might be a detective trying to plant something on you." "That possibility," I replied, "has crossed my mind." When Oswald Schütte, the Chicago *News* correspondent in Berlin, who was the last American correspondent to leave there after the United States entered the war, returned home from Switzerland in 1918, and settled in Washington as the correspondent of *Leslie's Weekly,* he and I often exchanged letters. They were, of course, quite harmless, but Schütte soon discovered that they were being opened. One day he provided me with plain proof of it—the envelope of a letter from me that had been three days reaching him from Baltimore, and showed the stamp of the War Department postoffice. It had been diverted there, and after it was opened some careless clerk had remailed it in the building. I was, of course, hard beset by the promoters of the war loans, and of war charities, real and bogus, but I always managed to resist them. I never contributed so much as a cent to any of the latter, and I never bought any so-called Liberty Bonds—not, that is, until the slump after the war, when they sold down in the 80's.

The policy of the *Sunpapers* during World War I consisted simply in following Wilson, just as their policy in World War II was to consist in following Roosevelt. Adams, who was densely ignorant of foreign affairs, was caught unawares by the swift sequence of events following the assassination of the Archduke Franz Ferdinand on June 28, 1914, and for a month his editorials were devoted largely to pious hopes that war would be averted. On August 3, following Wilson's neutrality proclamation, he wrote the following for the *Sun:*

> The *Sun* will do its best to follow the policy which it is now endorsing, and endeavor to preserve the spirit of those who gaze as dispassionate onlookers at a great world-spectacle, which thrills while it saddens and which creates in the breast emotions of pity and horror, but not of hate or unkindness.

But this was only Pecksniffery, and a fair match for Wilson's own. Already on August 1 the *Evening Sun* had printed an editorial denouncing the Kaiser, and on August 3 it was followed by a long and oleaginous paean of praise for England. Before the end of August there were many protests from readers regarding the pro-English bias of both papers, and on September 5 Monsignor W. T. Russell, a former rector of the Baltimore Cathedral who was then rector of St. Patrick's Church in Washington, sent in a vigorous letter objecting not only to their editorials but also to their presentation of news. "Since the war began," he said, "the *Sun* has not been fair to the Germans. . . . The headlines are often misleading and in the manipulation of the news is apparent a desire to bias public opinion against the Germans." For this manipulation, of course, Kent was responsible rather than Adams, but Adams undertook to answer Russell in an editorial. In it he said:

> However strongly our sympathies may be with the British and the French, no one can deny that this is one of the most wonderful campaigns in the history of the world, if not the most wonderful in military annals, considered purely from a scientific and strategic point of view.

But these appreciative words for the German Army, which had already won the Battle of Tannenberg and was about to meet the French at the Marne, did not satisfy Russell, and he continued his criticism. Adams's frank admission of sympathy with the Allies showed the way the *Sunpapers* were actually headed, and he continued on that line to the end. His mind, at bottom, was a great deal like Wilson's, and so he found no difficulty in supporting both Wilson's protestations of neutrality and his steady efforts to get the United States into the war on the English side. He supported Wilson in the "He kept us out of the war" campaign of 1916, and was still praising his "toleration and forebearance" in February, 1917, just before the American declaration of war. As I have said, I was convinced before the end of 1914 that Wilson would go to the rescue of England soon or late, and said so very frequently in the Free

Lance. Thus I dissented sharply from the course Adams was taking, but seldom discussed it with him after the beginning of 1915. When Wilson finally went before Congress on April 2, 1917, with his "the world must be made safe for democracy" blather, Adams accepted it at its face value, and proceeded to a vigorous belaboring of Robert M. La Follette, Gumshoe Bill Stone and the other Senators who were critical of it. I can recall but one conversation with him on the subject after I returned from Europe: it must have been toward the end of 1917. A violent spy-hunt was in progress, and one day I suggested casually that it was bound to bear heavily upon many German-Americans who were completely innocent, and had been perfectly correct in their behavior. His reply startled but did not surprise me. What he said, in brief, was that they deserved it for being Germans. Their sufferings, he told me, did not interest him. This reply seemed to me to be so thoroughly typical of a Puritan that I could not help chuckling inwardly. But after that I never discussed the war with him, and in fact saw little of him. It was not until 1920 that I had any contact with him, and at that time, as this narrative will show, we came into sharp conflict.

Both *Sunpapers* took an active hand in the spy-hunt in their news columns, for Kent was quite as Anglomaniacal as Adams. They were largely responsible for the dismissal of a German named Schumacher, who was professor of his native language at St. John's College, Annapolis. Poor Schumacher was turned out to the tune of a dreadful din, though he was guilty of nothing save being a German, and during the year or two following, as I heard from his friends, he had great difficulty in making a living. The *Sunpapers* were also mainly responsible for the ruin of the *Deutsche Correspondent,* a German daily that had been published in Baltimore since 1841, and was thus almost as old as the *Sun* itself. On April 16, 1918, the *Sun* printed a story describing it as intensely and openly pro-German prior to this country's entrance into the war," and hinting that it was about to be suppressed, though since April, 1917, it had printed no criticism of American policy in the war. This story scared away all of its advertisers and many of its subscribers, and twelve days later it suspended publication. It was owned at the end by Annie V. Raine, a niece of Frederick Raine, the founder. Her loss was naturally very heavy; in fact, it brought her to virtual bankruptcy. One of the members of the *Correspondent*'s staff, Frederick Strehlau, was taken on the *Evening Sun* as music critic, but the rest had hard sledding. Two or three were eventually given minor municipal jobs by sympathetic politicians. They were familiar and popular figures in the journalistic life of Baltimore, and not a few *Sun* men were thoroughly ashamed of the paper's vicious and cowardly assault upon their paper and their livelihood. One of these *Sun* men, I believe, was Patterson. Almost his first act, when he became president of the A. S. Abell Company in November, 1919, was to order Kent to cease referring to Germans as Huns in news stories and headlines.

4

My Ex-Best Girl Has
Designs on You

1919–1920

My intimacy with Patterson, which went on developing during the
war years, though from the Spring of 1917 to the beginning of 1920 I
wrote nothing for the papers, was due primarily to an accident. When he
entered the *Evening Sun* office as managing editor, on April 11, 1911, he
was given a desk next to mine in the old library on the second floor,
overlooking Redwood street, and I naturally made some effort to show
him the office ropes. It was plain at once that he was a very competent
newspaper man, and moreover, a charming fellow. His situation was not
unlike what mine had been in 1906. That is to say, he was taking a job
that was inferior to the one he had just lost in Washington, and he was
working in a strange and more or less hostile office. Indeed, his situation
was worse than mine, for he had been lately married, and his wife was
expecting, and his pay from the *Evening Sun* was a great deal less than
he had been getting in Washington. During his first year in Baltimore he
was so short of money that he had to borrow from the Morris Plan
Bank, for all his savings had been put into the furnishing of his Washington apartment. He still had the furniture, but his income was much
reduced. What he had been paid in Washington I do not know, but it
could hardly have been less than $10,000 a year. From the *Evening Sun*
he got at most, $60 a week. He and his wife took a tiny house in Roland
Park, and there I often dropped in on them. He and I hit it off at once,
for we were both keenly aware of the deficiencies of the *Sunpapers,* and
especially of the new evening edition. We came together, I suspect,
largely because there was no one else in the office, save only Harry

Black, for either of us to talk to: the rest were either old *Sun* men with a Bourbon incapacity to learn anything or forget anything, or newcomers without any ideas. In and out of the office we talked shop, and always our talk was directed toward improvements. Patterson actually made plenty of them while he was managing editor of the *Evening Sun,* but they were all minor ones, for there was not enough money to pay for anything better. When, in the Autumn of 1913, he was transferred to the business-office as business manager, he and I continued to see each other frequently, and our intimacy became deeper and more confidential. The transfer did not change him: he remained essentially an editorial man, with most of his ideas running toward improvements upstairs. Through him I learned of the really desperate position of the *Sunpapers* in the last days of the Grasty régime, and through him, during the years following, I was kept informed of the progress of their rehabilitation under Van Lear Black. Inasmuch as I was notoriously devoid of any desire for executive authority, he could gabble to me freely, just as Grasty had done before him. We were both still young—he was 36 in 1914 and I was 34—and so we put in many hours planning a wholesale renovation of the papers, both in organization and in policy. We had little hope at that time that any of our schemes would ever be realized, and I think that both of us were greatly surprised, in the years after 1920, when some of them were.

After my return from the war in 1917 I saw Patterson constantly, and heard at first hand all the difficulties he and Van Lear Black were having in the business office. His eye, as I have said, was always wandering toward the editorial department, though, under the ancient rules of the *Sun,* he now had no voice in its operations. He was greatly discontented with Kent as managing editor, and also (though much less so) with Adams as editor. I agreed in both cases. But all we could do in those days was to talk, for the papers had to be put on a sound financial basis before there could be any hope of materially improving them, and they did not reach that position until the war was over. I also saw a good deal of Harry Black—that is, before and after his war service.

It was Black's return from the war, just before Christmas, 1918, that started the *Sunpapers* upon their new paths. He had had plenty of time to think about their present state and future prospects during the long days of his tedious ferrying of coal from Wales to France, and, what is more, a chance to consider things without any distracting pressure of daily events and emergencies. By this time it was plain that his brother Van Lear's reorganization was a success, and that the papers would soon be showing a very substantial profit. Their situation, in fact, was growing better every day. In advertising lineage the Sunday edition was going ahead of General Agnus's *Sunday American,* the morning *Sun* was shoving his weekday *American* to the side-lines, and the *Evening Sun* was making substantial inroads upon the *News,* still owned by Munsey. A great deal of new advertising was coming in, largely because the larger national advertisers, confronted by heavy war taxes, preferred putting their excess profits into promotion to paying them to the government. The *Sunpapers* got their share of this money, as all other American newspapers got shares of it, but they did better than the average, for the news that they were on the up and up had gone about, and advertisers always prefer papers that are moving ahead. Black and I sat down together, a few days after he reached home, to discuss this agreeable state of affairs, and there and then began a series of sessions that went on for years.

Black in those days was a teetotaler (as he told me, drink was the curse of his family, and he was afraid of it), but he always provided beer for me, so we got on very comfortably. We met at intervals of no more than a few weeks, and got over a tremendous area by the Summer of 1919. Meanwhile, I was seeing Patterson quite as often, and the three of us soon began amalgamating our sessions. It turned out that we were pretty well agreed on every essential point. We all believed that the *Sunpapers,* with money beginning to flow in, should invest an increasing proportion of it in the improvement of their news service and their editorial pages. We agreed that their make-up needed a thorough overhauling, and that the old *Sun* practise of printing advertising on the first page should be abandoned, and we agreed that Grasty's scheme of operating both of them under one editor and one managing editor had outlived its usefulness, if indeed it ever had any. Finally, we agreed that they needed new editorial blood, and a lot of it. These confabs went on without any consultation with others; neither Adams nor Kent was taken into them. After Patterson became president of the company, on November 11, 1919, it was possible to proceed more rapidly and more effectively. The first of the objectives just mentioned could now be attained by his simple fiat, and the advertisements disappeared from the first page of the *Evening Sun,* which had very few of them, at once, and on November 22 from the first page of the *Sun* as well. {Virtually all other American newspapers of any pretensions had taken advertising off their first pages long before this, and Munsey had done so on his *News* in Baltimore. Patterson had to consent to continue advertising on the last page (the chief local news page) of the two *Sunpapers,* and it is still printed there (1942).

At election time, when manifestoes are numerous, it sometimes almost crowds news off the page.} The other aims had to be approached slowly and often by indirection, for reaching them involved invasions of the prerogatives of various functionaries, and moreover, the effort had to meet and overcome that stupendous inertia which marks all large organizations. The effects of this inertia will be exhibited more than once hereafter. At the start Patterson always led the attack on it, but in the long run he became a part of it, and even Black succumbed to it more or less. As for me, I denounced it to the end, but long before the end I had become convinced that, in certain areas at least, it was irresistible. Time after time it was strong enough to break up schemes of improvement so obviously worth while that no one ventured to challenge them openly.

Soon after Patterson became president he asked me to resume writing for the *Sunpapers,* as of January 1, 1920, and proposed to put me on the payroll of the evening edition at $3000 a year. I had by this time reduced my magazine interests in New York to such a point that I had some free time on my hands, so I accepted. It was arranged that I was to write one signed article a week for the *Evening Sun,* sit in on all editorial conferences, and in general give the program of rehabilitation whatever help I could.

On January 15, 1920, Albert Cabell Ritchie was inaugurated Governor of Maryland, and there began at once a kind of alliance between him and the *Sunpapers,* and especially the *Evening Sun,* which was to continue until the end of his fifteen years in office. The papers had supported him in his campaign, and it was generally believed in the office, and correctly, that he was a man of ability, but he was criticized very sharply when he seemed to deserve it, and during his first term he lamented the fact frequently and publicly. What Ritchie became in the end was mainly what the *Evening Sun* made him. He was a man of intelligence, and a lawyer of high capacity, but at the time he took office he had given relatively little thought to the graver questions of the day, and sometimes it called for hard tugging by the *Evening Sun* to get him in line. Like Frank Kent, he was disposed, in 1919, to accept Prohibition as a *fait accompli,* and to assume that it would quickly eliminate the Anti-Saloon League from politics. Personally, he was against the Eighteenth Amendment, and in the course of the years he was to evolve some powerful arguments for its repeal, and to take a leading part in the war upon it, but during the first half of 1920 he was disposed to hang back. After Stanley M. Reynolds became editor of the *Evening Sun* and its guns began to bear on him he came over to its point of view; but it was not until half his first term had gone by that he showed any genuine energy in the cause.

Throughout his extraordinary career as Governor of Maryland he took most of his ideas from the paper, and it supplied him with both the impetus and the rationale for his attempts upon the Democratic presidential nomination in 1924, 1928 and 1932. The whole Maryland Free State scheme of things, though he appeared before the country as its fugleman, was actually fashioned, not in the Executive Mansion at Annapolis, but in the *Evening Sun* office, and not only in its general outlines but also in every detail, including even its name. I had some hand in Ritchie's development myself, but Harry Black had more, and Hamilton Owens, who became editor of the *Evening Sun* in 1922, had most of all. Curiously enough, all three of us rather disliked him—I for his indolence, Black for his weakness for puerile political intrigue, and Owens for his cold and calculating selfishness. I often wonder how far he would have got if he had been able to conquer these defects. His indolence often held him back when concentrated diligence might have forced him ahead, his political manoeuvering tended to make him cautious when boldness was what he needed, and his selfishness bred so large a crop of enemies in Maryland that in the end they were able to wreck him. He had many good qualities, and a number of fortuitous advantages. Among the first was a gift for effective advocacy, once he had made up his mind or had had it made up for him. Another was a fundamental integrity that somehow survived all his politicking, and might be relied on in a crisis. A third was a capacity for logical analysis that was unusual in a politician, and set him off sharply from such evangelists as Wilson and Roosevelt, not to mention Al Smith.

But of his natural advantages the chief was a singularly handsome person. Tall, straight, slim and with hair that began to gray after 1924, he looked more like the ideal statesman than any other politician of his generation that I can recall, save only James A. Reed of Missouri. The best blood of America was in him, and he had a natural dignity that always impressed strange audiences. His only natural handicap was a somewhat weak physique. After any considerable effort—say a set speech—he was in a state of collapse, and had to go to bed. But his indolence usually saved him from overexertion, and many persons who knew him quite well were not aware of his lack of robustness.

Things began to hum in the *Sun* office during the late Winter of 1919–20, and by the end of the year the papers were safely launched upon that upward course which was to continue until the devastating impact of the Depression at the beginning of the next decade. Patterson was full of energy, and bursting with plans of reform and rehabilitation. His task naturally had two halves. The first was to clear the ground of the incompetent men and dubious practises that had accumulated during the *Sunpapers'* ten years on short commons, and his second was to find better men and formulate better practises.

My own first contribution to the editorial page of what Patterson, Black and I hoped would soon be a rejuvenated *Evening Sun* was printed on February 9, 1920, under the title of "A Carnival of Buncombe." It was a review of the candidates then preparing in their paddocks for the national conventions of the coming Summer, and it treated them with a kind of realism that had been strange to the *Evening Sun,* and indeed to the *Sun,* since the American entrance into World War I. A. Mitchell Palmer, who was then the principal contender for the Democratic nomination, I described as "a political mountebank of the first water," and General Leonard Wood, who was the favorite of what remained of the old Republican organization, I called "a simple-minded dragoon, viewing all human phenomena from the standpoint of the barrack-room." It was not until August 30 that I settled down to Monday afternoon, and became a fixture on the *Evening Sun* editorial page of that day for eighteen years. Some of my early articles were purely literary in theme, but I began to denounce Wilson from the start, despite Adams's support of him, and especially his "brigades of informers, spies, volunteer detectives, perjurers and complaisant judges," still raging in 1920. In my first article, on February 9, I described him hopefully as a "corpse" and a "cadaver," and by May 12 I was sneering at his "austere and incomprehensible imbecilities." But it was not until May 28 that I got any really powerful reaction. On that day, under the title of "The Armenian Buncombe," I printed an article belaboring the English effort to saddle the mandate for Armenia on the United States, and in it appeared the following:

> Just what Lloyd George and [Etienne-Alexandre] Millerand told Wilson when they heaved the foundling at him is hard to determine. His own accounts of such transactions are never to be taken seriously; he suffers from a congenital incapacity for telling the truth; his statements, transcending mere mendacity, take on a sort of fourth dimensional preposterousness.

In view of Wilson's bold lying about the Secret Treaties this was perfectly justified, but it provoked a double-headed attack that gave Paul Patterson something to think about for days. The first half, which came from Arthur O. Lovejoy, professor of philosophy at the Johns Hopkins and a bitter and notorious Anglomaniac, was relatively easy to dispose of, for when he was given space to denounce me on the editorial page he quickly subsided. The other was more serious. With my article in his hand Adams rushed into Patterson's office and demanded that I be dismissed instantly. If this were not done, he said, he would resign himself, for he could not in conscience work upon a newspaper which allowed a member of the staff to question the veracity of the President of the United States. Simultaneously, John Owens, Frank Patterson (who had passed my copy!) and several other office Wilsonistas held a meeting in the library, and resolved to back Adams to the limit. Here was a really uncomfortable situation for Patterson, for he was new in his job and not eager for an office war in the grand manner, but he stood up to the assault manfully, and refused Adams's hysterical demand. The truth, he argued philosophically, probably lay in the middle ground, as was its immemorial habit. Perhaps it was a fact that my denunciation of Wilson had been rather too forthright for a great Democratic newspaper, but on the other hand maybe he (Adams) had been supporting Wilson somewhat more ardently than the plain facts made plausible. When Patterson told me of the row the next day, I offered, of course, to resign myself, and what is more, I meant it. For one thing, I did not want to involve him in a nasty unpleasantness at the beginning of his administration; for another thing, I did not need my job, and was still in some doubt that it would work out to my satisfaction. But he refused to be browbeaten, and the upshot was that Adams soon cooled off and the other Wilsonistas were heard from no more. Patterson's show of resolution, in fact, was all that was needed to put them in their places: they had no stomach for a fight that showed any threat of being dangerous. I don't recall discussing the business with any one of them, and in all probability they assumed that I never heard of it. All I remember is that we were on good terms—at least outwardly—when we started for the Republican national convention together in June—Adams, Owens, Frank Kent, Stanley M. Reynolds of the Washington bureau and I. By the time we got to Harrisburg a jug of rye that I had brought along had produced a feeling of downright brotherhood, and we started a poker-game in which I drew a royal flush. Patterson was to join us in Chicago to act as editor in the field: he had gone ahead a bit earlier for a brief visit to his boyhood home in central Illinois. He was delighted when he got a telegram from Reynolds saying that the war was over.

He had asked me back in February to join the *Sun*'s staff of correspondents for the two conventions, and I had arranged with Nathan for the necessary time off from my *Smart Set* editorial work. We were joined in Chicago, not only by Patterson, but also by Essary, and by two newcomers, Stephen Bonsal and Henry M. Hyde. Bonsal was a Baltimorean, then 55 years old, who had behind him a long career on the New York *Herald,* chiefly as a war correspondent, and had also been in the American diplomatic service. He had been an occasional contributor to the *Evening Sun* editorial page during the early months of 1920. Hyde, who was a year older, was an old Chicago newspaper man, lately retired to a farm at Charlottesville, Va., after some years as London correspondent of the Chicago *Tribune.* Bonsal, I believe, was chosen at the suggestion of Van Lear Black—one of the very few times that Black ever made an editorial suggestion. Hyde was Patterson's choice, and a good one it was. Indeed, there have been few better men on the *Sunpapers* in their whole history.

The first of the two conventions of 1920 was the Republican one. Patterson had taken quarters for the *Sun* delegation at the Congress Hotel, but there was not room enough in the suite for all of us, so Adams, Kent and I had to move to the Virginia, a small hotel north of the river. I roomed with Kent, and had two disconcerting surprises the first night. The first came when he got down on his knees beside his bed and began to pray audibly and volubly, clad in an old-fashioned nightshirt. The second followed soon afterward, as he fell asleep. Never in my life have I heard more appalling snoring. All the ordinary sounds were there, but in addition there were others—for example, a series of *crescendo* gurgles ending in what seemed to be strangulation, with both the performer and me leaping up in our beds. The next night I managed to have Kent bunked with Adams, and so got some sleep. Ben Hecht, who was still living in Chicago, brought me a market-basket full of excellent bottled beer of his own making, and I looked forward to pleasant refreshment, but Kent not only drank a large part of it but brought in a gang of Maryland politicians, headed by W. Bladen Lowndes, the Blacks' cousin, to drink the rest.

The weather was extremely hot, and the old hall wherein the convention was held was an inferno, for it had a glass roof that acted like the top of a hothouse. It was the unbearable heat, far more than the machinations of the master-minds on the scene, that gave Warren G. Harding the nomination. On the first ballot, cast on Friday, June 11, he got but 64½ votes to 133½ for Hiram Johnson, 211½ for Frank O. Lowden and 287½ for General Leonard Wood. There was no effective leadership, for Boise Penrose, the accepted heir to Mark Hanna, was ill at home in Pennsylvania, and his orders, transmitted by long-distance telephone, were much easier to evade than they would have been if he had been present in person, roaring as was his wont. The more Liberal Republicans, a relatively small party, were in favor of Johnson; the Southern blackamoors, in large part, had been bought by Lowden, and the Eastern professionals leaned toward Wood. After four ballots on Friday it was apparent that a deadlock was in the making, for though Wood had climbed to 314½ votes, Lowden and Johnson had climbed also, and not one of the three showed any sign of picking up a majority. When the convention had to be adjourned to Saturday, with no candidate nominated, the delegates and alternates began to be uneasy, for they were in no mood to go into a second week. The horrible heat was chiefly responsible for this reluctance, but there was also the question of cost, for delegates to a national convention pay their own expenses.

The so-called leaders held a great many conferences Friday night, but failed to come to an agreement. On Saturday morning Wood was still in the lead, with Lowden and Johnson following him as on Friday, and the three held these relative positions until the eighth ballot. The delegates, meanwhile, were growing more and more restless, and many of them began to talk of deserting the convention and going home. In the middle of the morning the Harding backers, led by Harry Daugherty, later to become Attorney-General and infamous, made vigorous propaganda for their candidate, mainly on the ground that he had stood clear of the bitter fighting on the floor, had no enemies either inside or outside the convention, and was thus the only candidate who could hope to go before the country with a united party behind him. It is the legend that his nomination was arranged Friday night at a conference in the smoke-filled hotel rooms of Col. George W. Harvey, and in the year following Harvey himself labored hard to disseminate this story. But my own belief is that the log-jam was broken at last, not on Friday night but on Saturday morning, and not by Harvey or even by Daugherty, but by Myron T. Herrick, ambassador to France from 1912 to 1914 and later to be ambassador again. While the seventh ballot was being taken, he left his place with the Ohio delegation, came up to the platform, and engaged in a long and vehement palaver with Henry Cabot Lodge, the permanent chairman. When it was over, he went about the floor whispering to the heads of the principal state delegations, and on the eighth ballot Harding's vote rose to 87. On the ballot following Lowden blew up and Harding polled 374½, and on the tenth and last ballot Wood blew up and Harding polled 674⁷⁄₁₀, which was enough to nominate him.

When the progress of the rollcall showed that he would win all the women reporters in the press-stand, their make-up melted into unearthly streaks, rushed off to find and interview Mrs. Harding. They found her in the Harding hotel room preparing to go back to Ohio, with Harding himself, in his shirt-sleeves, sweating copiously over the packing of the family bags. Neither of them, it appeared, had really believed that the lightning would strike them: they wanted to get back to Ohio as soon as possible, where Harding was also a candidate for reëlection to the Senate. Mrs. Harding, in those days, was almost the perfect model of a small-town American matron, despite her five years in Washington as a Senator's wife. The women reporters, returning from her hotel, reported that her clothes had been plainly made by a provincial modiste, and were adorned with bands of ruching to hide her somewhat scrawny neck. Her legs, from the knees downward, were extraordinarily thick and ungraceful—what the Germans call Stössel (stampers or rammers). After Harding was elected, in November, some of the fashionable ladies of Washington—now suddenly become aware of her—took her in hand, and she was turned over to a French man-dressmaker in New York. The results were made brilliantly visible at the Willard Hotel in Washington on the night before inauguration day of 1921. Harding, who was a newspaper man by trade, announced a private reception for his colleagues of the press, and I went to it. The guests gathered in a large reception-room, and there was a considerable wait until the President-elect and his consort appeared. When they entered at last there was a gasp of astonishment, for Mrs. Harding tripped in wearing a dress in the most advanced style of the day, with a low neck and short skirts. Moreover, her face was brilliantly made up, and her hair showed the labors of a scientific frisseur. The last time most of us had seen her she looked like the president of the Christian Endeavor Society of Middletown, but now she almost suggested the Whore of Babylon. Moreover, her manner had changed with her clothes, and she was full of new and somewhat kittenish ways. The newspaper gals would have laughed at her if it had not been for the presence of Harding himself, who enchanted them. He was, in fact, a singularly handsome man—dark in color, well set-up, and graceful in his movements—and his clothes always fitted him perfectly, for his figure was God's gift to his tailor. The party quickly degenerated into a back-slapping match, with Harding calling most of the male reporters by their first names and Mrs. Harding making a great fuss over the females. I departed as soon as it was seemly.

Harding's chances had seemed so slim when he went to Chicago that he did not open the usual candidatorial headquarters. All the other candidates had vast reception-rooms in downtown hotels, and in them they held frequent press conferences. Hoover, in advance of the convention, had got more publicity than all the rest put together, for he was still, as a consequence of his war work in Belgium and elsewhere, a public hero of the first chop. Unhappily, he had not learned the elemental lesson that what a candidate for a presidential nomination needs is not so much popularity in the country as votes in the convention. Having neglected to round them up by the usual laborious and expensive devices, he found himself out of the running before the race on the floor began. On the second or third day of the convention, when it was already plain that he was nowhere, I dropped into his headquarters to have a look. The scene was sad indeed. Most of his hired whoopers had already deserted, and the huge reception-room was quite empty. In one corner I found two or three barrels of Hoover buttons, now worth less than a millionth of a mill on the dollar. All the portraits on the walls were hanging awry. This bitter experience taught Hoover a lot, and when he went out for the nomination again, at Kansas City in 1928, he had all the delegates he needed, bought, paid for, and safe in his pens. He had gone about rounding them up in a diligent and highly discreet manner, so that many of the professionals refused to believe, even after they got to Kansas City, that he had enough to win.

I attended all of the press-conferences at Chicago, and came away from them with a low opinion of the eminent men who gave them. Lowden, who was a heavy drinker, was always three sheets in the wind, and Wood both looked and talked as if he were insane. As for Johnson, he was so bitter against his opponents that it was next to impossible to get any rational gabble out of him. I recall that at one of his conferences he spent the whole time denouncing some obscure politicians in Georgia for failing to deliver a few delegates that he had been counting on. It seemed impossible for him to formulate the idea that anyone might be against him for anything save nefarious reasons. The convention itself was destined to augment vastly his natural venom, for when Harding was nominated he was offered the vice-presidency, and if he had accepted he would have become President on Harding's death. But he was so sore that he refused with indignation, and when Harding died in 1923 he became a sort of walking boil. Johnson, I believe, was an honest man, and he had no mean abilities, but his choleric disposition was always a great handicap to him. Lowden, a boozer of the expansive type, had married the daughter of George M. Pullman, and it was Pullman money that bought the delegates with which he came to the convention. As the early rollcalls showed, he had a formidable number, but there was so much scandal about the way he had acquired them, mainly fomented by Johnson, that large numbers of them, prompted by a healthy fear of the hoosegow, were ready to desert him at the first chance. The scene during the ninth rollcall on that blistering Saturday morning, when he at last blew up, was very dramatic and not a little painful, for his wife and daughters were present. Worse they sat in the first row of the gallery, so that the rest of the audience could witness their agonies. I could not help recalling a similar scene at Baltimore in 1912, when J. Harry Preston was booed down, also in the presence of his wife and daughters.

The Maryland delegation at Chicago had been instructed for Wood, but it had a member, Senator Joseph I. France, who was strongly for himself, and had high hopes of winning the compromise victory that went to Harding. I met him aboard the train on his way to the battleground, and he at once buttonholed me with irrefragable proofs that he would win. I had some respect for him, for he was a good Senator and had made a gallant fight against the Wilson-Palmer-Burleson *Gestapo* immediately after the war, but his arguments on this occasion seemed to me to be insane, and I hinted so in a dispatch to the *Evening Sun*. France's only active worker was his younger brother. They had headquarters in a downtown hotel, and tackled everyone who would listen to them, but not many did. France was very indignant because the Maryland delegation refused to give him a complimentary vote. Ten of its members stuck to Wood to the end; of the rest, one went to Hoover and five flopped to Harding. Wood was greatly damaged by a speech in his favor made by Mrs. Corinne Roosevelt Robinson, a sister to Theodore Roosevelt. The delegates to national conventions, in those days, were not yet used to female orators, and so her cocksure and saucy discourse, with its raucous refrain of "*We* want Leonard Wood," made them unhappy. They could not boo her down, for she was Roosevelt's sister, but they managed nevertheless to show their disapproval of her hollering. Wood was in favor of the League of Nations, and found himself out on a limb when the convention, flogged by the isolationist Johnson, adopted a platform plank that was predominantly against it. "Johnson," said a *Sun* editorial on June 12, "scored nine points out of ten." W. Bladen Lowndes and various other members of the Maryland delegation were also for the League, but they quickly subsided when the majority decided against it.

Once Harding had been nominated the delegates were eager for home, and so the selection of a candidate for Vice-President got even less than the usual meager attention. When Johnson refused the nomination it was offered to William E. Borah and one or two others, and when they also refused it the word went about on the floor that it was to go to Calvin Coolidge. Most of the delegates knew nothing about Coolidge save that he was Governor of Massachusetts, and had somehow broken the Boston police strike of the previous September, but they were quite willing, on that infernal afternoon, to vote for anyone in order to complete their business and escape. Coolidge got 674½ votes on the first ballot, which was many more than he needed to be chosen. Senator Irvine L. Lenroot, of Wisconsin, got 146½ and Johnson 22½. Just before the result of the ballot was announced I went to the catacombs below the hall to get a drink and stretch my legs, and there encountered a picturesque Irishman named Michael J. Hennessy, for many years political reporter of the Boston *Globe*. He was somewhat in his cups, and was making a speech to half a dozen idling delegates and correspondents. "I offer you four to one," I heard him say, "that Harding will be assassinated before he serves his four years." Along with one or two others I tried to shut him off, for the war psychosis had not yet abated, and the hall was reputed to be swarming with secret agents looking for subversion. But Mike stuck to his bet. "I am not saying anything against Harding," he declared. "I wish him well. But I know Coolidge—and he is the luckiest goddam son-of-a-bitch in the United States." Returning to the press-stand, I told the story to Henry Hyde, and it was overheard by Arthur Brisbane, who was sitting directly in front of us, writing an interminable play-by-play report for the Hearst papers. Brisbane must have passed it on to Edna Ferber, who was a row beyond, and to Oswald Garrison Villard, who slid into the Hearst row, a little while later, to whisper to him. Both La Ferber and Villard, nineteen years afterward, printed the story— and both ascribed Hennessy's prediction to other men. Villard credited it to Robert Lincoln O'Brien, another Boston Irishman, and Ferber to William Slavens McNutt. When I read their accounts I was struck once more by the fallibility of human memory and the unreliability of history—and began to develop doubts at once whether my own recollection was accurate. To test it I wrote to Hennessy, and he replied that he remembered the episode perfectly. A year later I met him during the Willkie campaign in New England, and he confirmed every detail. He added that he still stood by his prediction that Harding would be murdered, and recalled the fact that the notorious Gaston B. Means once published a book declaring that it had actually happened.

The *Sunpapers'* reporting of the Chicago convention apparently made a good impression in Baltimore, and helped to spread the notion that both papers were moving forward. Hyde and I sent daily dispatches to the evening edition, and the others wrote for the morning. Unhappily, the big day fell on a Saturday, and its principal events were too late for the evening paper, so I got no real whack at them. On my way home by train I happened to travel in the same car with Henry Cabot Lodge, and enjoyed the singular privilege of seeing him walking up and down the car corridor in his shirt-sleeves. He was ordinarily a very correct and even prissy fellow, but the inordinate heat had fetched him. Contemplating him, I was led to meditate upon his probable reflections, for he had just had a leading hand in nominating a candidate he despised, and his age was such—seventy years—that it was improbable that he would ever get a chance at the great prize himself. He had itched for it for years, but now it was gone forever. I put all this into an article printed on the editorial page of the *Evening Sun* on the following Tuesday, June 15. Some time later I was told by someone or other in Washington that Lodge had read it and liked it, though its irreverent tone was a bit upsetting to him.

When I proceeded to San Francisco for the Democratic national convention I traveled alone, for Essary, Reynolds and John Owens had gone on before me. During the lay-over in Chicago I met Edna Ferber, and with her was her mother, Julia. One day Edna and I took a promenade in Michigan avenue and dropped in at the propaganda headquarters of the suffragettes. We were not recognized, and as we left we were asked to sign the visitors' book. Edna signed "Edith Wharton" and I signed "Joseph Conrad." Old Julia, who was a prime cook, professed to believe that the food served on the Union Pacific was poisonous, and so came down to my train with a large basket full of fried chicken, prepared by herself. On the train I found Arthur Krock, then of the Louisville *Courier-Journal,* and with him was a wealthy Louisvillian named Wylie, who had in his baggage a stock of prime Bourbon whiskey. We were presently joined by a fat and jovial fellow named Augustus Owsley Stanley, then a Senator from Kentucky, and the four of us communed with the chicken and the Bourbon during the three days' trip to the Coast. There were many other politicoes on the train, including Senator

Thomas J. Walsh of Montana and Mrs. J. Borden Harriman. La Harriman was a rich and bustling widow, had a big house in Washington, and nursed political ambitions which were to come to flower, in 1937, in her appointment as American minister to Norway. She had her eye on Walsh, who had been a widower for three years, and pursued him with great assiduity on the train. One night he fled to the rear platform to get rid of her, but she followed him there, and when I turned in myself she had him backed up against the railing, and was blowing sweet nothings in his ear.

George Sterling, the poet, had known since March that I was coming to San Francisco, and had been making somewhat elaborate preparations for my entertainment. He wrote to me on March 9: "Holy Ghost! Come on out! I've not much booze left, but shall begin adding to it at once, and by the time you're here there should be enough to last through the convention." On March 23 he followed with: "I'll have some gin for you, and all the white and red wine you want. Mostly Californian—but they are not so bad when you get them *here*." On April 15 came this: "Our dry wines are sadly inferior to the French, but I really like them, as I do anything with alcohol in it." Then, on April 29:

> I'm putting by booze for you steadily, and now have port, sherry, Burgundy and sauterne. Also, Jack Newbegin, our leading bookseller, says you may have (with him) any kind of booze you want, including even absinthe. I know another person who guarantees plenty of gin, claret and sauterne . . . I suppose I'm impossible, for I like *anything* with alcohol in it. My preference is wine, though. Rhine wine is the best stuff I ever tasted. [Jack] London could afford to buy it freely, and we used to drink quarts of it at a sitting.

On May 13: "My ex-best girl has designs on you, and is saving hooch against your advent. She is a big-hearted, handsome creature, but, I fear, a bit too tall for you. Let me know if you'd prefer a pony—sans hooch. 'Our aim is to please.'" On June 11: "Your girl waits you with impatient hips." After all this, I was prepared for a somewhat rowdy reception, and that is what I got. On the night of my arrival Sterling gave me a large dinner at an Italian restaurant named Begin's, much patronized by the local literati. There was endless red wine and also a large supply of a raw brandy called grappo. As the guest of honor I had to go along, and the result was that when I came to my senses the next morning I found myself in bed with a strange woman—not the "ex-best girl" mentioned in his letter of May 13. I was considerably astonished, for I did not recall seeing her at the dinner, but it quickly appeared that she was a friend of George's who had come in after I had succumbed, and volunteered to look after me. She was a charming woman, and made no reference to our situation. She drew a bath for me and brewed a pot of strong tea, and in a little while I was on my way, with no dent in the chastity of either of us. When I got to the St. Francis Hotel I found that Owens, Essary and Reynolds were much disturbed by my disappearance, and were, in fact, on the point of notifying the police. I went to bed again and snoozed until the early afternoon. When I awoke I found Reynolds sitting at my bedside. I knew him only slightly, but we were soon in the midst of an earnest discussion, chiefly of politics. He objected vigorously, it appeared, to some of the ideas that I was merchanting in the *Evening Sun*, the *Smart Set* and elsewhere, but he argued against them with intelligence and showed not the slightest sign of the moral indignation of such men as Adams and John Owens. Altogether, he seemed to me to be a very engaging, if somewhat misinformed fellow, and I had a number of other sessions with him during the following week. When I returned to Baltimore, and Patterson began going over his plans to separate the *Evening Sun* from the *Sun,* and bewailing the fact that no likely candidate for the editorship of the former seemed to be available, I at once suggested Reynolds, and Patterson decided to give him a trial. He turned out to be precisely the man for the job, and in a little while he had completely rehabilitated the editorial page of the paper, and given it the smart, sophisticated, intelligent character that it was to hold until the catastrophe of the New Deal demoralized and ruined it. By that time, unhappily for the paper but perhaps happily for his own peace of mind, poor Reynolds was dead.

The San Francisco convention was a most amusing one, and covering it, to me at least, was a great lark. We were 3000 miles from home, and the telegraph service over the mountains was so limited that at the start there was talk of holding down every reporter present to 1000 words a day. The New York *Herald-Tribune,* in alarm, leased a wire running up the coast to Vancouver and down through Canada to New York, and several other papers made other such expensive arrangements. This relieved the burden on the regular wires, and after the first few days I got all the space I wanted. In this matter the four hours' difference in time helped, for it made it impossible for me to get any considerable amount of today's news into today's *Evening Sun.* I therefore confined myself, on Patterson's instructions, to writing at night reviews of the day's doings for next day's paper, and they were sent after midnight, when all the morning paper stuff was off the wires. I was usually free after 10 P.M., and spent most of my evenings with George Sterling and his friends. At the end of the week I gave him a dinner at Begin's, and came close to succumbing as I had succumbed to the dinner he gave to me. Toward daylight I found myself on the beach at Half Moon Bay, 25 miles below San Francisco, with the burble of a female voice in my ears and a waiting taxi chugging nearby. The voice belonged to his "ex-best girl"—a handsome Irish wench who was, at the time, leading woman in a San Francisco stock company. Later on she moved to New York, and I saw her off and on. An old woman accompanied her in the rôle of mother, and there was a little boy who passed as her nephew, though he was probably her son. She had a very comfortable and even luxurious apartment in New York, and I was considerably astonished when, after a couple of years, she was taken by the police on a charge of obtaining its furnishings by fraud. She was convicted and sent to prison, and on her release got into trouble again and was sentenced again. The last time I heard from her, circa 1938, she had just been liberated, and asked me to come to see her. I declined politely.

All national conventions before that in San Francisco were held in bare and hideous halls—usually militia armories—and their only decorations were flags and bunting. But the one I was now covering was staged in the beautiful municipal auditorium of the town, and the decorations were simple and in excellent taste. The weather was magnificent, and the delegates sitting in their places could look out through the open doors at palm trees glittering in the clear yellow sunshine. The arrangements for their entertainment were perfect. There were none of the usual barbecues, steamboat excursions and so on; instead, the celebrated James Rolfe, Jr., who was then mayor of the town, appointed a committee of discreet, humane and presentable women to look after them, and in particular to keep them supplied with the refreshments that Prohibition had just cut off. These women toured the hotels in small parties, waiting on the delegates, alternates and newspaper correspondents, and inquiring their wishes. A request for a bottle of whiskey was followed by its delivery within half an hour. When the convention was over, the Methodists of the town made a loud pother over this Christian system, and produced evidence that Jim had bought fifty barrels of Bourbon at the city's expense. They proved further that he had charged it to the town smallpox hospital—and that there had not been a case of smallpox in San Francisco for years. Jim ran for reëlection as mayor on the strength of this exposure during the Autumn following, and won by an immense majority. He remained in that office until 1931, when he was promoted to the dignity of Governor of California.

The principal candidates before the convention were William Gibbs McAdoo, A. Mitchell Palmer and James M. Cox. McAdoo, who was then married to Woodrow Wilson's daughter Eleanor, was supposed, at the start, to be the White House candidate, but it quickly appeared that Wilson was in hopes that the convention would reward his own services to humanity by giving him the nomination for a third term. In order to promote this great end he sent a number of confidential agents to San Francisco, among them four members of his Cabinet—Josephus Daniels, Bainbridge Colby, Carter Glass, and Albert Sidney Burleson. Daniels, who was Secretary of the Navy, arrived in San Francisco Bay on a battleship, with its guns banging so loudly that the crowd in the convention hall was alarmed. In a little while it became evident that all of these confidential agents were traitors who hoped to collar the nomination for themselves. I well recall a press conference given by Colby immediately after his arrival. It was behind a large clump of potted palms in the lobby of the San Francisco Hotel, and while it was going on the orchestra in the nearby dancing-room was playing "It's a Long, Long Trail," then a novelty. Colby was in liquor, and let it be known that McAdoo, Palmer and Cox were all done for, and that the prize would go to a dark horse. "I can tell you right now," he said, "who that dark horse is. His name is Bainbridge Colby." Another comic candidate was James W. Gerard, who has already appeared in this chronicle. He had bought the small delegation from one of the Northwestern cow states, and was put in nomination by a Swede in a mail-order suit who could barely speak English. He never got a vote outside his boughten delegation, and even his Swedes quickly deserted him. I encountered him just outside the convention hall as his spokesman was haranguing and amusing the delegates. He looked extremely sick, and I confess that I enjoyed his discomfiture, for I had and have a very low opinion of his abilities and also of his integrity. Until the era of the New Deal no trashier fellow had ever risen to high office in this great Republic. He had married the daughter of Marcus Daly, an immensely wealthy mining magnate, and used her money to promote his career. With it he bought a New York Supreme Court justiceship from Tammany, though he knew no more law than a cat, and out of it came the large contribution to the first Wilson campaign fund which got him the ambassadorship to Germany. The Swedes in that cow state had taken his shilling simply because no other candidate had bothered to enter their primary. They deserted him as soon as possible.

On the first ballot, on July 2, McAdoo had 266 votes, Palmer had 256, Cox had 134, and Al Smith of New York, then making his first appearance on the national scene, had 109. There was little change until the twelfth ballot, when Cox leaped ahead with 412 votes. Unfortunately for him, he needed 730 to win, for there were 1094 delegates and the two-thirds rule was still in force. By Saturday night he got to 430, and there he seemed stuck. In Chicago, as I have related, the sweating and impatient delegates, confronting a like situation, refused to adjourn over the week-end and instead nominated a dark horse. But in San Francisco the weather was so agreeable and the brethren so pleasantly liquored that they adjourned not only willingly but eagerly, and that night hundreds of them started out to have a time. Many parties, traveling in taxicabs, found themselves by Sunday night a hundred miles or more from San Francisco. One party, in fact, is said to have gone all the way to Los Angeles. But they all drifted back during Monday, and on Tuesday, on the forty-fourth ballot they nominated Cox. The Maryland delegation, on that ballot, cast 13½ votes for Cox and 2½ for John W. Davis, but most of its members, I believe, were actually for Al Smith. Unfortunately, he was not yet ripe for national honors.

With Cox nominated, the Tammany delegation tried to put Colby in second place on the ticket, but William Jennings Bryan and his yokel followers made such an uproar that the plan had to be abandoned. Some one to me unknown then proposed Franklin D. Roosevelt, assistant Secretary of the Navy, and he was put over with the dizzy dispatch with which nominees for Vice-President are usually named. The arguments in favor of Roosevelt were, first that his name would attract many followers of his cousin Theodore and perhaps fool a large body of morons; second, that he was from New York; and third, that he was satisfactory to the drys. They were much perturbed by the nomination of Cox, who was known to be dripping wet, though he was willing to speak for Law Enforcement, and many of them threatened to bolt the ticket. Both Roosevelt and his wife Eleanor were very friendly to the Anti-Saloon League, and she had done some speaking for it in New York state. Roosevelt, however, was not put forward by the League; indeed, its chief agent on the ground, Bishop James Cannon, Jr., was strongly against taking responsibility for any candidate. But Cannon told me years later in Baltimore that Roosevelt was trusted by the League, and had sent more satisfactory replies to its questionnaire than any other candidate that it had quizzed. Thus his flop to the wet side in 1932, of which more anon, greatly enraged the drys, and they tried in vain to beat him. But they were for him in 1920, and his popularity among them took some of the whiskey smell off Cox, and undoubtedly accounted for many of Cox's 9,143,000 votes.

The Republicans, after nominating Harding at Chicago, got into a panic when they belatedly recalled (or perhaps it would be more accurate to say discovered, for few of the leaders knew much about him) that he was married to a divorced woman, and that her first husband was still in circulation, complaining that he had been robbed of his wife. This, of course, was hardly true, for the first husband, a drunkard, had lost her before ever Harding saw her; moreover, she had done all the courting. The story is that she fell in love with Warren on seeing him sitting at a second-story window of the Marion *Star* office, majestically spitting tobacco juice into space. He was then, as always, a very handsome fellow, and she immediately set siege to him. At first he was disposed to throw her off, but when he began considering her money—she was the daughter of the town banker—he took a more favorable view of her charms, and in 1891 they were married. Harding was then 26 and she was some years older—perhaps five or six. It was with money supplied by her father that he bought the *Star* and launched himself upon the political career that eventually took him to the White House. A lazy fellow, he would have fallen by the wayside at an early stage if it had not been for her constant prodding. Her drunken first husband was pensioned by now, and her two children by him were farmed out, but his moans were still occasionally heard, and they greatly dismayed the Republican bosses. Fortunately for them, the nomination of Cox in San Francisco took the question of domestic morality out of the campaign, for Cox was a divorced man, and his late wife's charges against him, on file in Dayton, Ohio, were of a very sensational nature. His friends alleged that they were false; that she herself was the guilty party—but there was the record. The leaders of both parties, considering these grave facts, came to an agreement to avoid the subject in the campaign, and that agreement was kept faithfully. But when whispers began to go about that Harding had some Negro blood—an allegation reasonably supported by his swarthy complexion—the Democrats helped them on, and the Republicans could find nothing comparable to allege against Cox. I was told by Ohio newspaper men who should have known that one of Harding's great-grandmothers was actually an octoroon. He never took any notice of the whispering, which continued after he was in the White House. If he was actually a shade coonish the fact did not interfere with the wet and carefree life he led there. No President ever had a better time in office. Every afternoon he staged a booze and poker party with Harry Daugherty and his other buddies, usually at a hide-away nearby. Meanwhile, Mrs. Harding gave endless afternoon parties *à la* Marion, Ohio. She would send for four or five members of the Marine Band, a dozen or two young Army officers and as many nurses from the government hospitals, and put on a tea dance. The refreshments were always ice-cream and cake. At the start the newspaper girls of Washington were also invited to these parties, but they soon began to make excuses.

As I have said, the convention at San Francisco was a singularly pleasant one—in fact, it was the best national convention ever heard of, and during the years following it the Democratic National Committee, and likewise the Republican National Committee, was constantly besought to have another in the same place. Fred Essary and I both took hands in these agitations. They came to nothing because the delegates to a national convention have to pay their own expenses, and the cost of a trip to San Francisco alarmed too many Easterners and Southerners. The politicoes of the Coast are so accustomed to coming to Philadelphia or Chicago that they no longer protest. The high day of the San Francisco convention came on June 30, when the various candidates were put in nomination. The leader of the band, as usual, had been instructed to play something appropriate as each was named, and also to greet the orators, whenever possible, with suitable music. Lady politicians were just coming in in 1920, and he regarded them rather as females to be flattered than as publicists to be honored. Thus when a woman named Mrs. Susan W. Fitz Gerald, of Massachusetts, arose to say her say he and his men played "Oh, You Beautiful Doll," and when a Mrs. Izetta Jewel Brown, of West Virginia, followed, he put on "Oh, What a Pal Was Mary." La Fitz Gerald was surely no beauty, but La Brown was really a good-looking woman: she had been a stock-company actress when she married a decayed United States Senator, and was now his well-heeled and oompheous widow. Both ladies were somewhat disconcerted by the band leader's choices, but when the crowd began to cheer they recovered their composure, and got off their speeches to great effect. {It was probably at this convention, though I am not sure, that the leader greeted a Georgia orator with "Marching Through Georgia."}

But the real show came when Al Smith's name was presented to the convention. He was put in nomination by W. Bourke Cockran—not in any hope that he would be named, but simply as a sort of compliment from the New York delegation. That delegation had prepared no demonstration for him: it had no whoopers ready and had brought no flags or banners. When Cockran launched his name the band played "Tammany," and there was only moderate applause. But then, by a happy inspiration, the leader followed with "The Sidewalks of New York," and a really big show was on. "In five minutes," as I wrote years later, "the convention had been transformed into a carnival. In ten minutes all politics was completely forgotten. In fifteen minutes every delegate was on his legs, his voice raised in sentimental song. In twenty minutes they were all dancing." All the familiar waltz songs of that sentimental era followed "The Sidewalks of New York"—"The Bowery," "Maggie Murphy's Home," "A Bicycle Built for Two," "After the Ball," "Annie Rooney," and so on—and to them the merry delegates and alternates danced and sang. In any other convention such a fiesta would have become rowdy, but not in San Francisco. There was a different air there. No one was sweating. No one was crowded. The hall was lovely. The music was not blaring, but charming. I have never, in all my newspaper days, seen another scene to match that one. For a few minutes I almost believed in democracy, and, even more, liked it. Jim Rolph's supply of Bourbon, of course, had something to do with setting the tone of the exercises—but in any other convention alcohol would have produced jawing and fights, not harmony and amour. Many a lady politico was well hugged during that lovely hour, and not a few of them, I suspect, received more confidential attentions after adjournment. When I got home I wrote a piece for the *Smart Set* predicting that with women coming into politics, adultery would take the place of drunkenness as the favorite entertainment of American politicians gathered in herds. Unhappily, I was wrong. As bootlegging developed the brethren returned to their traditional hard boozing, and meanwhile the pulchritude of the sisters steadily diminished. Today the aphrodisiac stateswoman of the first days has been displaced by a hard, go-getting and usually bulky female who inspires only alarm in the male. Save in hotel rooms that are very dark and stuffy, and from fellow-Democrats or Republicans of low IQ's and worse technic, she can't hope to get any balm for her biological urges, if any.

Despite the gaudy time that I had in San Francisco with George Sterling and his friends I put in hard licks on my job, and sent home some stuff that seemed to me to be pretty fair. Patterson liked it, too, as I found when I got home, but something I wrote about Franklin D. Roosevelt had the unfortunate effect of wounding Van Lear Black. I knew, of course, that Black was acquainted with Roosevelt, but I had no idea that they were on terms of intimacy, and that Black was already thinking of offering him, in case of his defeat in November, a job with the Fidelity & Deposit Company of Maryland, which the Blacks controlled. After the Al Smith carnival that I have just described Roosevelt arose to second Al's nomination—and killed the Smith boom then and there. The chance before him was superb: if he had met it as it deserved he might have started the uproar all over again, and shoved Al among the leading contenders for the nomination. Instead he made a long, pompous speech on the heroic doings of the Navy during the war—a double anti-climax, for the delegates wanted to hear more about Al, and were tired of the war and eager to forget it. Here is what I wrote:

> The man to second Cockran's speech was young Franklin D. Roosevelt, and young Frank D. Roosevelt botched and butchered the thing in two minutes. What was demanded by the golden opportunity was a flash of genuine eloquence, a ringing appeal to the delegates to turn from the cadavers of Palmer and Cox and cast their votes for Alfred. But all that Roosevelt had on tap was a line of puerile and ineffective bosh about the great achievements of the Navy. As the delegates listened to him all their enthusiasm oozed out of them.

When I got back to Baltimore Black questioned me somewhat diffidently about Roosevelt's unfortunate speech, and I gathered that he was disappointed that Roosevelt had done so badly, but he made no protest against my report, and either he was too shy or I was too obtuse for me to gather that they were really close friends. Nor did anyone else in the office give me any warning. Thus I was still in the dark so late as December 27, for on that day I printed an article on the *Evening Sun*'s editorial page which rehearsed Roosevelt's great flop in a really cruel manner, speaking of him bluntly as "an ass" and "a pale and somewhat pathetic caricature of his late relative, Theodore." It must have been only a short while later that his appointment as vice-president in charge of the New York office of the Fidelity & Deposit Company was announced, greatly to my surprise and embarrassment. Neither then nor later did Van Lear Black show me any resentment of my low opinion of his friend, which has continued unbroken to this day, and gone on gathering accretions. I was never close to Black, as I was to his brother Harry. We met occasionally, but I don't recall ever sitting down with him for a palaver of any consequence. He was always very polite to me, but I hardly knew him.

Adams's dudgeon over my denunciation of Wilson as a liar wore off quickly, as I have said, but only on the surface. He and I, in fact, were too far apart on all fundamentals ever to be genuine friends, and our relations were always more or less formal. He was a liberal of the mushmouthed school, with a strong flavor of English Pecksniffery in him, whereas I was a libertarian, and hated every pretense to moral superiority and authority. Thus most of Adams's principal heroes—Wilson, Lloyd George, Borah, and so on—seem to me to be complete frauds and hence abhorrent; indeed, I was against them even on the rare occasions when they appeared to be right. My belief is that Adams was a drag on the *Sun* so long as he was in active service as its editor, and that when illness forced him to withdraw as editor his bad influence continued for a long while, and is in fact still evident.

My own contributions to the *Evening Sun*'s editorial page began to appear regularly on August 30, 1920: thereafter they were a fixture of the Monday paper, and so continued until the Spring of 1938. My first, in the regular series, headed "God Help Us All," was a discussion of the Supreme Court's order of May 15, 1911, dissolving the Standard Oil Company: I showed that the retail price of gasoline, during the nine years following, had risen from 10 cents a gallon to 30. My second, on September 6, was a warning to the triumphant suffragettes that what they had got [in the Nineteenth Amendment] was "little more than a severe case of *Katzenjammer*," for their victory had come "at the precise moment when all thoughtful members of the senior sex . . . have begun to doubt that the right to vote, at least in a democracy, is really worth a damn." My titles during the weeks following show how my mind was running: "The Bonus Banshee," "Government by Blackleg," "Free Speech-Truth-Justice-Idealism," "The Blue-Nose at the Bat Again," "The New Taxes," and so on. In the campaign I supported Harding against Cox, but only ironically. My final article before election day was headed "The Last Gasp" and began "Tomorrow the dirty job. I shall be on my knees all night, praying for strength to vote for Gamaliel. What ass first loosed the doctrine that the suffrage is a high boon and voting a noble privilege?" On November 20 I predicted that the new administration would never actually jail any of the war profiteers—too many contributors to the Republican campaign fund were among them. On November 29 I analyzed Cox's campaign, and came to the conclusion that he had made two capital mistakes. "First, he went to Washington, closeted himself with Woodrow, and then announced that he and the White House were at one on the League of Nations. Secondly, he tried to bamboozle the drys, and so managed to scare off the wets, who had nominated him. Neither gesture, of course, was honest, but that was no objection to them. What ailed them was that neither was wise." And on December 13 I undertook to extract some moral from the campaign, and among them ventured on this one: The party that gains and holds the moral offensive always wins. This sort of stuff naturally shook up the *Evening Sun*'s editorial page. The letter column began to bristle with letters denouncing my cynicism and undertaking to refute it.

5

Fruits of Versailles

1920–1922

Patterson was a man of enormous energy, and had many excellent ideas, but he was handicapped not only by the intransigence of Adams and Kent but also by a certain lack of coherence in his own plans. What was needed was a comprehensive thinking out of the new position of the *Sunpapers,* with a careful consideration of their future course, both in news enterprise and in editorial policy. Toward the end of 1920 Harry Black suggested to me that the two of us draw up a sort of protocol on the subject, embodying our own views. Needless to say, I was delighted, and for some weeks we sat almost nightly debating the details at great length. The result of these palavers was a document headed "An Editorial Memorandum" but recalled in the legend of the office as the White Paper. Black drew up the first draft and I made long additions, and then rewrote the whole.

Writing the thing gave me a fine chance to work off my discontent with the way Kent and Adams had carried on the *Sunpapers* during the war. I could not denounce them openly, but I was nevertheless able to attack their fundamental position, and I think I did it to some effect. I believed then, as I believe now, that it is the prime function of a really first-rate newspaper to serve as a sort of permanent opposition in politics, and I tried to show that the *Sun,* because of its geographical situation, had a superb opportunity to discharge that function effectively. Baltimore was but forty miles from Washington—and the Washington papers were all third-rate, and seemed doomed to remain so forever, for the overwhelming majority of their readers were petty Federal jobholders, which is to say, half-wits. In consequence of their badness all Washington officials in the higher brackets had to read out-of-town papers, and not a few of them, including Wilson, read the *Sun,* for that was in the days before airships, and the *Sun* could get to Washington with news nearly five hours earlier than the news in the New York morning papers. I took a crack at Adams's slavish support of Wilson, and another at the blowsy Liberalism he professed. The rudiments of the New Deal were already visible in those days, and I did not neglect to sneer at the "utopian ideas, economical, political and ethical" that were going about—most of them with Adams's support. Finally, I criticized the press associations from which the *Sunpapers* were getting their foreign news, for I had had a chance to judge their competence and good faith during my brief stay in Berlin in 1917, and had a low opinion of both. The Associated Press, in 1920, was rapidly going downhill under the management of Melville E. Stone, who was more than seventy years old, and quite unfit to handle the burdens put upon it during the post-war era. In 1921 he was retired and four years later Kent Cooper, who was his assistant in 1920, became general manager. Cooper was an able man, and quickly introduced far-reaching reforms and improvements.

Black made no objection to any of my oblique animadversions upon the conduct of the *Sunpapers* during the war years. He had been, to be sure, earnestly pro-English, but I suspected then, and still suspect now, that he was ashamed of the way the papers had snuffled for democracy and ranted against the Germans, for his admiration for all things British involved a strong distaste for moral indignation. Whatever the fact, he adopted the whole White Paper as his own, and presented it to Patterson as his own. Despite its obvious evasions and its occasional muddiness, Patterson liked it, and it soon reached Adams. What he thought about it I do not know, for he never mentioned it to me, but he at least undertook no answer to it, and during the two or three years following he gave a more or less willing hand to the efforts made to execute this or that article of it. {In 1940 John W. Owens, who succeeded Adams as editor of the *Sun* in 1927, told me that he (Owens) had a low opinion of the document. In view of what will follow toward the end of this narrative it is unnecessary for me to say that I was not surprised.} There was not much immediate effect. Reynolds went on improving the *Evening Sun* editorial page, and Murphy continued to do the best he could on its news pages with the service of the United Press, but the *Sun* continued flabby. On December 1, 1920, Frank A. Munsey bought the Baltimore *American,* and soon thereafter he put in a managing editor who made the first page of the *American* enormously superior, day in and day out, to the first page of the *Sun*. Patterson was greatly disturbed by this, and he and I frequently discussed ways and means of meeting the new and devastating competition, but nothing could be done so long as Kent remained managing editor of the *Sun*. Some good men were on the staff of the paper in those days—for example, James M. Cain—but Kent never utilized them to any advantage, and most of the more important news was still handled by dunderheads. {Cain's novel, "The Postman Always Rings Twice," made a great success in 1934. He became an editorial writer on the New York *World* and still later managing editor of the *New Yorker*. He is now (1942) in Hollywood.}

The great events of 1921, in *Sunpaper* history, were the trip to England and France that Patterson and Adams made in the late Summer of the year, and the highly elaborate measures that were taken to cover the Naval Conference at Washington in November. The two were connected, for it was Patterson's desire to have the *Sun* do the conference better than the Washington bureau could be expected to do it that suggested going abroad to recruit experts and seek advice. I was not told about the plan until Patterson had decided on it, and though I acquiesced in it I had some doubts, for I feared that when he got to England Adams would be taken into camp by the English, and I believed that he was already far too susceptible to English influences. These forebodings turned out to be well justified, but I made no protest; instead, I fell back on the theory that my accretion of ideas, however dubious, might conceivably shake Adams out of his lethargy, and set him upon efforts to improve the editorial page of the *Sun* as Reynolds was already improving that of the *Evening Sun*. Van Lear Black, by this time, was already started upon the wanderings that were to engage him until the end of his life, and so the formal staff meeting, called to discuss the proposed expedition, was held on the *Sabalo* in New York harbor. This must have been early in August, and I recall that the day was infernally hot. Those present were Black, his brother Harry, Patterson, Adams, Murphy, Essary and maybe one or two others. We heard Patterson and Adams in the stuffy little cabin of the yacht, and then went on deck to discuss the business and get down a few drinks. We were at anchor in the East river, and past us floated the sewage of half New York. I remember a couple of dead cats, many clusters of toilet-paper, and some dismal-looking used condoms, bobbing along like jelly-fish. I listened with only one ear, and was glad to

return to shore. It appeared that Adam's chief hope was to get an interview with C. P. Scott, of the Manchester *Guardian,* an old-time English
Liberal and one of his idols. He said that he was in hopes of inducing
Scott to let us have the American rights to some of his special correspondence and editorials.

He and Patterson sailed on August 26 and returned about a month
later. They saw not only Scott, but also a great many other Englishmen,
including J. St. Loe Strachey of the London *Spectator,* Sir Campbell
Stuart of the *Times,* George Bernard Shaw, and J. M. Keynes, whose book,
"The Economic Consequences of the Peace," had made a sensation two
years before. They also went to Paris and saw Stephen Lausanne, editor
of *Le Matin,* and Vincent O'Sullivan, who was by now reëstablished as a
more or less regular contributor to the *Sun.* As I anticipated, they were
taken into camp by the English. All the journalists they called on were
full of friendly advice, and the burden of that advice always ran the same
way: it was that the United States, in the current parlous condition of the
world, ought to follow English leadership, which was backed by long
experience and marked by a singular disinterestedness. The first result
was that the conference was covered for the *Sun* by more Englishmen
than Americans—among them, Strachey, H. W. Nevinson, H. N. Brails-
ford, H. W. Massingham, Wilson Harris and Hector C. Bywater. The second was that there ensued an intimacy with the *Guardian* which bore
fruit, three years later, in the establishment of a London bureau of the
Sun, quartered upstairs of the *Guardian*'s office at 40 Fleet street, and
strongly under the influence, from first to last, of its London editor, James
Bone. Of this there will be more later.

I was a member of the conference staff myself, but confined my writing to the editorial page of the *Evening Sun.* My first article, headed, significantly, "The Impending Buffoonery," was published on October 17,
1921, nearly a month before the sessions began, and I kept on hammer-
ing away at the dishonesty and futility of the proceedings until the treaty
was signed on February 6, 1922. The whole show, it seemed to me,
was simply an English device to take advantage of the American fear of
Japan—already growing acute—to rope Harding and his Secretary of
State, Charles Evans Hughes, into agreeing to an arrangement that
would insure English control of the seas. The British Foreign Office sent
Lord Riddell, publisher of the pornographic and immensely prosperous
News of the World, as its chief press officer, and in the choice there was
all the evidence that was needed for its contempt for everything American. Riddell gave press conferences that were attended by hundreds of

the country editors who had swarmed to Washington for the conference, which had been advertised as a final blow for eternal peace in the world. These poor fish knew nothing about the *News of the World;* all they knew was that Riddell was a real English lord (he had been given his barony only a year before) who was willing to talk to them familiarly and answer their imbecile questions. His replies, two times out of three, were only ponderous kidding: he made no attempt to conceal his low opinion of his customers. But every word that fell from his lips was received as gospel, and everything he said that had any sense at all was naturally directed toward promoting the advantage of England.

The conference bored me to excess, and after the first week I avoided it as much as possible, but it produced two parties that I enjoyed. The first was given by Van Lear Black on November 20, 1921, at his country place in Howard county, Maryland, Folly Quarters by name. All the correspondents in attendance upon the show—save, of course, the representatives of country weeklies—were invited, and they were brought from Washington in a long string of motor-cars. Black, who was a lavish entertainer and greatly delighted in his own parties, had made preparations on a grandiose scale. Two barbecue pits were dug and there were four or five bars scattered about the grounds. The principal entertainment was a rodeo, and with it came a group of Indians in full war-paint. Black was especially eager to have the foreign correspondents on hand. All of them accepted save H. G. Wells, who was covering the conference for the New York *World.* He declined on the ground that he had luncheon and dinner engagements in Washington. Inasmuch as I was the only member of the *Sun* staff who knew him, I was detailed to try to rope him. I told him that if he would come, and could be trusted to keep quiet, we'd stage the burning of a Negro toward the end of the afternoon. Whether or not Wells believed this I do not know, but he turned up with the rest, and hinted several times during the day that he was looking forward with keen sociological interest to the main bout. As the day wore on to dark I told him that it would have to be postponed—that certain persons who would blab could not be got rid of—and he returned to Washington looking disappointed. Many of the guests got drunk, but the *Sun* men present carried themselves very well, and only three out of perhaps thirty or forty succumbed—Frank Patterson, the Bentztown Bard, and Boardman Robinson, who had been employed to do cartoons during the conference. Robinson was overcome by the fumes as he sat on the top row of the bleachers that had been erected for the rodeo, and after a violent attack of emesis fell through the structure and landed in his own vomit. He was not hurt, but it took half an hour to clean him up. The rodeo was rather a failure, for the wild steers that the cowboys were supposed to throw turned out to be very tame and refused to resist. Several of them ran away instead, and a dozen colored boys spent the rest of the afternoon running them down in Black's woods. Two whole oxen, a dozen hogs and scores of chickens were barbecued, and the bars got rid of thirty or forty cases of whiskey. During that first miserable year of Prohibition, with bootlegging still undeveloped, it cost $125 a case.

It was my fixed policy, through all those early post-war years to avoid any argument that could be distorted into a plea for decency to prostrate Germany, for I had been denounced as a German during the war and did not want to appear to be asking for quarter. But I managed nevertheless to get my opinion of the war before the customers from time to time, and especially my opinion of the pious pretenses of Wilson. On August 8 I offered "one million dollars cash to any American citizen, beyond ten years old by the Simon-Benet test, who will swear on the Holy Scriptures that he believes the world to be now safe for democracy, and that he is of the opinion that there will be no more wars," and another million to anyone "willing to write and sign his name to a paper certifying that he believes that all or any of the money now due the United States by Great Britain, France, Belgium, Greece, Rumania, Serbia, Portugal, Liberia or any other collaborator in the struggle for democracy will ever be paid, or that the interest on the interest will ever be paid," and on September 8 I predicted formally that in the inevitable next war "the United States, for the first time in its history, will face an antagonist able to hit back."

In the early Spring of 1922 I decided to make a trip to England and Germany. I had not been abroad since my return from the war in 1917 and was eager to have a look at the fruits of the Treaty of Versailles. When he heard of my plan, in May, Patterson proposed that I go as the correspondent of the *Sun,* and at its expense, but I wanted to be free, and so refused this offer. I had it in mind, however, to do a few articles for the paper, and so I took its credentials. I sailed in August and came back in October, first visiting England and then Germany and what had by now become Czechoslovakia. When I landed at Plymouth the chief customs officer received me very politely, and I was interviewed by several English newspaper men. This reception amused me no little, for only a short while before Hendrik Willem van Loon had been refused an English visa. Van

Loon, during the war, had done a great deal of howling for the English and was commonly believed in New York to be on their payroll, whereas I had been against them from first to last, and was still against them, and made no attempt to conceal it. Yet now they were polite to me, an avowed enemy, and suspicious of van Loon, a vociferous partisan.

One day H. W. Nevinson, hearing that I was in London, invited me to lunch, and when I got to the restaurant appointed I found ten or twelve men assembled—mainly English journalists, but with a few of the younger men of the Foreign Office. I sat next to one of the latter, and toward the end of what turned out to be a long meal both of us somewhat alcoholized and hence in confidential moods. To this man, whose name I forget, I imparted a notion that I had lately set forth in the *Evening Sun* of June 12, 1922—that the United States had gone into World War I on the wrong side—that it would have got more out of the business, and at much less cost, if it had ganged with Germany against England, and so insured a German victory, and got a fat share of the loot. The Englishman admitted at once that this was probably true, and so I was emboldened to argue that England also had made a mistake. "If you had come to terms with the Kaiser," I said, "it would have been easy to make a deal with him to share the world—he taking the Continent of Europe, and you all the rest. Now you have a swollen and truculent France on your hands—and the certainty that Germany will try for revenge at the first chance." The Foreign Office gentleman looked at me sidewise, took thought for half a minute, and then said "We have thought of all that ourselves."

From London I went to Berlin, and then to Prague, where I met my old friend Adolf Torovsky, for many years leader of the Naval Academy Band at Annapolis and a member of the Saturday Night Club in Baltimore. Torovsky was a native of Czechoslovakia and spoke the language, so I had a good guide. He must have reported my approach in official quarters, with a hint that I was to be shown some attention, for I had barely got to town before I was waited on by one of the secretaries of President T. G. Masaryk, who informed me that His Excellency would receive me the next morning. Inasmuch as I was on a holiday, and knew that I would be expected to write something about Masaryk, whose grandiose politics did not impress me, I determined to get out of this nuisance, and did so by telling the secretary that I was leaving Prague immediately. Two days later Torovsky and I actually started on a pilgrimage to Pilsen, the home of the best beer on earth and hence one of the great shrines of the human race. There Torovsky did some more whispering,

At the beginning of his great decade, H.L.M. palavers with the British author Hugh Walpole. 1920. Janvier.

and we were invited to visit the principal brewery as the guests of the management. Deep down in the earth, in a cellar both dark and cold, we were served some Pilsner beer that I recall with a glow to this day. It was unutterably perfect. Torovsky and I put in a day or two in Pilsen trying the other local brews and feasting on roast goose. I then set off for Munich via the Böhmerwald, and had a grand day on the train, enchanted by the fairy-tale scenery.

At Munich I stayed for two weeks with Dr. Wilhelm Sohler, whom I had met in Baltimore at the end of 1914. Sohler was an ophthalmologist, and before the war had been a man of considerable wealth. Early in 1914 he started on a tour of the world, and was at Kiauchau [Kiaochow] in China when the war broke out. He volunteered for service as surgeon of one of the German raiders that started out from there, and arrived at Norfolk on it when it put into Hampton Roads in the late Autumn, out of coal. During the weeks following he came to Baltimore to observe the work of his fellow eye specialists at the Johns Hopkins, and I there met him. As I have hitherto recorded, Paul and Elsie Patterson and I spent *Sylvesterabend* [New Year's Eve] with him and his shipmates at Norfolk at the end of 1914. When the United States got into the war they were all sent to an internment camp at Fort Oglethorpe, Ga. I kept Sohler supplied with clothing, tobacco and other necessaries while he was locked up, and he invited me to be his guest in Munich as a return for these offices. The inflation had now begun in Germany, and his fortune was gone. Most of it had been invested in a Munich apartment-house worth 600,000 marks. At the time of the Communist revolution in Bavaria a Jew offered Mrs. Sohler that price for the building, in cash. Sohler himself had not yet been released and sent home, so she turned to a family friend, a Munich judge, for advice. He advised her to take the money, for the Communists were apparently preparing to confiscate all real estate. By the time Sohler got home they were overthrown, but the apartment-house was gone, the inflation was on, and the 600,000 marks were worth only about 3000 American dollars. He accepted his huge loss philosophically, invested the still dwindling money in the best ophthalmological equipment obtainable, opened an office at the Karlstor in downtown Munich, and prepared to resume practise. Inasmuch as he had picked up English in America he hoped to get some American patients, and when tourist travel was restored he did so. I sent a number of them to him during the later 20's.

The Sohlers lived in a large and charming second-story apartment (not in their own former building) in the Widenmeyerstrasse, with the green-lined river Isar in front of them and the great wooded sweep of the Englisher Garten to the rear. I had a lovely room with a private bath, and was very comfortable. The weather was wet and dismal, but the Oktoberfest was in progress while I was in town, and Sohler and I had a grand time visiting its sessions, and watching the Bavarian mountaineers booze and fight. I heard much from Mrs. Sohler about the events of the communist revolution, and saw the marks of its gunfire on many buildings. The Communists, who were mainly Jews, carried on with great savagery, confiscating and destroying property, dragging innocent people out of their homes and chasing them like wild animals, and even taking and shooting hostages. When the Bavarian soldiers, demobilized after long delays, got home at last, they punished these crimes vigorously, but most of the principal Marxians escaped. Munich remembered them and was already ripe, in the Autumn of 1922, for reaction against democracy in all its forms. The Bavarian state, in fact, was spoken of by sportive Müncheners as *die königliche bayerische Republik*—the royal Bavarian republic. I came away from Munich convinced that the days of that republic, and of all the other German republics, were numbered. "Outwardly," I wrote to Patterson on September 9, "everything looks serene, but every intelligent man looks for a catastrophe. If it comes, then there will be a colossal massacre of Jews." Adolf Hitler was in the city while I was there, but as yet he was only a minor figure in the ferments of the time, and I heard nothing of him. A year later, on November 8, 1923, he staged his famous beer-garden *Putsch,* which though it failed launched him upon his melodramatic career. Sohler, in the days before the war, had leaned toward the democratic side in politics, but in 1922 he was cured, and his hope was that the Wittelsbachs would be restored to the Bavarian throne. Whether or not he supported the Nazis on their rise to power I do not know, for I lost contact with him after 1933. By that time he was a *Medizinalrat* [senior medical officer] and very successful in his practise. The Sohlers had a servant named Kuni—a stocky, immensely strong country girl who thought nothing of hauling in the coal to feed their kitchen stove and hot-water heater. As I was leaving I proposed to give her a present, and asked Sohler for advice. He suggested cash, for Kuni was engaged to a *Heitzer* (stoker) at one of the Munich factories, and was to be married in a few months. I gave her a $20 American gold-note, which worked out to more than 3000 marks. Sohler protested that so much money in hand would ruin her, so he took charge of it, and agreed to dole it out as she really needed it. Several years later he wrote to me that Kuni had finally got all of it, that her *Heitzer* had spent most of it on drink, and that she was looking for a job.

From Munich I went to Berchtesgaden, since famous as the retreat of Hitler, to spend a night with Dr. and Mrs. Henry Wood of Baltimore. Dr. Wood, a native of New Bedford, Mass., had been professor of German at the Johns Hopkins from 1892 to 1920, and was now retired. Mrs. Wood, whose maiden name had been Clothide von Kretschman, was connected by blood with a large part of the German aristocracy, and stood on an intimate footing with the Hohenzollerns. She and the doctor had taken a charming villa in a forest near Berchtesgaden, and there they were entertaining half a dozen elderly and penniless noble ladies from Potsdam. Their income, derived from the United States, amounted to almost a million German marks a year, and they were looked upon as Croesuses by their friends. Their house, though large, was so crowded that I had to be quartered in a *pension* half a mile away. The doctor had discovered a bottle of Maryland rye in a tavern in Berchtesgaden, and after dinner and the retirement of the ladies we sat up to get it down and discuss the issues of the hour. He was, as befitted his academic dignity, a somewhat stuffy man, but nevertheless he was intelligent, and from him I learned a great deal about the state of German opinion, especially in the higher military circle. He told me that the Germans did not waste any time mourning the result of the war: it was, in their view, simply bad luck. But when they thought of the blockade that England had maintained *after* the Armistice they were full of a blind and berserker rage, and out of it flowed plans for revenge. That blockade cause the death of at least half a million Germans, most of them aged people and children; it was responsible for a great increase in rickets, which had come to be called "the English disease." If the chance ever offered, said Wood, for survivors of the late war to strike another blow at England, it would be struck without mercy. When at three o'clock or thereabout, the doctor's bottle of Maryland rye was empty, and I started back to my *pension* a heavy rain was falling, and I got lost in the woods surrounding the house. Fortunately, one of the servants heard me threshing about, and the doctor turned out to show me the way to the highroad. I started off with alcoholic confidence, but quickly discovered that I couldn't recognize the house in which I was quartered. All I recalled was that my room was on the ground floor, and that there was a porch outside my window, giving on to the road. After a long and futile search I picked out a house that answered these specifications, opened a window, climbed in—and found myself in my room. I often wondered afterward what would have happened if I had got into the wrong house.

Mrs. Wood suggested that, on my return to Bremen to take ship for home, I drop over to Holland and visit the German Crown Prince, who was interned on the island of Wieringen. I decided to do so, but first stopped in Berlin for another week of its feverish, and indeed almost delirious life. There I met a number of German authors, including Walter von Molo and Franz Blei. Blei had just finished translating my book "In Defense of Women," into German under the title of "Verteidigung der Frau," and though the book was not yet out I saw the proofsheets and was properly delighted by his excellent translation. One day old Dr. Alois Brandl, professor of English at the University of Berlin, called me up and said he wanted to see me: he had been greatly interested, it appeared, by the first and second editions of "The American Language," published in 1919 and 1921. I was naturally flattered, for he was a distinguished scholar—and all his American colleagues had either sneered at the book or ignored it altogether. After some parley I told him that I was giving a cocktail party that afternoon at the Bristol Hotel, and invited him to come. With one of his students as his aide-de-camp he showed up promptly—an immense Tyrolean with a long beard, probably six feet four inches in height. He was then 67 years old, but he fell upon my

American cocktails, mixed by myself, with great zest, and was soon very mellow. We came to terms quickly, and I maintained contact with him for fifteen years afterward. He sent me a number of his books, autographed, and continued to show interest in "The American Language". He was the president of the German Shakespeare-Gesellschaft, and was the author of a standard work on Shakespeare in German, besides many other scholarly books.

In Berlin I put in a good deal of my time with Herman George Scheffauer, a strange American who had been living there since the early days of the war. He hailed from San Francisco, and had been, in his early days, one of the young poets in the entourage of Ambrose Bierce, but he was now devoting all his time to promoting a cultural *rapprochement* between Germany and the United States. As a minor means to that end he was translating some of my *Evening Sun* and *Smart Set* articles into German, or procuring their translation by other hands. One of his aides in this work was a Jewish woman named Frau Noah, whose husband was extremely wealthy. When he took me to see her I was astonished to find a Botticelli (and a very lovely one) hanging on the wall of her drawing-room. Scheffauer was married to an English poetess named Ethel Talbot. They had a charming little daughter, and despite Mrs. Scheffauer's nationality and the fact that Scheffauer himself was violently anti-English they seemed to get on amicably. In 1926 he began to show signs of mental aberration, and in 1927 he committed suicide in Berlin. He took himself off in a really gaudy manner, first cutting the throat of his woman secretary and then jumping out of a window. Whether or not he had a love affair with the secretary I do not know: there were the usual rumors, but they seemed to have no basis in fact.

One day while I was in Berlin I dropped in on Martin Breslauer, a bookseller from whom I had been buying books before and after the war. I was trying in those days to fill out my collection of books by early Menckens, and also run down some family documents—chiefly files of letters in German libraries. Breslauer had put me into contact, in 1920, with Dr. Stephan Kekule von Stradonitz, and now introduced me to him. Kekule was the son of August Kekule, the discoverer of the benzene ring and the founder of modern organic chemistry, and was a man of distinction in his own right. He was the leading German genealogist of his time and had published a great many books. In preparation for the Bismarck centennial in 1915 he had made an extensive investigation of Bismarck's genealogy, and in the course of it had turned up a great deal of interesting matter about the Mencken family. All this he placed at my disposal, and later on he undertook various further investigations for me. As a result of his labor I acquired copies of four Mencken portraits in oil at the University of Leipzig, a large number of engraved portraits, an even larger number of Mencken books and pamphlets, and copies of many Mencken letters and other documents. I was in frequent communication with him until his death in 1933 or thereabout. I saw him again when I visited Berlin in 1930. He was a courtly and charming old man and I was very fond of him. Breslauer, who was a Jew, moved his business to Amsterdam when Hitler came to power, and afterward to London. During an air-raid on London in 1940 he suffered a heart attack and died.

Two New York acquaintances, Philip Goodman and Charles Recht, were in Berlin when I got there, and I saw much of Goodman, whose tastes, save for his anesthesia to music, were exactly my own. When I first met him, in 1917, he was an advertisement writer, but in 1918 he set up as a publisher, and did two books of mine, "In Defense of Women" and "Damn!" He had by now become a theatrical manager, and was very prosperous. I had not visited Berlin on my previous trips to Germany, so he served as my guide, and a good one he was. Recht, a radical lawyer, was in Berlin on mysterious business for the Russians, and one day proposed to me that I go to Moscow. He said that he could get me an invitation from the Bolsheviki, and that I'd be treated very politely, and have a chance to dig up some interesting stuff. But I was eager to avoid work as much as possible—and the Germans told me that Moscow was filthy beyond expression and full of fleas, so I refused. Not, of course, through Recht, but in some way I forget, I met a number of the White Russian exiles who were then swarming in its West End, with many restaurants, bookshops and even theatres of their own. One of them was Prince Kropotkin, a nephew of the famous anarchist of that ilk, then a prisoner of the Bolsheviki in Russia. The prince was an author himself, though what he wrote I do not recall and maybe never learned. I put in several evenings with him and his friends, rolling about the West End and observing the saturnalia that was in the making. The inflation was now well under way, and had already produced a spirit of half-insane recklessness. Berlin was dotted with *Likörstuben* selling strange and fiery drinks, all the downtown bookshop windows were full of pornographic books {Mainly the product of Jewish quacks who had set up as so-called sexologists. Nine-tenths of them were disguised as "scientific." These were the books that Hitler ordered burned when he came to power.}, and naked women were beginning to appear in the arty cabarets along the Kurfürstendamm—years before the dawn of the strip-tease in America.

In the Adlon Hotel one day I encountered Dr. Karl Muck, who had been conductor of the Boston Symphony Orchestra until professional patriots forced Col. Henry Lee Higginson, its backer, to dismiss him. I had met Muck in America, and we sat down for a friendly chat. He had been interned after his dismissal, and he told me that in the camp he was sent to, somewhere in Tennessee, he found more than a hundred other German musicians. Most of them had their instruments with them, and they soon formed an orchestra, with Muck as its leader. He said that they gave some of the best concerts he had ever conducted, though their only audience consisted of fellow prisoners. Once, on a very hot day, they played Beethoven's Eroica Symphony stark naked. "It was," said Muck, "a really magnificent performance, though the heat was hard on the violin strings. Beethoven would have been proud of it." Muck was a schoolmate of Count Johann Bernstorff, who had been German ambassador in Washington up to the time the United States entered the war. Bernstorff was now back in Germany, had joined the Democratic party, was a member of the Reichstag, and served as chairman of the German League of Nations Union. All this [was] anathema to Muck, who was an irreconcilable monarchist. He told me that some time before he had met Bernstorff in the Adlon lobby and denounced him publicly. He said his philippic ended with the words "Johann, du bist ein Verbrecher!" (Johann, you are a criminal!) This brought all the elegant loafers in the lobby to their feet, and in the old days would have meant a duel, but Bernstorff took it quietly. His later career was a sad one, for he lived long enough to see the German republic fall into the hands of the Jews, but not long enough to see Germany revive, rearm and tackle its enemies once more.

On tiring of Berlin I went to Oldenburg in the far west of Germany, the original home of the Menckenii, there visited the crumbling tombs surviving in the St. Gertrud churchyard, and then continued to Amsterdam in preparation for the trip to Wieringen. Mrs. Wood had smoothed my way. A note to the Crown Prince brought a prompt reply from his adjutant, Major Müldner von Mühlheim, inviting me to come two days hence, and the next day I began my journey, which was long and somewhat laborious. First I had to go by train to Den Helder, a small town at the northern tip of the province of North Holland, and then proceed by motor-car to De Haukes, the small port on the Zuyder Zee from which the motor-boat to Wieringen started. When I got to the island Müldner met me with the Crown Prince's car, and after a visit to the *burgemeester* [mayor], who insisted upon interviewing all visitors, we drove to the *kaiserlichekönigliche* [imperial royal] cottage at the tiny hamlet of

Oosterland on the north coast of the island, with the waves roaring against the dike only a few hundreds yards away. Mrs. Wood's recommendation got me a hearty welcome from the Crown Prince, and we quickly came to terms. He spoke English fluently, and so we were able to talk without any serious interference by the watchful Müldner, who knew only a few words of the language. The three of us had lunch together, and the Prince and I then settled down for a frank palaver. He turned out to be an extremely intelligent and amusing fellow, and what he had to say about the effects of the insane Treaty of Versailles, not only in Germany but all over Europe, was substantially what American Liberals and college professors were saying in retrospect ten years later. It was soon apparent that he differed from his father on important matters, and that his information was considerably wider than his father's. Over and over again he would say to me: "My father says so-and-so"—outlining the old man's theory about this or that in great detail, and then concluding with "What do you think of that?" Three times out of four I had to answer that his father seemed to me to be misinformed, which plainly pleased him. He readily gave me permission to put the more formal parts of our conversation into an interview for the *Sun*, but suggested politely that he had better see the story before I cabled it. This seemed reasonable to me, so I went down to the village at the Wieringen landing, hired a room in the four-room hotel, wrote my interview, and then took it back to Oosterland. The Crown Prince approved it without changing a word, and I filed it in Amsterdam the next morning. At the end of it I appended this note "to editors":

> Text interview passed by prince. Absolute promise no extension or paraphrase. Careful with the headlines. Do not insert ex before Crown Prince.

The Crown Prince had a respectable library in his little house, largely made up of books in English. He told me apologetically that his favorite American author was [the adventure-story teller] James Oliver Curwood. But he also had many better books, and seemed to know what was in them. He gave me an autographed copy of his own autobiography, "Erinnerungen des Kronprinzen Wilhelms" {It had come out in an English translation in July, 1922, and I had written an article on it for the *Evening Sun* editorial page of July 22. In that article I had praised the book, but the Crown Prince, of course, had not seen my notice at the time I visited him.}, and also a leather cigarette-case and various other trifles. I parted from him sincerely sorry for the loneliness that he was suffering in his bleak exile, and was glad to hear of it a year later when news came that he had gone back to Germany, Allies or no Allies, and taken up residence in Silesia. Mrs. Wood wanted me to visit the Kaiser also, but I was by now eager to return home, and went to Bremen to board ship. There I met Captain Paul König, who was by now marine superintendent of the North German Lloyd, and he quickly got me good accommodations on the first ship out. I never got to Doorn to see the Kaiser, but when my book, "Notes on Democracy," came out in 1926 I sent him a copy of it at the request of Mrs. Wood. It made a great hit with him, and he not only wrote me a letter of thanks, but also sent me two large autographed photographs of himself, tinted by his own hand! Until his death in 1941 he kept on whooping up my book as the leading authority on the crimes and imbecilities of democracy and usually advised the Americans who visited him to read it.

In Berlin, and later in Bremen, I had had several palavers with O. J. Merkel, a German whom I had met in New York during the early years of the war. He was a business man of wide acquaintance and considerable influence. In New York he had been the American representative of Kaffee Hag, but now he was preparing to go into airships, and wanted to come to the United States to try to interest American capital. It seemed to me that it would be a good idea for him to consult Van Lear Black, who was already greatly interested in air travel, and I offered to bring the two together. Unhappily, Merkel had been interned in America when the United States entered the war, and the consulate at Berlin was unable to give him a visa without direct orders from Washington. I wrote to Patterson suggesting that the Washington bureau ask the State Department to let him in, but nothing seems to have come of this, and Merkel did not visit the United States until 1931 or thereabout. By this time he was the head of one of the largest of the German airship companies, and was on his way to South America to extend its routes there. I met him again in 1938, in Berlin. He was now engaged in the manufacture of airships on an immense scale, and from him I learned a great deal about the German preparations for the war then impending. He talked freely, for he knew that I would write nothing indiscreet; as a matter of fact, I wrote nothing at all. Merkel hoped, at that time, that the war would not come until 1940. He told me that the Germans would be ready, by then, to meet and throw off the threat from Poland, which was being armed to the teeth by the English and would probably have the aid of the Russians. He said that the German military believed that the Russians would be more formidable than the English, if only because of their closer proximity, but that there was every confidence that they could be crushed in the end. He laughed at the supposed might of the Polish army. Two or three German corps, he said, would dispose of it in a couple of months. But there will be more about this in its proper place. I sailed for home October 11. I recall that I was completely free from hay-fever, my old pest, in Europe, but that when I reached New York it almost floored me, though the usual season was at end. Having developed no immunity, I was an easy victim of the small amount of pollen remaining in the air. I wrote little for the *Sunpapers,* save my interview with the Crown Prince, about my observations in Europe. In particular, I was always very careful, then and afterward, to write nothing that could be interpreted as a protest against the Treaty of Versailles. I was convinced that its imbecilities could never be corrected by argument—that only blood and iron could rectify them—and I was convinced too, especially after my trip to Germany in 1938, that the German people would see to the business in due time, and with a reasonable chance of success.

6

That Man in Baltimore

1922-1924

When Hamilton Owens became editor of the *Evening Sun* early in 1922, as successor to Stanley M. Reynolds, I did not know and in fact had barely heard of him. He was married to Olga von Hartz, who had lived in Hollins street as a child, so I had known his wife, as I had known Murphy's wife, before he knew her himself. But though Owens began newspaper work on the Baltimore *News* in 1909 and continued there for four years, I had never encountered him. On leaving the *News* he joined the staff of the *Press* in New York, but resigned in 1917 to become managing editor of the Foreign Press Bureau of the Committee on Public Information, under George Creel. At the end of the war he went to work for the Guaranty Trust Company, which sent him to its London office early in 1921. He was in charge of the company's press relations in England, and in that capacity encountered a great many English newspaper men, including James Bone, London editor of the Manchester *Guardian*. He was proposed as Reynold's successor by Murphy, who had been managing editor of the Baltimore *News* and then of the New York *Press* during his service on those papers. I recall entering a protest against making a press-agent editor of the *Evening Sun,* but Murphy was so sure that he had the man he needed that I did not press it. When Owens came into the office I was very favorably impressed by him. He was then 33 years old, unusually handsome in person, of pleasant manners, and obviously intelligent. His editorial experience, of course, had been mainly in the lower ranks, but he seemed to have a sharp, active, unconventional mind, with some sense of humor, and so he was a great relief after such adamantine dogmatists as Adams and Kent. On talking to him at length I made a report to Harry Black. "He is," I said, "a clean white page. Go write on him anything you want."

Black had the same impression of him, and proceeded to the writing at once. Thereafter, for seventeen years, the two worked in a symbiosis recalling that of Grant and Adam Badeau [U.S. Grant's secretary and champion in print], and their joint operations gave the *Evening Sun* editorial page a character that was not only new to the *Sun* office, but also extremely uncommon in journalism elsewhere. The groundwork of their philosophy came out of the White Paper: it was the doctrine that public officials, under democracy, were predominantly frauds, and hence did not deserve to be taken seriously. To its exposition Black brought a great deal of skill at concocting elaborate ribaldries, and Owens a deft hand for putting them into terse and effective words. They went into conference every afternoon, and in addition Black usually called up Owens of a morning. The result was a long succession of gaudy buffooneries, some of them attracting national attention. The *Sun* editorial page, under Adams, went on merchanting moral indignation, but that of the *Evening Sun* ran to a cynicism that not only scoffed at politicians, but also at the reformers seeking so vainly to unhorse them. It took over not only all the iconoclastic principles of the White Paper, but also all my Free Lance stock company of hobgoblins. Nor were its editorials the whole of it. Owens gradually accumulated a staff of occasional correspondents, and their contributions were often excellent. Many of these correspondents were put to work at my nomination—for example, Grover C. Hall of Montgomery, Ala., David Warren Ryder of San Francisco, Ralph Coghlan of St. Louis, R. Charlton Wright of Columbia, S.C., Duncan Aikman of El Paso, Tex., Gerald W. Johnson of Greensboro, N.C., and W. G. Clugston, of Topeka, Kansas—for my work for the *Smart Set* and later for the *American Mercury* brought me into contact with large numbers of bright young men, most of them still unknown outside of their own bailiwicks. But Owens also unearthed some competent ones on his own—for example, Louis Graves of Chapel Hill, N.C., Robert Lathan of Asheville, N.C., and Louis I. Jaffé of Norfolk, Va., the last-named one of the few Jews ever to work for the *Sunpapers*. These auxiliaries were mainly Southerners, for the South was our special field of interest, but there were also some from the Middle and Far West, and indeed every part of the country was represented save New England.

Some of the projects invented by Black and executed by Owens are described in "The *Sunpapers* of Baltimore," Chapter XX, but the list given there is very far from complete. Not only was Black constantly ready with novelties; he was also fertile in schemes to keep old ideas going with unflagging vigor. It was a day of excellent opportunities for the kind of journalism he and Owens practised. The Anti-Saloon League, the Ku Klux Klan and the American Legion were all easy and obvious marks, and the hang-over of official oppression from the war years turned up endless outrages, and hence chances to perform. For thirteen long years Black kept the *Evening Sun* in the forefront of the fight against Prohibition, always with fresh ingenuity and vitality, and for almost as long he kept it battling against the multiplication of laws and jobholders, and the shams and frauds of the politicians of all parties and factions, including especially the Liberals that Adams admired. His scheme to array both papers against the two major parties had been rejected, as I have recorded, but he revived it under a hundred specious guises, and banged away unceasingly. He was responsible, I believe, for the *Evening Sun*'s standing definition of a Liberal as "one who stands for more laws, more jobholders, higher taxes, and, in consequence, less liberty," and he certainly had a good deal to do with launching the concept of the Maryland Free State in 1923, though the actual name was devised by Owens. {To my frank envy. It was a masterpiece, and I still mourn that I did not think of it myself. Its effects were immediate and profound. In a year or two even the country editors of the state, most of whom were actually reactionaries, were whooping up free speech and all the rest of it. The notion that Maryland was somehow more liberal and enlightened than any other state spread from end to end of the country, and even extended abroad. The generality of Marylanders, at the start, held back, but eventually they began to be proud of their citizenship in the Free State, and even to make efforts to live up to it. The whole phenomenon was an impressive proof of the power of a phrase to influence the minds of men. The Free State, fundamentally, was purely imaginary, but the *Evening Sun* pumped a certain appearance of reality into it. Another excellent invention of those days was *Baltimoron*. This, again, was not mine, but Harry Black's.} He had been the begetter of the *Evening Sun*'s most successful editorial page feature under Reynolds, "The Mirrors of Maryland," and under Owens he devised countless others. Some of them died early deaths, but others ran on for years. He usually provided the cash prizes that the *Evening Sun* was always offering for this or that—for example, the best definition of the difference between a Democrat and a Republican, the best draft of a plank on Prohibition that both wet and dry politicians could approve, the best drawing of a Baltimore scene sent in by a Baltimore artist (1922), and the best new building erected in Baltimore during the year, regardless of its character.

My own contributions to the *Evening Sun* editorial page went on in 1922 as in 1921 save for the interruption caused by my trip abroad. I covered my usual range of topics. On February 6, for example, I denounced certain pedants who had objected to the English in Joseph Hergesheimer's "Cytherea" and bade them study it and teach it; on February 13 I reviewed the situation of labor in the United States, and discussed some of the rascalities and imbecilities of its leaders; on February 20 and 27 I noted the continued violation of the Bill of Rights by government snoopers and censors; on March 6 I hailed the news that the police of Baltimore were resorting to spiritualism for aid in running down crime; on March 20 and 27 I analyzed some of the fallacies of Socialism; on April 24 I reviewed the English translation of A. W. Thayer's monumental life of Beethoven, then lately published; on June 5 I paid a tribute to the Enoch Pratt Free Library of Baltimore, the source of most of my own education, such as it was; and on July 17 I printed a treatise on marriage, arguing that in most cases it was happy. Twice during the year I printed articles reporting on the continued effort of a minority of civilized Southerners to lift the South out of its intellectual wallow, and from time to time I gave a hand to other strivers against the prevailing darkness in the United States. On June 12, 1922, I printed the first of an intermittent series of "Notes for an Honest Autobiography," later to be transferred to the *Smart Set,* with a book in mind that never got itself written. By this time Adams's moral dudgeon over my denunciation of Wilson in 1920 was so far abated that no uproar followed the following paragraph: "The most shameless liar I have ever encountered was a President of the United States." Nor was there any audible objection in the office to these "conclusions about the late war":

> (*a*) that the American pretense of neutrality down to 1917 was dishonest and dishonorable;
>
> (*b*) that the interests of the United States were actually on the side of Germany, and against both England and France;
>
> (*c*) that the propagation of the notion to the contrary was a very deft and amusing piece of swindling;
>
> (*d*) that the American share in the war, after 1917, was carried on in an extremely cowardly manner.

But though these dicta passed the office censors, they aroused some fever among readers of the *Evening Sun,* and a great many letters of protest and denunciation flowed in. To these I paid no attention whatever, for it had been my rule from the resumption of my articles in 1920 to engage in no controversy with my inferiors if I could help it—and nearly always I could. The American Legion was in full blast in 1922, and its agents watched eagerly for every sign of treason to the official theology. I simply let them roar. It was during this era that I became That Man in Baltimore, rather to the soothing of my vanity. I had no desire to degenerate into a local worthy, and always resisted efforts to draw me into Baltimore activities. I refused all invitations to sit on committees, go to banquets, or make speeches. {As I have said, there were exceptions to this. I sat on no committees, but now and then I had to go to a public dinner, and once in a while I made a speech. On December 3, 1922, I succumbed to an invitation from Harry T. Baker, then an assistant professor of English at Goucher College, Baltimore, to harangue the girls to whom he was supposed to be teaching the art of short-story writing. One of the girls present was Miss Sara Powell Haardt, of Montgomery, Ala. She had graduated from Goucher in 1920, and was now teaching there. This was our first meeting. We were married on August 27, 1930.} I knew, of course, large numbers of Baltimoreans, but I kept away from them as much as possible, and my social life, if it may be so called, was led mainly in New York. I went there every third week on *Smart Set* business, and after the beginning of 1924, with the *American Mercury* on my hands, I went there even more. In Baltimore I seldom saw anyone save a few of the executives at the *Sun* office and the members of the Saturday Night Club. To the latter Raymond Pearl, professor of biology at Johns Hopkins, was added in 1919, and thereafter, until his death on November 17, 1940, he was my most intimate Baltimore associate, and indeed almost my only one, save for Paul Patterson. We have a common bond in music, but we were both also interested in many other things, ranging from good eating to the congenital infirmities of the human race. I got a great deal out of Pearl, first and last, and I believe that he was appreciably influenced by his association with me. His death was a great blow to me, and no one else has taken his place, or will ever do so. {One of my last articles for the editorial page of the *Sun,* printed November 24, 1940, was devoted to him. I also wrote the *Sun*'s editorial on him, printed November 18, and the obituary of him in its news columns, printed the same day.}

I attended, for a while, both the *Sun* and the *Evening Sun* editorial conferences, but the doings of the latter paper, then at its high point under Black and Hamilton Owens, interested me far more than those of the former under Adams, and so I gradually gave its business first place. The *Evening Sun* conferences were usually attended by Black, Owens, Murphy and Patterson, with myself added whenever I was in town. Inasmuch as the *American Mercury,* after the middle of 1923, began to take up a great deal of my time and took me to New York very often, I fell into the habit of confining my attendance to Monday afternoons. Whenever possible, all problems to which I could contribute anything useful were put off to these Mondays. There was complete frankness in our discussions. Black was always for fresh enterprises, some of them very daring, and Murphy usually took the side of conservatism, with Patterson acting as moderator between the two. In theory, Owens was Murphy's equal in the office hierarchy, but in actuality Murphy, who was his elder and had brought him to the paper, retained a kind of suzerainty over him, and exercised it frequently. Whenever I encountered Owens or Black, I heard of some editorial that the two of them had concocted with high enthusiasm, only to see it fall to Murphy's veto. They always took this in good part, and I can't recall them ever appealing to Patterson. Murphy also acted as censor of my own contributions to the *Evening Sun* editorial page, commonly printed on Monday afternoon. Sometimes he would strike out a few passages and sometimes, though not often, he would suppress a whole article. In March, 1921, while Reynolds was still editor, Murphy thus killed an article that I had written on Cardinal Gibbons, who had just died. In it I protested against the tendency of the obituaries to depict His Eminence as a pious old papa and nothing else; I argued that he was actually a man of acute and profound worldly wisdom, and that his usefulness to the church had been largely manifested by his skill at affairs, for example, in the so-called American and labor controversies. Murphy knew that all this was true, but he feared that printing it so soon after the cardinal's death would bring in protests from Catholics, and I incline to believe that he was right. It is possible, also, that his own pruderies as a Catholic had something to do with the matter. Whatever the fact, I made no protest, and Murphy and I always got on very well, though on most questions at dispute I sided against him and with Black and Owens.

During all my days of writing for the *Sunpapers,* I never made any objection to the cutting of my copy. It seemed to me then, and it seems to me now, that what goes into a newspaper ought to be determined by the editors thereof, and that they should not be burdened with contributors beyond their control. When, as occasionally happened, an error in an article of mine got into the paper, I refused to take any responsibility for it. No man, I argued, could be expected to read his own copy; it was a psychological impossibility. Some one should be told off to go through it, and that some one should be responsible for undetected slips. Nine times out of ten the man who read my copy was Hamilton Owens, and whenever he encountered anything that upset him he would call me up—if I were in town—and tell me the changes he proposed to make. I invariably invited him to do his damndest, and usually refused to listen to his reasons. He was the editor, not I.

It must have been in 1922 or 1923 that I was visited at my house one day by two reporters of the Baltimore *News*—Henry R. Luce and Briton Hadden, both of Yale, '20. They had a scheme to start a weekly digest of the news in competition with the *Literary Digest,* then at the height of its circulation and influence. I recall only that I warned them of the difficulties of the undertaking, and pointed to the failure of *Current Literature,* a competitor of the *Digest* that had but lately come to grief. I heard no more of them until they launched *Time,* and I confess that I was surprised by its immense success, for it was marked at the start, as it is still marked today, by a pretentious and puerile style of writing and a pervasive ignorance and inaccuracy. Some years later, when Hadden died, I did Luce a favor that he has probably never heard of. Hadden owned a large block of stock in *Time,* and his mother, who was his only heir, had consulted a New York broker about its sale. This broker, in turn, consulted an acquaintance in Baltimore named Arthur W. Hawks, Jr., who was a school-days friend of mind, and Hawks came to me to get the advice of one with some experience of magazine publishing. I told him that Mrs. Hadden should be advised to offer the stock, and at a moderate price, to Luce—that if it got into strange hands the new owner might embarrass him greatly, and perhaps wreck the magazine. This advice was followed.

I not only sent a long series of candidates for reportorial jobs to Reynolds and Murphy; I also, at Patterson's suggestion, invited those who were put to work to come to see me at my house, and tried to impress what I conceived to be proper *Sunpaper* doctrine and policy upon them. I enjoyed these meetings well enough, though they took up a lot of my time, but after a few years Murphy objected to them on the ground that they tended to interfere with discipline, and they were abandoned. Since 1926 or thereabout I have had only infrequent contact with the younger reporters of the two papers, and most of them I have never even met. This has been a disadvantage at times when news enterprises were under discussion, and men had to be selected to carry them out. In 1936 Patterson suggested that I resume talking to the youngsters, but before anything could be done about it the shadow of the Newspaper Guild and then of the National Labor Relations Act fell over the office, and since then it has been dangerous for any of the elders to show politeness to reporters.

My contributions to the editorial page of the *Evening Sun* continued unbrokenly through 1923. I began the year with a blast at the uplifters who were then promising to cure all the sorrows of the world with birth control, and proceeded to onslaughts upon many of the other do-gooders of the time—for example, the New York Comstocks, then at the height of their puissance; and the idiots who whooped up world peace. On April 16, under the title of "Educational Rolling Mills," I printed an article on the decay of the Johns Hopkins University which greatly upset R. Brent Keyser, who was both a trustee of the university and a director of the *Sun*. What I said in that article had long needed to be said, for the Hopkins was in a really lamentable state, but no one had ever said it. Keyser was, in the best sense of the word, a gentleman, so his discontent did not take the form of a demand that I be fired; he simply turned sad eyes on Patterson. A few weeks later Dr. Henry S. Pritchett, president of the Carnegie Foundation, published an article in *Scribner's* in which he said of the Hopkins almost precisely what I had said of it. On May 16 Hamilton Owens printed an extract from his article and an extract from mine, with an editorial note calling attention to the fact that "from different viewpoints" they reached "virtually the same conclusion." This disposed of poor Keyser, and on July 23 I returned to the subject and stated my case again. In May, 1923, I went to Bethlehem, Pa., with Joseph Hergesheimer to hear the Bach Choir, and on May 30 I had an article in the *Evening Sun* on its performance. Thereafter, for ten years, I returned to Bethlehem every May, usually with Alfred A. Knopf, but after the death of the old leader of the choir, J. F. Wolle, in 1933, we found the pleasant atmosphere vanished, and stopped going. I was already making plans for my book, "Notes on Democracy," in 1923, and on February 12 and 26, under the titles of "Democratic Reflections" and "More Democratic Reflections," I printed articles containing material that eventually went into it in 1926. Also, on March 19, under the title of "Forty Years of Baltimore," I printed some notes that finally took shape, in 1940, as "Happy Days." These were followed, on September 10, by "Notes of a Baltimorean," mainly devoted to deploring the current rapid growth of the city—a source of pride to most of its other citizens. "Roughly speaking, " I wrote, "about 250,000 men, women and children have been added to the population since the fire of 1904. Of this number probably 175,000 are newcomers, born somewhere else. How many of them reflect any honor upon the city, or make it, in any rational sense, a better place to live in? How many of them are worth a damn? I challenge anyone to make up a list of 100." This, of course, was unpopular doctrine, and brought in the usual flood of protesting letters.

From the middle of 1923 onward I was busy with two outside enterprises—getting rid of the *Smart Set* and setting up the *American Mercury*—but the story of the tribulations that they brought to me belongs to the chronicle of my magazine adventures. When the *American Mercury* at last came out (its first issue was dated January, 1924) I expected to move into smoother waters, but its extraordinary and unexpected success kept me on the jump. Worse, I was quickly confronted by the discovery that my colleague as editor, George Jean Nathan, was completely incompetent, so my expected work was doubled, and I was thereupon further beset by my long effort to get rid of him, not successful until 1925, and by his furious resistance. That story bears on the present narrative only because, when I undertook to cover the national conventions of 1924 for the *Evening Sun,* I had to find time between their sessions to do my double stint of magazine work. The Republican convention at Cleveland, which renominated Coolidge, was an extremely dull affair, and what I remember of it chiefly is the rigidity with which Prohibition was enforced in the town. It was generally believed in advance that, as a sort of gesture of respect to Coolidge, the Prohibition agents would let up for the duration of the convention, and so most of the delegates and newspaper correspondents took no supplies along. But when they got to Cleveland they found the place almost bone dry. Indeed, it was so dry that some of the Cleveland reporters came to see us in the Hollenden Hotel and begged for drinks: they were quite unable to get any themselves. Dan Hanna, then publisher of one of the Cleveland papers, had set up a house-of-mirth for visiting journalists in a hotel, but the local men were not admitted to it.

My friend Harry Rickel, of Mt. Clemens, Mich., hearing from me of the unexpected drought, loaded a motor-boat with bottled beer at Detroit and started it down the lakes to my rescue, in charge of several of his retainers. When it arrived off the Cleveland breakwater, these retainers got word to me, and I sent out Paul de Kruif, who was hanging about town, to arrange for the landing of the cargo. But when he got to the motor-boat he found that the crew had drunk all save a few cases of the beer on the way down, and that they wanted to keep those few for the return voyage. So de Kruif came back indignant and I got no beer. Patterson and I, as usual, had brought a supply of gin and whiskey, but there were so many demands on it that we had to put all hands on rations, and if the convention had lasted a day longer we'd have gone dry. One of the reporters covering the convention was Ring Lardner, a heavy and steady whiskey drinker. He brought his whiskey in gallon jugs, and remained in his room to guard them. Not once during the convention did he ever enter the hall, though he wrote about the proceedings daily. One day, coming down the street that runs past the Hollenden Hotel, I encountered William Allen White, and he told me that he was suffering from a severe bellyache. He was a supporter of Prohibition, but when I suggested that a stiff drink would probably cure him he agreed at once. For some reason that I forget I did not take him to the *Sun*'s quarters, but to the room of Lardner, who was sitting at his typewriter in a pair of dingy pajamas, working away at his convention story with one of his gallon jugs on the floor beside him. I introduced White, and Lardner poured out a massive drink. It cured White instantly, but left him groggy for the rest of the day.

The loud-speakers that now make a hideous roaring of all large gatherings were just coming in in 1924, and at the Cleveland convention one of them played a very amusing trick. The convention, having no business before it save the formal renomination of Coolidge, was very dull, so a song-leader was borrowed from the local Y.M.C.A. to pep it up. This leader, a tall and thin fellow in horn-rimmed spectacles, labored hard at his job, but the delegates and alternates were too depressed to respond. One gloomy afternoon, as he worked away on them with loud shouts and frantic gestures, I sat in the half-deserted press-stand idly watching him. Six or eight rows ahead of me sat Gustav J. Karger, Washington correspondent of the Cincinnati *Times-Star*, an amiable Jew with a bald head, reminding me very much of my old tutor, Al Goodman of the Baltimore *Herald*. Presently Karger turned round, caught my eye, and shouted, "I'd like to shoot that son-of-a-bitch." By some accident the loud-speaker system caught up his wish, and it went roaring over the hall, to the great delight of the sparse audience. But the Y.M.C.A. brother kept on undaunted, and after half an hour of hard effort he induced the crowd to tackle "My Old Kentucky Home." Thereupon I noted once more something that has always interested me at large gatherings: the crowd refused to follow his baton, but sang at a tempo of its own. How that tempo is established I have often wondered. In some mysterious way a crowd seems to agree on it unanimously, though the leader is sweating hard to make it sing either faster or slower.

The Coolidge convention ran from June 10 to June 14. It was not only the first national convention to be outfitted with a loud-speaker system; it was also the first whose proceedings were broadcast by radio. In addition, it was the first in which any considerable number of women sat, for the Nineteenth Amendment had gone into effect on August 26, 1920, just after the conventions of that year. There were 397 of them at Cleveland—118 as delegates and 279 as alternates. Most of them were jobholders who had got places at the trough since 1920, and nine-tenths of them were about as appetizing as so many midwives. Looking over the list of the convention notables I can't help reflecting upon the transience of public eminence in America. The key-noter was Senator Theodore E. Burton of Ohio, the permanent chairman was Frank A. Mondell of Wyoming, and the orator chosen to put Coolidge in nomination was Dr. Marion Leroy Burton, president of the University of Michigan. All are as completely forgotten as the politicians of the Polk administration. Hoover, whom Coolidge greatly disliked, was a candidate for second place on the ticket and got 334½ votes on the third ballot, but was beaten by "General" Charles G. Dawes, who was destined to make a place for himself in American history as a comic character. Hoover had spent a good deal of money on his campaign for votes, but his real chance was not to come until 1928, when he spent much more.

After the convention adjourned—or maybe it was before it began—I went to Mt. Clemens, Mich., to spend a couple of days with my friend Rickel, lately mentioned. I had got acquainted with him through his reading of my books. He was a lawyer, but his family business had been malt, and when Prohibition dawned he sent me materials and instructions for home-brewing. I soon became adept at it, and presently had a long string of pupils in Baltimore, each of whom taught others in turn, so that by the time the country was really dry the town was flowing with quite drinkable malt liquor. Rickel now staged a gaudy party for me at his house in Mt. Clemens, with both beer and wine on tap in unlimited amounts, and I came near succumbing to it. After the two of us recovered we made a motor trip to Ann Arbor, where Dr. Robert Bridges, the British Poet Laureate, was serving a term of unhappy servitude in the University of Michigan. I had made contact with Bridges because of his interest in my book, "The American Language," and he received me very cordially. He was, however, much out of humor with the university, for he objected to the fact that it and all Ann Arbor were dry, and protested bitterly because he was not permitted, as a medical man, to write prescriptions of whiskey for his own use. He had agreed to spend the whole academic year in residence—the idea was that his presence would inspire the campus poets—but he had arrived late and left for home early. I was in constant correspondence with him until his death in 1930, and in January of that year visited him at his home in Oxford.

When I returned to Baltimore in June, 1924, it was to put in a hard week on my *American Mercury* work. Then I went to New York for the Democratic convention, which assembled in old Madison Square Garden on June 24 and ran on until July 10. It was a good show, but it lasted too long, and before it was over I was pretty well exhausted by my effort to cover it for the *Evening Sun* and at the same time look after my heavy magazine job.

This is no place to rehearse the proceedings. Suffice it to recall that there was a long and bitter battle over the platform, centered on minority proposals that the convention endorse American entry into the League of Nations and denounce the Ku Klux Klan by name. Both proposals were voted down in the platform committee, but when they were taken to the floor the plank naming the Klan was lost by but five votes out of 1098. The fight against this plank was led by William Jennings Bryan, then making his last appearance as an important factor in American politics. The old boy had begun to look extremely mangy, and made a pathetic figure as he bawled from the speakers' stand, with the Tammany gallery hooting him and at least half the delegates and alternates joining in. One day, as he was thus under fire, I looked up the main aisle and saw a beautiful young woman slowly walking down toward the speakers' stand, her arms folded and her eyes fixed upon Bryan with such a gleam of malicious triumph on her face as I have never again seen. She was Genevieve Clark Thomson, daughter of Champ Clark, and she was having her sweet revenge for Bryan's ruinous opposition to her father at the Baltimore convention of 1912. I met her the next day, and found her a very gentle and charming young woman—but Bryan's débâcle had brought out in her all the venom of all the women of all the centuries.

The Tammany boys in the galleries had all sorts of noise-makers with them, including fire-engine sirens, and when they cut loose the din was deafening. In the places reserved for distinguished guests Roman collars were numerous. We were in Al Smith's *Kaiserstadt* [imperial domain]; he was a candidate for the presidential nomination, and his friends, clerical and lay, were turning out to help him. It was really amazing to note the devotion to him among the common people of the town. When Henry Hyde and I would leave the Biltmore of a morning, with our press-badges revealing our connection with the convention, bellboys, chambermaids, doorkeepers and taxi-drivers would press us for inside stuff about Al's chances. He was then at the very apex of his popularity in New York, and was, indeed, almost the town god. The rise of Roosevelt II was due wholly to the fact that he was for Al. In himself he was only a minor relative of the great Teddy, but as the man chosen to put Al in nomination he borrowed something of the glamor of the hero, and if he had been a candidate for Governor of New York in 1924 he'd have been elected as certainly as he was in 1928, and probably by a larger majority. But in proportion as Al seemed almost divine to the New Yorkers he appeared diabolical to the Ku Kluxers from the South and Middle West. The man they followed was William Gibbs McAdoo, Wilson's son-in-law and a fellow of highly dubious ways and means. He had tried to get the nomination in 1920 in the character of Crown Prince; now he was trying again as the candidate of the Klan. This last, of course, he denied, but he was a liar and everybody knew it. His chief press-agent was George Fort Milton, editor of the Chattanooga *News,* another transparent fraud. McAdoo took no part in the battle over the League. He knew that the overwhelming majority of Americans were against it, regardless of party. The plank advocating American entrance was beaten on the floor by 742½ votes to 353½.

The long balloting was a bore, and also involved some hard work, but it had its moments, and, as usual, I enjoyed the show. McAdoo polled his largest vote—530, which was only 19 short of a majority, but 202 short of the necessary two-thirds—on the sixty-ninth ballot, and Al Smith made his high score—368—on the eighty-third. As the hundredth ballot drew near, on July 8, Smith announced through Roosevelt that he was willing to withdraw if McAdoo would do the same. Late that evening, after the hundredth had been cast, McAdoo released his delegates, and the long combat was over. John W. Davis was nominated next day, on the one-hundred-and-third ballot, to the horror and humiliation of Bryan, who had been denouncing him violently as the candidate of Wall Street, as indeed he was. But when the leaders, with a stroke of humor, gave second place on the ticket to Bryan's ridiculous younger brother, Charlie, the Commoner became suddenly silent, and during the campaign he returned to the fold. Every ballot took an hour or more, and it was a trying business keeping a record of them, for the weather was hot and the press-stand was very uncomfortable. One day Frank Kent came in with the news that we of the *Sun* were invited to make use of the Manhattan Club, across the street from Madison Square Garden, where we could sit in upholstered chairs and listen to the balloting by radio. During the next afternoon, as Kent and I and one or two others were thus lolling in the club, we were startled to hear the words "Oh, shit!" come over the air. We rushed back to the hall to find out what had happened, and discovered that they had been spoken by Thomas J. Walsh, the permanent chairman. Some delegate had come up from the floor with a vexatious parliamentary question, and old Tom had indicated his displeasure by the classical Montana formula. The radio was still a novelty in those days, and people had not yet learned that it was dangerous to talk too near the mike. Tom's exclamation went out over the whole United States, but to his great relief the speaker was not identified. Nor did the radio public apparently recognize the fact that the "Twenty-four votes for Underwood!" which opened every roll-call save the last were delivered by Governor W. W. Brandon of Alabama in a state of liquor. His Excellency headed a predominantly dry delegation, but unless my observation was grossly in error he was tight from end to end of the convention.

Governor Albert Ritchie of Maryland was one of the minor candidates. He was sure of only the 16 votes of Maryland, but he picked up others from time to time, and on the eighty-sixth and eighty-seventh ballots he rose to 23. His campaign, such as it was, was in charge of Dr. Hugh H. Young, professor of urology in the Johns Hopkins Medical School, an amateur whose enthusiasm was matched only by his lack of political experiment. Ritchie, who was a handsome fellow, went to the platform at various times to make reports or motions, and on one such appearance, while the naming of candidates was still going on, his pulchritude inflamed the libido of a lady delegate from Hawaii. She was a native Hawaiian of very dark complexion, and had on the native garb of the islands. In the course of his roving about the hall Young got news that she was planning, when Hawaii was reached near the end of the roll-call of delegations, to go to the platform and make a speech seconding Ritchie. This greatly alarmed Young, for though he was glad of her support he was afraid that the Ku Kluxers from the South would mistake her for a colored woman, and that her advocacy would ruin Ritchie. He came up to the press-stand to consult Frank Kent and me. We advised him that the only way out was for Ritchie to wait on the lady, invite her out of the hall for refreshment, and keep her there until Hawaii had been passed on the roll-call. This was done. Ritchie plied his admirer with Coca Cola and hot-dogs until Young gave the signal that the coast was clear. The lady was upset when she learned that she was too late to make her speech, but there was some consolation for her in the memory of Ritchie's cooing. The next day she came back for more, and he had a hard time dodging her during the rest of the convention.

As the proceedings dragged on toward their third week many of the Southern delegates began to run short of money, for they were mainly yokels, and delegates have to pay their own expenses. They complained bitterly of the high cost of living· in New York, and reported that they had been charged as much as 75 cents, and even $1, for meals. When news of their plight reached the home-folks of the Bible country meetings were held in the Baptist and Methodist churches to raise funds for their succor. These yahoos were in great terror of the Tammany whoopers in the gallery, and believed in all seriousness that an effort would be made to nominate Al Smith by strong-arm methods. One day, during a loud uproar, I noticed that one of their leaders, Congressman William D. Upshaw, of Georgia, had left his place in the Georgia delegation and was making his way toward the platform. Upshaw was a cripple and usually used crutches, but now he was leaping along very nimbly, and dragging them behind him. I dropped out of the press-stand to find out what he was up to, and when he ducked down the runway leading under the hall, followed him. I came up with him at last in the tar-paper office of the *Sun,* where he had taken refuge. He was white and trembling. "What's the matter?" I asked, thinking he was ill. "They are about to bomb us!" he exclaimed. "Who?" I demanded. "The Catholics," he replied. "Didn't you see all those priests come in? When they give the signal the Tammany murderers will throw the bombs." It took me some time to quiet him, and even then he refused to be convinced that there was no danger. Apparently he had given no warning to his fellow Georgians: all he had thought of was his own safety. But soon afterward he must have got word to them, for they left the hall in a body, walking very briskly. After that I had a lot of fun spreading such alarms among the delegates from the Pellagra Belt. Whenever one of them came up to the press-stand in search of inside stuff (the delegates to a national convention seldom know what is afoot) I would hint that the Al Smith goons were preparing to rush the hall in force, and chase all Protestants out of town. I was told that some of them, fearing for their lives, had given up their rooms in New York and gone over to New Jersey to sleep. But here a desire for cheaper quarters probably reinforced their forebodings. The *Sun* got some *kudos* out of the convention. All the New York papers, including the *Times,* were biased in their reports, and put so much confusion into them that they were often downright unintelligible. The *Sun*'s clearer and more objective reporting was quickly noted by the delegates and alternates, and before the convention ended we were selling 1000 copies daily in the New York hotels.

My contributions to the *Evening Sun* editorial page in 1924 covered my usual wide range. I opened the year with a theological discussion, "What Is a Christian?" on January 7, and closed it with "Reflections on Journalism" on December 29. This last was the second of two articles on journalism, the first having been printed on February 18. The two later furnished me with materials for the opening chapter, "Journalism in America," in the last volume of my "Prejudices" series. In the first of them was this:

> The normal, typical, average American journalist of today, like the normal, typical, average American journalist of the days when I began at the trade, seems to me, on the whole, to be a decidedly inferior fellow. He knows very little and what he knows is mainly not worth knowing.

On March 31, under the heading of "Morals and the Moron," I had at Patterson for the dreadful comics that were appearing in the *Sunday Sun:* the article was a detailed analysis of a Mutt and Jeff page that had been printed on March 23, showing that the story it told would have inevitably brought down the Comstocks if it had been used for a bawdy farce in New York. On January 21 I discussed "The Progress of Moral Endeavor," on February 4 the current Teapot Dome scandal, on July 28 the whimwham that was getting into the discussion of a project to set up a public art gallery in Baltimore, and on December 8 chiropractic, one of my favorite butts in my Free Lance days. Since 1924 was a presidential year there were many articles on politics. On April 28 I had an article on the Tammany leader, Charles F. Murphy, lately dead, in which I voiced once more of my favorite theories, to wit:

> Obviously, government by Tammany is far from ideal, but equally obviously it is better than any alternative that is commonly offered. Certainly it is vastly better than government by professional reformers.

My discussions of the presidential campaign began with "The Clowns March In" on June 2, just before the two national conventions; proceeded to "Post-Mortem" on July 14, after they were over; and then went on to "The New Woodrow" (*i.e.,* John W. Davis, the Democratic nominee) on August 18, "Notes on the Struggle" on September 15, "The Coolidge Buncombe" on October 6, "Mr. Davis's Campaign" on October 13, "The Voter's Dilemma" on November 3, just before election day, and "Autopsy" on November 10, after the returns were in. If I remember rightly, I voted for Davis, but I was certainly under no illusions about him, and my treatment of him was quite as rough as my treatment of the preposterous Coolidge. Coolidge I flogged steadily from the moment he succeeded Harding, on August 2, 1923, to the end of his own elected term on March 4, 1929. I had no special animosity to him; he was simply the sitting President of the United States, and in all my life I don't recall ever writing in praise of a sitting President. Finding virtues in successful politicians seemed to me to be the function of their swarms of willing pediculae; it was the business of a journalist, as I conceived it, to stand in a permanent Opposition. Prohibition, of course, got plenty of attention. On September 1, in an article entitled "One Lustrum," I reviewed its failures to date: it was to be five years old on January 16, 1925.

The year 1924 was the busiest of my whole life, and I marvel, looking back upon it, that I got through so much work. I was 44 years old, the age of my father when he died in 1899, but never before or since have I been in better form. My appetite and capacity for labor was really immense, despite that fact that I was often ill, and in addition was burdened by anxiety about others. In 1923 my brother Charlie's wife, Mary, had come to Baltimore for some very serious surgery, and after ten weeks in hospital was still returning frequently for treatment. Sara Haardt, whom I was to marry in 1930, came down with influenza in January, 1924, and when it was over began to show signs of tuberculosis. She had to go to Maple Heights Sanitarium at Sparks, Md., on February 1, and remained there until October 31, and on her return to Baltimore was sent to hospital for a tonsil operation. Her people were in faraway Montgomery, Ala., and I had the care of her until December, when she was well enough to go home. In addition, my mother began to show signs of the illness that was to cause her death on December 13, 1925, and I was naturally greatly worried about her, and on October 2 my brother August was seized with a fulminating appendicitis that needed immediate operation and came near killing him. My own physical state, meanwhile, was far from good. In March, 1924, I developed a lameness in the left foot that was both painful and disabling, and all during the Summer I took troublesome treatments for it. They failed to cure it, and on September 2 I went to St. Agnes Hospital for an operation by Dr. George A. Stewart. It gave me relief, but when I got home hay-fever, my old scourge, hit me a dreadful crack, and a month after it subsided I was beset by a queer form of hiccup influenza that was then epidemic in New York.

But despite all these troubles and afflictions my energy, during most of the year, was at its all-time peak, and I often put in days of work that were really astonishing. As I have said, the whole burden of the *American Mercury* was on me, for Nathan turned out to be far too narrow in his range of ideas to be useful to a general magazine: his world was limited by New York, and even of New York he knew little save Broadway. After the first few issues of the magazine I read all the manuscripts, carried on nearly all the negotiations with authors, and prepared manuscripts for the printer—this last often a laborious task. In addition I wrote editorials for each issue, a series of book reviews that sometimes ran beyond 5000 words, and most of the briefer notices in the Check-List. The magazine was a striking success, and I was sustained by that fact, but the labor of getting it out was really formidable. It was not, however, until the time of the Democratic convention in New York that I decided finally that Nathan was hopeless. I recall coming to that decision while the convention was going on, as I sat with him one day at lunch in Dinty Moore's. It was a hard decision, and his violent and long-continued resistance made executing it very difficult and unpleasant, but I stuck to it, and by January 26, 1925, Nathan was out and I had installed Charles Angoff as assistant editor and office manager. Angoff, a Harvard graduate then but 23 years old, had written to me asking me to get him a job on the *Sunpapers.* When, after examining the writing he had been doing for Boston suburban papers and talking to him at a Sunday lunch in Jack's restaurant, I offered him the far better place on the *American Mercury,* he was speechless with astonishment and gratitude. My subsequent experiences with him will be told in the chronicle of my magazine adventures— that is, if I ever get to the writing of it. He turned out to be a diligent and reasonably competent young man, but I still had undivided responsibility for the magazine, and it kept me jumping. In addition, I brought out the fourth volume of my "Prejudices" in 1924, did a weekly article for the *Evening Sun,* and began to sketch out my "Notes on Democracy" and the first of the two volumes of "Americana." Meanwhile, my mother had fallen ill, and I was greatly concerned about her.

Why, in the face of all these labors and troubles, I was willing to take on another weekly article—this time for the Chicago *Tribune*—I simply can't tell. It was certainly not any need of money that moved me, for my taxable income for 1924 was more than $8500. But when Joseph M. Patterson, then in charge of the *Tribune*'s editorial department, asked me to do a series of Sunday articles for it and its syndicate, I was somehow tempted, and when I consulted Paul Patterson he urged me to accept, saying that the series would greatly extend my audience, and so help the *American Mercury*. I sent in my first article on October 7, 1924, and it was published on November 9. I began by dealing with relatively harmless literary themes, but soon bulged into politics, and in a little while was writing things that caused some stir. The *Tribune* syndicate, run by Arthur Crawford, found that placing the stuff was not easy. First and last, many papers subscribed for it, but most of them dropped out the first time I took a hack at the Methodists, the American Legion, or any of the other inhabitants of my menagerie of hobgoblins. Once, when I was in Chicago, I dropped in on Crawford and he handed me a letter from a San Francisco paper, stopping the service. While we discussed it the editor of another San Francisco paper was announced, and in my presence Crawford induced him to take my articles on, so that I did not lose a day in the town. But in a little while this second paper, confronted by complaints from all the local evangelical pastors, also stopped printing me. The *Tribune* itself, more than once, omitted my article and so notified its syndicate customers—for example, when I argued that unsuccessful candidates for the Presidency were public nuisances, and ought to be put to death. The only paper that printed every article was the New York *World*. The *Evening Sun,* which got them for nothing as part of my contract with Joseph M. Patterson, would have printed them also, but now and then it had to omit one that was no more than a rewriting of something of mine that it had already published. I tired of the series after a year or so, and proposed to Joe Patterson that it be abandoned, but he protested, and I continued it until the end of 1927, when I finally insisted on quitting.

7

Make Tennessee
Forever Infamous

1925

The memorable events of 1925 in *Sun* history were the setting up of a magazine section in the Sunday edition, the trial of Hamilton Owens at Westminster, Md., for refusing to testify before the Carroll county grand-jury, the establishment of the group insurance scheme, the beginning of Van Lear Black's career as a playboy on a world scale, the effort of old E. W. Scripps to lure Patterson away from the *Sun,* and its elaborate covering of the Scopes trial at Dayton, Tenn. The true origins of the last-named colossal buffoonery have never been recorded in detail. When, on March 21, 1925, the Governor of Tennessee signed the act under which Scopes was charged, the event attracted only mild interest in the newspapers. {The act read: "It shall be unlawful for any teacher in any of the universities, normals, and all other public schools in the state, which are supported in whole or in part by the public school funds of the state, to teach the theory that denies the story of the divine creation of man as taught in the Bible, and to teach instead that man has descended from a lower order of animals."} Nor was there much more concern when news came that Scopes had been indicted, for no one had ever heard of him, and no one expected anything save imbecility to come out of Tennessee. {The prosecution was launched as a joke by a man named George Rappelyea, a New Yorker who was the manager of a nearby coal mine. He suggested to the yokels of Dayton that jugging Scopes would get the town a lot of free advertising—and neglected to mention that it would be unfavorable. He later moved North, and when I met him there was cackling over the stupendous success of his whimsey. He said that the town was ruined forever, and inasmuch as he detested it and its people, he was delighted.}

But when it was announced that William Jennings Bryan, whose political career had ended at the Democratic convention in New York, was going to Dayton to help the prosecution there was an immediate pricking up of journalistic ears, for Bryan was still good copy. This announcement came at a time when Joseph Hergesheimer, the novelist, happened to be visiting James Branch Cabell in Richmond. At the same time Clarence Darrow arrived there to lecture, and the next day paid a call on Cabell. The conversation fell upon the day's news, and Hergesheimer suggested to Darrow that he ought to volunteer for the defense, and have some fun. Darrow replied that he was too old for such amusements—he was 68— but finally said that he might undertake the job if he could get sufficient aid. He named Arthur Garfield Hays and Dudley Field Malone as the sort of helpers he had in mind—Hays to prepare the case from the legal standpoint, and Malone, who was a famous orator, to assist in the hollering. A few days later he looked up the two of them in New York, and both agreed to join him. Hays, it turned out, was already interested, for the American Civil Liberties Union, for which he was counsel, had just received an appeal for help from John Randolph Neal, a Tennessee dissenter who ran a small law-school in the state. But first he wanted to consult me about the strategy of the defense, for he knew that I was greatly interested in the political and theological pathology of the Bible country, and believed that I might be able to make some useful suggestions. At his request I made an appointment to see him in Baltimore within the next few days, but at the last minute he was detained in New York, and sent one of his partners instead, a man named Buckley, or something of the sort.

Buckley came to my house in Hollins street, and we put in an evening discussing the case. He told me that Hays, backed by the Civil Liberties Union, was bent on getting Scopes acquitted. This seemed to me a folly, and I said so. It would only put a quick end to the show, and leave the defense with an empty victory. The thing to do, I argued, was to use the case to make Tennessee forever infamous, and to that end the sacrifice of Scopes would be a small matter. Above all, the thing to do was to lay all stress, not on Scopes, who was a nobody, but on Bryan, who was an international figure—to lure him on the stand if possible, to make him state his barbaric credo in plain English, and to make a monkey of him before the world. Getting Scopes acquitted would be worth a day's headlines in the newspapers, and then no more, but smearing Bryan would be good for a long while. Buckley thought that this was sound doctrine, and when he got back to New York he easily convinced Malone and Darrow, both of whom had been Bryan men in the Commoner's great days, but now detested him as an idiot. But Hays, who liked to win cases, kept on insisting that Scopes could be acquitted, and ought to be acquitted, and when the trial started in July he actually spent a day or two offering demurrers, and arguing them with a fine show of learning. When the judge, John T. Raulston, overruled them there was an immense relief among the other counsel at the defense table.

The *Sunpapers* sent Henry Hyde, Frank R. Kent, Duffy the cartoonist, J. Fred Essary and me to Dayton. We put up at a hotel in Chattanooga, and planned to run out to Dayton daily, but after a few days we found that this was not feasible, for Dayton was fifty miles away, the road was hilly, with five grade-crossings and many sharp curves, and the local taxi-drivers were all maniacal hill-billies. At every grade-crossing one or another of the Chattanooga undertakers had a large bill-board, advertising his ambulance service, and at every curve the native Christians had set up a sign reading "Prepare to meet your God," or something even more disturbing. On July 9 we decided to move to Dayton, and thereafter we spent most of our nights there. Fearful that the Chattanooga cops might search incoming baggage, we took no jugs from Baltimore, but when we got to the hotel Kent and Duffy were told off to hunt for a reliable bootlegger. While they were gone three or four of my local customers showed up with packages under their arms, and when Kent and Duffy got back there were six or eight bottles of prime goods on the bureau in my room. Half an hour later we had a call from a former judge who lived in the hotel, and he invited us to make free use of his quarters, which turned out to be stocked to the ceiling. Every afternoon His Honor gave a free-and-easy party, with half a dozen friendly females in attendance. Unhappily, duty called us and we had to miss most of these pleasant affairs. {We were also invited to other parties by the antinomian moiety of Chattanoogans, but had to decline nearly all of them. One night, however, we went to a dinner in a country-club atop of Lookout Mountain. On July 8 I wrote to Sara Haardt: "They have a magnificent club half a mile in the air, with a jazz orchestra and all the other trappings of a nigger dive in New York. The usual story in the Confederacy (and Nawth): the women were mainly very pretty and some of them were amusing, but the men were unanimously unspeakable. They are all rich here, but money has done them no good."} The stuff that Kent and Duffy got from the bootlegger was much inferior to that brought in by my customers, and in the end we got rid of it by giving it to Michael Williams, then editor of the Catholic weekly, the *Commonweal,* and a boozer so insatiable that he would drink even hair-oil.

We were comfortable enough in the hotel, though the weather was infernal, but, as I have said, we had to spend most of our time at Dayton, and there Hyde and I were quartered at the home of the town dentist. He and his wife were newcomers to the town, and appreciably more civilized than its natives. They gave us to understand that they inclined toward Darwin, but they had to be very cautious, for even the slightest suspicion of heresy was dangerous. The dentist's wife set what is known in the country towns as a bountiful table. There were never less than ten dishes on the board, even at breakfast, and most of them were as heavy as lead. I recall one especially: cauliflower covered with a batter composed mainly of rat-trap cheese, and then fried. The poor lady—she was visibly pregnant—was so solicitous that it was hard to decline these masterpieces, but Hyde and I managed to do it by pleading that we had stomach ulcers and were on strict diets. In the end we subsisted mainly on fried chicken and sliced tomatoes, both of which were served at all meals. The dentist himself enjoyed his wife's provender, and entertained us with tales about the dreadful state of cookery in the surrounding mountains. Many of his patients, he said, ate so badly that they suffered from dental maladies wholly unknown in the school where he had been trained.

The first person I met when we got to Dayton was Bryan, who was parading the main street in a low-necked shirt of his wife's invention and manufacture, and basking in the veneration of the yokels. He greeted me effusively, and let it be known that I was a publicist of parts. His reason, which he did not mention, was that I had an article in the *Nation* of July 1 arguing that, whatever the unwisdom of the Anti-Evolution Act, the Legislature of Tennessee had a clear right to prescribe what should be taught or not taught in the public-schools, which were its creatures. {The title of the article was "In Tennessee," and the essential part of it was as follows: "No principle is at stake at Dayton save the principle that school teachers, like plumbers, should stick to the job that is set for them, and not go roving about the house, breaking windows, raiding the cellar, and demoralizing the children. The issue of free speech is quite irrelevant. When a pedagogue takes his oath of office he renounces the right to free speech quite as certainly as a bishop does, or a colonel in the army, or an editorial writer on a newspaper. He becomes a paid propagandist of certain definite doctrines and attitudes, mainly determined specifically and in advance, and every time he departs from them deliberately he deliberately swindles his employers."} This help from across the bloody chasm greatly pleased the old boy, and he continued to be polite to me until the first of my reports of the trial reached him. After that he withdrew his favor, and whenever, after the first week, he caught my eye in the courtroom he would glare at me as if I were Beelzebub. My reports reached him, not because he saw the *Evening Sun,* but because Patterson had rashly given the local rights in them to George Fort Milton, publisher of the Chattanooga *News,* who has already appeared in this chronicle as the press-agent of McAdoo and the Ku Kluxers at the Democratic National Convention of 1924. I knew Milton to be a fraud and objected to being in his paper, but he had been useful to the *Sunpapers* during the weeks before the trial began, and Patterson's promise had been given. In a little while my dispatches became so offensive to the local Christians that printing them became dangerous to Milton. At first, he got round his dilemma by seeing that they got into his paper so filled with typographical errors that large parts of them were unintelligible. Then he omitted whole paragraphs, and surrounded what was left by refutations written by the local clergy and the dunderheads of his own staff, including one of his office boys. Finally, he let them drop altogether, greatly to my relief. He was a knavish and nefarious fellow, and it always amused me when he was accepted in the North as a salient Southern Liberal, and even libertarian. During the Scopes trial he actually served as Bryan's press-agent, and all through Prohibition he supported it. {Needless to add, he was not dry personally. Once he visited me in Baltimore, and I took him to the Marconi Restaurant for lunch. Offered rye whiskey, he got it down so hoggishly that he was quickly drunk.} At a time when all the really courageous Southern editors—for example, Grover C. Hall of the Montgomery *Advertiser* and Julian Harris of the Columbus (Ga.) *Enquirer-Sun*—were making their valiant fight against the Klan, Milton was playing with it and trying to edge his way into public office with its support. When, in 1939, news came that his paper had gone bankrupt at last, and that he was on his uppers, I confess that I was delighted. Once more the ungrateful Tennessee Baal had thrown a palace angel overboard.

But though Milton did his best to conceal and obfuscate my observations on the trial, enough of them leaked through his guard to fever the local Christians. At the end of the first week there were whispers that I was to be run out of Dayton. I got them only at second hand and did not take them seriously, but some of the other correspondents, led by Lindsay Denison of the New York *World,* let it be known that if any affront were offered to me the whole gang would defend me. The only native

who ever approached me with anything that appeared to be hostile intent was the clerk of the court, who told me in the courtroom on July 16
that he and several other Daytonians would like to have a palaver with
me. I replied that I'd be in the lobby of the little town hotel that night at
8 o'clock. I was there on time, alone, but there was a heavy thunder-
storm and the Daytonians did not show up, and after waiting half an
hour I left, still alone. The clerk did not say what he and his friends
wanted to talk of. When I left Dayton at the end of the second week of
the trial, just in time to miss Darrow's cross-examination of Bryan, the
report spread that I had been forced to flee the town. This tale is still told
and believed in the South, but it is false. I had arranged with Patterson in
advance that I should stay only two weeks, for that was as long as I
could leave the *American Mercury* office. Frank Kent left at the same
time, tired of the farce. As a matter of fact, the Daytonians were outwardly polite to me, though I ranked with atheists and German spies in
their menagerie of monsters, and several years after the trial the mayor of
the place invited me to revisit it for the opening of the Bryan Fundamentalist University, which had been set up in a nearby cow-pasture. Unfortunately, I was busy and had to decline. Denison, who was an assiduous
boozer, was all set to stage a riot in case I were molested. There were at
least fifty newspaper correspondents and telegraph operators in town for
the trial, and they would have given a local mob something to think of.

What offended the Daytonians even more than my reports of the
trial was an article I wrote on the orgies of the Holy Rollers four or five
miles back in the mountains. I was told about them by a young woman
working for Milton's paper, and Henry Hyde and I were taken to the
place by a youth named O. B. Andrews, Jr., also of Milton's staff. This
Andrews was the son of a Chattanooga Legionnaire and Rotarian who
regarded me with horror, but the boy himself was for me, and through
him I met and came to formally friendly terms with his pa. We made several visits to the Holy Rollers, and on a hot Sunday afternoon, stripped
to my drawers in the hotel at Chattanooga, I wrote a long account of
their performances for the *Evening Sun*. That account, expanded and
embellished, appeared in my "Prejudices: Fifth Series" under the title of
"The Hills of Zion," along with a long discourse on the last days of
Bryan. It was thus, in those days, that I made one hand wash the other.
My gatherings as a contributor to the *Evening Sun* provided me with a
great deal of excellent material for magazine articles and books, and the
contacts that articles and books brought me were constantly useful to the
paper. My presence on its staff, in fact, brought it more publicity than

any other one thing—sometimes friendly, though usually hostile, but in any case publicity. As I have said, my enforced return to New York after two weeks of the trial deprived me of the chance to hear Darrow cross-examine Bryan—a deprivation that I have always regretted heartily. I also missed, of course, the subsequent death of Bryan—a magnificently macabre climax to the farce. Darrow's savage onslaught had made a comic character of him, and so ruined him, and some understanding of that tragic fact must have penetrated his head. In any event, he lingered on in Dayton to lick his wounds, and there, on July 26, he died. By that time only one or two reporters remained in the town, and they were quite unequal to the story, which was badly manhandled. If the old boy had died while the trial was going on he'd have been turned off much more competently, for many virtuosi were then on hand.

I made it a point to get acquainted with most of the evangelists who swarmed to Dayton for the show, and got on very friendly terms with one of them, the Rev. T. T. Martin, of Blue Mountain, Miss. He was an old-time Southern exhorter and a very picturesque and amusing character, wearing a long-tailed coat and a ragged white collar so large that he could pull his head into it like a turtle. One day Hyde and I met him on the street and I asked him if he had heard that a squad of Bolsheviks was coming down from Cincinnati to murder Bryan. He hadn't, but he was greatly upset, rushed off to warn Bryan, and then notified the town constable. Two hours later Hyde and I met him again, and he told us the whole story as news, and in the strictest confidence: he had already forgotten that he had got it from us. That afternoon a large squad of Chattanooga police arrived in town, a steamboat excursion that had been planned was abandoned, and heavy guards were posted at the railroad station. When the train from Cincinnati got in only one passenger alighted. He was a tall, solemn fellow who turned out later to be a Y.M.C.A. secretary, but the Chattanooga cops were taking no chances, and he was thrust at once in the town hoosegow—a one-room brick structure in the middle of a field, as hot in that infernal Summer weather as a boiler-room. There the Y.M.C.A. brother languished until acquaintances convinced the cops that he was not a Bolshevik. For cell-mate he had a man who had come to town to lecture on Darwinism, and brought along a sad-looking ape as Exhibit A. When the cops locked him up he began heaving circulars whooping up evolution through the bars of the jail. Lindsay Denison and I tried to convince the cops that they had no right to imprison him, arguing that the Anti-Evolution Act applied to the public-schools only. But their commander, a complete imbecile, maintained that it was his duty to defend the Bible in all situations. In the end, he let the Darwinian go on condition that he would leave town at once, taking his ape with him. As his train left the station he delivered a final defiance by throwing into the air all that remained of his stock of circulars. The cops ordered the crowd back, gathered up the circulars, and burned them.

Before I left Dayton Edgar Lee Masters had a handbill printed purporting to be the announcement of an evangelist who offered to drink poison and suffer the bites of snakes, scorpions and gila monsters—all without damage, and as proof of the truth of Mark XVI, 17, 18. This evangelist, so the handbill said, would appear at Dayton "during the trial of the infidel Scopes," and all comers were invited to bring in poisons and reptiles to test him. Masters sent me about 500 copies, and when I got to Dayton I hired a couple of boys to distribute them. They made absolutely no impression on the yokels gathered for the trial. This puzzled me until some one told me that the miracles announced were old stuff in the Tennessee hills. Many Holy Rollers pretended to the same powers. During the years following several such clients of the Holy Ghost were badly shaken by snake bites and one or two died. As a result some effort was made to discourage their exhibitions, but nothing came of it, and many are still in practise in the mountains. During the early days of the trial evangelists of a dozen sects roared in the courthouse square, led by the T. T. Martin I have just mentioned. I came to know the old boy quite well, and he used to write to me at length during the years following. It was his hope to convert me to the backwoods Christianity he professed, and to that end he did a great deal of praying. His prayers fetched me no more than those of Dr. Howard A. Kelly, though I always replied to him politely. After his death in 1939 or 1940 I had a pleasant note from his daughter, saying that the poor old man greatly valued my friendship. He had a traveling plant consisting of long rows of portable bleachers, a pulpit and a stock of Bibles and hymnbooks. This he dragged all over the South for many years.

The preaching in the courthouse square, which went on at all hours that the court was not sitting, entertained Hyde and me very agreeably. Unfortunately, it had to be forbidden when a Unitarian from New York horned into it. This was the Rev. C. F. Potter, of the West Side Unitarian Church, a bustling, go-getting fellow who had come to Dayton in search of publicity. In some manner or other he induced the Methodist pastor of the town, a poor fish named M. H. Byrd, to invite him to preach in the Methodist church—a curious home-made structure of brick, with courses so erratic that, as an amateur bricklayer, I observed them with critical fascination. It surprised me to hear of this invitation, for I had not yet learned that, down in the Bible country, the Methodists were regarded as theological Leftists, and that many of the Holy Rollers were former members of the sect who had deserted it in protest against its Liberalism. But in Dayton, it turned out, Potter was a shade too raw for Pastor Byrd's flock, and there ensued a bitter row which ended with the pastor being cashiered. When I met him on the street the next day he told me that he had packed his household goods and was going to Muscle Shoals to resume his former trade of electrical worker. Barred from the Methodist church, Potter preached on the courthouse lawn at the invitation of old T. T. Martin, following a powerful evangelical sermon by Bryan. He drew only a small crowd, but there was so much resentment of his denial of the divinity of Jesus that Judge Raulston ordered that all preaching on the lawn be stopped. The order was enforced with discretion. That is to say, all theologians whose orthodoxy seemed doubtful were chased away, but bearers of the True Faith managed to be heard. Raulston later tried to make amends by inviting Potter to open one of the sessions of the court with prayer.

The weather was very hot during the trial, but I was comfortable enough in the dentist's clean and roomy house. In the courtroom, as on the street, all hands were in shirtsleeves, including judge, jury and daily chaplain. The only exception was Dudley Field Malone. An elegant fellow, he usually wore a blue coat. But he threw it off one day when Darrow sent him in to make an argument. I forget the subject, but I'll never forget Dudley's hollering, for it was so loud that it shook the courthouse. The assembled yokels, all of them fans for oratory, dissented from the doctrine preached but delighted in the rhetoric, and presently they began to break in with applause. Soon even the jury was applauding. This dismayed Darrow, who was bent, as I have said, on getting Scopes convicted. Turning to me (I happened to be sitting beside him), he said: "If this goes on the scoundrel will get us a hung jury!" When the speech was over there was a loud and long roar, and Dudley, exhausted, staggered from the lawyers' enclosure to the side of the courtroom. There stood his wife, Doris Stevens, and a number of other people, including some officers from an army post nearby. Doris was a violent suffragette and Lucy Stoner, and had been insisting that everyone call her Miss Stevens, not Mrs. Malone. But at the moment of Dudley's triumph she ceased suddenly to be a reformer and became an orthodox female. Thus when some of the army officers asked me to present them to her and I whispered "What is it to be, Doris—Miss Stevens or Mrs. Malone?" she blushed prettily and replied "Mrs. Malone." It was a great day for her, and an even greater day for Dudley, who found himself almost a hero. Fortunately, his oratory, though it was acclaimed, did not hang the jury. Scopes was duly convicted and fined $100. The *Evening Sun* paid his fine.

There were two trials within the main trial, both of them grotesque. The first culprit was Darrow, who was charged with contempt of court. On the last day of the first week, as he rose to enter an exception to one of the judge's rulings, the judge said, "I hope you don't think the court is trying to be unfair." I can see Darrow yet as he thrust his arms under his suspenders—a constant gesture—and answered, "Your Honor has the right to hope." The judge instantly banged his gavel, and presently cited Darrow for contempt. His bond was fixed at $5000, but no one, so far as I know, provided it, and he was permitted to go about unmolested. The whole week-end was given over to debate among the Scopes counsel. John R. Neal, the local man, was in favor of Darrow refusing to apologize, and so, I believe, was Malone, and my own advice ran the same way, for jailing the old boy would make an immense sensation, and heap up new ridicule and contumely upon Tennessee. But Darrow had seen the oven of a hoosegow in which the ape's owner and the Y.M.C.A. brother from Cincinnati had been jugged, and he was not eager to fry and blister to death, so he made a grudging and equivocal apology on Monday, and it was accepted with alacrity by the now very uneasy judge. The other culprit was William K. Hutchinson, who was covering the trial for Hearst. One day the judge took some motion or other under advisement, and everyone was eager to forecast his decision. Meeting him on the street, Hutchinson got it out of him by asking an apparently harmless question: the judge was too stupid to detect the trap. But when Hutchinson's dispatch got back to Dayton he was full of indignation, and cited its author for contempt. The correspondents came to the rescue of the accused by sending a delegation to the judge to say that many complicated questions of journalistic ethics were involved, and that their professional experience and judgment were at His Honor's disposal. He responded by appointing a committee of inquiry with Richard J. Beamish of the Philadelphia *Record* as chairman. This committee carried out its duties by staging a poker game that night, and the next day Beamish was ready to report. He made a striking figure as he rose in the courtroom, for he was in his shirtsleeves like everyone else, and the shirt he had on was of stupendous gaudiness. {He had a large wardrobe of such horrors, and some of them were really appalling. He had names for them—the Dark-Brown Taste, Everybody's Sweetheart, the Wild Rose, the Volcano, and so on.} A lawyer by training, he made a long and unintelligible speech, full of references to cases that the judge had never heard of—most of them, in fact, were imaginary—and then, pausing dramatically and rolling his eyes, ended with "Your committee therefore recommends, Your Honor, that no more proceedings be had." "It is so ordered!" roared the relieved judge, banging his gavel. He was eager to show all the infidels from afar that he could not be monkeyed with, but he was well aware that jailing any of them might bring very embarrassing consequences. Hutchinson was a smart reporter, and full of tricks. The legend was that, when he got into a strange town to cover a difficult story, he usually began work by taking one of the local telephone operators to bed. Thereafter she eavesdropped for him, and brought all the news to his hotel room, where her reward was a kind of technical virtuosity that the resident yaps were incapable of.

The Tennessee politicians diligently avoided Dayton during the trial, and refused with great discretion to make any comments on it. This was especially true of Cordell Hull, who had been a jobholder in the state since the age of twenty-two and was then (1926) one of its congressmen. He sent an agent to Dayton to keep him informed on the low-down— a cross-eyed woman secretary who got tight on the train coming down from Washington, and was made love to in a heavy manner by Charles Michelson, then head of the New York *World*'s Washington bureau and later director of publicity for the Democratic National Committee and the chief smearer of Hoover. But Hull himself never appeared, or said a word, and neither did any other Tennessee politico, though the Scopes case was on the first page of every newspaper in the world, and Tennessee was getting a bath of infamy that would leave it begrimed for years. Hull, in those days, supported Prohibition, as did all the other politicians of the state, but when Prohibition blew up in 1932 he flopped overnight. It shocked me when the *Sunpapers,* in 1933, began to hymn him as a statesman: he was still, as Secretary of State under Roosevelt II, the same abject and shameless timeserver he had been as a congressman in 1926 and as a United States senator from 1931 to 1933. Incidentally, one of his successors as senator from Tennessee was a third-string politician, Tom Stewart by name, who was chief of the prosecution in the Scopes trial. This Stewart, in most states, would have been simply county attorney, but in Tennessee the local prosecutors are all called assistant attorneys-general, and rate the honorific of General for the balance of their lives. If the case had been tried on its merits, and before an intelligent judge and jury, Stewart would have been duck soup for Darrow, Hays and Malone, to say nothing of Neal; but, as I have said, the aim of the defense was to lose, and so he scored an easy victory, and became a demigod among the Fundamentalist simians of the hills. After long years at the public teat in lesser offices he finally got into the Senate in 1940. His chief aides at the trial were a salty old fraud named McKenzie, himself a former assistant attorney-general and hence still a General; McKenzie's young son; and a Dayton shyster with the strange name, for a man, of Sue Hicks. Hicks was an ignoramus, and entertained the visitors with frequent mispronunciations of common words—for example, architecture, with the first syllable rhyming with *march*. Ten minutes after my first appearance in Dayton some one took me to see old McKenzie, who had an office upstairs of a feed warehouse, reached by an outside staircase. The old man was very amiable, and pressed on me a glass of the local drink—corn whiskey and Coca Cola. I had to get it down in politeness, but that night, having returned to Chattanooga, I had so powerful a bellyache that it alarmed my colleagues. I learned in Chattanooga that the corn whiskey on tap at Dayton was famous locally for its badness. The mash of which it was made was fermented in tubs set far back in the mountains, and all sorts of wild creatures, including squirrels, bats and snakes, took nips of it, got drunk and were drowned. The yokels distilled the ensuing mess without removing the carcasses.

One of the most picturesque figures who turned up at Dayton was Colonel Patrick H. Callahan, of Louisville, Ky., then celebrated as the only Catholic Prohibitionist known to statisticians. Pat was the owner of a prosperous varnish factory in Louisville, and had plenty of time on his hands, so he devoted a large part of it to gadding about the country seeking publicity. He was an admirer of Bryan, and often traveled with him. One day in Dayton he told me this story: The first time he ever set out on a tour with his hero Bryan asked him to read and dispose of the telegrams that were constantly pouring in. There were thirty or forty a day, all from strangers, and Bryan had long since got an overdose of them. When Pat protested that he wouldn't know how to answer them Bryan said, "Read them for a day or two, and you will find out." Pat then tackled the job, and soon made a discovery that surprised him. No matter how many telegrams came in, they all fell into two simple categories. The type of the first was a night-letter reading about as follows:

Before retiring to rest tonight my husband and I are on our knees thanking our Heavenly Father that you exist. So long as He spares you the Republic will be safe, and atheism can never conquer the faith of Christ.

Mrs. John J. Robinson,
Hula, Okla.

The other was shorter, and read thus:

Why don't you jump in the ocean, you old baboon?

A Jeffersonian Democrat.

Pat looked up the reporters as soon as he got to Dayton, and was soon in all the papers of the country. His revelation was to the effect that the Catholic Church was incurably Fundamentalist, and hence supported the prosecution of Scopes. After three or four days he suddenly disappeared without saying goodbye, and was not heard of for a week, when he bobbed up somewhere in North Carolina. It was not until some time later that I found out what had happened to him: he had been ordered out of the diocese of Nashville by the ordinary thereof. That was in the days before the canon law against the expounding of Catholic doctrine by laymen had begun to be relaxed in favor of Catholic Action and its amateur street-preachers.

Hyde and I greatly enjoyed our visits to the outdoor tabernacle of the Holy Rollers, back in the woods. Getting to it was somewhat laborious, but young O. B. Andrews had a car, and it managed somehow to navigate the mountain roads. The chief preacher at the orgies which went on every evening was a tall, cadaverous yokel who passed under the name of Brother Joe. His discourse was always idiotic, but it was couched in archaic English that interested me very much. That English had survived in the mountains since the first settlements, and there were elements of it that were downright Elizabethan. Brother Joe preached three or four times of an evening, always briefly but always powerfully. While he raved on the faithful would move toward a bench in the center of the clearing and there fall on their knees. Presently they'd all be in trances and jabbering "in the tongues." When one of them happened to touch another both would leap up and begin to prance. The younger customers avoided the ringside, but sat watching from the surrounding shadows. I began to suspect that the electric effect of contact was largely a sexual phenomenon, and this was confirmed when I noticed its long-range effect on the youngsters. After a couple of such explosions in the ring a youth and his girl would slip away into the adjacent cornfield, and then another pair, and then another. After perhaps fifteen minutes they would come back—the boy looking droopy and sheepish but the girl with her face flushed and her eyes sparkling. When I got back to Baltimore I wrote to Sara Haardt (July 19):

> I wasted two weeks on the buffoonery, but I think there was some profit in it. For the first time in my life I was in daily contact with Christian people. I got to know dozens of them very well, and have enough material stored up to last me the rest of my life. The thing was downright fabulous. When Bryan began arguing that man was not a mammal I almost swooned. God help us all!

8

Grand Tour of the South

1925–1926

My advocacy of a better Sunday Magazine, from 1925 onward, was intermingled with promotion of another and much more ambitious scheme—the setting up of a *Sun* weekly. The old weekly, abandoned in 1904 after an existence of 77 years, was a stupid and dull sheet aimed principally at farmers and prisoners in penitentiaries; what I had in mind was something radically different, to wit, an organ of opinion on the order of the Manchester *Guardian* Weekly, but much better. The wide influence of such weeklies as the *Nation* and *New Republic* suggested it. They were read by the editorial writers of newspapers of all shades of opinion, and their ideas were thus spread far beyond the bounds of their actual circulation. If, as we then all hoped, the *Sun* was headed for the first ranks of American journalism, why should it not aim at the same nation-wide audience? If we sold 30,000 copies a week, or even but 20,000, we'd reach a majority of the country's makers of public opinion, and the influence of the *Sunpapers,* instead of being hedged in by their narrow territory, would cover the nation and even extend abroad.

Unhappily, this fine project came to nothing. Patterson was willing, in 1927, to take the financial risk, and in fact induced the board of directors to earmark $100,000 for the experiment, but I began to develop doubts myself. For one thing, it was plain that the *Sunpapers* were producing too little first-rate matter to make a really good weekly. The foreign correspondence of the *Sun,* at least in large part, was good enough, but the editorials of Adams and his associates were far too feeble to be effective. In the main, indeed, they were clearly inferior to the editorials in the *Nation* and *New Republic*. It had been my hope that the weekly, once established, would put the heat on the *Sun* brethren—that their eagerness to get into it would make them try to write better. But in the end I concluded that they were hopeless. Nor did the *Evening Sun* offer anything much better.

My contributions to the editorial page of the *Evening Sun,* ever since I resumed writing for it at the beginning of 1920, had taken on a considerably wider scope than my old Free Lance column, though they consisted, in the main, of the same denunciation of frauds. In particular, I began at once to pay some attention to affairs in the South, for it was, in a way, within the *Sunpapers'* special territory, and moreover, it was far worse ridden by such frauds than the rest of the country. In it the American Legion, converted by 1925 into a witch-hunting organization, raged as elsewhere, but in addition it was afflicted by the fact that virtually all its politicans had taken the shillings of both the Anti-Saloon League and the Ku Klux Klan. Its situation, in fact, was downright tragic. The whole region from the Potomac to the Gulf had become a sort of intellectual Bad Lands. There were, of course, plenty of intelligent men and women in it—for example, James Branch Cabell in Virginia, and Julia Harris in Georgia—but they led the lives of beleaguered troops in walled towns. Some time in 1920 I printed in the *Evening Sun* an article on its intellectual degradation which eventually became the chapter headed "The Sahara of the Bozart" in my "Prejudices: Second Series".* That chapter made a dreadful pother in the South, and brought me a great deal of violent denunciation, but all the more enlightened Southerners had to admit its truth, and in the course of time, it had some effect. Indeed, there are Southerners today who argue that it was mainly responsible for launching the literary renaissance that flowered ten years afterward. So early as 1922 I saw signs of the approach of that renaissance, and on May 15 printed an article hailing it, under the title of "Violets in the Sahara," followed by "Confederate Notes" on December 26. But the professional Southerners continued to belabor me, and when I struck back, as I often did, they belabored me only the more. In 1925 they got stout help from a Marylander, one Aristides Smith Goldsborough, a native of the Eastern Shore (which was even less civilized than the South), but now executive secretary of the Baltimore Association of Commerce. Goldsborough, in my Free Lance days, was secretary to J. Harry Preston, and, like his

*Mencken erred; see footnote, p. 70. With the term "bozart" Mencken of course laughed at the American rendering of *beaux arts*.

151

master, was one of my butts. I ridiculed him day in and day out, and managed, among other things, to convince all Marylanders that his middle name was not Smith, but Sophocles. He still smarted from these wounds, and he was now working for an outfit that smarted too, for the Association of Commerce was the heir and assign of the old Baltimore Merchants and Manufacturers Association, which I had renamed the Honorary Pallbearers and lampooned without mercy. His *modus operandi* in 1925 consisted in setting up the cry that my articles were ruining Baltimore's old trade with the South. Hamilton Owens gave him space on the *Evening Sun* editorial page to state his case, and on August 13, 1925, after my reports of the Scopes trial had made a fresh uproar, he did so at length. {I had added fresh gasoline to the flames on August 9, 1925, with a report in the *Evening Sun* of a great Ku Klux parade in Washington, holden the day before. It so happened that most of the Ku Kluxers in line were Pennsylvanians, but any ridicule of the Klan in those days was taken as an attack on the South, where it originated and was strongest.} He got a great deal of support in Baltimore, for the town was full of persons—and especially business men—whose toes I had trampled on in my Free Lance days. Then and thereafter, in fact, I was always unpopular at home, and to this day the overwhelming majority of Baltimorons {This term was invented by Harry Black in 1930 or thereabout.} would vote that I have always been a liability to the town, not an asset. But though Aristides Sophocles roared, and his friends both in Baltimore and in the South gave him eager support, I went on telling the truth as I saw it, and in the long run he had to give up. {Also, I occasionally helped along the good cause with attempts at practical joking. It must have been about this time that I had an old-time printer in West Baltimore, with dusty cases full of archaic type, set up a letter-head for the American Institute of Arts and Letters (Colored). This buffoonery was a double crack, first at the Southern Bourbons and then at the National Institute of Arts and Letters, always one of my favorite butts. I wrote letters on the letter-heads to all Southerners who denounced me, inviting them to a banquet of the colored institute in Washington. Such letters, indeed, went to friends as well as foes—among them, James Branch Cabell.} In this battle, though it threatened to strike at the business of Baltimore, and hence at the revenues of the *Sunpapers,* Patterson stood by me, and so did Van Lear Black. As for Hamilton Owens and Harry Black, they not only stood by me; they egged me on.

Meanwhile, I continued my active interest in the long, hard, and, in the end, vain effort to put genuine life and vigor into the *Sunpapers,* and in consequence saw a great deal of Patterson and Harry Black. "The morning *Sun*," I wrote to [Patterson] on January 8, 1925, "is picking up, but I see no improvement in the local news of the *Evening Sun*. It is still devoid of imagination, and padded with all sorts of banal stuff." In 1926 or thereabout I urged Patterson to issue an order that whenever an organization seeking public subscriptions asked for space in the *Sunpapers* it should be required to file a statement showing "(*a*) the total amount of money collected during its last fiscal year, and the names and addresses of all contributors contributing more than 1% each; (*b*) a list of its paid employés, with their annual salaries; (*c*) a list of its other expenditures, including separately every one that runs to more than 5% of the total; and (*d*) a list of its responsible officers and directors, and a statement of the manner in which they are elected." This proposed order was discussed at editorial councils throughout 1926 and 1927. Murphy was against it, and Adams and the two Owenses were indifferent, but Reynolds and Moore were in favor of it, and so was Harry Black. Finally, Patterson asked me to draw up the proposed questionnaire, and I did so. Its effects were immediate and excellent. Confronted with it, many of the frauds who had been grabbing space for years quietly disappeared from the office, and some of them went out of business.

Even at that time the Negro community in Baltimore numbered much more than 100,000 people, yet it got next to no serious notice. The papers reported every Negro murder and many Negro brawls, but they seldom gave a line to Negro cultural activities. Some of the Southern papers had begun to give the colored people a whole page once a week, but not the *Sunpapers*. I proposed that a Negro reporter be employed, and that we print occasional articles on Negro problems by intelligent journalists of the race, for example, George S. Schuyler. But no one in the office agreed with me, and there were some, notably Murphy, who opposed me violently. Even Patterson showed a great deal of prejudice against the poor blackamoors, though he was born at Jacksonville, Ill., only thirty miles from the Lincoln Valhalla at Springfield. Years afterward, when John Owens was on the lookout for likely reprint matter for the editorial page of the *Sun,* I sent him a number of clippings of articles written by Schuyler for the Pittsburgh *Courier.* They were excellent stuff, and vastly better written than any of the compositions of Owens's own editorial writers, but he turned them down with the half-concealed sneer that Schuyler was merely one of my imitators. To this day, though the colored population of Baltimore is now approaching 250,000, there is no Negro news in the *Sunpapers* save news of crime and misfortune.

The year 1925 ended in tragedy for me, for my mother died on December 13. She had been ill for a year or more, but at first her illness did not appear to be serious. But during the Summer Dr. Louis P. Hamburger told me that she was suffering from a rapidly progressive form of arteriosclerosis, and that there was nothing to do about it but make her as comfortable as possible. Unhappily, her chief symptom was a numbness in the hands, and I lived in terror that their circulation would be so far impeded that it might be necessary to amputate them. It was dreadful to watch her sufferings, though her actual pain was never great. Hamburger gave her codeine in large amounts to obliterate the tingling in her hands, but it made her so drowsy that she could neither sew nor read—the two occupations of her evenings for many, many years. As I worked in my third-floor office in Hollins street I would drop down of an evening to see her in her sitting-room on the floor below. I was trying to write my "Notes on Democracy" at the time, but the sight and thought of her made work almost impossible. My mind was filled with horrible imaginings, and I resented bitterly the fact that medicine could do so little for her. But she had been born under a lucky star, and in the end she escaped all the appalling consequences that the disease might have brought upon her. On December 9 I found her in her sitting-room in obvious distress, and on taking her temperature found that it was 103. The next day tonsillitis developed and on December 11 it was followed by cellulitis in the neck—the so-called Ludwig's angina. This was not painful, but Hamburger decided that it needed drainage, and so we took her to the Union Memorial Hospital, where Dr. John M. T. Finney performed the small operation the same day. She went willingly and even gaily: it amused her to think that she was having her first surgical operation at 67. All the rest of us, including the house dog, had been on the table, but she had always escaped. The blood examination made at the hospital showed that her white corpuscles were far below normal, and the next day the count showed even less. In brief, a general infection was under way, with the hemolytic streptococcus as the organism, and in forty-eight hours she was dead. Her death was completely peaceful and painless. She simply went to sleep and passed quietly out of life. Her last words to me were that she felt much better. This is no place for me to record my stupendous debt to her: I hope to do it elsewhere. My father's death in 1899 was really a stroke of luck for me, for it liberated me from the tobacco business and enabled me to attempt journalism without his probable doubts and disapproval to hamper me, but the loss of my mother was pure disaster, for she had always stood by me loyally, despite the uneasiness that some of my ventures must have aroused in her, and I owed to her, and to her alone, the fact that I had a comfortable home throughout my youth and early manhood. Her death filled me with a sense of futility and desolation. It was weeks before I was fit for any work beyond routine: that routine, happily, was so heavy that it rescued me from myself. To add to my distress, my uncle, Henry Mencken, now sole proprietor of my father's old firm of Aug. Mencken & Bro., seized the time of my mother's last illness to go bankrupt. I got my first news of his difficulties, in fact, only a little while before she died, and I was at great pains to prevent her hearing of them, for I knew how they would distress her. This was not because she had any concern about him, for she had always regarded him as lazy and incompetent; it was because she had much pride in the good name of the old firm. In my father's time it had been of excellent position in the tobacco trade, with a high rating in Bradstreet and a reputation for scrupulousness in money matters. But now, after 26 years, my uncle and his stupid son, John Henry, had brought it to bankruptcy, and for weeks after my mother's death I devoted myself largely to trying to settle its affairs without public scandal. This was finally accomplished, and the business founded in 1877 shut down at last. I well recall how, on one of my unpleasant visits to its last office, at Pratt and Greene streets, I found John Henry preparing to turn over to the junkman most of its old books. I rescued such of them as belonged to my father's time, had them bound, and sent them to the Pratt Library. Patterson and indeed all the *Sun* brethren were very sympathetic and understanding in those dark days, and I owed much to their company. {My father died on Friday, January 13, 1899, and my mother on Sunday, December 13, 1925. My wife, Sara Haardt, died on Friday, May 31, 1935, and my brother Charlie's wife, Mary Kline, on Sunday, October 13, 1940. On the family tombstone in Loudon Park Cemetery, Baltimore, are the four dates—three thirteens, one thirty-first (thirteen in reverse), and two Fridays.}

During the early part of 1926 Patterson and I, in our endless discussions of the situation of the *Sunpapers,* concluded that they were showing less influence than they ought to have in the South. We had some circulation down there, and were naturally interested in Southern problems, but our treatment of them was not always well informed, and I was the only person in the office who knew some of the principal Southern editors. My own discourses on sub-Potomac themes, as I have noted, had produced mainly bitterness, but I had got some support from the younger Southern writers, and even from a few of the more enlightened newspaper editors. In 1924 I had proposed that a Southerner of the new school be added to the *Sunpapers'* editorial staff, and had nominated Gerald W. Johnson, then of the Greensboro *Daily News.* Unhappily, Johnson had just accepted the post of professor of journalism at the University of North Carolina—though he knew nothing about journalism save editorial writing—and could not come to Baltimore. But in 1926 he managed to get rid of his job at Chapel Hill, and so joined the editorial-page staff of the *Evening Sun.* Meanwhile, I had suggested to Patterson that some one be sent on a grand tour of the South, to meet editors and look over the ground. This last was in January, 1925. The difficulty lay in finding the man. On January 15 Patterson wrote to me: "Outside of yourself, I don't know of anyone we have who would handle it in the right way, with the possible exception of Hamilton Owens, and I know Murphy wouldn't let him off." Thus the matter rested until the Summer of 1926, when Patterson proposed one day that he and I make the trip together. This seemed an excellent idea, and we were presently busy with plans for it. At the start Patterson—who loved to arrange such things— laid out an itinerary that would have taken us on a zigzag journey through Virginia, North Carolina, Georgia and Alabama to New Orleans, and then, after a few days there, to Texas and Oklahoma, with a return home by way of Chicago. But he soon discovered that he would be needed in the office before so large a swing could be completed, and so our trip reduced itself to a week, and we covered only Richmond, Raleigh, Chapel Hill, Atlanta, Columbus, Ga., Montgomery and New Orleans. At New Orleans we parted. Patterson returned home direct, and I continued west to Los Angeles, where I met Joseph Hergesheimer and put in a couple of weeks of pure holiday.

The journey was very pleasant, and I believe it did some good. Patterson had never been in the South before, and his quick mind got something out of friendly contact with Southerners. Our first stop was Richmond, where I introduced him to James Branch Cabell and other local notables and we were pleasantly entertained at dinner by Mrs. William Meade Clark, the widowed step-mother of Emily Clark, editor of the *Reviewer.* That night we left by sleeper for Raleigh, N.C., where we found Josephus Daniels *non est,* but picked up his political reporter, Ben Dixon McNeill, and by him were taken to Chapel Hill, where the president of the University of North Carolina, Harry W. Chase, entertained us at lunch. I had some acquaintance on the faculty—for example, Howard W. Odum and Archibald Henderson {Henderson was professor of mathe-

Visiting southern California in 1926, Mencken enjoys a flirtation with actress Aileen Pringle, who here stands between him and the famous Lionel Barrymore. Renée Adorée, another of H.L.M.'s admirers, joins the group on Mencken's left.

matics at Chapel Hill, but occupied himself on the side as a literary critic, and it was in that capacity that I knew him. He wrote books on Mark Twain and George Bernard Shaw. In 1933 he brought out one on Shaw in which he made the preposterous claim that he had discovered Shaw and taught him how to write. This imbecility I reviewed tartly in the *American Mercury* for April, 1933, and since then I have heard nothing from Henderson.]—and that night Henderson, who was the richest professor in the place, gave a large party in our honor. I recall nothing of it save two things—first, that the chief refreshment was a local corn whiskey that Patterson and I found hard going, and second, that among the guests were Dr. and Mrs. Fred M. Hanes, to whom we both cottoned at once, and who have remained good friends of mine to this day. From Chapel Hill we proceeded to Atlanta, and were there entertained by Major John S.

Cohen, publisher of the Atlanta *Journal* and later a United States Senator from Georgia. Cohen's party was given at a country club, and only newspaper men were present. We had a large time, and met a good many pleasant fellows, including a reporter named Fuzzy Woodruff whose tales of Georgia politicans were capital. The next day we went to Columbus, Ga., where Julian L. Harris, son of Joel Chandler Harris, was struggling to make a go of the Columbus *Enquirer-Sun*. Harris had been making a gallant fight against the Ku Klux Klan on its home grounds, and in 1925 I had pulled the wires which got him the Pulitzer Prize for that service. But he was notoriously in financial difficulties, and it was Patterson's idea that a little friendly advice might be of some help to him; indeed, Patterson was willing to go to the length of offering him a loan in the name of the *Sun*. But it didn't take long to discover that he was a hopeless case. The Pulitzer Prize had converted him into a starry-eyed reformer in general practise, and he was engaged, among other things, in a gratuitous and wholly foolish war with his local advertisers. They were mainly Jews, and as such were grateful for his onslaught on the Klan, but he insisted upon treating them cavalierly, apparently on the ground that even common politeness to them would compromise his editorial chastity. We had dinner with him and his wife in their apartment, and put in the evening listening to them. We came away convinced that she was the better man of the two, and by far. She was a charming woman and showed a great deal of common sense, but Harris himself seemed to be hardly more than a journalistic evangelist, *à la* Adams, full of high-sounding words and moral indignation. Nothing was said about a loan from the *Sun*. We left Columbus the next day convinced that Harris was bound to come to grief. He did so in 1929. The *Enquirer-Sun* was sold to a chain, and he was given a job by Clark Howell, of the Atlanta *Constitution*. In 1934 or thereabout he moved to the Chattanooga *Times*, where he is now (1942) executive editor. He was an excellent editorial writer, and he had plenty of courage, but fundamentally he was a damned fool.

In Montgomery, the next night, I introduced Patterson to a much more competent Southern editor—Grover C. Hall, of the Montgomery *Advertiser*. Hall had also fought the Klan, and just as bravely as Harris, but he kept his feet on the ground, and was devoid of messianic delusions. In 1928 I pulled wires again and he received the Pulitzer Prize that Harris had received in 1925. He was on friendly terms with the family of Sara Haardt, whom I was to marry in 1930, and had been extremely kind to her in the days of her beginnings as a writer, when all the rest of Montgomery viewed her with suspicion. He had arranged a dinner for us at the Exchange Hotel, and when we got there we found Sara's sister Philippa and her brother John in waiting for us. I gave Philippa a bottle of wine for her mother and she vanished but John remained for the dinner, which was wet and gay. Of the other guests I recall only Dr. C. Hilton Rice, now dead, and the cartoonist of the *Advertiser*, whose name I forget. The trip from Columbus, Ga., to Montgomery was a long one, involving a change of trains at a little place called Union Springs (where colored pedlars offered Patterson and me huge sandwiches of country ham on homemade bread at 5 cents, and half-chickens with bread at 25), and by the time we got to the hotel we were ravenously hungry and even more thirsty. When, toward midnight that night, Hall and his merry men loaded us aboard the train for New Orleans we were barely able to stand up. The next morning I found that I had lost my hat and acquired Dr. Rice's. At New Orleans we were greeted by Marshall Ballard, editor of the *Item;* Clarke Salmon, its managing editor; and James M. Thomson, its publisher. Ballard was a Baltimorean, and I had known him since my early reportorial days. He was married to an extraordinary woman who was the daughter of a distinguished German surgeon of New Orleans, and herself an M.D. Ballard told me that he had married her because she was the only woman epicure he had ever encountered; he himself had originally gone to New Orleans because of its reputation for good eating. They lived with their five children at Bay St. Louis, Miss., in an old house directly on the shore of the gulf, and he commuted to New Orleans every day, nearly sixty miles each way. We went out to the place for dinner—and what a dinner it was! I recall especially that it began at 4 P.M. with a round of sandwiches and beer, and kept on continuously until 9. There were two separate fish courses, both superb, and so many other magnificent dishes that, though I can eat with the best of them, I was almost stalled. After dinner Mrs. Ballard went to the piano, and we sang German songs with her children. On the way to Bay St. Louis Patterson had developed a sudden diarrhea. Mrs. Ballard took him in hand at once, prescribed absinthe in large doses, and soon had him completely recovered—but very dizzy. In New Orleans we were entertained by Thomson and his wife, the latter a daughter of Champ Clark: my encounter with her at the New York convention of 1924 I have already recorded. Ballard also introduced us to a Catholic monsignor who had a hunting lodge down the Mississippi, forty or fifty miles below New Orleans, and he invited us there to dinner. It was a wet and gaudy meal, and I well remember our hair-raising ride back to New Orleans in the middle of the night, driven by a man who took all curves at full speed.

Altogether, we had a grand time in New Orleans, and I was sorry to see Patterson leave for home. The next day I started for Los Angeles by the Southern Pacific and by the time I awoke on the morning following the train had crossed the great stretch of Texas and was running along the Rio Grande, and I was looking across the river at the dusty wilderness of Old Mexico.

Our brief tour, I believe, was profitable to the *Sunpapers*. We met a great many Southern newspaper men, and got upon friendly terms with not a few of them. Everywhere we went we were bathed in publicity, and I was interviewed four or five times a day. In each state I told the local reporters that some native bigwig was prime presidential material, and predicted ironically that he would probably get the Democratic nomination in 1928—Governor Harry F. Byrd in Virginia, Governor Angus W. McLean in North Carolina, Major John S. Cohen in Georgia, and so on. Hamilton Owens printed a selection of the ensuing stories in my usual place on the editorial page of the *Evening Sun* on Monday, October 25, 1926, along with a two-column cut showing me in New Orleans, standing beside the chief of the fire department and wearing a fire helmet. A convention of fire chiefs was meeting there when we arrived, and our publicity and theirs were thus commingled. When I got to Los Angeles I received a letter from Patterson, dated October 28, which included the following:

> I was bowled over by the exhibit of clippings which Hamilton Owens had amassed reflecting the Grand Tour. The seriousness with which the presidential booms were taken, particularly in North Carolina, is of course screamingly funny. Most of them were quite serious in their discussion of the McLean boom. One suspected it was a diabolical plot on the part of the *Sunpapers* to put Al Smith over. The clippings are being held for you and I know you will enjoy reading them.

I stopped over in El Paso to see Duncan Aikman, then chief editorial writer of the El Paso *Times* and a contributor to the *American Mercury*, and he and some of his friends gave me a gaudy dinner in the Mexican town of Juarez, across the Rio Grande. They were in the habit of dining there often, for Mexico was magnificently wet. Before dinner they told me that it was the rule of their club that a round of cocktails should be served for each member and guest present. There were twelve of us at table, so dinner was begun to the tune of loud merriment. When it was over the brethren put me aboard the train for Los Angeles, and when I came to the next day we were approaching Yuma, Ariz., on the California border. My adventures among the movie folk and at San Francisco do not belong to this narrative. They came to a melodramatic climax with the suicide of George Sterling on November 18. This brought me a lot of unpleasant publicity, for the rumor went about that Sterling and I had quarrelled. This, of course, was not true. I cleared out of San Francisco before the funeral, returning to Los Angeles, and a little while later I started for home. Gouverneur Morris and his wife, who were also in San Francisco, were even more upset than I was. They departed at once for Seattle, and on arriving there sailed for New Zealand.

My contributions to the editorial page of the *Evening Sun* during 1926 were mainly devoted to denouncing two things: the interferences with free speech and like common rights that were hanging over from the Wilson administration, and the growing complacency and imbecility of the country under the so-called Coolidge Prosperity. I began on January 11 with an article headed "The New Despotism," and went on to "Innocent Bystanders" on January 25, "Liberty with Reservations" on February 8, "The Natural History of Service" on February 22, and "Farm Relief" on May 31. There was an agitation in Maryland at this time for the abolition of capital punishment, and I was against it. On the night of August 13 I attended the hanging of a notorious bandit, Russell Reese Whittemore, at the Maryland Penitentiary, and on August 16 printed an article about it under the title of "Finale of the Rogue's March." On May 21 Senator James A. Reed of Missouri, with whom I was on very friendly terms, came to Baltimore to harangue a large meeting of wets at the Alcazar, and three days later I paid my tribute to him in an article entitled "The Turn of the Tide." On May 3 and again on December 6 I discussed Ritchie's prospects in the campaign of 1928, on May 10 I whooped up Sinclair Lewis for refusing the award of the Pulitzer Prize for his "Arrowsmith" (he had done so at my instigation), and on October 4 I argued for a scheme to detach the Eastern Shore counties from Maryland and amalgamate them with Delaware and the Eastern Shore of Virginia, under the style or appellation of Del-mar-va. Early in August I had a chance encounter with Rudolf Valentino, the movie actor, in New York, and when he died soon afterward I wrote about him in the *Evening Sun*—"Valentino" on August 20.

I was kept jumping in those days by my other business. My "Notes on Democracy," after being delayed by my mother's illness and death, by the bankruptcy of Aug. Mencken & Bro., and by the "Hatrack" case [in which Boston authorities sought to ban sale of the April 1926 issue of *American Mercury*], came out at last toward the end of 1926, my

"Prejudices: Fifth Series" was published at about the same time, my "Prejudices: Sixth Series" followed in 1928, and during the same year I began the long and heavy labors that produced "Treatise on the Gods" in 1930. Meanwhile, I was putting in a lot of time in 1927 gathering material for a book, to be called "Homo Sapiens," that never got itself written. All sorts of visitors interrupted me, and I was plagued constantly by illness—both my own and that of others. In January my publisher, Alfred A. Knopf, came down from New York for a nose operation by my old friend, Dr. Franklin Hazlehurst. Hazlehurst, who was somewhat rough in his technic, hurt Knopf badly, and for a week or so he remained in hospital, suffering severely. On April 16 my brother August had a similar operation, and it was followed by hemorrhages so alarming that I had to rush him back to hospital. In June my sister-in-law Mary returned to Baltimore for a second operation, and it turned out so badly that she did not go home until October 6. I had the care of her while she was laid up, for my brother Charlie's engineering duties with the Pennsylvania Railroad required him to stay in Pittsburgh, with only occasional visits to Baltimore. Sara Haardt was ill off and on all through 1927, and when, on September 28, she went to Hollywood on a commission to write movies, I had to advise her about getting medical assistance there as best I could by mail and telegraph, beside steering her through a characteristically long and vexatious battle with the movie magnates. On November 17 my old friend William W. Woollcott had a stomach hemorrhage which came close to finishing him and kept him in hospital for weeks, and on November 24, which was Thanksgiving Day, my sister Gertrude became seriously ill, and the house in Hollins street was in turmoil. The year of misfortune came to a grotesque finale on December 7 when I was in a head-on taxi collision in Washington, but escaped with only a few bruises.

9

The Knavish Dishonesty
of Politicians

1928

Three major enterprises for the *Sunpapers* had my attention in 1928. The first was covering the Pan-American Conference that met in Havana on January 16, the second was an effort to get an Associated Press franchise for the *Evening Sun,* and the third was covering the two national conventions of the Summer. I went to the Pan-American Conference at the urging of Patterson, and without much anticipatory interest, for I was convinced in advance that it would be dull and dishonest. The *Sun* delegation consisted of Patterson, Reynolds, John Owens and myself, along with a reporter (I forget his name) who alleged that he could speak Spanish, and turned out to be mistaken. I recall that as we left the Pennsylvania Station in Baltimore for Key West on January 11 we saw copies of the New York *Daily News* with the whole front page given over to a photograph of Ruth Snyder in the electric chair. She had been electrocuted at Sing Sing, with her lover, Judd Gray, the night before. Joe Patterson, the publisher of the *Daily News,* had given an undertaking [promise] to Lewis E. Lawes, the warden of Sing Sing, to attempt no photograph in the death-chamber, and then violated it by sending in a reporter with a Leica camera strapped to his leg. The result was a picture that sold 500,000 extra copies of the paper, and kept Patterson explaining for months afterward. His chief apologia was printed in *Liberty,* which he still owned. It was so feeble that I was glad my relations with him (through my contributions to the Chicago *Tribune*) had been terminated at the end of 1927.

We got to Havana just too late to hear Coolidge open the conference with a speech. We had quarters in the Plaza Hotel, and Patterson had arranged with the United Press for the use of one of its leased cables for four or five hours every day. My own contributions to the burden of this cable were not heavy, for I had come to Havana convinced that the conference was a fraud and everything I saw and heard there confirmed me in that opinion. The chief American delegate was Charles Evans Hughes, then Secretary of State. His job was to shut off all discussion of Yankee imperialism, and with the aid of the ineffable Gerado Machado, then president of Cuba, he undertook it with great success. Many of the delegates from the smaller so-called republics were simply American goons—for example, those from Nicaragua, where American marines were still engaged in "police" duty, and those from Santo Domingo, where they had set up a subservient government in 1924. From Haiti, where they were in full control, there came two delegations. The first, made up of stooges, was received with honor by Machado, and given a full voice in the conference; the second, made up of disaffected Haitians, landed from a sailing vessel on the south coast of Cuba, and was jailed by Machado's gendarmes. Many of the delegates from the larger Latin-American countries, face to face with these disturbing facts and remembering also the bombardment of Vera Cruz in 1914, came to Havana with blood in their eyes, but the suave Hughes managed to hornswoggle them into silence and acquiescence, though many of them did a great deal of muttering behind the arras. In this benign business he was greatly assisted by Antonio Sânchez de Bustamante, the Cuban chosen to preside over the conference. In Havana itself the revolt that was to drive out Machado and his assassins on August 12, 1933, was already in the making, and one evidence of it was the fact that the University of Havana was closed, its faculty and students dispersed, and its buildings guarded by troops and surrounded by barbed wire. But despite these embarrassing exhibits the conference was held in one of the halls of the university, and Hughes made a resounding speech, full of brotherly love, from the top of the long flight of stone steps leading up to its main entrance.

My own view of him had been low since he stepped down from the Supreme Court in 1916 to run for the presidency, but John Owens regarded him with more confidence. One day he received Owens at his quarters at the Hotel Nacional, and Owens came back to the *Sun* bureau filled with enthusiasm. The result was an interview with him so long that it kept our leased cable busy all afternoon. Patterson read the copy as it poured from Owens's typewriter and then passed it to me. All I could discover in it was a vast flow of words, most of them without rational meaning. But Owens, by that time, was titular editor of the *Sun*, and Patterson, as usual, refused to censor him, so the whole inchoate mass appeared in the *Sun* of the next morning. Our Spanish-speaking reporter having turned out to be incompetent, it was necessary to find other interpreters of the proceedings, which were in both Spanish and English at the open sessions, but mainly in Spanish alone behind the door. I quickly found two in Henry P. Fletcher, formerly ambassador to Chile and Mexico, and then ambassador to Italy, and Dwight W. Morrow, then special ambassador to Mexico. Morrow had no Spanish, but Fletcher spoke it fluently. Moreover, he was an honest man, and yet more, I had known him for some years. From him I got a great deal of useful information, but most of it went to waste, for the *Sun*'s dispatches had to follow, more or less, the lead of John Owens. After a few days I gave up my job as hopeless, and began to devote my space to extraneous matters— for example, the swinish revels of the American Babbitts who came into Havana on tour ships, and celebrated their furlough from Prohibition in Sloppy Joe's bar. For the rest, I tried to enjoy myself in the town, which I remembered pleasantly from 1917. There were many amusing fellows among the assembled correspondents, including Dick Oulahan of the New York *Times* and Will Rogers, who was covering the conference for a syndicate. We had some gaudy parties at the Plaza, the Casino and elsewhere, and dined almost every night at the Paris restaurant in the O'Reilly, then one of the best eating-houses in the Americas. One night my waiter told me that the proprietor desired to speak to me before I left, and when I stopped at his desk on my way out he addressed me in excellent German. I observed in German that this surprised me, whereupon he told me that his father, the founder of the place, was a German.

I had several long palavers with Morrow, whom I had not met before. During the sessions of the conference, which bored him excessively, he would wander out of the hall and pace up and down the terrace. There I joined him, and he talked very frankly, but not much that he said could be published. Dick Crooker, a paper man who was a friend of Patterson's, made the trip to Havana with us for the holiday, and joined in our parties. One night he, Reynolds and Owens, having got an overdose at the Casino, started to sing together in Owens's bathroom. Inasmuch as the bathroom was tiled to the ceiling and all three had powerful bass voices they made a fearful din, and in a little while the manager of the Plaza came rushing up, protesting that all the other guests on the floor were complaining. In the bar of the Sevilla-Biltmore Hotel we found an old colored waiter who was the living image of Cardinal Gibbons. We addressed him as Eminence and speculated as to whether it were conceivable that his real Eminence had ever, in youth, taken a false step, but finally put away the notion as abhorrent.

The two national conventions of 1928 were deficient in dramatic interest for on the Republican side Coolidge had refused to run again and thus left the way open to Hoover, and on the Democratic side Al Smith, after two vain attempts, was plainly destined to get the nomination at last. The Republican convention met at Kansas City in June, and Hoover was nominated on the first ballot, with 837 of the 1084 votes cast. He had profited by his bitter lesson in Chicago in 1920, and came to town with a sufficiency of boughten and reliable delegates, and to spare. How much it had cost him to round them up never appeared officially, but the gossip at the convention put his outlay at nearly $1,000,000. In all probability he actually spent less, but it is hard to figure him spending less than $500,000. The professionals, including Coolidge, were all against him, but he had the delegates, and everyone knew it—everyone, that is, save some of the professionals. Led by old Charlie Curtis, then a Senator from Kansas, these imbeciles launched a stop-Hoover movement, and Charlie filled the newspapers with anti-Hoover invective. With my own ears I heard him declare the day before the convention opened that the nomination of Hoover would not only ruin the country, but also shame it. But when the boughten Hoover delegates duly did their stuff, and Charlie was offered the vice-presidential nomination as a gesture of conciliation, he suffered an instantaneous change of heart, and left Kansas City proclaiming that Hoover was a genius and would make the greatest President ever heard of. This exhibition, I need not say, I vastly enjoyed. Never, within my experience of American politics, had the knavish dishonesty of politicians been more dramatically displayed. It was a magnificent revelation of the true character of government under democracy. Hoover's easy victory, of course, owed something to the fact that no candidate of any size appeared against him—or, as the politicians say, to the fact that "you can't beat something with nothing". The only other open aspirants—the alcoholic Lowden, the preposterous Jim Watson, and the uplifting George W. Norris—were all too feeble to make much of a show, and Lowden, in fact, pulled out before the ballot, alleging that the refusal of the convention to endorse a subsidy for farmers made it impossible for him to support the platform. But what really won for Hoover was the plain fact that his agents, led by the mysterious Lawrence Richey (*geb.* [born] Ricci), had been corralling delegates for months past. Whenever a state organization indicated that a little financial help would be welcome, Richey appeared with plenty of money, entered Hoover in the state primary, and so had the state delegation instructed for him. No other candidate had enough funds to play this game, so it was virtually a walkover for Hoover. When he got to Kansas City he had all of the big delegations save those of Indiana, Illinois and Ohio, the first of which supported a favorite son, Watson; the second of which was split between Hoover and Lowden, with 17 of the 57 delegates still so uncertain that 13 of them voted for Coolidge and 4 for Watson; and the third of which gave 10 of its fifty votes to Curtis and 4 to Coolidge. New York, Pennsylvania, New Jersey, Massachusetts, Michigan and California were all in line, and so was Maryland.

Kansas City is usually an inferno in Summer, but while the convention lasted the weather was cool and lovely. The town was dry (though not as dry as Cleveland in 1924) and the convention itself adopted a platform plank advocating "the observance and vigorous enforcement" of the Eighteenth Amendment, but a local worthy, Col. Conrad H. Mann, had thoughtfully set up a house of mirth in the Muehlebach Hotel, and let it be known that all thirsty delegates, alternates and newspaper correspondents were welcome. Mann was a retired brewer and very rich, and he now devoted most of his time to fostering and glorifying the Fraternal Order of Eagles, the national headquarters of which were in Kansas City. His chief of staff, both at these headquarters and at the house of mirth, was an old-time Baltimore labor leader named Ed Hirsch, whom I had known for years. Hirsch was the most incorrigible cynic I have ever encountered, and hence amusing and instructive company. Starting out as a linotype operator on the Baltimore *News* in Grasty's day, he had become president of the Baltimore Typographical Union, and then, in 1897, of the Baltimore Federation of Labor. He remained in this latter office until 1912, and accumulated a competence. Whenever there was a strike in Baltimore he undertook to settle it, and in the course of getting the poor strikers back to work (sometimes on worse conditions than they had struck against) he managed to put himself upon excellent terms with their employers. It was his boast that he never took bribes in actual cash, but everyone knew that he loved precious stones, and so his collection of them grew larger and larger. A considerable part of it he carried about with him in a trousers pocket, and he was fond of bringing forth its diamonds, rubies and emeralds, and voluptuously admiring them. Hirsch pressed me to patronize the Mann house of mirth, but I declined for Patterson and I had brought our usual supply of refreshments from Baltimore. The house of mirth supply had come from New York: Mann had sent Hirsch there in a private car to bring it out to Kansas City. How much the emissary got from the bootleggers in the way of commission I do not know, but he hinted that it was a plenty. He complained to me bitterly of the hoggish boozing done under his eye by dry delegates to the convention, mainly Southerners or Middle Westerners. The worst of all, he said, was Henry J. Allen, of Kansas, once Governor of that state and soon to be appointed United States Senator to succeed Charlie Curtis. Allen had come to Kansas City to promote old Charlie's ill-starred presidential boom, and when it blew up he seized the chance to make some speeches. All of them were eloquent arguments for Prohibition, and the strictest sort of law enforcement. I myself heard him make one at a lawn-party of female politicos from the cow country. Having thus discharged his duty to humanity, he would go to the Mann house of mirth, and there immerse himself in whiskey until it shut down for the night. Getting rid of him, according to Hirsch, was a very difficult business; in fact, it could be achieved only by giving him a bottle of rye to take with him.

Since its result was known to everyone save the Charlie Curtises before it was called to order, the Kansas City convention offered little for journalists to get their teeth into, so Henry Hyde and I, who were covering it for the *Evening Sun,* devoted a good part of our time to visiting around. Oswald Garrison Villard, then editor of the *Nation,* was present in the press-stand, and sweating his usual moral indignation. Every time we encountered him we gave him some false but plausible news tip, and set him off upon a wild goose chase. One day we called on a curious character named Walter Cohen, who had been for many years the Republican boss of Louisiana. He was a man of color, but his authority over the white members of the Louisiana delegation was not diminished by the fact, and he delivered eleven of its twelve members to Hoover. Cohen turned out to be an amusing fellow, and was full of interesting tales of his political adventures. "Imagine my situation," he said, "in the days when the Klan was running Louisiana! I was a Republican, I was colored, I was a Catholic—and my name was Cohen!" One day, sitting in the press-stand, I saw Louis B. Mayer, the movie magnate, in the front row on the floor. He was a member of the California delegation and was wearing a large Hoover button. I had met him in Hollywood in 1926, and so dropped down for a palaver with him. To make conversation I asked him how, as a Jew, he could be for Hoover: wasn't Al Smith about to get the Democratic nomination, and wasn't Al Smith the fugleman and hero of all the racial minorities, including especially the Jews? Mayer

Mencken reads in the parlor at 1524 Hollins Street, where he entertained
Theodore Dreiser and George Schuyler. The secretary to the left of the fireplace
houses the copy of *Huckleberry Finn* that Mencken devoured as a boy. It
changed his life. 1928. Edgar T. Schaefer.

admitted that this was so. "My heart," he said, clasping his bosom, "is
all with Al—but we Jewish business men must think of our property.
Only Hoover can protect it for us. He is a business genius." I often wondered, after 1930, what Mayer thought of Hoover's genius then. He invited me to drop in for a drink at his rooms in the Hotel Muehlebach;
when I did so the next day I found that he was living in a suite reserved
by the hotel for movie stars, many of whom then broke their eastward
and westward train journeys at Kansas City. It was as large as the average church, and was furnished with lavish fittings, including two grand
pianos.

Among the women in attendance upon the Kansas City convention
was Alice Roosevelt Longworth. I had never met her, but I was well acquainted with her husband, then the Speaker of the House of Representatives, and had entertained him several times at the Rennert Hotel in

Baltimore. At those parties, which tended to be very wet, he was accompanied by his girl, Lucile McArthur, the widow of an Oregon congressman and herself a boozer of large gifts. Longworth, who was fond of music, liked to boast, when he was in his cups, that he had played the piano in a Cincinnati bawdy-house in his youth, and in fact stood at the head of the profession. Inasmuch as I had also done some piano-playing in Baltimore houses of sin, we fell into the habit of addressing each other as Professor. When I was presented to Mrs. Longworth at Cincinnati I naturally asked after her husband, who was not on hand. I spoke of him as the Speaker. "To whom do you refer?" she replied, pretending to be puzzled. "I mean," I said, "your husband." "Oh," she replied, "you mean the Professor." Mrs. Longworth and I, on this basis, became good friends at once, and have remained so to this day. Nick was full of amusing tales of his days as a pianist in Cincinnati. One had to do with a girl named Ivy, the youngest intern in the house he served. The ladies of the faculty always had a large fried fish for breakfast on Sunday morning, and Nick often joined them, with the madame at the head of the table. The madame did the carving—and poor little Ivy invariably got the head of the fish, with the eyes still in it. Nick said that he often tried to slip her a better cut, but the madame frowned him down. It was the rule in Cincinnati, he said, that the youngest girl in a bawdy-house should get the piece with the eyes in it. I once heard him tell that story to a dinner party of fifty or sixty men. He was then Speaker of the House and a power in Washington, but he didn't care. He was a great music lover, and often slipped out of his chair of a late afternoon to hear a violin recital or a string quartette.

My *American Mercury* work followed me to Kansas City, as it followed me everywhere. This time it included a nuisance in the form of an acrimonious exchange of letters and telegrams with Upton Sinclair. In 1927, when she was in Hollywood, Sara Haardt had met Jim Tully, and when she returned East she did an article on him for the magazine, printed in May, 1928. It described Tully's early struggles as a writer, and among other things told of his effort to enlist the interest of Sinclair, to whom he sent one of his early manuscripts. Sinclair kept it so long without reporting on it that Tully finally dispatched a boy to Pasadena to recover it. Thus the tale, as told by him to Sara, and by her recorded:

Mr. Sinclair's yard was filled with fierce watch-dogs to keep off the desperadoes of Wall Street, and the small boy who fetched it [the manuscript] away counted himself lucky to escape with it, and the clothes on his back.

To this Sinclair, who was always a vain ass, objected violently, alleging that he had never owned any fierce dogs, and demanding a full and abject apology. When I refused it he began to make threats of a libel suit, but I knew that a show of firmness would stop him, so I sent him a curt and insulting telegram, and that was the end of the row.

The convention adjourned on June 15, and the Democratic convention was to open at Houston, Texas, on June 26. Patterson, Hyde and I had two invitations for the interval. One was from Edison K. Bixby, editor of the two papers in Springfield, Mo., and the other was from Amon G. Carter, publisher of the Fort Worth, Tex., *Star-Telegram*. Hyde and I knew neither of them, but Patterson was well acquainted with both, so we accepted. Bixby drove us to Springfield in his car, and we enjoyed the trip very much, for it took us through the heart of rural Missouri. We paused for lunch at a small eating house on the courthouse square of a little country-town called Butler. The greasy bill-of-fare that the waitress produced looked unpromising, but when I saw pigs' feet on it suggested that we order them, for pigs' feet ought to be good in the hog and corn country. They turned out to be magnificent. At Springfield we met Bixby's wife, a tall, handsome, charming blonde from North Dakota, obviously of Scandinavian blood, and she entertained us most agreeably. Because of the shortness of the Kansas City convention we had got away with some of our Baltimore bottles, so we gave her and her husband a return dinner at the Kentwood Arms Hotel, and broached them. It was a fine party, but in the midst of it one of Bixby's reporters rushed in with the news that a mob was collecting around the town jail, and proposing to lynch one of the prisoners. What the prisoner was charged with I forget, but I recall that we all rushed out to see the lynching, and were greatly disappointed when the cops on duty announced that it would not take place. But when we got back to the hotel the bottles were still there, and the evening was a large one.

Bixby hailed from Minnesota, and had inherited his papers from his father. There was another one in Muskogee, Okla., operated by his younger brother. Bixby was a pleasant enough fellow, but his wife was much his superior intellectually—a very common situation in this great Republic. After we had put in a couple of days with them in Springfield we started out with them for Muskogee, to visit the other Bixby. We traveled by motorcar, and our route led through the Ozarks from end to end. The weather was fine, the roads were smooth, the scenery was lovely, and I had a fine time, though the dust in Arkansas and Oklahoma set me to sneezing violently. I recall that we had lunch on the way at a little mountain hotel which straddled a trout stream, and that hundreds of its fish were disporting in a pool just outside its door. During the afternoon we crossed the line into Arkansas, and there encountered the most barbaric white people I have ever seen. Some of the straggling villages that we passed through actually had no streets: the houses in them were simply set at random. In one of them we saw "Drugstore" on a house, and Hyde dropped off to buy some cascara. He came back with the news that the so-called druggist had never heard of cascara, though he stocked Cascarets. In several places we met migratory families camped by the roadside, and more than once we saw a mother sitting on a log with a child clasped between her knees, and busily engaged in picking lice from its head. We got to Muskogee late and tired, but considerably edified. The other Bixby had prepared a buffet supper for us, and all the town notables were invited. One of them was a surgeon. In the course of the evening another guest told me that this savant, in the heyday of the Ku Klux Klan, which raged with great violence in Oklahoma, had performed a number of castrations on its victims. He was greatly respected, for he had always done the operations in the grand manner, and had not lost a life.

We left Muskogee by sleeper for Fort Worth, and were there received by Carter. He was an assiduous entertainer, and had developed an elaborate ritual. On reaching town every guest was presented with two hats, one a huge Stetson and the other an elegant Borsolini. We were expected to put on the Stetsons at once, and them submit to being photographed for Carter's paper—alone, in groups, and with cow-girls who seemed to be kept for the purpose. This photographing was done on the main street, and I recall that I had to stand for a picture in front of a bronze tablet announcing that the building it adorned was a Methodist church. Carter put us up at the Fort Worth Club, in a roomy and airy suite including a cupboard stocked with whiskey, gin and cigars. That night we dined on the roof in pajamas—on T-bone steaks, the pride of Fort Worth, and well may it be proud of them—and the next day there was a large party at Carter's ranch, some miles out of town, with Will Rogers as one of the guests. Rogers came in from Oklahoma by air, and I went out to the airport to meet him. It was hot weather, and he was proceeding to Houston for the convention, but his entire baggage consisted of one small suitcase. As he shaved in the washroom at the airport I sat with him, and could not help seeing its contents. They embraced an extra suit of clothes, two shirts, a simple suit of cheap underwear, and three pairs of socks. As I was to learn later, he always traveled thus. One of his suits, brown in color, he used for day wear; the other, of blue, was for the evening. Both looked as if they had come from Sears-Roebuck. How he managed about laundry I never found out. He seldom, if ever, paid for his transportation by air. He would go out to an airport, find a pilot who was setting off in his general direction, say "Damned if I ain't got a mind to go along," and then climbed in. The result was that he traveled mainly in planes of the third, fourth and fifth class: they were dangerous, perhaps, but they cost nothing. It was this craze for free rides that finally cost him his life. When he encountered Wiley Post in August, 1935, and found that Post was just about to take off for Alaska and Russia in a homemade plane, he could not resist the temptation to climb aboard. On August 15 the plane cracked up in a remote part of Alaska, and both were killed. The night after the party at Carter's ranch the Junior League of Fort Worth gave a musical show at one of the theaters, and we all had to go. The night was appallingly hot and the show was dreadful, but Carter soon induced Rogers to give one of his speeches, and in five minutes the sweating audience was roaring with laughter, and Patterson, Hyde and I were sorry that we had to leave before he finished to board a train for Houston.

While we were in Fort Worth Hyde and I called upon the Rev. J. Frank Norris, pastor of the First Baptist Church and a famous ecclesiastic of those parts. We had heard that he was predicting that Hoover would carry Texas, and we wanted to hear his reasons for believing in that miracle. Texas had gone Democratic at every election since the Civil War, and by stupendous majorities: in 1924 Davis had beaten Coolidge there by a vote of 3 to 1, and in 1916 Wilson had beaten Hughes by 4 to 1. But Norris, when we found him, insisted that if Al Smith were nominated at Houston Hoover would carry the state by at least 250,000. We left him convinced that he was half insane, but when the votes were counted in November it turned out that he was more than half right. To be sure, Hoover's majority in Texas was not 250,000, but it was more than 25,000, and that was certainly revolution enough. Hyde and I found Norris to be a fellow of extraordinarily forbidding appearance and manner, with shifty eyes set too close together, a hard and cruel mouth, and the clipped, sidelong speech of a movie villain. Only two years before, on July 17, 1926, he had shot and killed a man in cold blood. This man, one D. E. Cripps, had called upon him to protest politely against accusations that he was making against H. C. Meacham, mayor of Fort Worth. There was no evidence whatever that Cripps had offered him the slightest menace, but he knew the Texas law which made it a sufficient defense to swear that he was in fear of his life, so he pulled a pistol and let go. All this happened in his study, beneath the very roof of his church. Put on trial, he got a change of venue to Austin, and was there acquitted under the law aforesaid. Hyde and I left him almost shivering: he was the most evil-looking man that either of us had ever encountered, though we had both met many criminals. His vicious character was known to all the decent people of Fort Worth, but he had so strong a hold on the morons that there was no way of getting rid of him.

When we got to Houston the next morning, June 23, we found a band playing in the station, and learned that it was there to welcome [the New York Democrat] James W. Gerard, who had come in on our train, not to attend the convention, but to harangue a gathering of West Texas Babbits. A large committee of welcome was present, and the plan was that the open automobile bearing Gerard should head a parade following the band. But when Patterson, Hyde and I jumped into a taxicab the driver barged in directly behind the band, and so we proceeded to the Rice Hotel, with Gerard looking daggers at us for stealing his spot. I had spoken to him in the station, but saw no more of him after the parade was over. He had by now shrunk to nothing, politically speaking, and none of the assembled politicos paid any attention to him. Our quarters on the eleventh floor of the sixteen-story Rice Hotel were comfortable enough, but we had run out of alcoholic refreshment, and looked forward to a dry week. Relief arrived quickly from two directions. First the Hogg brothers, sons of a former Governor of Texas, sent word that they had opened a house of mirth in another hotel, and invited us to use it. Secondly, Amon Carter arrived from Fort Worth the next day with an immense stock of liquors, and these he laid out for his friends in rooms near ours, with the sheriff of Fort Worth, elegantly bebadged and heavily armed, in charge. The Hogg brothers had converted a ballroom into an old-time saloon, with a wooden bar and sawdust on the floor. It served beer only. Hyde and I set out to investigate it at once, and came back with the melancholy report that everything was lovely save the beer, which had been made in Texas and was quite undrinkable.

The convention, like that at Kansas City, was without suspense, and hence rather flat, for everyone knew from the start that Al would be nominated without serious opposition. There was a short delay while he made it plain by long distance that while he was willing to accept a Law Enforcement platform he would endeavor, if elected, to procure the repeal of the Eighteenth Amendment, but after that things went almost too smoothly to be interesting. At the end of the first ballot Al was within ten votes of the two-thirds necessary to nominate him, so many states flopped at once, and before the count was announced he had polled 849⅔ and was the nominee. The only other considerable candidates were James A. Reed of Missouri, Walter F. George of Georgia, and Cordell Hull. It was obvious that Reed had no chance against Al; indeed, his effort to get the nomination was almost ludicrous. Nor did he help himself when he issued a statement proposing in substance that the Prohibition issue be shelved. On June 27, sitting in my room at the Rice Hotel, Frank R. Kent and I fell to discussing the old boy's situation, and presently several others joined in. While we talked some one brought in a strange young man and introduced him as a cub reporter on one of the Houston papers. We should have shut down at once, but it never occurred to us that the young stranger would write anything about what he heard. The next day his paper came out with a story in which all of Kent's and my lamentations over Reed's follies were set forth at length—with every line of them credited to me. It was an immensely embarrassing situation. I could not go to Reed with a disclaimer, for the youngster had reported the conversation accurately. I could not even explain that Kent's words had been put into my mouth, for I had agreed with them. Greatly upset, I consulted Reed's secretary, Hicklin Yates. He told me that, so far as he knew, the old man had not seen the story, and promised to keep it away from him if possible. There I had to let the matter rest. The young man's city editor, hearing of it during the day, offered gallantly to print a piece repudiating the story as false and apologizing for it to Reed and me, but that I could not permit, for it would have been grossly unjust to the reporter, whose only offense was the inexperience that led him to break what he didn't recognize as a confidence. Whether or not Reed actually saw the story I never learned.

I had to endure a number of other unpleasantnesses at Houston, and left it at last with a considerable distaste for it, and in fact for all Texas. The Texans were simply not my kind of people, and even when they were trying to be nice to me I found myself unpleasantly conscious of that difference. Amon G. Carter's hospitality at Fort Worth, though it was earnest and lavish, was more of a nuisance than a joy, and at Houston his attentions were worse. He came into my room two or three times a day, usually accompanied by his friend and retainer, the sheriff of Fort Worth, and the two of them wasted a great deal of my time. I had plenty to do to cover the convention for the *Evening Sun,* but in addition I was hard beset by *American Mercury* business, for several large packages of manuscript were waiting for me when I arrived at the Rice Hotel. One day the Fort Worth sheriff dropped in on me alone, with a copy of the *American Mercury* for July, 1928, under his arm. He had just read an article in it by Jim Tully, entitled "Shanty Irish," and wanted to discuss it. He had no objection, it appeared, to the article itself, but he considered the title an insult to the great race of Irishmen. Inasmuch as he was drunk, it was impossible to argue with him; moreover, I was too busy. I finally got rid of him by telling him that Tully, an Irishmen himself, looked upon "Shanty Irish" as an epithet of honor. He went away muttering, and tried to resume the debate every time I met him thereafter. He was a gigantic fellow, always drunk, and carried in a holster a huge pistol studded with rubies—a present from his admirers among the Fort Worth bootleggers.

Carter himself dropped in on me every few hours, and often brought strangers to be introduced. They were always tight, as was Carter himself. One afternoon, as I was sitting in my undershirt trying to knock out a dispatch for the *Evening Sun,* he appeared alone in very ebullient spirits, and refused to be got rid of. Finally, I had to turn my back on him, and resume my work. Suddenly he pulled a pistol and fired three shots out of the window. The aim of his volley, as I learned, was simply to entertain me pleasantly in the Texas fashion, but what ensued was an uproar that kept me busy for two hours. The cartridges, it quickly appeared, had been loaded with ball, and the three bullets hit a hotel across the street, close to the window of a room in which the Ku Kluxers were holding a caucus, with one of the town judges of Houston presiding. The Ku Kluxers, headed by the judge, rushed out howling that Al Smith had turned loose the Pope's sharpshooters on them, and in five minutes the Hotel Rice was swarming with Texas Rangers. As I found out afterward, some of them had to hoof all the way upstairs to the top floor, for the elevators, as usual, were jammed. Working downward they then began a systematic search of the whole building, to the tune of a great deal of shouting and running about. When a party of them knocked at my door Carter slipped his pistol under the mattress of my bed, and made off through the room adjoining, leaving me to engage them alone. I pretended, when they barged in and explained their business, to be greatly surprised, and protested that I was a hard-working newspaper correspondent, as they could see by my costume, and carried no arms, and knew nothing about any shooting. I had pretty well convinced them when one of them, smarter than the rest, espied the three bullet-holes through the fly-screen of my window. They then announced that I was under arrest, and would have to go to the lockup at once. While I was still arguing with them, the town judge, who had been following them, came in, and on his heels came Carter.

Carter had become miraculously sober, or so, at least, he seemed, and he proceeded at once to tackle both the judge and the cops. If I were cast into jail, he said, the whole country would ring with the scandal, and Texas would be made ridiculous. I was known as a peaceable and virtuous character by millions of people, and the charge that I had tried to shoot up Houston would make the whole world laugh. But what of the bullet-holes? demanded the cops. It was easy, replied Carter, to explain them. Eminent though I was, I was still subject to the calls of nature. Obviously, some miscreant had sneaked into my room while I was in the bath relieving my bladder and then fired at the Ku Kluxers and run off. It was, as everyone knew, a way that such enemies of the Southern *Kultur* had. And how came it that I had not heard the shots? Because the toilet made a noise, the bands playing outside in the street made more, and the convention hubbub in the hotel made still more. The town judge admitted that there was something in this defense, but insisted that my room was no place to try me: I should be taken before the proper authorities, and heard according to law. Meanwhile, the rangers searched my baggage, my writing table, my typewriter case, my bureau drawers, and even the clothes hanging in my closet, but by great good fortune they overlooked the bed, though the pistol under the mattress made a visible lump. I was in fear that they would find the last bottle of our stock of booze in the closet, but it did not appear, and I learned later that Patterson had taken it away that morning. While they searched Carter wrestled with the town judge, and finally, to my considerable astonishment, His Honor ordered the rangers to go no further. He was convinced, he said, that I knew nothing of the shooting. It must have been done by prowling Catholics from the North. He advised the rangers to round up all such persons then in town, and to give them brisk work-outs. I should add that His Honor, like nearly all the other Houstonians I met, was in liquor. But the cops were sober, and went away reluctantly and in bad humor. The instant they were out of sight I got Carter's pistol from under the mattress, handed it to him, and desired him to clear out at once.

Later in the day he fired it again—this time through a glass elevator door. As I have said, the hotel elevators were all jammed, and often a passenger waiting for one would have to wait while half a dozen went past him. This irritated Carter, and his protest took the form of firing through the door after the fifth or sixth elevator had flitted by. This time

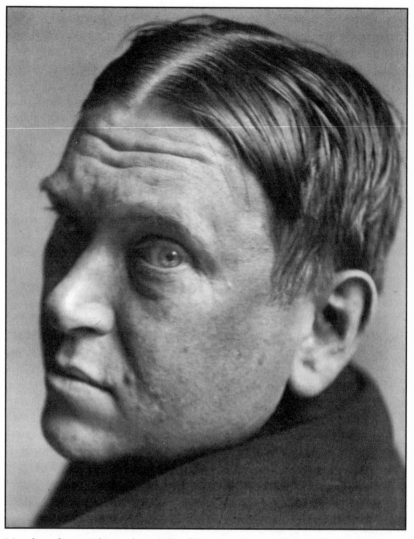

Mencken, forty-eight, at the zenith of his career. 1928. Robert H. Davis.

he was seized by bystanders, but the city cops, not connecting him with his first offense, let him go on the ground that no one had been hurt, and that firing a pistol was a natural sign of discontent in Texas. Later on the fact that he had fired the three shots from my window were known, but by that time he was back in Fort Worth and safe under the protection of his sheriff. All sorts of legends grew out of the two episodes. It was widely reported and believed that Carter and I had got into a quarrel, and that either I had fired at him or he had fired at me. It was also reported that he had fired through the elevator door into an elevator full of people, and wounded several of them. I suspect that he propagated these stories himself. He was a vain fellow, and eager to be respected as an exponent of Texan truculence. Indeed, he always spoke of himself, not as a simple Texan, but as a West Texan, which connoted a familiarity with firearms and a willingness to use them. After we got back to Baltimore Patterson wrote to the manager of the Rice Hotel asking him to send on the fly-screen with the three bullet-holes in it. This was done, and a segment of it showing the holes was framed. For some years thereafter it hung in Patterson's office.

At Houston Patterson and I called on Franklin D. Roosevelt, who placed Al Smith in nomination there and was staying at the Rice Hotel. We had no business with him, but paid him that small attention to please Van Lear Black. He was, at the time, almost completely disabled, and needed the constant care of his son Jimmie, then a tall, slim youth with nothing to say. He received us with his characteristic haw-hawing and back-slapping, and we stayed with him for an hour. I remember little of the conversation save that he was sure that Al would be elected in November. He predicted that anti-Catholic feeling in the South would wear itself out by election day, and that Al would carry all the Southern states. When I told him of the Rev. J. Frank Norris's prediction in Fort Worth he laughed at it as insane. As I have said, that was my own view of it at the time—and the view, I may add, of nearly all the politicos assembled at Houston, including the Texans. Everyone knew that Roosevelt hoped to be nominated for Governor of New York in succession to Al, and that he was counting on Al's support, but he choose to keep up the pretense that he was not seeking the nomination. When, on October 2, it was given to him by the New York state convention at Rochester, he telegraphed from Warm Springs, Ga., to its chairman, Oliver Cabana: "Every personal and family consideration has been and is against my becoming the candidate of the convention, but if by accepting I can help the splendid cause of our beloved Governor I will yield to your judgment." In 1939 or thereabout, meeting Al at a small dinner given by Samuel Kaplan in New York, I heard his bitter comment on this bogus reluctance. The problem confronting the New York Democrats, he told me, was to find a candidate free from any overt connection with Tammany, for he himself was a Tammany man, and it was feared that two Tammany candidates would provoke an alliance between the Republicans and the anti-Tammany Democrats. Al said that there were a dozen aspirants, but that one after the other had to be rejected for this reason or that. Finally, only Roosevelt remained, and so he was given the nomination. His chief qualifications were: first, that the name of Roosevelt was still glamorous in New York, and could be counted on to pick up some Republican votes; second, that Franklin's notorious complaisance made him satisfactory to Tammany, though he was not of it, just as it had made him satisfactory to the Anti-Saloon League in 1920; and third, that he had been one of Al's chief followers for some years, and his loyalty was supposed to be absolute. What that loyalty was actually worth was shown when he got into office early in 1929. From his first day at Albany he began to look toward the Democratic presidential nomination of 1932, and in a little while he was engaged in an elaborate and unscrupulous, and, as it turned out in 1932, successful effort to eliminate Al.

Soon after we got back from Houston Thomas J. McCartney, superintendent of the *Sun* Building, reported to Patterson that there had arrived a mysterious roll of news-print from the paper-mill the *Sun* patronized in Three Rivers, Canada. The mysterious thing about it was that it had been accompanied by a notice from John Chahoon, head of the mill, saying that it was not to be put on a press, but unwound by hand, and in the strictest confidence. Patterson ordered McCartney to open it—and inside was a full barrel of Pilsner beer. This beer was a present from Chahoon and his agent, Dick Crooker, the same who had gone to Havana with Patterson and me. In having it wound in a roll and sending the roll to Baltimore they had taken long chances, for if the customs officers had discovered the barrel there would have been a dreadful how-de-do. But now it was safe in Baltimore, and Patterson ordered it sent by night to his house in Guilford, where a select party of *Sun* men drank half its contents the same night, August 3, and bottled the remainder.

The *Sun,* of course, supported Al Smith in the campaign, though Frank Kent continued to hymn Hoover almost daily in his column on the first page. Unhappily, no one in the office believed that Al could win, and not many were convinced that he would make a competent President.

The best that could be said of him was that he was manifestly better than the shifty and inept Hoover.

When I complained to Patterson that the editorials of [John] Owens were feeble, and argued that we ought to do our whooping, not on the morgue-like editorial page, but on the first page, he got rid of me by asking me to prepare some specimens for such display. I did three and they were printed on September 5, 9 and 14. During the weeks following Owens himself tried his hand. I must confess that my three were almost though not quite as bad as his. {My first, printed in column two of the first page on September 5, displaced Frank Kent's The Great Game of Politics, which was dropped for the day. Patterson made only one small change. The phrase "a perfumer of scoundrels" in paragraph four was expunged and "an unprotesting associate of scoundrels in high places" was substituted. This, of course, was a reference to Fall, Harry Daugherty, Jesse Smith and company.} I had, in fact, little stomach for the campaign. I was against Hoover rather than for Al. Hoover seemed to me to be a plainly nefarious character—a schemer with a highly dubious business record who had entered the late war as an Englishman, and discovered that he was an American only when the prospect and promise of high political office began to excite him. For a year after his return to the United States he could not make up his mind whether he was a Republican or a Democrat. Now he had got the nomination by the use of money, and was trying to win the election by pussyfooting on the dominant issue of Prohibition. Al was at least a relatively frank man, and tried to tell the truth as he saw it. Unhappily, I became convinced, after listening to him day in and day out on one of his campaign tours, that he was, on most matters of national importance, a complete ignoramus, and that if he were elected he would be in the hands of a gang of New York Jews, all of them with something to sell. I continued to advocate his election in my Monday articles in the *Evening Sun,* but, as I say, that was mainly because I longed—though I did not expect—to see Hoover not only beaten, but altogether eliminated from public life.

I joined Al at Richmond, Va., on October 10 for his tour of the border states, and was accompanied by Henry M. Hyde, with J. Fred Essary covering the tour for the morning paper. It led through Tennessee to Kentucky and then into Missouri, with a final hullabaloo in Chicago. The routine of life on the train was the same nearly every day. Al would spend the morning and the early afternoon making brief impromptu speeches from the rear platform, and seeing the local politicians who swarmed aboard at every stopping place, bringing their local reporters and photographers. Meanwhile, the Jewish brain trust that he carried labored hard at its files and card indexes, concocting his formal speech for the evening. The principal members of this brain trust were Bernard L. Shientag and Joseph M. Proskauer, the former a justice of the City Court of New York who was to become, in 1930, a justice of the Supreme Court of New York State, and the latter a justice of the same Supreme Court. They had the usual battery of secretaries, and worked with great industry and a complete lack of humor. Toward the middle of the afternoon they would give Al his speech of the evening, and he would order a highball and sit down to study it. Two times out of three it dealt with matters—for example, the tariff—that were wholly beyond his ken, and not infrequently there were large sections of it that he could not understand at all. But he sweated through it faithfully, and made copious notes from it on cards. It was from these cards that he spoke in the evening—and often he wandered far from the brain trust's text. But inasmuch as that text was sent out by the press associations in time for the earliest editions of the morning papers, and was put into type at once, it usually appeared the next morning as Al's speech. What he actually said was taken down by stenographers, and issued to the correspondents in the press-stand, sheet by sheet, by a force of mimeographers at work under the speakers' stand. But these stenographic reports were necessarily late, and the correspondents of only a few papers ever sent them out. What the great majority of the American people took to be Al's speeches were the drafts prepared for him by Proskauer, Shientag and company. The *Sun* itself often printed these drafts, greatly to the discontent of Stanley M. Reynolds, then its managing editor.

Al was, in those days, a very effective mob orator, especially when stoked with Scotch, and his speeches went off with great effect, even in plainly hostile territory. This was true, for example, in Louisville, where the gallery was full of heelers of the Republican city administration, and the Republican cops actually tried to wreck the meeting by turning on the steam heat in the hall. Al sweated like a bull, and so did the rest of us, but he refused to give up, and before he finished he had the reluctant crowd applauding. In Sedalia, Mo., there was one of the largest and noisiest meetings I have ever seen. It was held in a vast building built for cattle shows, and yokels poured in for it in their Fords, not only from all parts of Missouri, but also from Kansas, Oklahoma, Iowa and Nebraska, and even from Texas and Colorado. In the front row, when Al began at 8 P.M., there were farmers and their wives who had been sitting there since

8 A.M., when the hall opened. What he discussed that evening I forget: all I recall is that his discourse was confused and unilluminating—and that the audience greeted it with such yells that they were actually deafening. Never in this life have I heard anything to match the roar when he first appeared. It was a mixture of bellow and screech, and fairly bruised the ears. Not even the Tammany heelers at the New York convention of 1924, for all their fire-engine sirens and other machines, had made so much noise. But when the votes were counted in November Hoover had carried Missouri by nearly 175,000, which was more than double Coolidge's majority in 1924. In Pettis county, of which Sedalia is the county-seat, Hoover won by a vote of almost two to one. On October 30 Al came to Baltimore for a meeting in the Fifth Regiment Armory. Once again the uproar was enormous, but, despite the heavy Catholic vote in the city and the eager support of the Jews, he lost it by nearly 10,000.

Throughout the campaign there was a great deal of whispering against Al's wife, Catherine. She was depicted in these calumnies as a gross and ignorant creature but little removed from a washerwoman, and there were countless stories of her social gaucheries and conversational malapropisms. There was little truth in them. It was plain at a glance, of course, that she was not a duchess, but she had been the governor's lady, by 1928, for seven years, and knew very well how to conduct herself and take care of herself. I saw her constantly on the campaign train and sat directly under her every evening—for my colleague, Hyde, being somewhat deaf, always went to the hall early and grabbed a seat directly under the speakers' stand, with another beside it held for me. Kitty was thus seldom more than ten feet from me. I must confess that her preference for purple dresses did not please me, but I am glad to record for posterity that she had slim and graceful legs. Her upper works were on the heavy side, but her legs were impeccable. The Democratic national committee had provided her with a social adviser in the person of Mrs. Charles Dana Gibson, a sister to Lady Astor and one of the famous Langhorne sisters of Virginia. Mrs. Gibson fluttered about the train, especially when female politicos came aboard, but I do not believe that her services were needed, for Kitty knew female politicos far better than she did. One day, as I was sitting in my compartment writing a dispatch for the *Evening Sun* and had just taken a large chew of tobacco to facilitate parturition, La Gibson walked in on me announced, and I nearly strangled before I managed to get rid of her. Al's chief woman confident, Mrs. Belle Moskowitz, a New York social worker, was not aboard: she was simply too fat to travel. Once, earlier in the campaign, I called on her in New York, and found her really himalayan. In 1933 her ever-increasing obesity finally killed her.

I greatly enjoyed the tour with Al, for he always gave a good show and travelling in the company of Henry Hyde was very pleasant. The days of crowded sleepers were now over, and Hyde and I had a comfortable compartment together. He was from Freeport, Ill., and deep down in him lurked a black Republican. He liked Al and probably voted for him, but could not get rid of a congenital distrust of Democrats, especially of Catholic Democrats. "This is a brave fellow," he would say, "but he is doomed. The American people simply won't stand for him." Inasmuch as I was of the same opinion, we did not quarrel. On the morning of October 13, somewhere in rural Kentucky above Bowling Green, he and I were minor figures in a charming interlude. Al had spoken in Nashville the night before and was to speak in Louisville the night of the thirteenth. The distance between the two cities was too short for an all-night run, and moreover, Al needed some quiet, so the train was side-tracked a couple of hours after it left Nashville, and remained dark and still until morning. When Hyde and I turned out we found ourselves in a lovely little valley in the Blue Grass country. There was yet an hour or two before the train would resume the journey to Louisville, and we accordingly decided to take a walk along the track. A little way down the line a white fence ran beside the right-of-way, and hanging over it we found two buxom country girls. They not only greeted us politely, but invited us to come to their house, which stood in a grove of trees nearby. When we got to the house they introduced us to their mother, who asked us to breakfast, and when we declined, insisted on us trying her home-made wine—at 6:30 A.M.! She was, it appeared, an ardent Al fan, and she and her two daughters would vote for him. All they asked in return was a Federal job for another daughter, not then present. This other daughter was now a schoolma'm, but yearned to be postmistress at the small village just visible down the tract. Hyde, a very gallant fellow, promised it to her on the spot. "I'll see the Governor," he said, "the minute he is astir, and your daughter will get the place the day he is inaugurated." What is more, Hyde actually saw Al when we got back to the train, and Al duly ratified the promise. Unhappily, he was never inaugurated, and during the four years of Hoover some Republican held the postmastership. But when the Democrats came to power in 1933 the fond mother wrote to both Hyde and me, suggesting that Roosevelt ought to make good on Al's promise. Hyde took this suggestion to Jim Farley, now Postmaster General, and Jim, after hearing the story, declared that it would be done. But when he issued an order for the daughter's appointment, it was returned to his desk with a reminder that postmasterships of the sort she wanted were now in the classified service. This meant that she would have to take an examination before she could be appointed. Jim ordered the examination at once—and the poor girl failed to pass it.

Ever since my return to the *Sunpapers* at the beginning of 1920 I had turned in no expense accounts. If I went off on an out-of-town assignment, of course, the office bought my tickets, and at national conventions and other such affairs it paid my hotel bills, but all other expenses I paid myself. This was mainly because I regarded myself as a sort of part-time worker: a good deal of my time, in fact, was always consumed by my magazine duties, and by my constantly increasing mail. It was not until the campaign of 1940 that I began turning in expense accounts. I did so then because, by that time, I had no other business in hand; moreover, I had begun to see the force of Patterson's argument that my compensation, whatever it was, ought to be clear, and that the paper, as in the case of all other members of the staff, should reimburse me for my out-of-pocket outlays. By 1940, alas, I had come to view the *Sun* less sentimentally than aforetime. Most of my old dreams for it had gone a-glimmering, and working for it had begun to seem less a glorious adventure than it once was and more a mere chore. I believe it is reasonable to say that, during my long connection with the paper, I never gave much thought to my pay. In my Free Lance days I worked for a decidedly lower salary than I could have got elsewhere, and after I resumed writing for the *Evening Sun* in 1920 it paid me much less than my constantly increasing market rate, as my contract with the Chicago *Tribune* from 1924 to 1927 demonstrated. All the advances in compensation that were made after 1920 were made by Patterson voluntarily, and not at my solicitation. There was never a time when I could not have gone to some other paper at much better pay. I stuck to the *Sun* for many reasons, and all of them seem sound in retrospect. Its office was a pleasant one to work in, it gave me a great deal of freedom, and it was in Baltimore, close to the base I did not want to leave. Moreover, the paper, in a large sense, was my own. I had helped to fashion it, and was proud of such progress as it had made, though I always complained that that progress had not gone far enough or fast enough. It was not until 1941 that Patterson convinced me at last that the future was hopeless. How that came to pass will be told in its proper place.

My Monday articles for the editorial page of the *Evening Sun* in 1928 were largely suggested by the two conventions of the year, the Al

Smith campaign, and the Pan-American Conference at Havana. The conference produced two—"The Spanish Main" on January 30 and "The Clowns Go Home" on February 21, the latter of which described the show as "one of the most idiotic futilities ever heard of." I began the discussion of the campaign on April 23 in an article with the perhaps unmatchably short title of "Al," and proceeded to "The Impending Combat" on May 28, "Al and the Pastors" on August 6, "The Hoover Manifesto" (his speech of acceptance) on August 13, "Real Issues at Last" on July 23, "Civil War in the Confederacy" on July 30, "Onward, Christian Soldiers" on August 24, "The Campaign Opens" on August 27, "The Show Begins" on September 3, "Der Wille zur Macht" ["The Will to Power"] on September 10, "Prophetical Musings" on September 17, "Al in the Free State" on October 29, "The Eve of Armageddon" on November 5, and "Autopsy" on November 12, after election day. I was strongly for Al, not because I had much belief in his fitness for the Presidency, but because I greatly disliked and distrusted Hoover. But I was well aware—perhaps much better aware than most—of the extent and virulence of anti-Catholic prejudice in the United States, and so I had but small hope of his victory in November, and none at all after the opening of the campaign. His defeat, of course, was anything but an unmixed evil in my sight, for a journalist thrives best in opposition, and is tremendously hobbled when his candidate wins, as the case of Frank R. Kent was presently to show once more. On November 7 I wrote to Sara Haardt: "Now for four years of the Anti-Saloon League and good hunting."

10

No Desire to Be
Admired by Morons

1929–1931

Despite the Hoover Prosperity the year 1929 was one of cataclysmic changes among American newspapers. The New York *World,* once so enormously profitable, was fast going downhill, and there were frequent rumors that it was to be sold or suspended. Finally, on January 31, 1931, the incompetent and cowardly heirs of its founder, Joseph Pulitzer, knocked down its remains to Roy W. Howard, who abandoned the morning issue and amalgamated the evening with what was left of the *Telegram,* once the evening edition of the New York *Herald.* The *Sun* had ceased taking its news service, which had been deteriorating for years, in 1928, and was now in miscegenous alliance with the New York *Herald Tribune,* with an office in the *Tribune* building, and young Dewey L. Fleming as resident correspondent. Another important paper that was notoriously wobbling was the New York *Evening Post,* and yet another was the Washington *Post.* Some one—I don't know who it was—proposed to Patterson that he take over the *Evening Post,* though without giving up his place on the *Sunpapers,* and he discussed the proposal with me at length. I was against it, and said so, and he soon agreed. About the same time there came a proposal that he take over the Washington *Post* on the same terms, and this tempted him more sorely, for he had been general manager of the Munsey paper in Washington before coming to Baltimore, and liked the town. Moreover, he believed that the *Post,* properly managed, might be converted into a really first-rate newspaper. He went so far in the matter as to propose that I join him by taking its editorship, but when I refused he dropped it.

I did less writing for the *Sunpapers* in 1929 than I had done in any year since 1920. Patterson proposed, in August, that I go down to Charlotte, N.C., to cover the trial of Fred E. Beal and the other labor radicals accused of the murder of Chief of Police O. F. Aderholt, but when the time came I was glad that a severe attack of hay-fever made it impossible for me to do so. The year was shadowed for me by the continued illness of Sara Haardt, whom I was to marry in 1930. After her bout with tuberculosis of the lungs in 1924 she had so far recovered by the end of 1927 that she was able to go to Hollywood and attempt some writing for the movies, but in 1928 she was ill again and had to have some major surgery, and in the late Spring of 1929 there followed another and quite unrelated illness which required even more severe surgery. The day she went on the table at the Union Memorial Hospital was one of really infernal heat, and both the patient and the surgeon, Dr. Edward H. Richardson, were almost overcome by it. She made a slow and painful recovery, and it was not until September that she was discharged from hospital. Dr. George Walker, whom I have previously mentioned, was very kind to her during her long illness, though he was not in professional attendance upon her, save as a consultant to Dr. Richardson. Unhappily, he took a gloomy view of her chances of recovery, and one night he called me up in Hollins street, and told me that he thought she would die. I was trying, at the time, to finish my "Treatise on the Gods," but this news wrecked me for a week. By that time Walker had become more optimistic, and so I resumed my writing. My own health was not at its best in 1929, for in addition to my usual spell of hay-fever in the Autumn I suffered nearly all year from a troublesome sinus infection, the lingering product of my trip to Havana early in 1928. This sinus infection, in fact, bothered me off and on until 1940, when it finally cleared up. I finished "Treatise on the Gods" on Thanksgiving night, 1929. By this time Sara was nearly recovered, and thereafter, for several years, her health was better than it had been since 1924. My contributions to the editorial page of the *Evening Sun* in 1929 covered my usual range, and were of small importance. I wrote an obituary of the Coolidge administration, under the title of "Exit," for March 4, but devoted less space during the year to politics than to Prohibition. Unlike John Owens, I believed that the Anti-Saloon League would be unhorsed soon or late, but I suspected that the battle would be a long one, and so I kept banging away. On May 6 I protested in my space against the unfairness of the trial of Harry F. Sinclair, the oil magnate—and incidentally got a letter of thanks from Sinclair after he was in jail; on May 20 I printed a piece, by now an annual, on "Bach at Bethlehem"; on June 10 I took another hack at the decaying Johns Hopkins; on June 17 I discussed the Mooney case; on November 25 I denounced "The Charity Racket," and on November 18 and December 9 I printed two more installments of my projected "Notes for an Honest Autobiography."

The stock market crash of October, 1929, did not surprise me, and thus made less impression on me than on most. I had been looking for it, in fact, ever since the rise of the Coolidge Prosperity, and had been at pains to keep my own money out of speculative investments. The result was that when the blow fell at last I lost comparatively little: indeed, I was enchanted, a year or two later, to learn that my losses had been much less, per dollar of net worth, than those of J. Pierpont Morgan & Company. It seemed to me then, and it seems to me now, that the explosion of October 23 and the long Depression that followed were the natural and inevitable effects of American entrance into World War I in 1917—a folly so stupendous that the American people will probably be a century realizing its full imbecility. Early in the Spring of 1928 [1929], fully convinced that major disaster was in the offing, I made plans for another trip to Europe, but Sara's illness forced me to postpone it, and I did not get off until December 28, when I sailed from New York in the *Columbus* of the North-German Lloyd. We had become engaged a little while before this, but our engagement was not announced until the Summer of 1930. In the *Columbus* I spent my second New Year's Day at sea. Also aboard was Dudley Field Malone, along with his fiancée, a Swedish girl from Chicago, obviously of the stage and by name Edna Louise Johnson. His marriage to Doris Stevens had blown up soon after the Scopes trial, and he was to take La Johnson as his third bride in London on January 29. I put in most of the voyage gabbling with him, for he was excellent company. Fritz Kreisler, the violinist, was also aboard, with his American wife. Dudley, La Johnson and I celebrated New Year's Eve with them, and Mrs. Kreisler, as I recall it, got considerably lighted up. I landed at Cherbourg and went to Paris, where my friend Goodman, then at the height of his success as a theatrical manager, was staying with his wife and daughter. I put up at their quiet hotel, the Tremoille, and for the next week he and I spent most of our time together, eating, drinking and walking about. There was at that time a great fashion for German beer in Paris, and we tried all the brews on tap, including the incomparable Kulmbacher at the Reine Pedoque restaurant. Goodman knew Paris a great deal better than I did, and he showed me many things that I had missed in the past, for example, the incredibly lovely stained glass of the Sainte Chapelle. I also saw a number of other friends, among them, Ludwig Lewisohn, Régis Michaud (my French translator), and the J.A.M. de Sanchez who had helped to play the practical joke on Aristide Briand at Washington in 1921. I also called on Emma Goldman, the anarchist, who was living in a Paris suburb, and met Blanche Knopf, my publisher's wife, who handed me my first copy of "Treatise on the Gods," which had been brought out by her husband in record time. I found La Goldman occupying a luxurious studio, lent to her by some rich and admiring artist, and served by a secretary and maid. I was accompanied on my visit to her by Stanton Leeds, formerly Washington correspondent of the New York *Evening Mail* and an old friend. She had tea brought in and we drank it in an exceedingly refined and bourgeois manner.

On January 10 the Goodmans left for Cherbourg and home, and the next day I boarded the Orient Express for Vienna. I knew no one there save Mrs. Paula Arnold, the *Sun*'s correspondent, and Dr. Andor Juhász, my Hungarian translator, so I looked forward to spending a quiet week, but after a few days a woman reporter for the Chicago *Tribune* (Paris edition) discovered me at the Bristol Hotel, and after that I was kept jumping. The American correspondents insisted on introducing me at the Foreign Office, and there, to my considerable astonishment, I was assigned a desk in the press-room. Among them I recall M. W. Fodor, then working for the *Nation* and afterward an occasional *Sun* correspondent, and Whit Burnett, who was the New York *Sun* correspondent. Burnett and his wife, Martha Foley, founded the magazine, *Story*, in Vienna a year later, and in 1933 moved it to New York; both contributed to the *American Mercury* after my return home. I had to go to several newspaper parties, but managed to hear some capital music, and also saw something of Vienna. I well recall my emotions when I came upon the grave of Beethoven in the Central Friedhof, with its incomparable guard of honor—Mozart, Schubert, Gluck, Brahms, Hugo Wolf and Johann Strauss! Mrs. Arnold took me to see Schönbrunn (now a sanitarium for the proletariat), and the huge blocks of workers' flats that the radical city administration had erected in one of the suburbs, but I was not much interested in such things. On January 14 I wrote to Goodman:

> The china washbowl and pitcher put in by Metternich after the Congress of Vienna are still in service in the men's washroom of the Opera House. But who gives a damn? I heard "Cosi Fan Tutti" last night, done with

Modernist decorations and superbly sung. It was, in fact, a gaudy evening, and I got lost afterward trying to find a Hungarian eating-house in the Spiegelgasse. Today I searched for it again, and had to give it up. Maps are useless in such a place. The streets seem to be moved from day to day.

My hotel room costs $8.40 a day. But what a room! The bathroom hardware, put together, would probably touch 200 lbs. There are two telephones, a day bed that breaks into two halves, 18 lights, and five mirrors. All the light pushbuttons are in triplicate. The wallpaper shows roses, carnations, tulips, orchids, parrots, canaries and birds of paradise, all in full colors.

As for the victuals, I put Sacher very close to the Petit Durand. True enough, the head-waiter looks like a head-waiter, and not like an American statesman, but I don't think of it when the pork goulasch, with sauerkraut, comes on. Or the goose-liver omelette. Or the chocolate cake with the coffee. I spent two days here thinking that the Schilling was at 7 cents. Now I find it is at 14. The shock is serious, but I have decided to go on eating as usual.

After a week or so in Vienna I proceeded to Budapest, but stayed only a few days, for the weather was wet and cold. Knowing no Hungarian, I employed a Jew who spoke more or less German as a guide. This Jew took me, among other places, to the great church at Buda, in which the right hand of St. Stephen, the patron saint of Hungary, is preserved. When we got there the church was deserted, and he led me behind the high altar for a close view of the hand in the glass reliquary. The light being somewhat dim, he opened the reliquary, grabbed the hand, brought it forth, and bade me admire it. I got him away as quickly as possible, trembling lest some priest or verger come in and turn us over to the police. But no one appeared. On January 19 I wrote to Goodman:

> Just a line to report that the Paprika-Huhn at the Spolarich [restaurant] is absolutely, superbly, magnificently *kolossal*. I got down a whole chicken—all save the neck and one leg. I shall go back to eat the rest in an hour. What paprika! What *Spätzle!* And what chicken!
>
> The beer that goes with it is Hungarian, and almost perfect. It is what Spaten used to be when we were young—rich, creamy, caressing. There is no gas in it, but only malt and hops. The belch that follows is no vulgar blast, but a soft, refined little pooplet. . . . In two days I'll be on my way to London. It will be like moving from Paris to Cherbourg.

And on January 20:

> If you laugh I must bear it patiently: in such matters ignorance is an excuse. What I mean to say is that the *Székely gulyás* at the Spolarich stands clearly ahead of any victual obtainable by ordinary barter in Paris—not far ahead, perhaps, but still ahead. I go further: it is probably the noblest dish obtainable in the civilized world. And why? Simply because everything perfect is in it—the incomparable paprika of the Magyars, the exquisite sauerkraut (with a few aniseeds) of Vienna, and the honest hog-meat that is the hallmark of Christian culture everywhere. I got stuck in the middle of the second order; with your aid and example I might have gone into a third. The ensuing belch had a magnificent recoil. I fell back in my chair, breathing heavily like a man who has just mastered an Alp. With it goes Paracelsus *Dunkles,* on which I reported in my dispatch of yesterday. It has merit. The *Helles* of the Spolarich, Haggenmacher by name, is much inferior. In fact, it tastes precisely like Moerlein, and has the same curious fetor.

The Naval Conference scheduled to meet in London on January 21 was a sort of second act of the Washington Conference of 1921. Patterson planned to cover it in what, by now, had come to be the usual elaborate manner of the *Sunpapers*. He had asked me to join their staff, writing for the *Evening Sun,* and I accordingly left Vienna on January 21, the day the conference opened.

In London I found Patterson established in a large and expensive suite at the Savoy Hotel, overlooking the Thames. With him were John W. Owens, Dewey L. Fleming (then the *Sun*'s London correspondent) and Drew Pearson, who was a member of the Washington bureau, covering the State Department. My low view of the 1921 conference had led me to expect nothing of this new one. "I shall make short work of it," I wrote to Goodman on November 27, 1929. "It is bound to be a swindle, and it will take me no more than ten days to write all I care to about it". The most it could accomplish, it seemed to me, was to postpone for a few years the inevitable World War II. The American delegation, headed by the fanatical Anglomaniac Henry L. Stimson, then Secretary of State under Hoover, was easy hunting for the English, who were now looking forward uneasily toward that next war, and already making plans to rope the United States as their banker and gunman once again. At Washington in 1921 their main effort had been to regain control of the seas; but now, having regained it, they devoted themselves to lightening the burden of maintaining it. To that end they proposed various schemes of ship-scrapping, all of them designed to favor their own navy. Stimson, a dreadful ass, was no match for them. They got him socially, and they got him every other way. On the editorial page of the *Evening Sun* for March 31, after I had returned home, I described him as "one of the sorriest representatives ever sent to discuss a grave matter by a great nation." He looked, I added, "like a plate-pusher in a somewhat fashionable suburban church." All the other delegates were heavily beset by social attention, and all of them save Dwight Morrow quickly succumbed. The English, on such occasions, do a gang job. The visitor who fails to fall for duchesses is tried by bankers, and if the bankers can't fetch him the literati or scientificoes or fox-hunters or artists take a hack at him. If he still holds out he is tackled by stage stars, movie queens and kept women. In London in 1930 this diverse and protean camorra was turned upon the newspaper correspondents as well as upon the delegates. I myself received invitations to at least half a dozen swell parties, two of them given by duchesses, before I had been in town three days. I dropped the large and elegant cards of invitation into my waste-basket at the Savoy, but a week or so later, curious to see how the game worked, I accepted a summons to luncheon from one of the Guiness women. She turned out a gaudy feed (for England) and gave the other guests (some of whom were very beautiful women) to understand that I was an author of parts and very influential in the United States. Seeking to do my share of the entertaining, I ventured upon a few anecdotes of my travels, and among other stories told the one about the Hollander on a visit home which I was to retell years afterward in a sketch called "Old Home Day." My previous tales had gone well, but this one was an obvious flop. I did not discover the reason therefor until I got back to the Savoy. There I learned that the fourth husband of the hostess, sitting at the far bottom of her table, was himself a Hollander, though he now lived in London, well nourished by the Guiness money.

The French delegation to the conference was headed by André Tardieu, a highly dubious politician, and, next to the Rev. J. Frank Norris, of Dallas, Texas, the most evil-looking man I have ever seen. The chief Italian spokesman was Dino Grandi, then Mussolini's Foreign Secretary: he wore the fan-shaped beard that was just coming into fashion in Italy, and was in all ways the most picturesque figure at the sessions. Some time afterward Grandi fell out of Mussolini's graces and was consigned to the dog-house. Tardieu survived until the fall of France in 1940, when the new Petain government either locked him up or chased him out of the country—I forget which. The boss of the English outfit was J. Ramsay

Macdonald, then Prime Minister, with A. V. Alexander, First Lord of the Admiralty, as his first aide. They were assisted in their labors by a great swarm of lawyers, "experts," press-agents and back-scratchers, including the duchesses, bankers, literati and whores aforesaid. The idiot Stimson was aided in presenting the vague and uncertain American case by Charles G. Dawes, Vice-President under Coolidge and in 1930 ambassador to England; Charles Francis Adams, Secretary of the Navy; two Senators, David A. Reed of Pennsylvania and Joseph T. Robinson of Arkansas; and two ambassadors, Hugh Gibson (Belgium) and Dwight W. Morrow (Mexico). I got enough by February 13 and sailed for home on the *Bremen*. The conference dragged on until April 22, and the ensuing treaty was dutifully ratified by the Senate on July 21. I wrote in the *Evening Sun* on February 21:

> The English have definitely renounced their dream, so enchanting in the first years after the late war, of pulling down and disposing of Uncle Shylock. They have discovered suddenly that the business is a sheer physical impossibility. Their aim now is to make terms with him, to keep in his good graces, and to get him on their side.

As a slave, of course—not as a possible rival. With the aid of his agents they managed to trim the French and Italian fleets, but they did not neglect to trim his fleet also, at least in spots where it threatened danger to them. By the treaty the United States agreed to scrap four battleships, beside many other craft. In 1939, again at the behest of England, whose control has by now been perfected, it began feverish preparations to replace them.

But despite the fact that the conference rapidly degenerated into low comedy I enjoyed my three weeks in London. I shared a room with Patterson in the lordly suite at the Savoy, and had a great deal of time on my hands, for I wrote very little for the *Evening Sun*. John Owens and I searched London for good eating-houses, but found them scarce. The best was Simpson's in the Strand, but even Simpson's quickly palled, and when we essayed to find out how many successive dinners we could eat in it we blew up after the third.

One of my principal duties was to help Patterson entertain the voracious Englishmen who swarmed in our suite at the Savoy, attracted by the free drinks on tap and the off chance of making some money out of visiting Americans. One of the most assiduous of these customers was Hector C. Bywater, naval correspondent of the London *Daily Telegraph*,

Five years after the trial of John Scopes, Mencken entertains Clarence Darrow at 704 Cathedral Street, Baltimore. 1930.

who had been writing for the *Sun* since 1921, and was contributing to our daily grist now. Once he got into our rooms his thirst was such that it was almost impossible to get rid of him. On several evenings he sat until long after midnight. This sponging finally irked Patterson, and he adopted various devices to keep Bywater out. When we got home he was notified that his contributions to the *Sun* would be no longer required. On January 29 Dudley Field Malone was married to La Johnson at a swagger hotel in the presence of a large party. Dudley, in those days, was a successful international lawyer, and had many acquaintances in London. His best man was Sir William Jowitt, Attorney General in the current Labor government. Will Rogers was covering the conference for his papers, and he and I went to the wedding together. I sent the bride a piece of silver bought in Regent street, but to this day I have never had any acknowledgement of it from her. Van Lear Black was in London when the *Sunpaper* brethren came in, preparing to start out on another crazy journey in his airship. A few days before he sailed we gave him a farewell cocktail party at the Savoy, and invited all the American notables then in town. It was a large affair, and I spent four or five hours mixing the cocktails. How many I made altogether I don't know, but I remember that I used up several cases of gin.

James Bone invited Patterson and me to spend a Sunday with him at his hide-away at Hankley Common, near Aldershot, but the weather was raw and cold and I had heard that the heating and plumbing arrangements at Hankley were those of Inner Mongolia, so I pleaded that I had work to do. That work consisted in signing the flyleaves of a *de luxe* edition of "Treatise on the Gods." The flyleaves had been sent to London from New York. There were 375 of them altogether, and 365 copies were for sale. The job took me a couple of hours, but I was very well paid for it, for my royalty upon the 365 copies, all of which were sold, was $1 a copy. When Patterson and Owens arrived back from Hankley they were far gone in liquor. Their excuse was that Bone's little cottage was as cold as an ice-house, and that there was nothing to drink save Scotch. When they sobered up they were full of amazing specifications. There was no way to take a bath, for the only well on the place was polluted. There was also no toilet save an outdoor Chick Sale. The roof of the house was of thatch, the windows were so small that they admitted hardly any light, and the nearest provision-shop was so far away that food had to be taken down from London. Jim drank Scotch, with occasional small dilutions of bottled soda, but his wife Annie, who preferred water, had to get it in bottles from a neighbor half a mile away. When I was in London in 1935 with my brother August Jim invited us to Hankley, but I again refused.

But though I thus escaped Hankley I had to go when Patterson, Owens and I were invited to spend a week-end at Manchester as the guests of the *Guardian*. Bone, who was and is a director in the paper, accompanied us, and we were very hospitably received. Old C. P. Scott, the editor of the paper, entertained us at an excessively formal dinner at his house, with his charming daughter, the widowed Mrs. C. E. Montagu, as hostess, and the Lord Mayor of Manchester and other notables among the guests. The next night the staff of the *Guardian* dined us at the National Liberal Club, much more informally. I happened to sit next to a Manchester cotton man, Thomas D. Barlow by name, who turned out to be a Rhine wine fan, and he invited me to dine with him at the Savage Club in London the following week. There were six men at that Savage Club dinner, and six bottles of the most magnificent German wine I have ever tasted. The food, English-like, was to the windward side of indifferent, but the wines were super-colossal. When I heard, in 1935, that

Barlow had been knighted I sounded a hearty Amen. The night following
the Scott dinner, which was dull but short, the editorial writers of the
Guardian gave us a party at the Manchester Press Club which lasted
until 5 A.M. I noted, some time after 3 o'clock, that the bar was still open,
and asked one of the Manchester city councilmen, who had been invited
to help entertain us, how that had been managed, for the general closing-
hour in England was 11 P.M., and even the most favored West End restaurants in London had extensions that expired at 1 A.M. The councillor,
who was tight, confessed to me confidentially that the club really had
no liquor license at all. It simply bootlegged, trusting to the fact that the
Manchester police would hardly raid a place frequented by city councilmen, who were their bosses. This was but one of the many evidences I
picked up that the celebrated rigidity of English law was largely imaginary. The saloons in London, even in Fleet street, closed at 11 P.M., but
Rule's and a few other chop-houses nearby had extensions good until
midnight, the principal West End restaurants got extensions to 1 A.M. in
rotation, two by two, and anyone rich enough to stop at a big hotel
could get drinks in his room all night. Patterson and I often tested this at
the Savoy. Once we ordered a pitcher of beer at 3:30 A.M., and got it
without question. At Manchester we were put up at the Midlands Hotel,
a place so vast that it had three barrooms on the ground floor. But there
was no central heating and there were no private baths. One bleak afternoon John Owens and I, who roomed together, ordered a coal fire in our
room. It took the maid half an hour to set it going—and then it almost
roasted us. The same maid brought us hot water for shaving in the morning—about three gallons in a huge copper pitcher. There were two groups
of communal toilets on every floor, and near the grand staircase was a
sort of traffic cop, to direct guests to vacancies.

Ted Scott, son of old C. P., and his lovely wife took us on an automobile trip to Chester, and we enjoyed it very much. Poor Scott, a few
years later, was drowned in Lake Windermere—a serious loss to the
Guardian, for he was a highly competent fellow, and his father, by that
time, was also dead. Mrs. Scott took me to her house to show me the
kitchen arrangements. The house was large and the Scotts were well-to-
do, but there was no refrigerator in the kitchen, and the stove burned
coal. When Mrs. Scott wanted a piece of ice she had to send to the fish-
monger's for it, and she told me that it usually smelled of fish. She had to
buy butter in quantities sufficient only for a few meals, for there was no
way of keeping it sweet. On February 3 I wrote to Goodman:

I spent the week-end in Manchester. It is a story verging upon the fabulous. You shall hear it when I return. If you don't bust into a giggle now and then I'll be astounded. Manchester is really a museum piece. The very towels in the hotel are Gladstonian.

The *Guardian* brethren were extremely polite, but I must confess that they made only an indifferent impression upon me. John Owens seemed to believe that they were masters of journalism, but I dissented sharply, then as always. The truth is that they got out a very poor paper. There was very little spot news in it, and most of its so-called correspondence was so obviously biased that it was of little value. They asked me to write a piece for the *Guardian* myself, and I had to comply, but the job went against the grain and I found it difficult. Various other English papers made demands on me while I was in London, but I managed to throw them all off. The most pressing overtures came from Ralph D. Blumenfeld, the American-born editor of the *Daily Express*. He wanted me to undertake a series of articles from America, but I told him that I hadn't the time for them.

As I have hitherto recorded I went to Oxford one day to visit Dr. Robert Bridges, the English Poet Laureate, then 86 years old and on his last legs. When I got to his house on Boar's Hill his wife, who was in her 60's, and seemed almost a flapper compared to him, warned me that it might be necessary for him to leave the table several times during lunch. This, in fact, he did. In the midst of a brisk conversation he would suddenly lose the thread of his discourse. Mrs. Bridges would then take him out of the room and in ten or fifteen minutes he'd return, restored. There were several other guests, all of them Oxford dons. The old man during his rational intervals was very entertaining, and even amusing. After lunch, as I prepared to return to London, he went with me to the house door. I naturally told him that I hoped to see him soon again. He replied gravely that it was impossible. "I am now," he said, "very near the end. I have had a pleasant life, but it is virtually over. Every day I feel myself slipping further downhill." He died before the end of the year.

The really big event of our stay in London was Van Lear Black's farewell dinner the night before he set off in his new airship. His plan, it appeared, was to attempt a flight around the world. He actually flew as far as Tokyo and then took ship for San Francisco. From San Francisco he flew to Baltimore. The dinner was an elaborate affair, with probably thirty guests. Most of them were Englishmen bent on selling Black something. Sir Robert Witt, the lawyer, was there with his wife, and so were several English officers who apparently had something to do with the airship business. The evening was chilly, and the only heat in the dining room was provided by a coal-fire at one end. Those who sat at that end of the table were almost roasted, but the women who were at the other end were so cold that they had to put wraps around their bare shoulders. I sat about midway, and was thus fairly comfortable. Opposite me sat Will Rogers. He had come to the dinner at my solicitation, and Black had placed him between two middle-aged Englishwomen with buck teeth. Let us call them Lady Augusta Waltsingham and Lady Gwendolyn Snively-Snooker. Rogers showed up in his usual evening costume, which was his blue suit. The two Englishwomen regarded him with the utmost amazement and suspicion. I could see them shrinking away from him all during dinner. But after the coffee came on Black, who had by that time got considerably tight, began calling for speeches, and finally reached Rogers. Rogers got up and gave his usual show, chewing gum all the while. The two Englishwomen shrunk even further away from him at its beginning, but in a little while one of them gave a cautious snicker. Presently the other began giggling behind her handkerchief. Within ten minutes he had won both of them with his old stuff, and they were grinning so widely that all their buck teeth showed. When Rogers finally sat down one of them was hanging on to each of his arms, and they were both demanding that he go on. It was an extraordinary exhibition of the power of his peculiar humor. Three-fourths of his jokes must have been quite unintelligible to his audience. Nevertheless, he won it—all, that is, save several of the Englishmen who were too drunk to understand anything.

The dinner, save for Rogers, was a dismal affair. Most of the guests were obvious harpies. From Sir Robert down, they were all engaged upon separating Black from his money. Jim Bone's loose niece was present, along with her mama, but Jim himself was not. Her presence in the house was naturally a great shame to him and his brother David, and Patterson and I never mentioned it in his presence. The next morning Jim showed up, but not the niece, at Croyden, where Black was taking off. His two Dutch pilots were running the ship and he was accompanied by his comic valet, Leo. It was early in the morning when we got to Croyden, and we had to eat breakfast at the airport. The sky was overcast and there was a sharp chill in the air. Finally, without much ceremony, the pilot started the engines of the ship and in a few minutes it disappeared in the fog. Patterson and I were half convinced that we'd never see Black again, but, as I have said, he actually got as far as Tokyo. A few days later, on February 13, I went to Southampton and boarded the *Bremen* for home. I was sick of the conference, and especially of John Owens's insistence upon taking it seriously. I was convinced that it was phoney, and that conviction I still entertain. From Southampton I sent the following telegram to Patterson at the Savoy:

> My hope and prayer on leaving England is that your patriotic labors and those of your esteemed associates will not be in vain. We stand at the threshold of a new day. May our Heavenly Father bless and prosper your endeavours.

Patterson was much of my opinion about the conference, and had tried to get passage on the *Bremen* for himself. But it was so crowded that he failed. Aboard the ship were Ernest Boyd and Herman Oelrichs. I had encountered them both during my stay in London, and the three of us ate and boozed together on the voyage home, along with Richard Barthelmess, then a popular movie actor. I had with me a curious souvenir of the conference. In the quarters allotted to the press at St. James's Palace there were somewhat elaborate wash-rooms. In them all the toilet-paper was stamped on each sheet "For Official Use Only." I lifted a packet and after I got back to the United States enclosed specimens in letters to friends. The press-room at the palace was a large and gloomy apartment, and in it, at least in theory, there was a desk for every correspondent. But there were a great many more correspondents—I think about 300—than desks, and inasmuch as I needed none I asked for none. In this room, at noon every day, a one-eyed agent of the Foreign Office read a solemn communiqué. Once or twice we had press conferences with J. Ramsay Macdonald, then Prime Minister. He turned out to be a very gabby fellow, and answered questions readily enough, but his replies were not illuminating. These press conferences were held in the armory of the palace—a room whose walls were decorated with pikes, swords, daggers and other such ancient arms. The plenary sessions of the delegates were held in a room so small that only twenty or thirty correspondents could be accommodated at a time. I got in only once, but did not repine, for the sessions were extraordinarily stupid. Every speech had to be translated into several languages, and this consumed a lot of time. I was especially interested in the speeches of the Japs, who always spoke in their own language. To my astonishment it sounded like a European language. While the ambassadors were hollering in the conference room those correspondents who could not get in were offered tea in an antechamber. I tried it once, but only once.

On May 9, 1930, after Patterson had returned home, he and I drove to Charlottesville, Virginia, to visit our colleague, Hyde. Hyde had a place four or five miles south of Thomas Jefferson's "Monticello," on the other side of the mountain. Patterson and I took a supply of limes with us, and Hyde turned up a bottle of gin, so the three of us put in the evening drinking gin-rickeys on the lawn. The next day Hyde took us to visit Prince and Princess Pierre Troubetzkoy, who lived on the other side of Charlottesville. I had met the prince before, but the princess was new to me. She was formerly Amélie Rives, in her time a famous novelist. At the time we called on her she was by her own confession 67 years old, but her blond hair was still thick and bright and her skin was that of a healthy woman of 35. The prince greeted us barefooted. He told us that Russians of the upper classes, when in the country, commonly imitated the peasants by taking off their shoes. The old boy had in reserve a prime bottle of Maryland rye, and the four of us took a whack at it. The house was notable for the enormous growth of boxwood in front of it. The bushes were so high and so dense that the automobile road made a sort of tunnel through them. Inside, the thing I most noticed was the display of paintings. Troubetzkoy himself was a portrait painter, but the canvasses on the walls had all been done by his wife in her earlier days. They were extremely bad, but we had to admire them. Patterson, Hyde and I traveled to Charlottesville from Washington by way of Fredericksburg, and there we saw Marye's Hill, with the sunken road under it, and marvelled at the imbecility of the Federal commander who had ordered his troops to charge up it. Along the road between Fredericksburg and Charlottesville we came to the place where Stonewall Jackson had been mortally wounded on May 2, 1863. There was a small monument directly beside the road, and we got out to look at it. Directly behind it was a wild wood, mainly made up of scrub pine. I retired into the wood briefly, and discovered the next day that I had picked up several chigger bites.

As I have said, I became engaged to Sara Haardt at the end of 1929, but it was not until the first days of August, 1930, that our engagement was announced by her mother in Montgomery, Ala., her home. She was, by early Spring, almost completely recovered from the serious surgery of 1929, and in April she was greatly bucked up by the news that Doubleday, Page & Company had accepted her novel, "Career," afterward renamed "The Making of a Lady." I had, of course, told Patterson of my projected marriage long before it was announced, and with characteristic energy he assumed charge of the press arrangements. My fear was that the newspapers would play it up as sensational news, for I had long been one of their principle examples of a confirmed and incorrigible bachelor. It was Patterson's job to get something approaching decorum into their reports, and this he achieved with great skill. On August 3 I wrote to him: "It was a masterpiece. No publicity has been better handled since the Snyder-Gray case. I have been beset all day by queries from New York, and have told everybody that you order me to keep silent." The wedding was set for August 27, and once more he elected himself stage manager and press agent. He was busy with this business when, on August 18, there arrived news of the death of Van Lear Black. It was a shock, undoubtedly, but, as I have said, it was not altogether unanticipated. When Patterson and I had seen Black off at Croydon on February 9 we had both half believed that we were seeing him for the last time. It seemed inevitable that, soon or late, his wild journeys by air would bring him to disaster. But he had somehow completed his tour safely, and had been back in Baltimore for several months, temporarily fed up with aviation and giving over most of his time to trips on his yacht *Sabalo*. Now he had fallen overboard from the *Sabalo* in the night, and was done for at last.

The facts about his death are set forth briefly in "The Sunpapers of Baltimore" and that account is accurate so far as it goes, but it does not go all the way. Black had a companion on his last voyage—a tall, thin, acidulous woman named Mrs. J. Walter Lord, the widow of a Baltimore lawyer. His carryings-on with this unappetizing baggage had given his virago of a wife plenty of effective ammunition for months past, and she had been exploding it to the dreadful distress of his brother Harry and the alarm of Patterson and the rest of us. The problem now was to so color the newspaper reports of the accident that the scandal would not come out. To that end Patterson and Joe Blondell rushed to New York by air, and managed to get aboard the *Sabalo* before any of the reporters for the press associations and New York papers. It had been searching for the body all night, and did not reach New York until late in the afternoon of August 19. Patterson and Blondell met it down New York harbor, and before the reporters found it they had spirited Mrs. Lord ashore and started her back for Baltimore by train. They could not conceal her presence on the fatal voyage, but they succeeded deftly in planting the story that she was an elderly woman, and a cousin to Black. This lie the reporters swallowed, and Patterson also managed to induce them to omit her name. He and Blondell did a good job, and returned to Baltimore the next day much relieved.

The search for Black's body went on for a couple of days afterward, but was then abandoned. Some weeks later a report came in that his yachting cap had been discovered afloat off the Jersey coast, but it turned out not to be his. The report spread in Baltimore, by whispers, that he had committed suicide, but I could never discover any reason to believe it. To be sure, he was hard pressed for money, and his two women—La Lord in America and La Bone in London—were probably giving him plenty of trouble, with his wife meanwhile making a constant uproar, but the alcohol in which he was immersed kept him optimistic, and he was, in point of fact, in excellent spirits during the weeks before his death. He had long since developed a powerful appetite for public notice, and that was what was mainly at the bottom of his silly journeys by air. He had been getting plenty of it since his return from his round-the-world tour, and was planning new projects on a grandiose scale. It goes without saying that Patterson, who had been living in terror for three or four years past, lest the huge cost of this folly bring Black to downright bankruptcy, was relieved by his death, but I should add that, like all the rest of us, he was also saddened by it, for Black was an extremely amiable fellow, and we all liked him. The distress of Harry Black touched everyone. He had watched his brother's degeneration without showing a sign, and his loyalty never wavered. Even in the face of a death almost ignominious Van was still his hero.

With Van Lear Black dead, the pressure for high dividends disappeared, and that for the year dropped to $6.50. This, of course, was still high, for it amounted to 65% on the par value of the old common stock, but it was at least materially lower than the dividends in 1929 and 1930. I was busy with the *American Mercury,* which had begun to give me serious concern, but nevertheless I attended the editorial conferences nearly every Monday, and saw Patterson and Black very often in the intervals. Early in the year Patterson decided to adopt a new face of body type for all of the *Sunpapers,* and after a long investigation decided on Textype, which was larger than the face in use for years past. It appeared in the *Sun* and the *Evening Sun* on June 22. He also made renewed but futile efforts to improve the editorial page of the *Sun.* After my fruitless survey of it in July, 1929, I resigned it to statistics and the Devil, but I had to listen to Patterson's projects, and did not spare praise when it was plausible. Once, when John Owens wrote an effective editorial against Amos W. W. Woodcock, the Federal district attorney in Baltimore, I described it (as I find in a letter to Patterson in his files) as "magnificent." On another occasion (November 4) he asked my judgment on an article opposite the editorial page by H. N. Brailsford, bitterly denouncing J. Ramsay Macdonald. "It is," I said in a note now in Patterson's files, "one of the best pieces ever printed in the *Sun*. In fact, I think that any paper should be proud to get such stuff into its columns. What a picture of Macdonald! He is obviously ten times worse a rat than I ever suspected." This was quite sincere. Brailsford, at his best, was the most competent writer among all the English journalists of his time, and he was here preaching a doctrine that I naturally applauded. Any telling of real names and washing of dirty underwear among the English always had my approval, for in those days I still lived in hope that the *Sun* would eventually throw off the English influence, and essay to think things out for itself. But between the two world wars, as while they raged, it remained Anglophile, and whenever it printed an article on an English politician or an English scheme of grab that told the truth, it was usually some heretical Englishman that did the job. I kept a lookout, during 1931, for likely recruits for the staff, but turned up no new ones. The only candidate I can recall recommending was Robert S. Allen, who had lately resigned as a member of the Washington bureau of the *Christian Science Monitor*. I had met him on the Al Smith campaign tour, and had been favorably impressed by him. I wrote to Patterson on September 14, 1931:

> He may be worth looking at. He has a fiery energy, is a thorough Liberal, and has a talent for unearthing unusual stuff. He had an important hand in "The Washington Merry-Go-Round." Working for the Eddyites, of course, he has been horribly repressed and handicapped. On a decent newspaper he would probably show very good qualities. If we took him it would be necessary to hold him in a bit—but holding a good man in is surely less onerous than building fires under the tail of a bad one. . . .

"The Washington Merry-Go-Round," which came out anonymously earlier in 1931, had made a big success, and was, in fact, full of pertinent and amusing stuff. I did not know it at the time, but Allen's collaborator in the book was Drew Pearson, then still a member of the Washington staff of the *Sun*, assigned to the State Department. In 1932 Pearson had to be fired for turning in false and libelous stuff. A little while before this he and Allen had brought out a second volume, "More Merry-Go-Round," and Pearson alleged in Washington that he was fired on account of this book. This was not true, though it is a fact that Moore remonstrated, as a decent journalist and a man of honor, against some of the

In his fiftieth year, Mencken returns aboard the *SS Bremen* from the London Naval Conference. February 1930. Kingstone View Company.

contents of the book, especially a passage dealing with the alleged adultery of an army officer's wife, in which she was named by name. Pearson seized upon that fact to posture as a martyr to free speech, and induced a number of publicity-seeking politicians, including Fiorello H. La Guardia, then a congressman from New York, to denounce the *Sun*. I knew La Guardia, and had once been his guest in Washington—he was a capital spaghetti cook—but when, shortly afterward, he called me up in Baltimore, I refused to see him, and have never spoken to him since. Pearson also persuaded Arthur Sears Henning, Washington correspondent of the Chicago *Tribune* and a somewhat shady character, to write an article for the *Tribune* accusing the *Sun* of seeking to censor books written by members of its staff. For all this Moore was mainly to blame. In those days, as later on, he sometimes showed a considerable imprudence, born of his Irish impetuosity. He should have fired Pearson for writing the libellous stuff, and have done: it was quite unnecessary to mention the bounderish passages in "More Merry-Go-Round." Some time later Allen told me that he was ashamed of them, and had objected to their inclusion, but despite his qualms he continued as Pearson's partner, and presently they set up a daily newspaper column, mainly made up of back-stairs gossip, that still survives (1942). Pearson departed from the *Sun* full of bitterness, and has searched and longed for revenge ever since. When, in 1938, Roosevelt attempted his purge of Senator Millard E. Tydings of Maryland, Pearson backed the Administration candidate, David J. Lewis, and wrote most of the violent attacks on the *Sun* that appeared during the campaign. The defeat of Lewis was a great blow to him, and vastly increased his acrimony. It was thus fortunate that nothing came of my suggestion that his partner Allen be taken on the *Sun* in 1931.

The one really important acquisition of 1931 was Neil H. Swanson, a Minnesotan then 34 years old. He was Murphy's discovery and came to the *Sun* from the Pittsburgh *Post,* where he had been managing editor for two years. He proved his competence from the start, and has kept up his pace ever since, though often in the face of discouraging impediments. Of all the young men who came to the *Sunpapers* in my time he was, and is, the best, and by far. He has energy, good judgment, a plentiful boldness and originality, and a high capacity for getting on with other men, whether subordinates or superiors. When Murphy finally became incapacitated Swanson was made acting managing editor of the *Evening Sun* and at once made a number of radical improvements in its organization and makeup. Among other things he devised a new system of news headings that attracted attention among newspaper men from end to end of the country: they were immensely simpler than the old ones, and hence could be written easier and more quickly, but at the same time they set forth what was under them more clearly. In 1939, when Murphy finally retired, Swanson succeeded him as managing editor, and at the end of 1941, when Moore died, Patterson made Swanson chief of all save the editorial page of both papers, with the title of executive editor. He is the only editor in the office of whom I can say honestly that I have never known him to do anything or advocate anything that did not have the single aim of making the *Sunpapers* really intelligent, enterprising and independent newspapers.

The great stock market crash of 1929 had only slight repercussions in the *Sun* office, largely, I suppose, because it had only slight repercussions in Baltimore. The town was in a favorable position to withstand the shock, and in truth it actually withstood it better than any other large American city. This was mainly because its activities were widely diversified, and few of them depended upon Wall Street financing. The *Sun* itself made a great deal of money in 1930 and paid the largest dividend in its history. Thus there was no disposition to alarm in the office. Hoover's efforts to deal with the situation, though they were criticized in detail, were accepted as fundamentally rational all through 1930 and well into 1931. As a matter of fact, they appeared to be working reasonably well, and all the professional optimists of the country were filling the newspapers with predictions of an early recovery. In Baltimore the first whiffs of serious disaster were not noticed until the Summer of 1931, when whispers began to go 'round about the largest local bank, the Baltimore Trust Company. This institution, under the guidance of a go-getter named Donald Symington, had been sky-rocketing for some years—absorbing smaller banks, extending its loans to all sorts of hazardous enterprises, and reaching out for the distinction of being the largest bank south of Philadelphia. Of late it had put millions of its resources into a monumental office-building, the largest in Baltimore. But down to the middle of the Summer of 1931 there was no serious doubt of its solvency. At the opening of the year its report showed resources of nearly $98,000,000 and deposits of more than $76,000,000, and on July 1 the former were within $80,000 of $100,000,000 and the latter had grown to $85,250,000. But before July was out a run started, and in a little while deposits were below $80,000,000, and then below $75,000,000, and then below $70,000,000. I had met Symington, the president of the bank, some time before (he had been the guest of Patterson at a somewhat elaborate luncheon in the *Sun* boardroom), and my impression of him was highly unfavorable: he seemed to me to be the archetype of all the gaudy gamblers with other people's money who raged during the Coolidge prosperity and the first delirious years of Hoover. Nor was I reassured when he became chairman of the bank's board in May, 1931, and was succeeded as president by James Bruce, the same speculative young Baltimorean who had sold the Keyser *Sun* stock to Patterson. I was thus full of doubts when I began to hear talk in the *Sun* editorial conferences of the need of giving aid and encouragement to the Baltimore Trust Company. If we had any duty at all in the premises, I argued, it was to tell the plain truth about it, no matter what the consequence. It needed a thorough housecleaning and perhaps a reorganization, for it had become infested with a large gang of adventurers of the Symington-Bruce variety, and if its crazy career were not checked it would come down in a crash, mulcting thousands of Baltimoreans of their savings—for it had many branches and did a large neighborhood business—and spreading ruin throughout the town.

When I argued thus I little knew the extent of the mess it was in. Its alleged assets, in fact, were largely imaginary, for its funds were laid out in all sorts of wild speculations. It had advanced money in large amounts to timber exploiters in Florida, to a steamship line from Baltimore to London and Bremen that lost money from the start, to Glenn L. Martin, a go-getting Iowan who had set up an airship plant near Baltimore in 1929, and was destined to become one of the prime curses of the community, and to almost countless other such dubious risks. Suddenly, in September, 1931, a really formidable run started, and within a few weeks the company's perilous situation was obvious. I now argued that its collapse was inevitable, and that trying to stave it off by concealing the facts would be a kind of fraud on the readers of the *Sun,* many of whom were its depositors. I believed that it would be best for Baltimore to let it die and take the loss, for if it were propped up its débâcle could only be postponed, and in the end it might involve other banks, and make a first rate disaster. We had some very hot debates on this subject in the *Sun* office, but I could make no impression on either Patterson or John Owens.

The Baltimore Trust's troubles made it plain even to such optimists as John Owens that the Depression was really a serious matter, and that Baltimore would not escape its effects. On August 27, 1931, Mayor Howard W. Jackson of Baltimore, a very competent official, had a meeting with the principal *Sunpaper* executives at the *Sun* office, and informed them that the city's relief burden was fast outrunning its resources. Various schemes of raising money were discussed. I forget what they were, but recall that they were presently found to be inadequate. The load was then thrown on the state of Maryland, and the Governor, Albert C. Ritchie, retired to Annapolis for one of his intermittent spells of serious cogitation. When he emerged he had concocted a plan to raise the money by taking it out of the receipts from automobile licenses and the gasoline tax, which were supposedly earmarked for the use of the state roads. This caused some protest, but Ritchie was the sort of man who could not be diverted, once his mind was made up. The result was that, before he went out of office, the state roads were in a sad condition, and to this day (1942) they have never been completely restored. Ritchie, in 1931, was giving serious thought to his presidential chances, which had been brightening since it became evident, after the election of 1928, that Al Smith was out of the picture. To be sure, Franklin D. Roosevelt, now Governor of New York, was making quiet efforts to get the nomination in 1932, but it was not apparent, as yet, how far he had gone. The first tour of Jim Farley, who actually organized his campaign, was not begun, in fact, until July, 1931. Moreover, it was still the general impression that Roosevelt, who owed his governorship to Al, would not come into the open unless Al withdrew, which appeared unlikely. Thus the way seemed to open for Ritchie, who was free from factional entanglements in the party and had made an excellent record as Governor of Maryland. I urged him, beginning in 1930, to show himself as often as possible, and got him a number of invitations to make speeches. He always made a good impression on these occasions, for he was a singularly handsome fellow and he knew how to talk effectively, once he had primed himself by careful preparation in his study. Unhappily, making speeches was one thing, and rounding up delegates was another. What Ritchie really needed was an agent as competent and as fanatical as Jim Farley was to turn out to be; also, he needed a large sum of money for expenses, *i.e.*, for buying the organizations in the states where they were for sale.

I was, of course, not in politics, but I believed that Ritchie had earned a right to a run for the money, and so I helped him as much as I could in 1931, principally by trying to formulate a coherent body of doctrine for him. As I have said, the Maryland Free State scheme of things was not his, but the *Sun*'s and he needed constant tutoring in its articles. Himself, he had no fundamental ideas, and had little to say to the country save that he was against Prohibition and had balanced the Maryland budget.

He dropped in on me often at my apartment in Cathedral street. Sara, who disliked him, would go to bed, and he and I would sit for hours—with bottle after bottle of my home-brew oiling my pipes and glass after glass of straight Maryland rye oiling his.

A few days later [after one such meeting in early September, 1931], going to New York, I encountered [Howard] Bruce on the train, and we discussed Ritchie's situation at length. He told me that he was too busy with the affairs of the Baltimore Trust Company to undertake a tour of the country, but that he believed he could raise a sufficient campaign fund—say, a million dollars. He had a lot of money himself, and he was intimate with men in New York and elsewhere who had much more—all of them now falling away from Al Smith and bitter against Hoover. I had no confidence in Bruce, but I knew he packed a powerful yearning to be Governor of Maryland himself, and I tried to insinuate into him the notion that the best way to clear Ritchie from his path would be to shove him upstairs to the White House. He plainly cottoned to this fancy, but he did nothing to further it, and Ritchie actually entered the convention of 1932 with but 21 votes—Maryland's 16, four from Indiana and one from Pennsylvania. Nevertheless, he had plenty of admirers among the delegates, and if Roosevelt had blown up, and there had been a free-for-all, he might have got the nomination. As some one said at the time, he was the favorite second choice. But Roosevelt did not blow up. I should add that his nomination, which blasted Ritchie's presidential aspirations forever, did not really grieve me.

My contributions to the editorial page of the *Evening Sun* in 1931 were mainly of small importance, for I was already beginning to lose interest in both the page and my job, and moreover, I was incommoded for a large part of the year by illness, both Sara's and my own. Nevertheless, I helped, in December, to lead the *Sunpapers* into a row which raged savagely for years afterward, and still has repercussions. This uproar followed a lynching at Salisbury, on the Eastern Shore of Maryland, on December 4—the first lynching in the State for twenty years. The gentleman hanged and burned was a blackamoor named Matthew Williams, and he well deserved his fate, for he had murdered his employer, a white man named Daniel J. Elliott, in a barbaric manner. Nor were the people of Salisbury without some excuse, at least by their lights, in taking the law into their own hands, for another atrocious murder on the Shore, performed by a Negro named Euel Lee some time before, was still unavenged, and the intervention of various highly dubious busybodies, including some Jewish Communists in Baltimore, made it seem likely that the culprit would escape the gallows for a long while, despite the fact that he had twice confessed. But though I was thus more or less sympathetic with the lynchers in the specific case I was strongly against them in general, and with them the whole Eastern Shore scheme of things. For some years past, as I have noted, I had been actually proposing that the Shore be detached from Maryland, and joined to Delaware and the Eastern Shore of Virginia in a new State to be called Delmarva, with the Methodist Book of Discipline as its constitution and Prohibition as its great glory. I therefore seized the chance that the butchering of Williams provided for whooping up that scheme, and on December 7 printed on the editorial page of the *Evening* Sun, under the title of "The Eastern Shore *Kultur*," an article which made every Shoreman, at least below the Choptank river, my sworn enemy forever. A few specimens:

Not many observant Marylanders, I take it, were surprised by the news of last Friday's extraordinarily savage and revolting lynching at Salisbury. Something of the sort had been plainly hatching down in that forlorn corner of the State for a long while. There was a time, years ago, when it was the seat of an urbane and charming culture, dominated by an enlightened and public-spirited gentry, but of late it has succumbed to its poor white trash, who now determine its ideas and run its affairs. The Ku Klux Klan, which was laughed at in all the more civilized parts of Maryland, got a firm lodgment in the lower counties of the Shore, and the brutish imbecilities that it propagated are still accepted gravely by large numbers of the people, including not a few who should know better. The whole area is a lush stamping-ground for knavish politicians, prehensile professional patriots, and whooping soul-savers. It is, quite naturally, a stronghold of Prohibition (and of the rot-gut liquors that go therewith) and within its bounds tin-pot revivalism is making its last stand in Maryland. . . .

Certainly it would be silly to think of the lynching as if it were an isolated incident. It was, in fact, nothing of the sort. It was the natural culmination of a degenerating process that has been in progress for years. At least since the World War the lower Shore has been going downhill, mentally and morally. It has been sliding out of Maryland and into the orbit of Arkansas and Tennessee, Mississippi and the more flea-bitten half of Virginia. Time and again the whole State has been menaced by the peculiar swinishness of its boozing dry politics, and now it holds us all up to the contempt of the nation and the world by staging a public obscenity worthy of cannibals. . . .

It has become an Alsatia of morons, which is to say, of lynchers. What it cries for without knowing it is more attention from the rest of the State. We have let it sweat in its own juices without paying anything more than casual attention to it. We have even allowed it to arrogate to itself a political power and importance altogether out of line with its state of civilization. Baltimore City sends one delegate to Annapolis for each 22,300 of its population, but Wicomico county of which Salisbury was the county-seat sends one for every 7,800. Baltimore, with 805,000 population, has six State senators; Wicomico, with but 31,600, has one. In other words, the vote of the president of the Johns Hopkins University or of the Baltimore & Ohio Railroad, when it comes to electing the lower House of the Legislature, is worth but one-third as much as the vote of one of the Salisbury witch-burners, and when it comes to electing the upper house, but one-fourth as much.

And so on, and so on. On the editorial page of the *Sun* John Owens lamented the lynching with some show of his usual moral indignation, but there was relatively little resentment of his editorials: what really set the Shoremen aflame was my attack on their whole *Kultur.* For weeks afterward I was denounced violently in every country paper south of the Choptank, and from almost every pulpit. The main charge was that I was an apologist for drunkards, whores and murderers, but there were also correlative charges that I was both a Communist and a German spy. This attack, which went to almost fantastic lengths, was largely fomented by one Truett [Charles J. Truitt], the editor of the daily newspaper in Salisbury. He was also the *Sun's* correspondent there, and after the night of the lynching (which he reported promptly enough) made elaborate efforts to prevent it covering the story adequately. All the reporters who were sent to Salisbury from the home office were threatened with violence, and one of the photographers, Robert F. Kniesche, was saved from rough handling, and maybe even murder, only by escaping in an airship. On March 28, 1932, I fanned the flames with another article entitled "The Lynching Psychosis," and they roared anew. A great many threatening letters reached me, most of them anonymous, and I was invited publicly to come down to the lower Shore and be lynched myself. To this day, in fact, I am *persona non grata* there, to put it mildly, and so recently as March, 1942, Paul Palmer found that I was still remembered and detested in Ocean City, which is on the ocean front about 25 miles from Salisbury. Inasmuch as I had no desire to be admired by morons I let the Shoremen howl.

11

Prohibition Was on the Rocks

1932–1934

The two national conventions of 1932 were the most fateful in American history, but no one knew it at the time. Most newspaper men, like most other Americans, believed before they began that their chief significance lay in their probable effect upon Prohibition. No one, in those days, had ever heard of the New Deal, not even Roosevelt. Nor was the Depression taken with too much gravity. To be sure, things had been fast going from bad to worse under Hoover, but it was generally believed that if he could be got rid of there would be a rapid improvement, and most authorities held that, in any case, the Depression would pass off soon or late, as all previous ones had passed off. I certainly believed that myself, and so did all the *Sunpaper* brethren. Both conventions were held in the Chicago Stadium, with that of the Republicans first, as usual. I had scarcely got to the *Sun* quarters in the Blackstone Hotel when news reached me that the elder Knopf had died suddenly. This, of course, meant a radical reorganization of the *American Mercury*, and in that job I'd naturally have to take a hand, but it could wait until the convention was over, so I did not go to New York for the funeral.

We were very comfortable at the Blackstone, and I greatly enjoyed both shows. Quartered with us was James Bone of the Manchester *Guardian*, who had come over to cover them for his paper, and also to do a small daily article for the *Sun*, setting forth a Briton's impression of them. These daily articles were very feeble stuff, but Jim labored at them diligently, writing with a pen. Some one was needed to copy his manuscript, so that our telegraph operators could read it. All the rest of us being busy, the job fell to John W. Owens. Thus the cheerful spectacle was presented of the editor of the *Sun* serving a visiting Britisher as amanuensis. Patterson saw in it only a proof of John's willingness to labor for the good of the paper in any capacity, however humble, but its ironical significance was not lost upon me. Jim's gigantic thirst made a large dent in the supply of hard liquors that Patterson and I, as usual, had brought from Baltimore. One afternoon, struggling with thoughts that came up muddy, he put away a whole bottle of gin. Like any other British patriot, he got an ill-concealed delight out of the evidences of hard times that were spread before the eye in Chicago. On the grass of Lincoln Park, below our hotel windows, hundreds of homeless men slept every night, and in the morning we would see them shaving and washing at the park fountains. When an especially bedraggled old tramp appeared we would tell Jim that it was Samuel Insull. One night we made a tour of the subway under the Wacker drive, and saw hundreds of men sleeping on the hard concrete platforms outside the basement doors of the adjacent warehouses. The Depression was making itself felt at last. Even the *Sun-papers*, though they were still able to pay princely dividends, were beginning to suffer in revenues.

But, as I have said, it was not the Depression that chiefly occupied the Republicans at Chicago, nor was it the choice of a candidate, for the convention was made up mainly of Hoover jobholders, and his renomination was certain. The real issue of the hour was Prohibition. Its predominance, I must confess, surprised me, for I had thought, like everyone else, that Hoover and his goons would be able to keep it under cover. It was plain by this time, of course, that there had been a great revulsion against the Eighteenth Amendment, and that it would probably have to be repealed, or, at all events, greatly modified, soon or late, but Hoover believed that there was one more campaign in Law Enforcement. His agents, when they got to Chicago, were greatly surprised by the extent of wet sentiment among the delegates pouring in, and so were the rest of us. "If the delegates were really free agents," I wrote for the *Evening Sun* of June 15, "they would vote the imposture out by a majority of at least five to one." But they were not free agents; they were simply, as I said in the same dispatch, a gang of "country postmasters, Federal marshals and receivers in bankruptcy, masquerading as the heirs of Lincoln." Dr. Nicholas Murray Butler was on hand to demand Repeal, but though the delegates cheered his excellent short speech, they voted as they were ordered from the White House. Even the White House, however, quickly grasped the fact that Prohibition was in serious difficulties, and so the plank adopted made some concessions to the wets, though its main purpose was to keep the drys in line for Hoover. Starting off with sonorous nothings about the sacred duty of Law Enforcement and the wickedness of Nullification, it went on to propose that there be submitted to the States, for consideration at "conventions called for that sole purpose," an amendment to the Eighteenth Amendment "which, while retaining the Federal government power to preserve the gains already made in dealing with the evils inherent in the liquor traffic, shall allow the States to deal with the problem as their citizens may determine, but subject always to the power of the Federal government to protect those States where Prohibition may exist and safeguard our citizens everywhere from the return of the saloon and attendant abuses." Who concocted this flubdub I do not know—in all probability, Hoover himself, for it was brought to Chicago by his Secretary of the Treasury, Ogden L. Mills, himself, incidentally, a convinced wet and once an assiduous boozer. The indomitable Dr. Butler tried to put through a substitute providing for the outright appeal of the Eighteenth Amendment, with a bone thrown in for the drys in the form of a promise to "effectively abolish the saloon, whether open or concealed," but though, as I wrote to the *Evening Sun*, at least 700 of the 1154 were in favor of it, and in fact for something even more drastic, only 472 got up the courage to vote for it, so the Hoover plank was adopted. This, in theory, was a victory for Bishop Cannon, and the other dry bosses, but they saw clearly the handwriting on the wall, and by the time the convention adjourned they were in a very low state of mind, and full of fears that the Democrats would walk out on them a fortnight hence.

The only opposition to Hoover that was heard of during the convention came from the before mentioned Joseph I. France of Maryland, now out of the Senate. France still had some of the money he had acquired by the death of his first wife in 1927 and had not yet got over the delusion that he was a candidate himself. Moreover, he had learned a lesson from Hoover's experience in 1920, and came to the convention this time with some actual delegates. He had picked them up in Oregon, where the State organization was short of money, and welcomed his contribution of $20,000. The spokesman for the Oregon delegation, a man with the curious name of L. B. Sandblast, put him formally in nomination on June 16, but only after a vigorous prodding, for all the Oregon delegates were eager to leap for Hoover as quickly as possible. The nominating speech so amused the crowd that poor France, realizing at last that his goose was cooked before it had really got on the fire, decided fatuously to try to launch a stampede to Coolidge. He went to the platform for this purpose with a proxy given to him as a sort of farewell present by his Oregon lieges. Unhappily, the permanent chairman of the convention, Bertrand H. Snell, did not recognize him, though he had been a United States Senator for six years, and so refused to let him make a speech. France, who was a big fellow, thereupon brushed Snell, who was small, aside, and strode for the microphone. Snell then bawled for the cops, and the upshot was that France was dragged off the platform and locked up in the convention hoosegow upstairs. This happened at a moment when, of all the *Sunpaper*'s staff, only Patterson and I were in the press-stand. The result was that I had to cover the story—a somewhat sweaty job, for it involved fighting my way through the cops to reach France to find out what had happened, and then writing my piece with a lead-pencil, for I had left my typewriter at the Blackstone. Somehow I managed to get through with it, and in very short time, and Patterson was so pleased that he returned home bellowing that I was one of the liveliest reporters in captivity. He sat beside me as I wrote, filing my copy paragraph by paragraph, and it got into the *Evening Sun* without a bull.

Once the convention was over I had to rush to New York for a palaver with Alfred A. Knopf, for the death of his father had thrown the affairs of the *American Mercury* into fresh and worse confusion. The night I got back to Chicago for the Democratic convention Frank Kent brought a visitor to the *Sun* bureau in the Blackstone Hotel. He was A. Mitchell Palmer, and he was in town, so he said, in the character of a confidential agent of Franklin D. Roosevelt, the only really formidable candidate for the nomination. In particular, he went on, he was charged with seeing that the convention adopted a plank on Prohibition that would be satisfactory to Roosevelt. This plank he had in his pocket, and after a couple of drinks he showed it to us confidentially, explaining at the same time that Roosevelt had written it in person, and would insist on its adoption. When he read it we were really astounded, for it was almost as cautious as the plank the Republicans had adopted at Hoover's orders ten days before. It provided, to be sure, for calling state conventions to consider the repeal of the Eighteenth Amendment, but it committed the party to no stand on repeal, and was full of the usual blather about preventing the return of the saloon and protecting dry States against the "importation of intoxicating liquors in violation of their laws." Patterson, Hyde and I argued with Palmer that this was an ignominious surrender to Bishop Cannon and company, and that it was not only ignominious, but also bad politics. The fact that Prohibition was on the rocks was by now plain to everyone. The very drys in

Chicago were admitting it freely. Roosevelt's one chance of beating Hoover, we contended, lay in yielding to the manifest demand of the country, leaving Hoover to hang on the fence. The wets were all against Hoover, and many of the drys were already beginning to howl against him for not ordering his convention to declare for straight Law Enforcement. Here was a golden opportunity. If Roosevelt would only throw the drys overboard altogether and come out flatly for Repeal he would probably win in November. But if he continued to play with the Anti-Saloon League as he had done at San Francisco in 1920, he would muddle the issue between himself and Hoover, and go into the campaign badly hamstrung. Palmer, himself a wet, admitted the cogency of all this, but said that Roosevelt could not be moved. The plank in his pocket would be the plank of the platform.

How the resolutions committee, on June 28, threw out that plank and substituted one declaring flatly for Repeal, and how this substitute plank was adopted by the convention by a vote of 934¾ to 213¾—this is a tale that has been often told. It deserves to be ranked, indeed, among the great dramas of American politics. I covered the meeting of the committee at the Congress Hotel—an extremely onerous job, for it was held behind locked doors and lasted six hours, and every time a member came out with news of what was going on inside the story had to be revised. Altogether, I sent four different versions of it during the day, and most of them were filed in four or five pieces. For a while I tried writing in the Western Union office in the hotel, but toward the end the crowd outside the committee's door became so dense and boisterous that I had to stick closer, and my final fragments were written by hand at a shaky writing-desk in the lobby, just outside the door. When the committee began its fateful session none of the correspondents on hand believed that it would actually reject the Roosevelt plank. Thus we were surprised every time a member came out and reported that some other State had plumped for it. In the middle of the uproar Jim Farley, acting for Roosevelt, tried to have the consideration of the platform postponed until after the nomination, but by that time the wets had the bit in their teeth, and refused any compromise. When the committee arose at 3 P.M. the news was that 35 States, Territories and dominions beyond the seas had voted for the wet-wet plank, and only 17 for the Roosevelt plank. The vote in the convention the next day was thus forecast clearly, but nevertheless the drys made a final stand on the floor, and it was not until one o'clock in the morning that Prohibition finally went out of the window. The chief whooper for the Roosevelt plank was Cordell Hull of Tennessee.

After the smoke cleared away the nomination of a candidate began to look almost like anti-climax. Roosevelt, of course, was the only aspirant who had a chance. To be sure, he had come to Chicago with more than a hundred votes less than the two-thirds needed to nominate, and for a day or two Jim Farley had made heavy efforts to have the two-thirds rule abrogated, but by the time the platform fight was over Jim had come to terms with the highly nefarious William Gibbs McAdoo, ostensibly leader of the Garner *bloc*, and knew that he could count on the Garner votes whenever they were needed. Against this combination the anti-Roosevelt forces, led by Al Smith, were completely impotent— first, because they had no really plausible candidate to rally 'round, but secondly, and most importantly, because Al was in a state of complete political, mental and moral disintegration. Indeed, he showed such mountainous imbecility that many of the correspondents who knew him best concluded that he must be either drunk or crazy. His rage against Roosevelt was really almost pathological. Roosevelt, his creature, was now turning on him, and trying to steal his goods. Roosevelt was a cuckoo planted in his nest. Roosevelt was a traitor surpassing Judas. At poor Al's first and only press conference he ranted thus for half an hour, and then went out to play golf with some Chicago politicians. Just before the balloting began he got word from William Randolph Hearst, who hated Roosevelt also and had carried California for Garner, that McAdoo was preparing to deliver the California delegation to Farley, and that Garner was probably a party to the operation. He thereupon put in a telephone call for Garner in Washington—and was told by Mrs. Garner that Jack had gone to bed and could not be disturbed. The next morning the Allies deposed Al and appointed James A. Reed of Missouri their leader, but it was too late, of course, to beat the Farley-McAdoo-Garner combination. Moreover, Reed was temperamentally unfit for the job—perhaps even more so than the now completely frantic Al. I met him in the space under the hall just after his appointment was announced. He was on his way to a tar-paper room wherein the Missouri delegation was holding a caucus. I left him at the door, but could not help hearing his first words to his lieges within. "If any of you sons-of-bitches want to go to Roosevelt," he roared, "you have my permission. I am asking nothing of you." Thus he began the great work of rallying the shattered anti-Roosevelt troops. When the convention reassembled, McAdoo went to the platform and announced with an oleaginous smile that California was leaving Garner for Roosevelt, and on the next ballot—the fourth—Roosevelt got 945 votes and was nominated. Al, by this time, had fled from Chicago in despair, but his faithful followers from New York, Pennsylvania, New Jersey and the industrial areas of New England held out to the end. On the first ballot they had given him 201 votes and on the fourth they were still giving him 190.

Garner's cool desertion of his Texas lieges was one of the most exhilarating episodes of the convention—but not, of course, to the Texans. The State's 46 delegates were with him to a man and to the death, and so were all the fans they had brought with them from their native steppes— a huge gang filling four or five special trains, and including several bands, each with a female drum-major who was at the same time a powerful sexual *agente provocateuse*, at least by Texas standards. When the delegates first heard that Farley and McAdoo were in treaty they refused to believe it. They were sure that Garner would never consent to any such betrayal of the Californians who had voted for him in the primaries. He was, they insisted, the soul of honor, politically speaking, and had never broken an agreement in all his eminent career. Thus it was a cruel shock to them when the news of his eager trade with Farley leaked in from Washington. One of the chief men of the delegation was the same Amon G. Carter who had fired his pistol from my room in Houston in 1924. When he was convinced at last that old Jack had sold out his friends for the vice-presidency he came to the press-stand and unloaded his woe upon Patterson and me with tears in his eyes. But in a little while the Texans began to take comfort out of the fact that Jack would get second place on the ticket, and by the time he was actually put through they were once more marching in the aisles, let by their bands and their she-gal drum majors. Jack thus duplicated the flop of old Charlie Curtis at Kansas City in 1924. The two were of a piece. Both were willing to give up anything, including especially honor, for a job. Jack was a thoroughgoing Bourbon, and when the New Deal began to unfold itself in 1933 it found it very hard to take, but he hung on to the vice-presidency for eight years, and would have been glad to serve four more. All the while he engaged in intrigues against Roosevelt behind the door. The more ardent New Dealers were for dropping him in 1936, but Roosevelt decided to keep him, and it was not until 1940 that he finally got his congé. During all his eight years as Vice-President he lived in fond hopes that Roosevelt would die. His routine of life, despite his teasing closeness to the throne, remained that of the yokel that he was. He appeared at his office in the Capitol every morning at 7 o'clock, and was in bed every night at 9. Henry M. Hyde, who kept much the same hours, used to drop in on him every morning to discuss the state of the nation, and old Jack was full of news tips to the discredit of Roosevelt and the New Dealers. Just before the Senate was called to order, at noon, he would get out his bottle of Texas forty-rod, and, as he said, "strike a blow for freedom." This, of course, was before the repeal of the Eighteenth Amendment became effective. One day Hyde took me in to wait on him, and he produced his bottle as usual. He told me then that every Texan who called on him expected a drink out of it. He said he didn't mind the cost of the whiskey, which was not much, but that the wastage of glassware was serious, for every visitor pocketed his own glass as a souvenir. He said that Mrs. Garner had to go to a ten-cent store every few weeks, and lay in a new supply.

Roosevelt, as historians will recall, rushed out to Chicago by air to accept the nomination—the first nominee in American history to do so on the spot. His speech was completely devoid of any reference to the vast congeries of perunas that afterward passed under the name of the New Deal. Like the platform that the convention had adopted he was orthodox on all the classical articles of Democratic doctrine—the reduction of governmental expenditures, the balancing of the budget, easy loans for the sweating farmers, and a downward revision of the tariff. He even followed the platform into a demand for sound money. His speech was hardly a success. He had been delayed by a storm on his air trip from Albany, and the delegates, who were eager to have done with their business and go home, were kept waiting. When, in his mellifluous tenor, he bellowed "We want beer!" there was very little applause, for everyone knew what efforts he and his agents had made to kill the wet-wet plank. It is, indeed, a sober fact that Ritchie got more applause from the delegates than Roosevelt. The latter went home in a predominantly gloomy frame of mind. The Southerners believed that the wet-wet plank would give them trouble on election day, and might be almost as costly as the nomination of Al Smith in 1928, and no one save Jim Farley had much enthusiasm for Roosevelt. He was elected in November, not for his own sake, but because the country was tired of Hoover. Hoover's speech of acceptance was a flop in the grand manner. His long dalliance with Bishop Cannon and company had over taken him at last. As for Roosevelt, he simply kept on repeating the lofty promises of his own speech of acceptance, none of which was ever carried out. The day after the wet-wet plank was forced into the platform I encountered Bishop Cannon in an upstairs corridor of the Congress Hotel, and sat down with him to discuss the situation of the Prohibitionists. He admitted freely that they were on the ropes, but insisted that they would come back. He regarded the Hoover platform as treason, and hinted that multitudes of Prohibitionists would vote for Roosevelt, if only in reprisal. While we sat talking one of the newspaper photographers discovered us, and soon half a dozen of the brethren came rushing up and began exploding their flashlights. It struck them as extraordinary that I should be engaged in an amicable palaver with the bishop. But despite our public disagreement, we were good friends in private, and have remained so ever since.

When I got back to New York Knopf suggested that my dispatches to the *Evening Sun* from the two conventions would make a saleable book. This seemed to me to be a bad idea. Those dispatches were already stale as news, and it would be a long while before they would have any value as history. But Knopf kept dogging away at me, and finally I consented, though still against my own judgment. I put it together in record-breaking time. The preface was written on a Sunday afternoon in Baltimore, and the text following was put together the next day. Knopf rushed the book through the printing-office and bindery, and it came out on September 1. It was a dismal failure—in fact, the worst I have ever had. Knopf, rather fatuously, sent a copy [of *Making A President*] to Roosevelt, who was treated rather roughly in my reports from the convention. He acknowledged it on August 26 in a letter saying "I am particularly happy to have it because I happen to know Mr. Mencken very well." This deceived poor Knopf, who was (and is) a political innocent, and knows nothing of the ways of politicians itching for high office.

I did not follow the candidates in the 1932 campaign, for I was kept too busy by the troubles of the *American Mercury*; moreover, my opinion of Hoover and Roosevelt was so low that I had no desire to travel with them. I voted for Roosevelt and gave him mild support, but only because, everything else being equal, I have always been against the sitting candidate.

My contributions to the editorial page of the *Evening Sun* in 1932 began with a review of "The State of the Nation" on January 4. Politics was my principal theme all year, with special stress upon the final states of the long battle against Prohibition. There was an interlude in the early months, when my trip to the West Indies produced two articles—"West Indian Notes" on January 25 and "Havana Revisited" on February 1—and another soon afterward, when the Japanese landed in Shanghai, and the idiot Stimson, then Hoover's Secretary of State, began beating his breast in moral indignation and talking darkly of war. I had been convinced since the Washington Naval Conference of 1921 that the United

States would goad Japan into war soon or late, and it seemed to me that 1932 was as good a time as another. On February 8, under the heading of "The Japanese Bugaboo," I wrote as follows:

> I confess frankly that it would not annoy me to hear that the Japanese ambassador had been given his passports. The war would blow up the Depression as neatly as a Prohibition agent explodes a still. Every factory chimney would begin to belch smoke, and the railroads would resume dividends. There would be good jobs at high wages for all the unemployed, and the busting of banks would cease. It would delight me, above all, to behold the pacifists, and especially the clergy among them, tearing up their pledges to object conscientiously, and howling for blood.

I returned to the subject on February 29, under the heading of "Blood Upon the Moon," and again on March 14, under that of "Tough Days for Pacifists." My estimate of the military prowess of the Japanese, in those days, was not too high. Remembering how a small force of German reservists had run rings around them at Tsingtao in 1914, I figured that they would be no match for any Western army (or navy). It was not until the end of 1941 that their almost fabulous successes in the South Pacific proved how wrong I was.

The campaign of 1932 was a dull one, despite the tremendous issues involved, for Roosevelt confined himself to orthodox promises, and nothing whatsoever was heard of the New Deal. Hoover started out in the fond belief that it would be sufficient for him to stick to the White House, continue his imbecile incantations for the cure of the Depression, and issue an occasional solemn pronunciamento to his lieges, but when, after his speech of acceptance, it began to appear that he was in peril, he took reluctantly to the stump. The reception that he got was anything but flattering, and he developed a fear of assassination. Meanwhile, Roosevelt was roving the country with his lyrical tenor voice, making powerful medicine. He whooped up all the time-honored economic planks that his party had adopted at Chicago—a reduction in governmental expenditures, the balancing of the budget, the abolition of useless boards and commissions, a revision of the tariff downward, the maintenance of a sound dollar, and so on. The country, up to election day, was still unaware that the Depression was unlike the others that had gone before it: both Hoover and Roosevelt proposed to treat it with the old remedies. But toward the end of the year it began to be apparent that something extraordinary was afoot, and soon afterward Hoover proposed that Roosevelt come to Washington to join him in more radical action. When

Roosevelt refused a genuine panic followed, and early in February, 1933, the banks began to wobble. The first of the bank holidays was proclaimed by Governor Ritchie of Maryland on February 25, and others quickly followed. A good deal of all this I missed, for at about the same time both Sara and I came down with influenza, and before the end of the month, at Patterson's advice, I took her to Sea Island, Ga. He had been there some time before, and recommended it as much superior to Florida. Just before Ritchie's bank holiday began I got word from Patterson that the Baltimore Trust Company was again in serious difficulties and would probably blow up anon, so I drew out the last of my balance with it. The result was that Sara and I had plenty of money during our trip to the South, which made us stand out sharply from all the other Northerners we met. There were bank holidays by then in nearly all the States, and the national holiday was to start on March 6. Many of the guests at Sea Island, most of them rich, had no money on them save a little small change, but the hotel took their checks: it actually offered to take mine *undated.*

Roosevelt's measures for dealing with the situation, at the start, seemed to me to be reasonable enough, but when Congress met on March 9 and he flooded it with palace legislation giving him all sorts of vast and irresponsible powers I began to be suspicious, for I had a very low opinion of his capacity for affairs. But the country was in such a mood that it was willing to accept any device that promised to give it relief, and so he had his way. No one, as yet, could see more than the faintest outlines of the New Deal. Nor did many Americans, in those electric March days, realize the importance of the news that was coming in from Germany. Hitler had become chancellor on January 30, and two days later he had dissolved the Reichstag. On March 5 there was an election, the Nazis won, and at once proceeded to chase and jail their opponents. A few days after the election there were attacks on American Jews in Berlin. It was impossible, at that time, to see any reasonable hope for the rehabilitation of Germany in the Nazi program: it looked to be no more than a scheme of ruffianism, quite indistinguishable from the ruffianism of the Ku Klux Klan and the American Legion in the United States. By May the Jews in the United States were hard at work on a new campaign of anti-German propaganda. This alarmed many persons who were friendly to Germany, and eager to see the venom of the first World War disposed of forever, and some of these persons formed an association under the name of the Friends of Germany. I was asked to join by Col. Edwin Emerson, but refused for two reasons. The first, of course, was

Mencken looks—and was—perturbed during President Roosevelt's first year in office. 1933. Ben Pinchot.

that I never joined anything, and the second was that I was convinced that Hitler's reckless operations were fanning enmity to Germany, and so undoing the work of its friends. On May 12 I wrote to Emerson:

> I appreciate your thought of me, but I must confess frankly that I am in no mood at the moment to join the Friends of Germany. It seems to me that the German politicians, by their extraordinary imbecility, have destroyed at one stroke a work of rehabilitation that has been going on since the war, and that they have made it quite impossible to set up any rational defense of their course. I can imagine no more stupendous folly. For ten years, thanks to the hard and intelligent work of both Germans and Americans, the American attitude toward Germany has been improving steadily, and there was a growing disposition to take the German view of the "reparations" obscenity, and of the whole Treaty of Versailles. But now, by talking and acting in a completely lunatic manner, Hitler and his associates have thrown away the German case and given the enemies of their country enough ammunition to last for years.
>
> I am well aware that the reports of what has actually gone on in Germany have been exaggerated by interested parties, and I am keenly conscious that this is the time, above all times since 1914, for those who know and respect the country to come to its defense, but I see no way to make that defense convincing to fair men so long as the chief officer of the German state continues to make speeches worthy of an Imperial Wizard of the Ku Klux Klan, and his followers imitate, plainly with his connivance, the monkey-shines of the American Legion at its worst.
>
> My belief is that all sincere friends of Germany can accomplish most in the present emergency, not by seeking to stay the anti-German propaganda now loosed again in this country, but by trying to convince Hitler and company that their course makes staying it impossible. If you are taking any steps in that direction I'll be very glad to join you. My sympathy for the German people is not diminished in the slightest. I believe today, as I have always believed, that the right was on their side in the war, and I am distressed beyond measure to see them exposed once more to their enemies, many of whom are obviously not honest. But I see no way to give them any effective help so long as their official spokesmen are such blatant and preposterous damned fools.
>
> I don't think I have been misled by the prevailing anti-German billingsgate. I have been the target of it myself too often to take it seriously. But the testimony of such old and tried friends of Germany as S. Miles Bouton is not to be disregarded, and there is incontrovertible

support for it in almost every day's news. I am in hopes that the present uproar will end quickly. But while it lasts it seems to me that there is nothing to do save to try to weather it with as much equanimity as possible.

I was, of course, not yet aware of Bouton's probable reasons for turning on Hitler, and hence swallowed his correspondence to the *Sun* too innocently, but there was enough corroboration from other sources to justify my uneasiness. It was plain from the start that the campaign against the Jews would set their brethren in the United States to howling mightily, and I well knew Roosevelt's friendliness toward them and his obligation to them. The tour of Jim Farley had been paid for largely with Jewish money, and Jews had contributed lavishly to the Democratic campaign fund in 1932. What I feared was that Hitler's doings would give the English an excuse for attaching Germany, and that they would have American support. Germany was then unarmed, and its position seemed precarious. No one, at that time, had any conception of Hitler's stupendous cunning. If I had been told that he would somehow manage to bluff and hold off the English (not to mention the French) for five years, and that in the meantime he would organize a mighty Germany army, find first-rate commanders for it, arm it with new and highly effective weapons, and so be able to challenge and stand off all Europe—if I had heard that in 1933 I'd have snickered like any other wiseacre. The only consequence I could see in the rise of the Nazis was a revival of anti-German agitation all over the world. But it was one thing to feel thus, and quite another thing to help the Jews foment that agitation. I got a great many letters and telephone calls from the more rambunctious of them, all demanding that I denounce Hitler in the *Evening Sun* categorically and at once, but therein they made a characteristic and often-repeated mistake. If they had let me alone I might have said in print substantially what I had already said in my letter to Emerson, but in the face of their attempt to browbeat me I could only refuse to write a line. They then tried to get at me by putting pressure on the *Evening Sun* itself, and finally, on May 25, that pressure became so formidable that it printed a letter from one of them. I thereupon sent Patterson a copy of my letter to Emerson, along with the following:

> I observe that a Jewish brother calls on me in today's Letter Column to write an article on Hitler. Other demands of the same sort have reached me, by mail and telephone, but none from any Jew I know, or from any of any apparent dignity. I shall, of course, write no such article. If I did so I'd have to discuss the causes of anti-Semitism in Germany (and in

the United States) and that would only provide a field day for all the professional kikes.

It occurs to me that you may be interested in knowing how the situation really looks to me. Enclosed is a carbon of a letter I sent to Col. Edwin Emerson two weeks ago, after he had notified me of my election as an honorary member of a society calling itself the Friends of Germany. This Emerson I don't know, but I have been in communication with him since 1914, and so far as I know he is an honest man. I have had no reply from him. During the past month or so I have sent letters of the same general tenor to 30 or 40 German acquaintances, including some high dignitaries.

Patterson, of course, agreed that I was right in refusing to print anything against Hitler so long as the Jews were trying to force me, and the net result of the attempt was simply a sharp rise in the anti-Semitism in the *Sun* office. Officially, to be sure, the paper sympathized with the German Jews, but the raucous bellowing of their Baltimore relatives produced a great deal of ill-feeling. They were, in those early days of Naziism, so alarmed as to be hysterical. Better than the rest of us, they sensed what was ahead for their people. But the imprudence of their devices for getting support only made them enemies in the *Sun* office. Of these the chief was William E. Moore, managing editor of the *Sun*. He remained implacably anti-Semitic to the end of his days, and any suggestion that he give a job to a Jewish reporter or copy-reader set him to howling. It was sometimes difficult for him to turn down an applicant supported by important influence, but he always managed to do it.

Some of the details of what afterward came to be known as the New Deal began to reveal themselves before Roosevelt was inaugurated, and so early as January 2, 1933, I was denouncing the underlying theory on the ground that it involved a "concept of the government as a milch-cow with *n* teats." But in those days before the actual miracle on Mount Sinai I was principally interested, not in economics, but in the liquidation of Prohibition, and followed eagerly every step of the process. It was plain by the middle of January that Congress would submit the repeal of the Eighteenth Amendment to the country (it was done on February 20) and that even before the States could vote on it 3.2% beer would be legalized (it was done on April 7). {These events gave the final quietus to a scheme that I had been agitating in the *Sun* office during all the years of

Prohibition. It was for a census of actual church attendance at all the Baltimore churches on a typical Sunday. My theory was that the evangelical churches, which were the strongholds of Prohibition sentiment, were very slimly attended—that they really represented a much less formidable body of opinion than their blood-sweating pastors alleged. I was convinced that the total attendance at a big Catholic church—say, St. Martin's— where nearly all the communicants were wets, would turn out, for all masses, to be greater than the total attendance in any 25 Protestant churches. Taking such a census, of course, would have been difficult technically, for it would have involved finding at least 150 enumerators capable of making counts without causing disturbances and honest enough to report them objectively. But this difficulty might have been surmounted, and the *Sunpapers* were rich enough to pay the high cost. What dissuaded Patterson and Black was the fear that announcement of the result might have launched a religious war in Baltimore. I had no fear of that, for I was convinced that the Methodists, etc. would get the worst of it, but I could never put my plan through. Now it was dead.}

Anticipating these events, I set myself the job of drawing up a licensing act for Baltimore city, and it was printed in the *Evening Sun* in three instalments, January 23, 24 and 25, and soon afterward reprinted by the *Sunpapers* as a pamphlet for free distribution. The principal features of this proposed act were two in number—first, an effort to get rid of stand-up bars for drinking, and to divert their trade to sit-down restaurants, and second an effort to set up a licensing authority that would be beyond the reach of politicians. So far as I can recall, it had no influence whatsoever upon the licensing act actually adopted in Maryland, though Governor Ritchie, who drew up the letter, asked for my aid while he was engaged upon it. What I chiefly remember of this consultation is that Ritchie turned out to be as completely ignorant of wines as a Methodist bishop.

I had a low view of Roosevelt, but he was at least better than Hoover, and so I was inclined to grant him every reasonable assumption when he was sworn in. But when, after calling Congress in extra session, he began reaching out for a vast congeries of extraordinary and often extraconstitutional powers, and, what is worse, filling Washington with a horde of bogus "experts" of a hundred varieties, I found myself on the opposition bench once again—my natural, most comfortable and apparently inevitable place. My first doubts got into the *Evening Sun* of March 13, under the heading of "A Time to be Wary": they were directed at the motley quacks of the Brain Trust rather than at Roosevelt himself. But on March 27 I began to object to the immense cost of the new legislation that was being rushed through Congress, on April 24 I was protesting against Roosevelt's conversion (in direct violation of his campaign promises) to debasing the dollar, and on June 19 I was predicting that a great increase in the Federal deficit and hence in the national debt was in the offing. Soon after the National Industry Recovery Act (N.I.R.A.) was passed in June I wrote an article pointing out some of its imbecilities, but this article did not get into the *Evening Sun* until November, and then only in a considerably diluted form. It was held up, and with it an analogous editorial for the *Sun* by John Owens, because Paul Patterson feared that if the *Sunpapers* attacked the N.I.R.A. with any vigor they would be accused of trying to protect their own withers. That charge, in fact, was soon made against other and less cautious newspapers by Roosevelt and his associates, and there began a battle over the Newspaper Code which went on until the Supreme Court finally liquidated the National Recovery Administration (N.R.A.) in the Schechter decision of May 27, 1935.

But the *Sunpapers* signed the Newspaper Code as of August 14, and decided to fly the Blue Eagle. It appeared at the top of the first page of both *Sun* and *Evening Sun* on August 17. I also flew it myself, though of course only ironically. Long before this time my mail had grown so heavy that the Baltimore Postoffice had given me the rank of a business concern, which allowed me, *inter alia*, to go to the main postoffice on Sundays and legal holidays, when there were no deliveries, and cart my letters home myself. When the N.R.A. began, the blanks for signing up were distributed to employers by the Postoffice, and so I got one. I signed it at once, hung a large blue eagle in my office window in Cathedral street, bought a Blue Eagle stamp, and used it on my stationery. My opposition to the N.R.A. did not extend to its administrator, General Hugh S. Johnson. He was a talented showman, and his uproars during the Summer and Autumn of 1933 greatly amused me. There was a big parade in Baltimore in the heat of August, and all the poor shop-girls of the town were forced to march in it. At the head of the procession rode Governor Ritchie in an open automobile. As he passed along Cathedral street Sara and I, looking from our third-story window at 704, noted with delight that His Excellency was far gone in liquor. In fact, he was so far stewed that he could hardly hold up his head.

John Owens, a born conservative, was suspicious of the New Deal from the start, and as its vast extravagance and multitudinous quackeries began to unfold he tackled it with some vigor in the *Sun*. But on the *Evening Sun* Hamilton Owens took a much more friendly view of it, and by the beginning of 1934 the two papers were widely at variance. There were several reasons for Hamilton's greater tolerance. The first was that there was a Liberal hidden in him, despite his long reviling of the puerile Utopianism that passed in the United States under the name of Liberalism. He had reprinted his familiar definition—"A Liberal is one who believes in more laws and more jobholders; therefore in higher taxes and less liberty"—so recently as November 24, 1932, nearly three weeks after Roosevelt's election; but in the face of the whoopla that began in Washington on March 4 he rapidly succumbed—if not to the highly dubious ideas behind it, then at least to the wild enthusiasm of the New Dealers, the noise and drama, the sheer exhilaration of the chase. Any gaudy show enchanted him, and he was naturally in favor of whoever was doing the flipflops and cracking the whip. Moreover, it is not to be forgotten that the New Dealers, in those first electric days, were pursuing quarry that he himself had been pursuing for ten years—the bankers, the big industrialists, the great herd of stupid Babbitts. I had myself engaged in the same sport, and greatly enjoyed it as it was carried on in the grand manner, though I never had any delusion about its wisdom or its probable effects: my belief, then as now, was that Recovery was still possible in 1933, and that it was impeded and prevented by the idiotic devices that New Dealers adopted to produce it. There was something else in Owens, to wit, a great itch for money, and hence a covert envy and dislike of men who had got it. In a little while he was accepting quite gravely the New Deal theory that all the blame for the Depression lay upon the rich, and thereby giving countenance to the worst demagogies of the wizards of the Brain Trust. When I took him to task for this course, late in 1934, he confessed frankly that the New Deal had fetched him, and defended himself on the ground that it had also fetched all the other younger man in the office, and, as he added, in the composing-room. This seemed to me a bad reason for swallowing buncombe that was growing more palpable every day, but it was not my business to police him, and so I dropped the subject.

He might have been brought to order very easily by Harry Black, for, as I have before remarked, he was hardly more than a function of Black—but Black, alas, was going the same way. Two things, I believe, moved him. One was a conviction, not without support in the evidence, that the men of money of the country, taking one with another, were hopeless idiots, and that it was thus good riddance to drive them to cover. The other was a sentimental feeling about Roosevelt, his dead brother's friend. So far as I know, his personal relations to Roosevelt were hardly closer than, say, my own, and I am sure that he never visited the White House; nevertheless, Roosevelt had had the confidence of Van Lear, and thus appeared to deserve his. Whatever the complex of causes, Hamilton Owens and Harry Black gave Roosevelt steady support, though often only by satirical indirection, during the whole of his first term. I can't recall a single editorial in the *Evening Sun* that denounced the New Deal in a forthright manner, as it was sometimes denounced in the *Sun*. Black and Owens were always finding excuses for its successive sure-cures, and when no such excuse could be fetched up they devoted themselves to sneering at its opponents. This last habit greatly diminished the effectiveness of the editorials in the *Evening Sun*, for it was hardly possible to adapt the methods of the old merry wars on Prohibition, Ku Kluxry, the Coolidge Prosperity and the Hoover New Economics to what was essentially a serious fight. Much that Owens wrote and printed in those days was downright silly, not only in thesis but also in manner. The *Evening Sun*, once shrewd and witty, began to seem hopelessly trivial: it had become like a third-rate college paper, run by campus pinks. I had been protesting against its deterioration for some years, and now, with that deterioration grown acute and unendurable, I protested every day and with violent earnestness. Patterson never made any answer to my argument save to agree with me; in fact, he seemed to be even more disgusted by it than I was. But his characteristic dislike of forthright acts and unpleasant scenes stayed him from doing anything about it, and it was not until 1936 that he lost his patience at last, and brought Hamilton Owens sharply to heel. When that time came he proceeded, very wisely, by tackling Harry Black, for Owens was still only a function of Black. The scheme he adopted will be described in its proper chronological place.

My contributions to the editorial page of the *Evening Sun* in 1933 began, significantly enough, with a piece entitled "The Men Who Rule Us," printed on January 2: in it I made my first onslaught on "the concept of government as a milch-cow with n teats"—an idea that I was to labor very often during the eight years following. On January 30, Coolidge having died, I discussed his dark and baffling character under the heading of "The Coolidge Mystery"; on February 6 I denounced the beginnings of the New Deal in an article entitled "Economy: 1933 Model"; and on March 13, during the Bank Holiday, I printed a piece called "A Time to be Wary." "The Tune Changes" followed on March 27—a brief treatise on the imbecilities in the Roosevelt Farm Relief programme. In the meantime, on February 13, under the heading of "Katzenjammer," I flogged the pedagogical quacks who were by now crowding to the front, and on March 30, under that of "Thirteen Years," I reviewed the history of Prohibition. On April 17, in "The Twilight of the Idols," I noted the collapse of the bankers of the country as objects of envy and admiration. "One by one," I wrote, "the old idols of *Pongo americanus* wither and fade away. Single-handed and alone, the late Lord Hoover finished two favorites—the Quaker and the engineer. Now the bankers carry on the sad process by committing *hara-kiri.*" On May 1, under the heading of "Vive le Roi," I responded to Roosevelt's voracious reaching out for power by proposing that he be made king, and several times later on I returned to the subject. On June 19, in "A Day of Reckoning," I discussed his threatened budget for the fiscal-year 1933–34 and denounced the Brain Trust; on June 26, in "Saving the World," I had my say about the World Economic Conference then meeting in London and soon to be wrecked by Roosevelt's sabotage; on September 11, in "Obsequies," I rejoiced in anticipation over the fact that Maryland was to go thunderously wet the next day, my fifth-third birthday; and on November 6, free at last to deal with the N.R.A., I had at it under the heading of "The Morning After." At other times I printed articles on familiar themes—for example, several on crime and punishment.

The most important of the last-named had to do with a second lynching on the Eastern Shore of Maryland. This occurred on October 18, 1933, the scene was the forlorn little town of Princess Anne, down near the Virginia line, and the victim was one George Armwood, a Negro accused of raping an aged white woman. Two days before this, on October 16, I had printed an article on the Euel Lee case, which had been dragging on since 1931. The Court of Appeals of Maryland, determined to get a fair trial for Lee, though he had twice confessed and was clearly guilty, had issued a remarkable declaratory judgment—something quite new in Maryland jurisprudence—notifying the Eastern Shore courts very solemnly that if anything even remotely resembling a legal lynching were attempted it would be heard from. This declaratory judgment was written by an old friend of mine, Chief Judge Carroll T. Bond, and I was naturally strongly for it, and praised it in the *Evening Sun.* But its effect on the Eastern Shore was simply to inflame the crackers the more, for the long delay in trying Lee, though it was due to their own acts, had greatly exasperated them. In all probability, their exasperation was the principal cause of the Princess Anne lynching, which seemed to their dark minds to be a brave gesture of defiance. Whatever the fact, they were in a violent state of mind, and when the *Sun* denounced the lynching and I followed on October 23 with an article headed "Revels in Transchoptankia" they raged and roared in a really dreadful manner. My article, it goes without saying, was not designed to placate them. It began as follows:

The civic pageant at Princess Anne last Wednesday night, technically speaking, was of a high order, and no doubt there is some quiet gloating when a Somerset man meets a neighbor from Wicomico today. By comparison, the evangelical ceremony at Salisbury two years ago was a crude and rustic affair; moreover, it took no warlike enterprise, for the victim was helpless in a hospital and not a soul went to his defense. But the brethren at Princess Anne not only had to bang their way into a stone jail; they also had to face a shock-troop of General Baughman's Cossacks, armed with lethal gases, firearms and the authority of the great Free State of Maryland. If Somerset is now palpitating with pride, then why not? And if Wicomico feels a bit let down, and Dorchester and Worcester stir uneasily, then why not again? Certainly the championship of the First Judicial Circuit has been won fairly by the gallant lads of Princess Anne.

Dorchester and Worcester both had the Hon. Euel Lee in their clutches at the time of the Salisbury fiesta, and each muffed its chance. There was some motion to dispatch him at Snow Hill when he was first arraigned but it petered out in a roughing of his counsel, the Hon. Bernard Ades, LL.B. A week or two later, when he was taken to Cambridge, the patriotic men of Dorchester began to assemble, but before they could work off their fear of the State cops the Court of Appeals induced the local judges to send the prisoner to the Western Shore, and they let him depart without the loss of an ear. What they had in mind was eloquently indicated by Pattison, C.J., a Dorchester man himself, when he proposed gravely that Lee be quartered on an armed boat in the Choptank river, heavily guarded during his trial. But the local boys lost their nerve, and so another felonious blackamoor lived to be hanged by due process.

I can't pretend to be in the confidence of the brave Bible students below the Choptank, but I am willing to risk \$2 at even money that Dorchester and Worcester will not wait two years to wipe out their shame. There is at all times a large supply of likely colored brothers in those latitudes, and local pride runs very high. Thus I look for a lynching in Dorchester before another year rolls around, and another in Worcester, and maybe a third in Wicomico, better and braver than the last one. Then the First Judicial Circuit, which is exactly coterminous with Transchoptankia, will be on an even keel again, its eminent jurists will be free to resume the chase of chicken-thieves, and a long while may pass before the cycle is resumed.

This sort of thing, of course, set the whole lower Shore to howling, and my mail was filled with tall threats. Going on, I proceeded to discuss the various plans that had been put forward, after the Salisbury lynching of 1931, to prevent other lynchings in Maryland, and rejected them all as ineffective.

The plain truth—I said—is that public opinion, in all that lush and pious domain of Moronia Felix, is almost unanimously in favor of an occasional lynching, with ears and pieces of rope for souvenirs, and a pleasant time for man, woman and child. There is, to be sure, a minority that dissents: but it is feeble and almost inarticulate. At the time of the Salisbury ceremony it was simply not heard from; all the noise came from the other side. I seem to recall that a clergyman in Cambridge protested, but if so he certainly did not protest long and loud. The rest of the holy men confined themselves to denouncing the city slickers who had ventured to offer opinions on the subject. As for the generality of the local patriots, they were openly exultant, and thousands of them outfitted their automobiles with signs reading:

I Am An

EASTERN SHOREMAN

And Proud Of It.

Governor Ritchie had sent the State police to Princess Anne when reports of a threatened lynching reached him, but the mob had defied them, and their commander, Baughman, was afraid to order them to fire. After the show was over Ritchie employed Pinkerton detectives to track down the lynchers, and in a little while four of them were collared and brought to Baltimore—a druggist named William H. Thompson, who was the leader of the mob; Irving Atkins, one of the town constables; William S. McQuade, a chain-store clerk from the nearby town of Pocomoke City; and William P. Hearn, a truck driver from the hamlet of Shad Point. Ritchie's employment of the detectives was decided on at a meeting at Patterson's house, at which Ritchie, his attorney-general (W. Preston Lane), the two Owenses, Harry Black, Patterson and I were present. Lane, who was a very courageous fellow, went down to Princess Anne to help in the investigation, though the yahoos there threatened to shoot him. Unhappily, it came to nothing, for a local judge eager for higher office, Robert F. Duer by name, ordered the four suspects—they were all obviously guilty—brought before him on a writ of *habeas corpus*, and then released them "for lack of evidence." Duer was urged by his customers to order John Owens and me brought before him also, and it was openly announced that our trip to Princess Anne would be a one-way ride, but this scheme was blocked when Ritchie let it be known that he would intervene as Governor and order our release before we could be removed from Baltimore. On October 30 I returned to the subject under the heading of "Plans to Put Down Lynching," and on December 4, after Duer had discharged the lynchers, I had my say again in a piece entitled "Victory." In the last named I called attention to a forgotten provision of Article IV of the Constitution of Maryland, permitting the Governor to remove any judge convicted "in a court of law of incompetency, of willful neglect of duty, misbehavior in office, or any other crime": I proposed that Duer and the other judges who had got lynching dust upon them be put on trial by the Court of Appeals. But nothing, of course, came of this. A curious feature of the whole uproar was that public opinion in Baltimore seemed to be predominantly on the side of the lynchers; in fact, I got more threatening letters from city people than from the simians of the lower Shore itself. One of these sympathizers was Harry C. Martin, warden of the Baltimore City jail. When he was required by Judge Duer's writ of *habeas corpus* to return the four lynchers to Princess Anne, he made quite a ceremony of the business, and soon afterward, in a speech before a Democratic ward club, praised them highly. Another partisan, as incredible as it may seem, was Dr. Joseph S. Ames, president of the Johns Hopkins University! When one of his professors, a radical named Broadus Mitchell, published a report on the Salisbury lynching in 1932, at the request of the Federal Council of the Churches of Christ in America, old Ames wrote a letter to the Salisbury *Times* saying:

> My whole reaction toward the civilization on the Eastern Shore is that *I think it is fine, and I have often said that I would like to live there.*

The italics are mine. Mitchell became extremely unpopular at the Johns Hopkins, and was finally forced out in 1939. Others who went to the defense of the lynchers were William T. Holloway, principal of the State Normal School at Salisbury, and E. Clarke Fontaine, supervisor of high-schools under the State board of education. In my final article, "Victory," on December 4, I recalled to the incandescent Shoremen what the Scopes trial of 1925 had done for Dayton, Tenn. I said:

The lower Shore now trembles with fatuous ecstasy on the verge of just such ill fame. Millions are aware of it who were never aware of it before, and the picture they have of it bristles with bayonets and drips with gore. Let it have another lynching, and it will be three strikes and out. Thenceforth, no newspaper reader, no radio listener and no newsreel customer on earth will ever see or hear its name without thinking at once of mobs roaring down village streets, helpless prisoners mauled, butchered and burned, and savages fighting for pieces of their carcasses. It may be that this is the sort of celebrity that the boosters of Salisbury and Princess Anne crave and will take pride in, but I doubt it. Certainly there must be plenty among them who know very well that a town may be ruined quite as easily by a man or a woman, and a whole region quite as easily as a town.

These cooler heads, I daresay, are reflecting even today, with the banners of victory still flying, upon the possible consequences, including the economic consequences, of the performance to date. The lower Shore, for years past, has been doing badly, and is very hard up. Of the eight counties below Cecil, six lost population between 1920 and 1930. There is an unhealthy crowding into the larger towns, especially Salisbury, just as there is a movement out of the region as a whole. Life on the farm and along the bay is not what it used to be, and the livelier spirits are all clearing out. The best come to Baltimore, or go to some other city, and the second or third best seek fortune and adventure in Salisbury, the Babylon and Gomorrah of all Transchoptankia. This resigns the villages, the farms and the dreary coastlands to the fourth-raters, and they made sad havoc of what remains of the old Shore *Kultur*, once so civilized and so charming.

The natural treasures of the lower counties are the beauty of their landscape, the fertility of much of their soil, and the prodigal riches of their waters. The first, in late years, has brought in some new and valuable residents—mainly well-heeled *rentiers* from the North, eager only to fish, gun, loaf and invite their souls. But not many will come hereafter, for such men have no taste for mob rule, and know only too well the perils of xenophobia. Thus the Shore will have to live by raising and catching things to eat. How will it be helped in that enterprise if the appetites of its customers are turned every time they hear its name by recollections of gruesome and revolting public rites, suggesting the dissecting room rather than the dinner table? Here is a kind of boycott that its bold Babbitts do not seem to have thought of.

That was in 1933, and there has been no lynching on the Shore since, nor even any threat of one. The dudgeon of the Shoremen flamed on for a year or two, and then gradually subsided. While it lasted there was a boycott of the *Sunpapers*, and they lost some subscribers, but not a great many. Their circulation men, like their reporters and photographers, were threatened with violence, but circulation men are tough fellows, and soon resumed operations, at least in the larger towns. The lower Shore, in truth, is territory that belongs to Philadelphia and Wilmington rather than to Baltimore. Getting papers to it from Baltimore is so difficult that for a while the experiment was attempted of delivering them by air. But it turned out to be too expensive and was soon abandoned. The Shore's Christian pride and sensitivity were soothed, in the long run, by two things, the first being the effect of time and the second being the diligent missionarying of Folger McKinsey (The Bentztown Bard), the *Sun*'s staff poet. The Bard had always been a favorite in rural Maryland, and whenever he appeared in a county-town the whole population turned out to hear him read his pious verses—the school-children in the morning, the local Rotarians, Kiwanians or Lions at lunchtime, the clubwomen in the afternoon, and the male dignitaries in the evening. Not infrequently he wound up a day of mellifluous poesy by getting tight with the town antinomians. In 1936 or thereabouts Patterson conceived the idea that this popularity might be well employed by the *Sunpapers*' promotion department. To that end he provided the Bard with motor-car and a chauffeur and sent him on long tours of the Maryland *Hinterland*. Sometimes he would be gone a week. Not only did he read his poems to the rustics; he also wrote highly complimentary articles on their towns, with plenty of pictures and flattering mention of all the local notables, and these articles were printed in early editions of the *Sun*, for distribution in the counties. The city readers of the paper never saw them. This scheme worked very well, even on the Eastern Shore, and after a year or two the *Sunpapers* were almost as popular again as they had been in the heyday of the Abells. But I did not share in that popularity. In 1934 I went on the *Nation*'s Roll of Honor for my denunciation of the two lynchings, but rural Maryland did not applaud. To this day it is clearly understood that my presence is not desired on the lower Shore, and that my appearance there would probably lead to unpleasantness.

12

Battle in the Grand Manner

1934

In February, 1934, Sara and I sailed for the Mediterranean in the
Columbus of the North-German Lloyd—our first holiday of any length
since our honeymoon in 1930. We were gone until April. When we left
New York the whole East was in the midst of the coldest weather for
years, there was floating ice in the ocean fifty miles from shore, and the
paint was flaking off the ship's hull; when we got back the temperature
was 80 degrees. I wrote enough *Evening Sun* articles in advance to keep
Hamilton Owens going until the first done *en route* could reach him, and
then went through the year without missing a week. I sent home five
from places along the way—the first from Madeira, where I looked into
the wine situation, and wrote a detailed report on it for the comfort of
the Baltimore winebibbers; the second from Morocco, the third from the
ruins of Carthage, and then two from the Holy Land.

During the hot Summer of 1934, before my election to the board, I
gave over weeks to the dismal job of getting the *Sunpapers* out of a gory
knock-'em-down-and-drag-'em-out battle with Michael J. Curley, the
Catholic archbishop of Baltimore, in the course of which he attempted to
force all the Catholics of the archdiocese to boycott them. The man primarily responsible for this row was S. Miles Bouton, hitherto encountered as the Berlin correspondent of the *Sun*, but Moore and John Owens
were also more or less to blame, and Owens's vanity introduced a
complication that was almost worse than the battle itself. Bouton's last

article from Berlin was dated May 17, and it appeared on the page opposite the editorial page of the *Sun* on June 1. Two weeks later he showed up in Baltimore with the news that he had been expelled from Germany by the Nazis, and a hint that he had got out just in time to save his skin. This story, as I have said hereinbefore, seemed suspicious to all of us, but inasmuch as he was now undoubtedly free, whatever the truth or nontruth of his tale of recent peril, Patterson, Owens and Moore decided to let him have his say. His first article was published in the *Sun* on June 15. It began on page one, and in it was this statement regarding his former high enthusiasm for Hitler: "I came to believe that he would be its [Germany's] salvation. I was cruelly mistaken, cruelly disillusioned." On June 18 there was a second article, beginning again on page one and jumping thence to page ten. The headline was "Hitler Described by Bouton/ As Impersonal Man, Not Vain,/ But Unswerving in Purpose." Toward the end of the article, on page ten, was the following paragraph:

> It has seemed to me at times that there is a kinship between him [Hitler] and Ignatius Loyola. One finds in both men the same complete faith in their mission, the same readiness and determination to exercise their power with utter ruthlessness and brutality in order to carry out that mission. No consideration of personal profit or glory ever entered Loyola's mind, and I believe that the same can be said of Hitler.

Obviously, this was hardly the sort of stuff that should have got into a daily paper in a city full of Catholics. For one thing, the comparison was a lame one, and for another thing it was bound to be challenged by those who both admired Ignatius and disliked Hitler. But the paragraph was passed by a copy-reader not too attentive to his duties, and when the proof went over Moore's desk he was napping and did not notice it. On June 18, the day the article was printed, the Rev. Henri J. Wiesel, S.J., president of Loyola College, Baltimore, wrote the following letter to the *Sun*:

> In his article this morning on Hitler, your former Berlin correspondent made an assertion, though he offered no proof or substantiation, that Hitler and Ignatius Loyola were alike in "their readiness and determination to exercise their power with utter ruthlessness and brutality in order to carry out their mission." No one wonders that the German government asked for his return to America when one realizes that this is a sample of his powers of observation, and his lack of regard for the truth.
>
> Why a gentleman and a seasoned newspaper man, who is supposed to have reason and judgment, must descend to such depths of untruth

as to bring up again the old and aged slander about Ignatius Loyola and the Society of Jesus, which times without number has been exploded, is beyond all power of comprehension. Let your former Berlin correspondent go to the library, ask for any of the non-Catholic biographies of Ignatius Loyola, Van Dyke, for example, or Sedgwick, and let him learn that neither Ignatius nor any of his members of the Society of Jesus have ever held or taught such a doctrine.

On the front page at the top of the *Sun* there is printed a small device depicting Justice, the American eagle, an anchor, a steamboat and a train. Above the group runs the legend: "Light for All." If your former Berlin correspondent is to continue to write along this line of untruth, then erase the "light" and substitute anything else. I suggest "darkness."

This was printed on the editorial page on June 20, under the heading: "In Protest Against Mr. Bouton's Reference to Loyola." Under it was printed a second letter from a Jesuit, also dated June 18: the author thereof was the Rev. Theodore E. Daigler, S.J., of Woodstock College, the Jesuit house of studies in Western Maryland. Both letters were mild in tone and neither made any categorical demand for an apology. On June 21 there appeared a third letter, this time dated June 19 and signed by the Rev. Thomas I. O'Malley, S.J., dean of Loyola College. It was even more conciliatory than the other two. It included a brief quotation from "Ignatius Loyola," by Paul Van Dyke, professor of modern European history at Princeton, a brother to Henry Van Dyke, and himself a former Presbyterian clergyman. So far only Jesuits had been heard from, and they were all very polite. The obvious way out, practised on newspapers since time immemorial, would have been to print a brief disclaimer of offensive intent, say at the end of one of the letters, and so adjourn the matter *sine die*. It was plain to any sensible newspaper man that comparing Ignatius to Hitler was a bad slip, if only because the letter columns of both papers were currently full of letters from Jews who compared Hitler to Beelzebub. But Owens, who was in charge of the editorial page, printed no disclaimer after any of the Jesuits' letters, and Moore, who was responsible for the Bouton article, printed none in the news columns. As for Patterson, he was a bit uneasy, but the conciliatory tone of the Jesuits reassured him, and he did not intervene. One of his reasons for doing nothing and hoping for the best was that Owens and Moore were at odds, and he did not want to set them to rowing. Moore, in fact, was on bad terms in those days with most of the other heads of departments. His infantile paralysis disabled him and made him irascible. He and Murphy, managing editor of the *Evening Sun,* scarcely spoke, and there was absolutely no coöperation between them. He was also at loggerheads with Schmick. And he greatly disliked Owens.

While all this was going on Archbishop Curley was at Woodstock, taking a Summer holiday at the Jesuit house of studies. Not much about him was known in the *Sun* office, though he had been archbishop for nearly thirteen years. All of us had known his predecessor, Cardinal Gibbons, but, as incredible as it may seem, not a single *Sun* executive had ever met Curley. He avoided association with Protestants, was engaged in reorganizing the archdiocese in a violent and ruthless manner, and was regarded by most of his lieges, including his priests, as a somewhat hard customer. An Irishman by birth, he found the Summer climate of the Eastern American seaboard unbearable, and was in the habit of returning to Ireland in June to spend July and August at his birthplace. He had put in seventeen years in Florida before coming to Baltimore, but he had never become acclimatized, so he had gone home nearly every year. He was even now preparing to sail on July 6. Meanwhile, he was not only beginning to lather under the Summer heat of Maryland; he was also entertaining a case of shingles, and had various other malaises. Moreover, he was an Irishman, and loved combat. Yet more, he had just had two easy victories—one over the Washington *Post* and the other over the Baltimore *Jewish Times,* both of which he had forced to apologize abjectly for articles that he construed as offensive to Catholics. He was thus ready to take on the *Sun,* and when he returned to Baltimore on June 26 he called up the office in high dudgeon and demanded an immediate and unqualified apology. As I have just said, he knew no one in the office, and hence did not ask for any responsible editor. Instead, he roared his objurgations into the ear of an alarmed office boy, and when the office boy turned him over to young Frank R. Kent, Jr., who was holding down the city desk in the morning *Sun* city-room, and Kent suggested weakly that he call again after noon, when some one with authority would be present to hear him, he dissolved in purple indignation and demanded that some editor of the highest rank be sent up to his house in Charles street to see him.

This demand was transmitted to Moore when he came to work in the middle of the afternoon, but he, too, was Irish, and refused absolutely to make the call. When Patterson heard of this he asked John Owens to wait on His Excellency, and after some hesitation Owens did so the next morning. He returned in an hour almost as purple as the archbishop. The two of them, it appeared, had had a dreadful set-to. On the one hand, the archbishop had roared and threatened, and on the other hand Owens had wrapped himself in a cold and aloof dignity. Owens's account of the discussion was so confused as to be almost unintelligible; all that was certain was that they had not come to terms. Patterson suggested prudently that there was still time to print a brief disclaimer of evil intent, and so get rid of the row, but Owens, by this time, was past conciliation, and so was Moore. Thus nothing was done, and on June 29 the archbishop printed the following proclamation to the faithful on the first page of his diocesan weekly, the Baltimore *Catholic Review,* in a three-column box:

THE MORNING SUN INSULTS CATHOLICS / LET US ACT, SAYS ARCHBISHOP / ARCHBISHOP'S HOUSE, / 508 NORTH CHARLES STREET, / BALTIMORE, MD. To the priests and Catholic People of the Archdiocese of Baltimore:-

The morning *Sun* on June 18 published an article by Mr. Bouton, its exiled correspondent from Germany. In it the *Sun* offered a gratuitous insult, not only to the Jesuit Fathers in this See and throughout the world, but also to every Catholic priest and every lay Catholic member of this Archdiocese.

Bouton, in his article on Hitlerism, dragged Saint Ignatius Loyola out of his four-century-old grave and held him up before his readers as a consummate blackguard. He instituted a comparison between Hitler and Saint Ignatius. He made the statement that the great Ignatius, like Hitler, did not care how he reached any particular end or by what means. He (Saint Ignatius), according to the *Sun*'s correspondent, was brutal and conscienceless like Hitler when it came to a question of means to an end. Any means—murder, rapine, fire or sword to reach your end. That, according to Bouton, was the mind and theory and teaching of Ignatius. Any man who is held up in that light is placed before the public as an ordinary scoundrel. That is exactly what the *Sun* permitted Bouton to do with Saint Ignatius Loyola.

We have no brief for Hitler. We are of the opinion, however, that Bouton lied about Hitler. {Curley, like most of the other Catholic ecclesiastics in the United States, inclined toward Totalitarianism, even though the Catholic churches in the Totalitarian countries were occasionally in conflict with it.} He certainly lied about Saint Ignatius. It was not a slip of pen or tongue. It was a lie out of whole cloth, and we defy the *Sun*'s infallible exiled correspondent to prove his statement.

Three hundred thousand Catholics of this Archdiocese repudiate the ignorance of Bouton and resent the publication by the *Sun* of Bouton's brazen mendacity concerning Saint Ignatius.

The *Sun* refuses to apologize. It has been stated that it might seem like repudiating Bouton. The latter is described as a man of courage and of a certain amount of brilliancy. Very well. The man of courage has not the courage to admit that he is wrong. Again we defy him to prove he is right. The *Sun* has not the courage to say that that statement of Bouton should never have been published. It might offend its special free-lance correspondent. The whole policy of the *Sun* has been, and is, that its special correspondents cannot err. No matter what they say, they are right.

I am not saying that Catholics of this Archdiocese should not buy the *Sun* and should not deal with its advertisers. I am saying, however, that our Catholic priests and people have no obligation in law or morals to buy the *Sun* or to deal with the *Sun* advertisers.

For twelve years and more the *Sun* has seen fit to offend Catholics by their editorials and news stories.

The priests of the Archdiocese are hereby ordered to bring this Bouton calumniation into their pulpits on Sunday, July 1, and to explain to their people the stupid insult flung at the Catholic priests and people of the Archdiocese by the *Sun*'s writer, Bouton, in his article published June 18.

We have stood enough of the insults of the *Sun*. We are now through. We ask no favors of the *Sun*. We demand justice. The organized Catholics of the Archdiocese know exactly how to act.

Catholics of the Archdiocese, let us have action!

Michael J. Curley, Abp. of Baltimore.

This blast was supported on the editorial page of the *Review* by an editorial reading as follows:

No apology has been made by the morning *Sun* for the insult contained in its issue of Monday, June 18, to the Founder of the Society of Jesus, to the members of the Society of Jesus in the Archdiocese of Baltimore; in the Maryland–New York Province of the Society of Jesus; all the members of the Society in the United States and throughout the world; all the Catholics of the Archdiocese of Baltimore and the United States and the hundreds of millions of Catholics throughout the world.

This insult, which found a place in an article written by the *Sun*'s former Berlin correspondent, likened Ignatius Loyola to Hitler and declared that Ignatius was ruthless and brutal, willing to go to any end to accomplish his purposes. Apart from the insult to the memory of Ignatius and all his spiritual sons and all Catholics, that statement is a revival of the infamous, damnable, slanderous statement that the Society of Jesus has preached the nefarious doctrine that the end justifies the means. In plain, unvarnished English the statement made in the *Sun* by an accredited correspondent was a Lie and for that Lie the *Sun* has not apologized.

His Excellency, Archbishop Curley, in today's issue, resents that Lie. He orders the priests in the Archdiocese of Baltimore, every one of them, to call attention from their pulpits to that Lie and to the refusal of the Baltimore *Sun* to apologize for it.

His Excellency hopes the alumni of Loyola College, Loyola High School and the alumni of other Jesuit institutions will make known their resentment to the Baltimore *Sun* quickly.

If the *Sun* has any sense of fair play, it will, without delay, publish an apology on its front page for the slander done to the memory of Ignatius Loyola and for the slander done to the spiritual sons of Loyola and all the Catholics of the world.

If the former Berlin correspondent of the *Sun* knows no more about conditions in Germany than he does of the life of Ignatius Loyola, it is no wonder he was invited to get out of Germany.

What is the *Sun* going to do about it? The Archbishop of Baltimore, the priests of Baltimore, the members of the religious sisterhoods and brotherhoods of Baltimore and the 300,000 Catholics of the Archdiocese want to know. If the *Sun* thinks it can defy the Catholics of Baltimore, the *Sun* is due for a sad and speedy awakening.

An early copy of the *Review* reached the *Sun* office on June 28. It was rushed there by Vincent dePaul Fitzpatrick, another Irishman, and one with a bitter personal grievance against the *Sun*. He had been on its local staff in 1917, and had hoped to be sent to France as its correspondent with the Maryland troops: when Raymond S. Tompkins got the assignment he was full of indignation, and soon afterward quit to join the staff of the *Review*. I had heard of the archbishop's demand for an apology, but knew nothing about his proclamation until Paul Patterson and John E. Semmes came to my apartment in Cathedral street on the afternoon of June 28 with a copy of it. Semmes was not only a director of the *Sunpapers,* but also their counsel in certain of their affairs. He was leaving for his Summer place in British Columbia the next day, and Patterson was planning to join him on July 18. They wanted to lay out a plan of defense at once, for it was obvious that the archbishop was launching a boycott against the papers, and no one had any idea how effective it might be. The Washington *Post,* as I have said, had been brought to its knees quickly and easily, but the *Post* was a feeble paper, whereas the *Sun* was strong, with an old and wide influence among the Catholics of the archdiocese. In the days of the Abells, who were themselves Catholics, it had been generally regarded in Baltimore as a spokesman of the church, and even after the passing of the Abells it remained on a close footing with Cardinal Gibbons. The Ku Kluxers, in fact, had often denounced it as a Roman hireling, and there was a legend in Baltimore that its real owner was a rich nun. Ever since 1922 or thereabout an alleged photograph of this nun had hung in Hamilton Owens's office, along with photographs of Bishop Cannon, the imperial kleagle of the Klan, and many of the other mock heroes of his Valhalla. But though this legend still persisted, there had been a certain change in the relations of the *Sunpapers* to the church after the exitus of the Abells in 1910, and a much greater one after the death of Cardinal Gibbons and the appointment of Curley as his successor in 1921. Gibbons had always played with the rich Catholics of the archdiocese, and they sat on all his boards, but Curley held them at arm's length and had supplanted most of them by priests. He apparently classed the *Sun* with them, and not illogically, as a representative of the lay influence that he detested. Moreover, he resented the fact that the *Sun* commonly printed more about the dead Gibbons than about the living Curley. This was his own fault, but nevertheless he resented it. He was, indeed, intensely jealous of the ghost of Gibbons, and showed it in various small ways. Thus his talk about "the insults of the *Sun,*" stretching over "twelve years and more." He was ripe for a battle in the grand manner.

When Patterson and Semmes came to see me I advised them that in my judgment the publication of the offending paragraph in Bouton's article had been a serious mistake, and should have been rectified at once, but that, in view of Curley's threat of a boycott, it was now too late for any attempt at conciliation. I proposed instead that two things be done—first, that a good man be assigned to go through the *Sun*'s files and dig up whatever they showed that might be construed as offensive to Curley's vanity, and hence responsible for his choler; and second, that efforts be made to reach the apostolic delegate at Washington, Archbishop Amleto Cicognani, who was Curley's superior and might be expected to want to avoid an open and dirty row. Patterson and Semmes agreed, and to the first end C. P. Trussell, of the *Sun*'s Washington bureau, was put to work on the files the next day. He did a good job and unearthed a lot of stuff showing that Curley had been engaged in frequent uproars, and that the *Sun* had reported them. The approach to the apostolic delegate presented greater difficulties. Essary, head of the Washington bureau, was assigned to undertake it. He reported that Cicognani kept to himself in Washington, and was virtually unknown to the newspaper men. But lines were laid to reach him through influential Catholic laymen, and though no direct word from him ever reached the *Sun* office I am convinced that he took a hand in the battle at once, and was largely responsible for its sudden end on July 19. Meanwhile, the more intelligent Catholic laymen of the archdiocese, both in Baltimore and Washington, were very much alarmed. What they feared was that if Curley really ordered a boycott, as his proclamation of June 29 threatened, the *Sun* would be forced into fighting back, and that the ensuing combat would put the Catholic church into a ridiculous light, awaken the Ku Klux spirit in the archdiocese, alienate all the other newspapers of the United States, and probably produce unpleasant repercussions throughout the country.

On July 4 a volunteer committee of Catholic laymen called at the *Sun* office to try to work out terms of peace. I was not there when they came in, and do not recall who they were, save that one of them was a man named L. J. Lebbehusen, a vice-president of the Calvert Bank. They were very much exercised over the dangerous possibilities of an attempt at a boycott, and proposed that the *Sun* print a belated disclaimer of the Bouton paragraph, and so give them material for an approach to Curley. Patterson called me up at 6 P.M. and asked me to draw up a draft of such a disclaimer. I did so at once, and had it at the office at 7.15. Patterson, Moore and Hamilton Owens were present. Owens had also prepared a draft, but it seemed to the rest of us to be too abject, so it was rejected and mine was adopted. Then John Owens came in with a third draft, prepared by himself. Hamilton Owens objected to it on the ground that it was too long, that there was in it too much abstract discussion of newspaper rights, and that it thus raised a number of fresh questions, possibly provocative of further uproars. But Patterson seemed to be inclined to it, and I finally consented to its substitution for mine, mainly because I did not want to be put in the position of arguing for my own draft. Moore then called up Monsignor Henry A. Quinn, rector of the Cathedral, and Quinn invited him to bring it to the archbishop's house at once. Curley had already gone to New York, preparing to sail for Ireland the next day. Quinn accepted the Owens draft as satisfactory, and volunteered to go to New York by sleeper that night to submit it to the archbishop. This was an heroic offer, for the weather on that July 4 was really infernal, and it was in the days before sleepers were air-cooled. Alas, the poor monsignor suffered in vain. The archbishop rejected the proposed disclaimer as evasive, insulting to his high mightiness, and, in large part, irrelevant. What he demanded was something categorical and ignominious.

On July 6 the *Catholic Review* let go with both barrels, and in a fashion reminiscent of an old-time Hearst paper denouncing the Interests. Powder and shot, of course, had been prepared before Curley left Baltimore; all that had to come from him just before he sailed was the order to fire. Across the top of the first page, above the flagstaff of the paper and in 72-point Gothic, was the streamer:

ARCHBISHOP DEFIES THE SUN TO PROVE IT DIDN'T LIE

All the rest of the first page, save for a brief notice of Curley's departure for "his boyhood home, Golden Isle, Athlone, Ireland" was given over to denunciations of the *Sun,* and one of these fulminations jumped to page eight. In addition, there were no less than six violent castigations on the editorial page. The most important of these assaults, of course, was the archbishop's own proclamation to the clergy and laity of his flock, printed on page one in a three column box under the following heading:

ARCHBISHOP DEFIES THE SUN AND BOUTON / TO PROVE THEY
DID NOT LIE ABOUT / SAINT IGNATIUS

In this proclamation Curley gave away again the secret of his animus: it lay largely in the fact that the publicity the *Sunpapers* had been giving to the Maryland Tercentenary, mentioned in his eighth paragraph, had devoted less space to the Catholic share in the State's early history than to other factors in its growth, and that in the Catholic parts a great deal more attention had been paid to the line of archbishops from Carroll to Gibbons than to Curley himself. No doubt many Catholic laymen, not to say priests, must have been astonished by the charge in his tenth paragraph ("The *Sun* has sinned against us on more than one occasion. We have stood it all for twelve and a half years. It began in 1921; it is with us in 1934"), for there had never been any such sinning, and it was, in fact, imaginary. But Curley himself had come to Baltimore in 1921, and now he admitted plainly enough that he had been dissatisfied from the start by the *Sun*'s failure to give him the adulation he thought he deserved, and its frequent reminders that he had been preceded by Gibbons.

On the same first page of the *Review* of July 6 was the following formal notice of a boycott:

CLERGY TOLD / TO PRESS HOME / THE CAMPAIGN / LETTER FROM BISHOP
MCNAMARA IS / SENT TO THE PRIESTS OF THE / ARCHDIOCESE / PEOPLE
TO LEARN ISSUES / FROM CHURCH PULPITS / ORGANIZATION WORK NOW
UNDER / WAY WILL REACH ITS CLIMAX / AFTER SCHOOLS OPEN

A letter has been sent out by the Most Reverend John M. McNamara, Auxiliary Bishop of Baltimore, to all the priests of the Archdiocese notifying them to speak again this Sunday on the insult which appeared in the morning *Sun* against Saint Ignatius Loyola.

EVERYONE WILL KNOW IT

Archbishop Curley has ordered that the campaign be kept up from the pulpits during his absence in Ireland. Every Catholic in the Archdiocese who has not read or heard Archbishop Curley's letter will hear that letter before noon next Sunday. Due to a misunderstanding the letter was not read in some churches.

At all the Masses next Sunday it will be made plain to the people of the Archdiocese that the campaign has just begun and that these are only the early days of organization. Priests will speak on the campaign Sunday after Sunday. . . .

The organization of the Knights of Columbus committees is under way. The eighty thousand Holy Name men in the Archdiocese will be organized as will all the other organizations, great and small, white and black.

The Catholic papers of the country read by more than 10,000,000 Catholics and representing the 22,000,000 Catholics of the country will tell the story of the *Sun*'s insult. It is further planned by committees now being organized that the insult will be made known to the non-Catholic citizens of the country and to the advertisers throughout the country.

This violent bombardment naturally caused some perturbation in the *Sun* office. We had plenty of assurance from the start that many of the more intelligent Catholics of the archdiocese bitterly resented the archbishop's billingsgate, and there was evidence indicating that some of them were making representations against it to the apostolic delegate. Moreover, we also had news that many priests were ashamed of the course the row was taking, and that a good many of them had conveniently forgotten to read the archbishop's proclamations at their masses. Nevertheless, Schmick and Patterson were considerably alarmed, for a good many cancellations of subscriptions were coming in from the more naïve and faithful sort of Catholics, and we were all wondering what would happen if the boycott were extended to the *Sun*'s advertisers, as Curley had plainly threatened. Only one advertiser had actually cancelled his contract by July 10: he was a pious Catholic named Martin J. Barry, a dealer in automobile tires. But there was no telling what might happen if pressure were put upon the big Jewish advertisers of Baltimore. Some of them promised Schmick that they would not yield, but he did not believe them. As I have shown, their own weekly paper, the *Jewish Times*, had just been brought to heel; moreover, they were all in a panic because of the daily reports of proceedings against the Jews in Germany, and the fact that Bouton's unfortunate paragraph had likened Loyola to Hitler might eventually put them on the archbishop's side. I was all for striking back, and so was John Owens, but Patterson decided to print nothing in the *Sun* until and unless its larger advertisers began to show signs of wobbling. Owens was in fear that Patterson would surrender if the storm kept up, and print a really abject apology, and one day he begged me to fight against this to the last ditch. I promised, but I was not too sure, for Patterson, by 1934, had lost his old fighting spirit, if indeed he ever had any. The journalistic possibilities of a battle in the grand manner did not appeal to him; he was thinking of the probable cost to the *Sun*, and searching for some way to make a reasonable peace. He was still planning to join John Semmes in British Columbia, and so early as June 28, when he and Semmes came to my apartment to discuss the business, he asked me to take command of the battle. I naturally refused, for its conduct would depend upon decisions that only he could make, but I continued to prepare materials for the counter attack that I hoped for, and carried on all the negotiations which ended eventually in peace.

Those negotiations began on July 12, when Patterson called me up to say that a priest named Edwin L. Leonard had come to the office and asked for a parley. This Leonard was in charge of all the Catholic charities of the archdiocese, and I had met him only once before—at a meeting of social workers at the *Sun* office, called so that they could tell us about the burdens the Depression had thrown on their agencies. He came to my third-story apartment at 8 P.M. sharp, much puffed by the dreadful heat and the long climb up the stairs. Patterson followed him half an hour later, delayed by a series of minor misfortunes: he was just getting over an attack of ptomaine poisoning, his wife and son had got home from Europe that day, and he had had to carry out a promise to make a radio speech at 6.30 P.M. He sat almost silent while Leonard and I discussed the situation. Leonard told me that there had been a meeting of the priests of the archdiocese at the Cathedral that morning—150 of them. A few, he said, had advocated war to the knife, but the great majority had favored conciliation, and of these last Leonard himself was one. At his suggestion a committee had been appointed to approach the *Sun* in an effort to make peace. This committee consisted of ten priests, but after a long discussion it was reduced to four—Monsignor Peter L. Ireton, rector of St. Ann's Church, Baltimore; Monsignor Henry A. Quinn, rector of the Cathedral; Father Ferdinand Wheeler, S.J., rector of St. Ignatius' Church; and Leonard himself. Wheeler, according to Leonard, was a firebrand, but the other three were for conciliation, and believed that Curley had attacked the *Sun* too violently. Finally, Leonard was appointed a committee of one to open negotiations, and if possible come to terms. He told me that he had assured the other priests, on the ground of his experience at the charity meeting, that a fair spirit prevailed in the *Sun* office, and that editorial policies were determined, not by the fiat of any one man, but by reasonable discussion.

He stayed until after 1 A.M., and we discussed the whole business at great length and very frankly. Patterson, who had been on the go since 6 A.M., took relatively little part in the conversation, and what he had to say seemed to me to be too conciliatory, so I had to do nearly all the talking for the *Sun*. I told Leonard that, if the billingsgate in the *Catholic Review* kept up, the *Sun* would have to reply, and that its reply would not be a defense but an attack. I called his attention to the fact that the Jesuits, who were supposed to be the persons chiefly aggrieved by the Bouton paragraph, were satisfied by the publication of their three letters, and that (despite the contrary example of one of them, Father Wheeler) they showed plainly that they wished the uproar were over. I also told him that the Methodists, Baptists and other evangelical Protestants of Baltimore would be glad and eager to give the *Sun* help if, when and as it struck back, and that it had already had some difficulty (this was a fact) in restraining a few of the more bellicose Methodist pastors. Leonard admitted that a headlong attack on the archbishop by the *Sun* would produce a grave situation in Baltimore, and perhaps do the Catholic Church serious and irreparable damage, but he argued in rebuttal that a really earnest Catholic boycott might also be immensely costly to the *Sun*. So far, he said, the church had not unlimbered its heavy artillery. The boycott, despite the howling of the *Catholic Review,* had been preached only mildly, and many priests had refused to preach it at all, or even to read the archbishop's two proclamations to their flocks. In reply, I argued that what this really showed was that the priests as well as the laity were divided on the subject, and that if we cut loose we'd have many of both groups with us, not to mention all the Protestants of the archdiocese, and every fair man in the United States. Leonard seemed to be impressed by this; in fact, he looked alarmed. The whole discussion was in very friendly terms, and there was not the slightest sign of anger on either side. Obviously, Leonard was eager to get rid of a situation that was full of dynamite, and equally obviously the majority of the priests of the archdiocese were with him. We paused for a few rounds of beer. It was a dreadfully hot night.

Finally, I proposed that the priests approach the *Sun* in the manner attempted without result by the volunteer committee of laymen—that is, that they write a letter to the paper, and it be printed with a reply. Various objections developed to this plan—mainly the one that it would be difficult, if not impossible, to draft a letter that all of the priests would approve. I then suggested alternatively that the *Sun* prepare a statement of the case, with an explanation of its failure to meet Curley's demand for an apology, and that the priests append a tail to it, saying that they accepted it. I insisted that we could not be expected to publish anything whatsoever on the subject without making some allusion to the violence of Curley's attack, and the subsequent fulminations in the *Catholic Review*. Leonard appeared to favor my plan, but after some discussion we both concluded that it would be impossible for the priests to accept anything that included criticism of the archbishop. When Leonard left Patterson left too, and there was no chance for the two of us to review the evening's proceedings. In the morning I called Patterson up, and told him a night's reflection had convinced me that it would be impossible to draw up a document that would be satisfactory to both the *Sun* and the priests, but he asked me to make the attempt nevertheless. I began work at once, and by 11 A.M. was at the *Sun* office with a draft. Leonard came in soon afterward, leaving the other three priests of his committee somewhere nearby. I told him I believed that it would be impossible for the *Sun* to print any statement of the case that the priests could agree to, but offered, off the record, to read him what I had written. To my great astonishment he said that he believed the priests would accept it.

He and Patterson and I then sat down to go through it in detail, and were so occupied until 4 P.M. Patterson tried to tone down every reference to the archbishop, but I always insisted that we must have our say. After a while John Owens came in, and the whole discussion was rehearsed for his benefit. When he left he called me outside Patterson's office, and urged me to stand fast. He objected vigorously to certain passages in the revised draft, saying that they allowed Curley too much and made the *Sun* appear too weak. With this I could only agree, but Patterson was eager to come to terms. Finally, Schmick was sent for, and the draft in its now mutilated form was read to him. He said he feared that, as it stood, it would have a bad effect on the Protestants of Baltimore: they would say that we had yielded too much to Curley. He told Leonard that the boycott, so far, had not done the *Sun* any serious damage, and that he was not afraid of a real war. He said that the Jews were against the archbishop because of his threat to order a secondary boycott, and so afflict them in a quarrel that was none of their business. He added that many Protestants of prominence were coming in offering the *Sun* help, and that many Catholics who had cancelled their subscriptions were renewing, or bootlegging the paper. Leonard admitted that this last was true. The very priests, he said, could not do without it. Only that morning one of them, having mislaid his memorandum of a funeral at his church, had had to send out for the *Sun* to find out the name of the deceased and the time of the service.

In the end, there was a sort of agreement on the revised draft, though Owens agreed to it grudgingly and I myself had doubts about it. When Leonard left he took a copy with him, saying that he now had the job of selling it to his committee. He was sure, he said, of the acquiescence of Ireton and Quinn, but he feared that Wheeler would baulk. In the end, of course, the auxiliary bishop, John M. McNamara, would have to decide, for he was in charge of the archdiocese in the absence of Curley. McNamara lived in Washington and was ill. Leonard offered to go to Washington to see him—that is, if the other three priests of the committee agreed—and promised to telephone to Patterson through the *Sun's* Washington bureau. If he could get McNamara's imprimatur by 8 P.M. we would print the statement the next day. It had to go to the composing-room by then to make the first country edition, which closed at 9. It would not do, of course, to print it in the city editions only, for then the country Ku Kluxers would allege that we had tried to conceal a yielding to the archbishop. Leonard called up at 8 o'clock to say that he was still going over the statement with his committee, and that it would be too late when they concluded to reach McNamara. Patterson told him to take his time. Leonard had been urging haste in order that all the priests of the archdiocese might be notified by Saturday morning, and so withhold the fresh attacks on the *Sun* that were ordered for their masses on Sunday. Now he volunteered to see that they would say nothing. The *Catholic Review,* to be sure, was already out with a fresh batch of inflammatory and libelous stuff, but it was too late to do anything about it. Leonard and I, at the meeting in the morning, had discussed the case of the *Review* at some length. I told him that I was in favor of the *Sun* suing it for libel, and would urge that plan in the event that our negotiations failed. He said that he believed the *Review* had taken legal advice, but admitted that its proceedings had been disgraceful, and hinted that most of the priests of the archdiocese agreed with him. We had plenty of evidence that many laymen were of the same opinion, for letters from them had been pouring in all week.

On July 14, two days after Father Leonard's visit to the *Sun* office and while we were still waiting to hear from him, Patterson, John Owens and I called on John J. Nelligan, a leading Catholic layman of Baltimore and a director in the A. S. Abell Company since 1892. Nelligan was on a hot spot, for his only son was a priest, and, what is more, secretary to Curley. Nothing had been heard from him, and we were somewhat uneasy about his attitude. We carried the revised statement with us, and he read it with great care. Then he cheered us mightily by saying that he thought it showed a fair spirit, and went as far as the *Sun* could honorably go. If it were not accepted by Bishop McNamara, he said, we would be free to defend ourselves as best we could. Later the same day Leonard was heard from. He proposed that Patterson, Owens and I go to Washington on July 16 and have lunch with McNamara. The priests of the archdiocese would be represented by Monsignors Ireton and Quinn. Leonard himself, he said, would be barred out because he was known to be "a *Sun* man." Patterson accepted, and he, Owens and I duly lunched with the bishop. The only person present, beside those already named, was his secretary, a singularly handsome young priest named Sweeney. The meeting was amicable, and the bishop showed a very accommodating spirit.

In this palaver Patterson and I did all the talking for the *Sun*: Owens confined himself to an aloof silence. On our return to Baltimore Patterson and I met at his house to discuss the text of the *Sun*'s proposed statement, with Owens not present. It was hot, we were growing tired of the subject, and so we came to no conclusion. I had, during the three days preceding, prepared at least four versions of the statement, and was pretty well worn out. The next morning Patterson called me up to say that he had decided to put aside all these versions, and put together one of his own. It arrived from the office half an hour later. It turned out to be a pastiche made up in part of fragments from my different versions, and in part of more conciliatory contributions from Patterson himself. It read rather roughly, and so I volunteered to put it into better English. This I did the next morning, July 18, and in the course of the job I made some changes in it, all of them in the direction of stiffening it. Patterson then suggested that his original draft and my revision be submitted to two or three men who had not been parties to the negotiation and could bring fresh minds to it. He specifically barred out John Owens, and for two reasons. The first was that Owens's stiffness and lack of adroitness at the time of his unhappy interview with the archbishop had been largely responsible for the whole row, and the second was that Owens had since shown a characteristic tendency to reduce the whole uproar to simple moral terms, and was too much disposed to deal with it, not as a nuisance to be settled in some practical manner, but as an excuse for enunciating and defending to the death a long series of more or less dubious ethical principles. In brief, John was suffering one of his recurrent attacks of moral indignation, and nothing could be got out of him save sonorous generalities. The men actually called in for advice were Moore and Schmick. They put together a composite made up in part of paragraphs from Patterson's original and in part of paragraphs from my revision, and Patterson finally approved the whole. This was printed in the *Sun* of the next morning, July 19, under the following preamble:

> For the past three weeks the *Sun* has been subjected to criticism because of a passage in an article written by Mr. S. Miles Bouton. The *Sun* has made no reply to these attacks, but since it appears that this silence leaves the *Sun*'s position open to misunderstanding, it presents the following statement regarding the matter.

Then came the text:

Mr. Bouton's Article—A Statement by the *Sun*

Mr. Bouton, for a long period of years a special correspondent of the *Sun* in Berlin, had been forced to leave Berlin because of his strictures upon Nazi excesses. Upon his arrival he was asked by the *Sun* to write a number of articles. In this series he included a character sketch of Hitler, with whom Mr. Bouton had had a close personal acquaintance. This article appeared on June 18, and in it was the following paragraph:

"It has seemed to me at times that there is a kinship between him and Ignatius Loyola. One finds in both men the same complete faith in their mission, the same readiness and determination to exercise their power with utter ruthlessness and brutality in order to carry out that mission. No consideration of personal profit or glory ever entered Loyola's mind, and I believe the same can be said of Hitler."

Obviously, there was unfortunate phrasing here. Mr. Bouton, writing hurriedly, used two words, "ruthlessness" and "brutality," in attempting to rehearse the strong virtues which historians attribute to Loyola. These words were badly chosen and are not in accord with the prevailing historical opinion. His error should have been detected by the sub-editor who prepared the article for publication, but again there was a lapse and the words got into the paper. That inadvertence was and is regretted by the *Sun*.

In dealing with such situations a newspaper is under the same obligations as an individual in his relations with his neighbor. It may not gratuitously wound devout people. And when through an oversight it does inflict wounds, it must make amends. That is the invariable custom of the *Sun*. And in this case amends were undertaken without delay. . . .

However, the *Sun* continues to receive requests from many sources for a statement that will give better understanding to its readers of the facts of the situation. They have urged that the *Sun* has always shown complete readiness to make prompt and adequate correction of the mistakes that have appeared in its columns. They have asked why the *Sun* should hesitate in this instance.

Most of those who made these inquiries have been surprised when the fact has been brought to their attention that the *Sun* published promptly in full the three letters from the leading Jesuits of the community, and the fact that no further communications with regard to the Bouton article were received for a full week following its publication.

The *Sun*, therefore, is publishing this review of the case in order to clear the minds of those who are interested. It bears no ill will for the temper that has been shown by some in the discussion of certain aspects of the present case. It believes so much in free speech that it is quite willing to accord the utmost liberty to its critics, and it recognizes that in the heat of controversy it is not always possible to give the fullest consideration to every word uttered.

But the *Sun* does not grant the truth of the allegations made against it in the *Catholic Review,* nor can it accede to demands which violate its general policy.

The *Sun* feels certain that its readers, of whatever faith, must realize that a newspaper in its position must be careful to maintain its complete independence and that it cannot accept suggestions, under duress, as to the conduct of its affairs.

This was printed on the page opposite the editorial page. To my amazement, and hardly less to that of Patterson, the *Catholic Review* accepted the statement as sufficient, and the boycott was called off. To be sure, the *Review* printed a long gloss on it, by the editor-in-chief thereof, Monsignor Albert E. Smith, in which some attempt was made to point out weaknesses in the *Sun*'s case—God knows, there were plenty of them—but that gloss was moderate in tone, and ended with "The controversy, for the *Review* at least, is now over." On the morning following the publication of the *Sun*'s statement Patterson dropped in on Father Wiesel, president of Loyola College and hence head of the Jesuits in Baltimore. Theoretically, he was the party principally aggrieved by Bouton, but as I have said he and his fellow Jesuits had kept out of the row between the *Sun* and Curley. Wiesel turned out to be very friendly, and made it plain that the Jesuits were by no means pleased by Curley's blackguard championing. The boycott, in fact, had been far from a roaring success. The maximum losses in circulation while it was going on were about 5000 for the *Sun,* 5000 for the *Evening Sun,* and 7500 for the *Sunday Sun,* but 60% of these losses were restored the moment it was over, and the rest were made good soon afterward. In a region so strongly Catholic as the territory of the *Sunpapers* this was a really remarkable record. At various times Curley claimed 250,000 and 300,000 Catholics in his archdiocese—many of them, of course, children, and others poor Poles and Italians who could not read English. Newspaper boycotts are often much more damaging. When, in 1922 or thereabout, the Indianapolis *Times* was boycotted by the Ku Klux Klan, it lost 17,000 out of a circulation of 55,000 {But the *Times* kept up the fight, and finally landed Stephenson, the boss of the Klan in Indiana, in prison for life}. Two things that kept up morale in the office during the fight were the attitude of Nelligan, and that of the Catholics on the editorial staff. All of the latter, without exception, were violently against the archbishop, and there was never the slightest doubt of their loyalty to the paper.

On July 18, after Patterson had put together the *Sun*'s statement of July 19, but before it was printed, I drew up a memorandum outlining the course we should follow, as I saw it, in case the priests of the archdiocese, in the absence of the archbishop, refused to accept the statement as sufficient, and the war thus went on.

Meanwhile, there fell a blow that was almost as devastating as the archbishop's attack. This was the resignation of John Owens as editor of the *Sun*. It came quite unexpectedly on July 19, the day the *Sun*'s statement was printed. To be sure, Owens had shown some discontent with Patterson's conciliatory attitude during the whole negotiation, and that fact had caused Patterson to bar him out of the final conference on July 18, but no one looked for him to walk out at so critical a moment. Two things apparently moved him to launch this blow *a posteriori*. The first was his honest belief that the *Sun* should have taken a firmer line from the start: in this view I inclined to agree with him. The second, and much more important, was the wound inflicted on his vanity when Patterson undertook to draw up the *Sun*'s statement without consulting him. Whatever his motive, he came to his decision wholly on his own, sent an angry letter of resignation to Patterson, and rushed out of the office.

> I hereby give you my resignation as editor of the *Sun* and, of course, as secretary of the A. S. Abell Company.
>
> As you know, the statement made by the *Sun* in the controversy with Archbishop Curley is not what I wished. I could perhaps have stomached the concessions contained therein if I believed they represented the composite judgment of a group of men acting for the best interest of the paper and of the community, and also acting in good faith and good will among themselves. But to my dissatisfaction with certain parts of the statement I must add the fact that in the final formulation of it I was allowed no voice beyond the privilege of expressing opinion on isolated sentences; and that it was printed without submission to me and without opportunity for me to consider it in its entirety. This circumstance I regard as one of the most deliberate discourtesies ever offered the editor of a newspaper.
>
> Throughout the long consideration of the issue presented by Archbishop Curley I have had but one purpose and that was to protect the freedom and the integrity of the *Sun* against the most brutal assault that any paper could suffer. . . .

This was subscribed "very truly yours." Owens sent me a copy of it, with a covering letter reading:

> Dear Henry: I think you ought to have a copy of a letter I sent today to Patterson. War is hell!

If I had been in Patterson's place I'd have accepted Owens's resignation at once. He had, to be sure, some excuse for it, but in the situation that then confronted us I could see it only as desertion in the face of the enemy. If news of it now got out—as it was bound to do—then the archbishop and his goons would have sound reason to gloat over us. I therefore decided to make some effort to induce him to withdraw it, if only temporarily, and to that end sent him the following note at his house:

> One archbishop at a time is enough. As the moralist who first raised the point of honor I forbid the banns, and ask for a hearing. Certainly you don't argue seriously that Paul *intended* any affront to you. He was completely flabbergasted, and no wonder. He thought, and so did I, that the programme had your approval at every step. He has been on a redhot spot. Don't put him on another.
>
> I get only one consolation out of a horrible situation on an unbearably hot day. Curley is to blame in the last analysis, and it will cost him another 1,000,000,000,000,000,000 years in Purgatory.

To this I received no answer. Owens had withdrawn into the silence. No one could reach him; no one knew where he was. Patterson and Schmick, in alarm, went to his house in Homeland, but he was not there, and after they had waited two or three hours he had not returned. His sister-in-law, who was his housekeeper, then told them that it would be useless to wait any longer: he would not come back. In all probability he was in the house all the while. This blow naturally demoralized the whole *Sun* outfit. No one knew, as yet, how the *Review* and the priests would take the *Sun*'s statement, and if news of Owens's desertion got out too soon it might buck them up immensely. Finally, Harry Black volunteered to track him down. A few days before he had promised to dine with Black on Sunday, July 22, and now Black called up his house. Somewhat to Black's surprise, he came to the telephone, and to Black's even greater surprise, agreed to keep the dinner engagement. Nearly all day Saturday I sat with Patterson and Black, discussing our course of action when the news got about town; already the members of the staff seemed to be aware that something dramatic was afoot. My final advice, reverting to my first impulse, was that the resignation be accepted. After all, there was no evidence that Owens would ever make a really competent editor for the *Sun;* on the contrary, the weaknesses that he had revealed already offered sufficient proof that he'd always be third rate. Moreover, I was not inclined, on reflection, to forgive desertion in the face of the enemy, and I was especially hot against forgiving the desertion of a man in an important place, whose treason might still be disastrous. If Owens had a grievance—and I believed that he had—he should have stated it to Patterson in plain terms, and given Patterson a reasonable chance to answer it. If he were now lured back, he would return triumphant, and it would be irrational and against human nature to expect Patterson to give him any confidence thereafter, or for their relations, for years to come, to be anything better than an armed and wary truce.

Nevertheless, Patterson and Black were so alarmed by the possible consequences of an open row that they decided for conciliation, even at the cost of submitting to what amounted to a kind of blackmail. What happened at Black's dinner on Sunday I did not learn until the Tuesday following, for I had to go to New York on Sunday, and when Patterson called me up there on Monday I was out. The next day he reached me, but his report was rather vague. All I could make out was that Black had induced Owens to withdraw his resignation, but only on the amazing condition that there be no further discussion of the matter in the office, and indeed no mention of it. These seemed to me to be harsh and even impossible terms: they left the office in the position of the culprit, whereas all the trouble had been made by Owens himself. I was still in favor of letting him go, but Patterson, always weak in a crisis and by now thoroughly shaken, was against it, and so was Black.

The office was in a state of almost pathetic demoralization. The *Review* had called the war off, but no one knew what Curley might do when he returned to Baltimore in September. Meanwhile, Owens held himself gloomily aloof, keenly conscious that he had brought Patterson to heel, and not at all inclined to bury the hatchet. Black and Hamilton Owens were seeing spooks behind every door. A harmless reference to the Jews in an article by A. D. Emmart, the London correspondent, set them to trembling. A reference to the Eastern Shore of Maryland in an article of my own was cut out, and another article that I has written, on the war upon syphilis, was held up. The situation had its comic aspects, but I was in no mood to enjoy them. It seemed to me that Owens's vanity had done a great deal more damage than the archbishop's choler, and that by taking it lying down we were only preparing the way for more troubles in the future. That foreboding was well borne out by subsequent events. When Patterson got back in August he was plainly in terror of Owens, and Owens was well aware of it. Hitherto the relations of the two had been on a first-name basis, but now Owens always addressed Patterson very stiffly as Mister, and every effort that Patterson made to resume the old friendly and easy terms—some of them very close to downright humiliating—was rebuffed. The editorial conferences that had gone on since 1920 were abandoned, and to this day they have not been resumed. Owens glowered in his office, and Patterson shook in his. It was a sad mess, and it was destined to have very unhappy effects upon the course of the *Sun*.

The archbishop, on his return to Baltimore in September, accepted the peace made by his lieges without any public sound of dissent: if he berated them in private I never heard of it. The whole episode, despite the discomforts of the negotiations and the unpleasantness engendered by John Owens, delighted me, for it provided a magnificent demonstration of the amount of Christian charity actually to be found in a salient ambassador of Christ. My belief is, though I have no direct evidence for it, that his caterwauling lost him a cardinal's hat, or, at all events, postponed his getting of it indefinitely. As the archbishop of the primatal see in the United States he plainly rated it, and every one (including apparently himself) assumed that he would get it; indeed, there were actual reports of the coming elevation in the Spring of 1934. But the indignation of the high-toned Washington Catholics over his unseemly bellowing undoubtedly had some effect on the apostolic delegate, and so he was passed over. His relations with the *Sunpapers* remained strained after the peace, and every smart young reporter on them waited patiently for a chance to smear him. It came at last on December 7, 1941, the day of the Japanese attack on Pearl Harbor. His Excellency, like most other members of the Catholic hierarchy, had been opposed to Roosevelt's long-continued war-mongering, and had often denounced it from the pulpit. On the evening of the fatal day a *Sun* reported called him up at his residence and asked him if he had any comment to make. The result was the following, conspicuously displayed in a two-column box on the last page of the *Sun* the next morning, December 8:

ARCHBISHOP CURLEY AND THE WAR

Archbishop Michael J. Curley, asked for comment on Japan's attacks on United States bases in the Pacific Ocean, said:

"We might as well have a war in the Pacific. We're out looking for war, aren't we? We're out looking for war in the Atlantic, so why not in the Pacific? In fact, we've got a war in the Atlantic. We've had one there ever since the order to shoot on sight went out.

"We're not satisfied. We're looking for war, so I see no reason why we should not have a war in the Pacific, on all the seven seas and everywhere."

Asked whether he wished this comment to be published, the Archbishop said: "Yes, go ahead, but I'm afraid you won't be able to keep the humor of it in the writing."

When His Excellency read this in the cold day dawn of the morrow he saw at once that he had committed a *faux pas* of the first calibre, so he made hasty and panicky efforts to extricate himself from its consequences. Unhappily, the best plan he could concoct was to issue the following statement, which was printed in the *Evening Sun* of December 8, and then, to rub it in, reprinted in full in the *Sun* of December 9:

I left my house at 3.30 P.M. on my way to Sacred Heart Church, High-landtown, to confirm 600 children. I was in the church from 4.00 o'clock to 6.15 P.M.

I heard nothing about war before I left Charles street and I certainly heard nothing about war during the two hours and fifteen minutes spent in the church. I returned to the rectory at 6.15 P.M. and there I heard nothing about war. I arrived home at 6.30 P.M. and heard nothing about war there. As a matter of fact, I saw no member of the household when I arrived.

At 6.35 P.M. I was called by a morning *Sun* reporter to ask my opinion on the fighting in the Pacific. I thought it was a matter of our coming into contact with another raider of some nationality, but I had no more idea than a man in the moon that war had been declared by Japan and that hundreds of our armed forces had been killed and wounded on the Hawaiian Islands. The *Sun* reporter took it for granted that I knew, of course. In my talking to him over the telephone, the word "Japan" or "Japanese" never entered into the conversation. It was not until 7.50 when I turned on the radio that I heard the announcement that all programs would be interrupted for news of the war between the United States and Japan. It was then and only then that I learned that war had been declared, that attacks by the Japanese flying forces had been made on the American possessions and American troops.

The above are the facts. I was no more prepared to hear about war being declared by Japan on America on Sunday afternoon, December 7, than was either the President of the United States or the Secretary of State. If the armed forces of our island possessions in the Pacific were taken by surprise, as they actually were, I certainly was taken by a surprise infinitely greater. It goes to show how quickly things happen and I would not be at all surprised to know that millions of our people knew nothing about the whole affair until, perhaps, they saw the morning papers, if they saw them.

There can be no discussion and no expression of opinion today except in one way—America has been attacked by Japan. Every American citizen, regardless of his views in the past, must be an American, and only an American, at this moment. Every man, woman and child in the nation must stand behind the United States Government in its defense of this nation.

Today, in this grave hour, in this really critical period of our history, there is no place for discussion between Isolationists and Interventionists.

There can be no question of any foreign policy condemnation regarding Japan. The die is cast—it is a matter of defense of the nation, its people and their rights. Our forces on the sea and in the air will now do their share and no American has any right whatsoever by word or deed to do anything but help.

This is the attitude today of the Catholics of the Archdioceses of Baltimore and Washington who number, by reason of the enormous increase of population in the capital city and its suburbs, close to half a million people.

No one, of course, believed his statement that he had been unaware that war had broken out when he gave out his interview of December 7. He was, indeed, palpably lying, for it was manifest to the meanest understanding that the *Sun* reporter must have told him the news on calling him up; there was no other excuse for calling him up. So the whole town laughed, and the *Sun* had its revenge after more than seven years of waiting. How it must have galled him that he could not put the blame upon the paper! Very few *Sun* men of any rank have ever met him to this day (1942); when he has business with the office it is carried on through underlings. He is given all due notice, and in rigidly polite terms, but nothing more. After the conclusion of the uproar in 1934 Nelligan suggested one day that Patterson and I drop in on His Excellency some morning, squired by Nelligan himself, who was the father, as I have said, of the archepiscopal private secretary. I was at first inclined to make this visit if only (*a*) out of sheer curiosity to see so bellicose a buck, and (*b*) because it seemed to me that, inasmuch as we had to live with him, it would be better for at least some of the *Sun* executives to have some sort of contact with him, but on reflection I concluded that he would probably misinterpret our call, and so refused to make it. Patterson then said that he would go with Nelligan alone, but no appointment was ever made, and the scheme was quickly forgotten. When Nelligan died on October 14, 1935, Curley preached his funeral sermon—a somewhat florid effort, delivered in very loud tones. But there was no mention in it of Nelligan's 21 years of service as a director of the *Sunpapers*. On November 7, 1934, I gave a small dinner at my apartment in honor of Monsignors Ireton and Quinn and Father Leonard, the chief negotiators for the archbishop in the war as I had been the chief negotiator for the *Sun*. It was a stag affair, for Sara was ill in bed. The other guests were Patterson and John Semmes. At Patterson's suggestion I also invited John Owens, but he refused. His letter, dated November 5, was as follows:

> I never supposed that anything could bar me when an opportunity appeared to sit at your board. But I can't make the grade. The iron went too deep for me to make merry, and what I am trying to do is to forget the whole thing. I count on you to suffer fools, if not gladly, at least with patience.

The dinner went off pleasantly enough, with the rev. and the right rev. guests eating and drinking heavily: in fact, a considerable hole was made in my cellar. I had come out of the war sore on many counts, but principally against John Owens for his brainstorm at the end of it. As I have said, I sympathized with him to his objection to Patterson's timorousness; his offense was not that of being wrong, but that of putting his personal vanity above the good of the paper, and at a highly hazardous moment. It seems to me that a newspaper man is never justified in doing that. My plans for fighting the archbishop in the grand manner were always hobbled by my conviction that, if the worst came to the worst, Patterson would not really fight. Schmick had the same opinion, and so also, I think, had Black and Owens. In all probability, Patterson was fundamentally right. The *Sun*—mainly because of the intransigence and bad judgment of Owens and Moore—had made some serious blunders at the very start of the fight, and a battle to a finish would have been very costly to it. Not many other newspapers would have given it any useful support: they were, and are, all enormously afraid of the Catholic church; indeed, they are quite as afraid of it as they are of the Jews. The *Nation*, the *New Republic* and maybe a few other weeklies would have howled for us but their help would have been of no value. Patterson's position was thus no easy one. Behind him lurked a Catholic director, Nelligan, and behind Nelligan lurked a good many Catholic stockholders, the Abells. To be sure, Nelligan stood firm so far as we actually went, but it was always a question whether he would have stuck through a really stand-up fight, with the *Sun* doing serious damage to the church. As for the Abells, it was not possible to trust them. This was especially true of Walter, though he was himself in bad odor with the church on account of his marriage to a divorcée. He hated Patterson, as he hated the Blacks (not to mention Nelligan), and it is hardly likely that he'd have supported them in a battle which was really costly to the *Sun*. It would have given him too good a chance to moan "I told you so." Moreover, there were the advertisers to consider—a notoriously jumpy lot. Schmick was confident that most of them would stick, if only to protect themselves against other secondary boycotts in future, but Patterson was not so sure, and neither was I. At the end of the year Patterson insisted on giving me a bonus of $750 for my services. Considering the infernal weather at the time I had certainly earned it.

13

Snake Charmers

1933–1937

My adventures with the radio began late in 1933, when William Lundell, of the National Broadcasting Company, asked me to do a broadcast on the repeal of Prohibition, mainly devoted to the charms of beer. The idea amused me, and I had several palavers with Lundell in New York. What he had in mind, it appeared, was a more or less formal speech: it seemed to me that a dialogue with stage effects, supposedly holden in a beer-house, would be more effective. We sat down with a stenographer and began to concoct it, and in the end I rewrote it completely. It was done on October 18, 1933, and went out over the whole N.B.C. network. Lundell and I were helped out by a couple of actors playing waiters, and by the N.B.C. orchestra under Frank Black, playing the elder Johann Strauss's "Radetzky" march and the younger Strauss's "Mein Schatz" waltz. John W. Davis was in the studio while the broadcasting was going on, and appeared to enjoy it. I got hundreds of letters from listeners during the next few days. But I had learned by this experience that radio work was not a little onerous; it involved writing a script, rehearsing it and instructing whatever aides it called for, and so it wasted a lot of time. I refused to take anything from the N.B.C. for the beer broadcast, not even my expenses: it was my contribution to the jubilation over the downfall of the Prohibitionists. During the next year or so, at Lundell's urging, I made three more N.B.C. broadcasts, but in each case I talked from Baltimore, for going to New York was too much trouble. The first was on January 14, 1934. It was a joint affair, in which Walter Damrosch, Mrs. Carrie Chapman Catt, Daniel Frohman, Will H. Hays and

Dr. Arthur H. Compton also spoke. On April 27, 1934, I delivered an ironical blast against the New Deal, and on February 26, 1935, I followed with another. By that time I had had enough of the radio, and never appeared thereafter save rarely, and under pressure from friends. On November 16, 1937, Cabell Greet, editor of *American Speech,* roped me for a dialogue with himself over the Columbia network, and soon afterward the Columbia people approached me with a suggestion that I try my wings as a news commentator. I got rid of them by saying that my minimum price would be $500 a broadcast. They protested that my first attempts would have to be on their sustaining programme, at their expense, and that it might be some time before a sponsor willing to pay $500 a broadcast could be found. I replied that I was not asking for the job, but merely stating my price. After that I heard nothing more from them.

In November, 1934, an old acquaintance, James L. Wright, Washington correspondent of the Buffalo *Evening News,* and then president of the Gridiron Club, asked me to make the speech at the dinner of the club at the Willard Hotel in Washington, on December 9, 1934. The club had two such dinners a year, one in December and the other in the early Spring. The President of the United States for the time being was almost always present, and there was but one speech beside his own. The other speaker was usually some one well known to be an opponent of the Administration, and inasmuch as the rule of the club was that "ladies are always present, reporters are never present," he was permitted to speak his mind freely. To his speech the President replied with equal freedom. These speeches came at the end of a long programme of more or less amusing skits and songs, in which the members of the club—along with the professional singers who were its associate members—poked fun at the President and the other high functionaries present. I had been to but one dinner of the club before this, and found it a considerable bore, for the amateur acting of the members was pretty bad, some of the skits were labored and dull, and the service of the dinner was spaced out in the intervals of the show, so that guests who got their *hors-d'oeuvres* at 7.30 did not come to their dessert until 11 o'clock or even later. The one speech was ordinarily short, and the President replied briefly, but even so the proceedings did not finish until 11.30 or thereabout. Before the dinner there were cocktail parties in various private suites at the Willard, most of them given by politicians or other persons eager for newspaper good will—for example, Eugene Meyer, publisher of the Washington *Post*—and afterward some of these parties were continued.

Wright's invitation rather surprised me, for I seldom made speeches: he explained that I was chosen because the club usually had a politico for its speaker and the members thought it would be a pleasant variation to put up a newspaper man. I consulted Patterson, and he urged me to accept, for my appearance, he thought, would identify the *Sun* as an anti-New Deal paper. I accordingly wrote to Wright that I would be on hand, and began work on my speech. Inasmuch as it would embody a criticism of the President to his face, I decided to make it light and amiable in tone, avoiding altogether the harsh words that occasionally got into my *Evening Sun* articles. I wrote two or three drafts before I got it as I wanted it, and then showed a copy to Patterson and sent others to Wright and to Essary, Washington correspondent of the *Sun*. All of them approved it as inoffensive. The tables at the dinner are arranged in the form of a huge gridiron, with seats for 490 guests. They are always crowded, and among the guests are usually a couple of justices of the Supreme Court, the Vice-President, a dozen or two Senators, forty or fifty congressmen, half a dozen foreign ambassadors, as many Governors of States, and a miscellany of other bigwigs, including newspaper editors and proprietors. The president of the club sits in the middle of the guest-table, which is elevated above the other tables. At his right hand sits the President of the United States and at his left the Vice-President. I was seated somewhere to the left of Wright, with Governor Ritchie at my right. There was a loud-speaker in front of me, but no desk for the typescript of my speech, and Ritchie, who had large experience in such matters, helped me to make one out of a couple of candlesticks. Just before the dinner began I went to the washroom beside the banquet-hall, and in a large room on the way encountered Roosevelt in waiting. He was sitting down, for his lameness made it necessary for him to keep off his legs as much as possible. He called to me as I passed through, and we had a short palaver, in the course of which I told him that my speech would be very mild. He was, as usual, bursting with amiability, and replied that his reply would be mild too.

Whether, at that time, he had read that reply I don't know. I heard afterwards that it had been written for him by one of his secretaries, Marvin H. McIntyre, a Washington press-agent turned statesman, but this I doubted, for McIntyre was almost illiterate. My guess is that its actual author was more probably Thomas G. Corcoran (Tommy the Cork), and the chief scrivener of the Brain Trust. Obviously, the author, whoever he was, expected me to make a somewhat savage attack on Roosevelt, for in substance it was a savage attack on me.* Its chief point was that, at some unnamed time in the past, I had denounced newspaper owners and newspaper men as violently as I was now (supposedly) denouncing the New Deal. In support of this point it embodied many extracts from the chapter on "Journalism in America" in my "Prejudices: Sixth Series," published in 1927. The reading of these extracts—they were certainly not chosen for their mildness!—was somewhat embarrassing, for I was the guest of newspaper men and there were many others in the audience. But there was nothing I could do about it save accept it in good humor, for the rules of the club forbade any reply to the President's speech. On the chance, however, that some happy accident might suspend this rule I made notes for an answer. Its chief point was the obvious one that whatever I wrote in 1927 I was still prepared to uphold in 1934, whereas there were other persons present who had made many categorical promises in 1932—for example, to balance the budget, to protect the dollar and to reduce the number of jobholders—and then repudiated them in 1933 and 1934. But no chance to answer was given me, so my notes went to waste. Roosevelt, in his speech, spoke of me, in his usual way, as his old and intimate friend, and referred to me always as Henry, but the text of his remarks certainly showed very little amiability. After he sat down Wright asked him why he had replied so ill-humoredly to my good-humored speech, and he replied that he couldn't help it, for the text was before him and he couldn't think of anything else to say. In all probability he read the text for the first time when he intoned it to the diners. As he passed out at the close of the dinner, and passed by my place at the guest-table, I arose, shook hands with him, and said "Fair shooting." He seemed somewhat taken aback, and had apparently expected to find me angry, but we parted on good enough terms.

Many of the guests at the dinner, as I met them afterward, denounced him for making a reply that had no relation whatsoever to my speech, and was altogether out of harmony with it—and likewise out of harmony with the usual Gridiron Club spirit. During the weeks following exaggerated accounts of the matter got into circulation, and it came to be believed that he and I had engaged in a slanging match. Unhappily, the rules of the club forbade me to publish my speech, but I sent copies in confidence to various newspaper acquaintances who asked for them.

---

* Among the president's papers at the Roosevelt Library in Hyde Park, New York, are notes—both typewritten and cursive—for this speech. See Appendix B, Note, page 370.

Certainly no one present who had ever read me could have been surprised by the doctrines dredged out of "Prejudices: Sixth Series." I had been belaboring newspaper men for their lack of intellectual courage for many years, not only in books and magazine articles, but also in the *Evening Sun*. So long back as March 16, 1920, I had denounced them on the *Evening Sun*'s editorial page, and on May 2, 1922 (to cite but one more example) I had returned to the attack under the heading of "A Gang of Pecksniffs." These onslaughts were well known in the trade, and had got me a considerable unpopularity among the sort of journalists I had principally in mind. During the period from 1925 to the end of 1940 I was the subject of a large number of editorials in American newspapers; in fact, they always averaged more than 100 a year, and often ran beyond 200. At least three-fourths of them were hostile, and not a few were extremely bitter.

It was during 1934 that I began to be seriously concerned about Sara's health. She had been in hospital several times since our marriage in 1930, once with pleurisy, and she had been receiving treatments, off and on, from Dr. Edward H. Richardson, and from a favorite nurse, Miss Ethalinda Handy, but on the whole she had been pretty well, and was almost constantly busy with her writing. While we were on our Mediterranean cruise, however, I noticed that she bore the fatigues of travel badly, and when we returned to the *Columbus* from Cairo, where we spent a week, she developed a slight temperature, and was put to bed by the ship's surgeon, Dr. W. Fischer. The temperature gradually subsided, but she reached home somewhat played out, and went to Dr. Benjamin M. Baker for advice. He reported that her lungs were clear, but that there were obvious indications of infection somewhere else—just where, he could not determine. Late in July she went to Montgomery to visit her mother, who was ill and was to die in January, 1935. From Montgomery she reported that she had a slight bronchitis. On September 17 she started for home by train, and the next day I met her at Greensboro, N.C., and the two of us proceeded to Roaring Gap, N.C., where we stayed a few days with Dr. and Mrs. Fred M. Hanes.

When she got off the train at Greensboro I could see at once that she was ill. Her face was pale and in the bright morning sunlight she looked almost transparent. When we got back to Baltimore Baker examined her again, and decided that she would have to go to bed. "It is perfectly plain," he said, "that she still has tuberculosis. Her lungs are quite clear and there is no sign whatever of further kidney infection, but somewhere or other there is a pocket—maybe in a lymph gland—and the only thing to do is to give her complete rest and watch her carefully." She took this disturbing news very bravely, and I bought her a hospital bed, that she might be more comfortable. For three months she remained in it, never complaining. After a little while Baker let her resume a certain amount of activity, and she wrote several short stories. At Christmas her temperature dropped to normal, and Baker told her she might leave her bed. But she was still weak, and when her mother died in January she was unable to go to Montgomery for the funeral. In March her temperature rose again, and Baker sent her to the Union Memorial Hospital. After a month there she returned home, apparently much improved, but in May she developed alarming symptoms and had to go back to the hospital. Baker told me at once that there were indications of tubercular meningitis— an agonizing and almost always fatal condition. On Sunday, May 26, she became desperately ill, and on Friday, May 31, she died. I saw her for the last time on Wednesday, May 29. She was then oscillating around the edges of consciousness, and for a few minutes she recognized me and talked rationally, but it was plain that she was dying.

Her death made the year 1935 a dreadful one for me, and it was not until the Autumn that I gave my considerable amount of attention to the *Sunpapers*. When she died, on May 31, my sister Gertrude had already gone to her farm in Carroll county, and August was living alone in Hollins street. He offered at once to move into Cathedral street with me, to remain until Gertrude returned from the country in November, and needless to say I was very glad and grateful. After the funeral I proposed to him that the two of us make a trip to England, if only to get away, for a little while, from the endless reminders of Sara in Cathedral street.

We had a quiet time in London, and saw very few people. August spent a large part of his days in the South Kensington Museum, studying the collection of ship-models there, or roving on foot through the East End. One day we went to Henley with James Bone and his wife, and had a long row on the river, with Bone at the oars. Another day I went to Norwich to visit my old friend H. W. Seaman, an Englishman who had had newspaper experience in the United States and was a frequent contributor, in my time, to the *American Mercury*. August and I also went to Oxford for a day, but in the main we stuck to the Savoy Hotel neighborhood. One afternoon there was a thunder shower, and the newspapers broke out with headlines announcing a "great tropical storm." Another day Newton Aiken, then London correspondent of the *Sun*, got us tickets to the visitors' gallery of the House of Commons and we heard a speech by Anthony Eden, and that night a young Irishman in the Foreign Office entertained us at a beer-party at his house in Kensington. The beer was warm and bad, but there were some amusing people present, and we had a pleasant evening. We ate our meals at Simpson's in the Strand, at Rule's, at the Hungaria in Lower Regent street, at the Spanish restaurant in Sparrow street, and at various pleasant places in Soho, and in the evenings we went to the theatre or the news-reel movies. We returned in the *New York,* and presently I resumed work in Cathedral street. Luckily, I had a heavy job in hand—the revision of "The American Language"—and it kept me occupied for long hours every day. In addition I put together a collection of Sara's short stories, under the title of "Southern Album," and it was published early in 1936 by Doubleday, Doran & Company, who had done her "The Making of a Lady" in 1931. After Gertrude returned from the country and August rejoined her in Hollins street I was very lonely, and fell into the habit of going to Schellhase's restaurant in Howard street every evening. The Winter of 1935–36 was very cold, with much snow, and my little office in Cathedral street had leaking walls and could not be heated sufficiently to be comfortable. The janitor of the apartment house stoked his furnace diligently, but the weather was too much for him. I tried working in the big drawing-room, which was warmer, but all my notes and files were in the office, and I needed them constantly. In the end I put in three electric heaters and managed somehow to get the job done. On many a day I worked from 9 A.M. to 10 P.M., with only brief intervals for meals and maybe a cat-nap late in the afternoon. When I plowed through the snow to Schellhase's at 10 P.M. my companion there was my old friend H. E. Buchholz, editor of the *Journal of Educational Psychology* and *Educational Administration and Supervision,* who sat there seven nights a week, and in fact kept on doing so until January, 1941, when he had a quarrel with Schellhase because his favorite waitress, Emma by name, had been dismissed. Buchholz was a godsend to me in those dismal days. At Christmas, 1935, my sister Gertrude suggested that August and I take over the house in Hollins street, and set up housekeeping there, with Hester Denby and Emma Ball to look after us. Gertrude was spending more and more time on her farm, and said that she would be content with an apartment for the Winters, for there was scarcely room in the Hollins street house for all three of us. This arrangement seemed admirable and we adopted it, and it has prevailed ever since. I took some of the household goods that Sara had assembled in Cathedral street to Hollins street, but the house was too small to accommodate all of them, and the rest had to be disposed of. I gave some to Sara's two sisters and some to Gertrude for her apartment. Breaking up the apartment in Cathedral street was a most depressing business, and I was glad when it was over.

The war clouds were beginning to roll up darkly in 1935, and I naturally took some notice of them. The Japanese crossed the Great Wall of China during the year and seized control of the whole Peiping area, and soon afterward Mussolini made his demands on Abyssinia. In both cases the English made efforts to mobilize American opinion in favor of their imperiled interests, and the *Sun*, as usual, adopted their point of view. Roosevelt, in those days, was still pretending to be a pacifist, and his Chautauqua speech was still ahead,* but I was already convinced that if a general war followed he would try to take the United States into it, if only to conceal the colossal failure of the New Deal. On September 2, under the title of "The Lion of Judah," I undertook to present the Italian case in the Mediterranean, on November 11 I wrote on "The War Against War," and on November 18, under the title of "The Next War," I said of the so-called pacifists: "How long would they stand up against another such assault as the one delivered on their midriffs of April 6, 1917? Perhaps three or four days." Various matters of domestic politics also engaged me during the year—among them, the continuing Red hunt. I discussed it in "Étude Upon the Red Keys" on February 4, "Chasing the Reds" on March 25, and "The Red Bugaboo" on May 20. I also devoted three articles (on January 21, February 18 and March 8) to Huey Long, who was then at the height of his puissance and seemed likely to give Roosevelt serious trouble in the not too distant future. Unhappily, he was assassinated on September 10. My trip to England produced two articles—"English Notes" on July 15 and "New Deal: English Model" on July 22. I also did a few pieces on themes of local interest— "The Johns Hopkins Hospital" on April 22, "The Pratt Library" on October 14, and "The Murray Case" on September 23. The last-named had to do with the application of a young colored Baltimorean, Donald Gaines Murray, for enrollment as a student in the School of Law of the University of Maryland. He was a graduate of Amherst with an excellent

---

* In early August 1936, a month after the beginning of the Spanish Civil War, President Roosevelt spoke at Chautauqua, New York, and said, "We shun political commitments which might entangle us in foreign wars. . . . I have spent unnumbered hours, I shall pass unnumbered hours, thinking and planning how war may be kept from this Nation."

record, but the school authorities rejected him because of his color. This seemed an imbecility and an outrage to me, and I wanted to say so, but I was uncertain about the attitude of John Owens, and so consulted him before writing my article. I found that he agreed with me, though he was a little uneasy about probable future attempts by Negroes to force entrance into the University of Maryland's other departments at College Park, where there was coeducation. He wrote to me on September 17:

> The only point that I have in mind is the one that I mentioned to you yesterday, and it is a little sharper after reading the documents. I think it would be extremely unwise if any attempt were made to break up the existing separation (of the races) in the lower schools, or even to attempt to break up the separation as between College Park and Princess Anne (a Negro "college" on the lower Eastern Shore, maintained by the state). It would lead to serious trouble and do no one any good. Insofar as liberal arts education is concerned, as distinguished from specialized professional training, the effort should be made to improve Princess Anne. When it comes to a specific issue here, that of admission to the law school or any other professional school, it seems to me absurd to say that any harm would be done by letting the Negroes in. . . .

So I went ahead with my article. The Baltimore courts, at that time, had already decided in favor of Murray, and presently the Maryland Court of Appeals sustained them. He thereupon entered the School of Law, and finished its courses without any apparent objection from his white fellow students. On the contrary, they all seemed to be in favor of him. The effort to avoid an attempt at a Negro invasion of College Park by improving the State Negro "college" at Princess Anne turned out to be hopeless, for the lower Eastern Shore was no place for an institution of the higher learning. In the end the State got rid of the problem by taking over Morgan College in Baltimore, a Negro seminary that had been in existence for years, supported by private funds. Colored students are now quite free to enter the School of Law of the University of Maryland, but so far none has been admitted to the Schools of Medicine, Dentistry and Pharmacy.

The Republican convention, always the first of the two, was scheduled to open at Cleveland on June 9, and we got there several days ahead, as usual. Up to this time I had been hopeful that Roosevelt might be beaten at the November election, but once I got to Cleveland I saw clearly that it was most unlikely, for the Republicans were thoroughly demoralized, and the only leadership visible was that of the Grass Roots brethren from the Middle West, most of whom were at least two-thirds New Dealers. The principal candidate from the start was Alfred M. Landon, Governor of Kansas. I knew nothing of him save that he had been brought out by Roy A. Roberts, editor of the Kansas City *Star* and formerly Washington correspondent of that paper. Roberts was an old acquaintance, for I had covered other national conventions with him in the past. I was strongly against newspapers or their editors taking an active hand in politics, and so would have been delighted if his candidate had been beaten in the convention, but it was apparent at once that that was not to be, for the other aspirants all lacked both public popularity and effective political support. The most competent of them was Senator Arthur H. Vandenberg of Michigan, but Vandenberg was too little the demagogue to appeal to any great number of voters. The others were Frank Knox, formerly of New Hampshire but now of Illinois; L. J. Dickinson, a former Senator from Iowa; Walter E. Edge, a former Governor of New Jersey, Senator from that State, and ambassador to France; Robert A. Taft, of Ohio, son of President William H. Taft, and after 1938 a Senator; and Harry W. Nice, Governor of Maryland. Nice, of course, was only a clown in the drama; he was running for the nomination in theory, because he was, as his placards said, "the only Republican Governor elected in a Democratic State in the Democratic landslide of 1934," but actually because his predecessor, Ritchie, had been a candidate for the Democratic nomination in 1924, 1928 and 1932, and it seemed a good custom to carry on. His vast capacity for attracting misfortune was in full operation. He arrived at Cleveland with a sort of crystal over one of his eyes, which was so impaired that it was extremely painful and had to be removed soon afterward. To present his name he had chosen, characteristically, a Baltimore retainer of the name of J. Cookman Boyd— a boozer who, only a short while before, had narrowly escaped being jailed for driving an automobile while drunk. When he got up to present Nice's name Boyd was so far gone that the gallery noticed it at once, and when it began to bait him he tried to bawl it down. The result was a very painful scene, comparable to that which finished the vice-presidential candidacy of J. Harry Preston at Baltimore in 1912. But Nice kept his head, and when the time came for all the disappointed candidates to go to the platform and whoop for Landon, he made a very good short speech, and it was so well received that he came down to the press-stand full of hopes that it might get him second place on the ticket. This, also, was not to be, for the Landon managers wanted Knox, an old Bull Mooser, as Landon himself was. Patterson and I waited on Knox on June 9, and had a pleasant session with him. The most conspicuous figure in Cleveland, however, was not any open candidate, but William E. Borah, who had come to town in his usual mysterious way and was supposed to be brewing powerful medicine. When he announced a press conference on June 8 the whole corps of correspondents turned out. It was, however, a fizzle, for Borah was a candidate for reëlection as a Senator from Idaho at the November election, and hence showed an excessive caution. I well recall the frantic efforts of Heywood Broun and other so-called Liberals to make him say something of a forward-looking import. The most they could drag out of him was a disconcerting defense of State's Rights and, even worse, of the Supreme Court—which had been playing hob, of late, with some of the favorite enterprises of the New Dealers.

Herbert Hoover came to Cleveland on the second day of the convention, and was invited to address it that night. This invitation was given to him very reluctantly, for the Middle Westerners in the saddle wanted to bury him and forget him, but he was still the titular head of the party, and so he could not be turned away. He made what, for him, was a fiery speech, and marked its points by thumping his belly with his right fist. When he finished his California friends tried to stage a demonstration, and began by shouting "We want Hoover!" The wags in the gallery, always eager for innocent merriment, presently joined in. Hoover himself, who had planned to board a train for the East, left the hall just as this mock demonstration began, but when he got outside he heard it roaring from the loud-speakers there and assumed at once that it was serious. He was all for returning at once, on the theory that he could wrest the nomination from Landon if he did so, but the friends with him—among them, Pat Hurley, his Secretary of War—managed to dissuade him, and he went to the Hotel Cleveland instead. There his hopes revived, and Hurley and the rest had a hard time restraining him from going back. Finally, they got him out of town, but on a later train than the one he had planned to use. We in the hall heard nothing of this until an hour later, by which time the convention had adjourned. The tip came in after Patterson and I had returned to the Hollenden Hotel. As usual, all the younger men of the staff had vanished, so I had to rush to the Hotel Cleveland to cover the story. By the time I got there Hoover had been packed off at last, but I wormed its outlines out of some of the members of his entourage. It was then, however, too late to add it to my story of the evening's proceedings. The details, in fact, had to wait until the next day, when Hurley and company began to blab. The episode was a shining demonstration of the vanity of politicians. If Hoover had actually returned to the hall, the ribald galleries would have hooted him, but he believed in all innocence that his reappearance would have electrified the convention and got him the nomination. In fact, he probably still believes it to this day.

The platform adopted showed that the Middle Western agrarians were firmly in the saddle. It swallowed at least half of the New Deal programme, and there was a hollow sound to its promises to balance the budget and protect the dollar against further raids. It even included a sop for the Townsendites, who were soon to have a national convention of their own, also in Cleveland. Landon not only accepted it in toto, but also telegraphed from his Kremlin in Topeka that he favored a constitutional amendment to put through its labor planks in case the Supreme Court declared the legislation they advocated to be unconstitutional. He received 984 votes on the first ballot against 19 for Borah. The next morning Knox was given second place unanimously. He was known to be against a large part of the platform, but he had an intense itch for high public office, and was willing to do anything or say anything to get it.

When the brief and dismal show ended on June 12 I wrote a résumé of it for the *Sun,* pointing out that, no matter which side won in November, the American taxpayer was in for a rooking. Landon, as a Grass Roots politician, was all for the farmer—and Roosevelt was for both the farmer and the city proletarian. The Republican professionals all went home in low spirits, and I pointed out in my review that Landon's chances of election were very slim—unless, perchance, he managed to save himself in his speech of acceptance, as Hoover had ruined himself in 1932. I started for home on June 12, but was there only a week, for on June 23 the Democratic convention opened in Philadelphia. It was, of course, a cut-and-dried affair, for there was no opposition whatsoever to Roosevelt's renomination. Al Smith and other old-timers had issued a manifesto against him on June 21, but no one paid any attention to it, for Al was a political corpse, and so were the others. Four-fifths of the delegates and alternates were jobholders under the New Deal, and the only sign of dissent from the floor came from Cotton Ed Smith of South Carolina, who stalked out of the hall when a colored delegate arose to second Roosevelt's nomination. There were, in all, 57 speeches that day, and it took from 1 P.M. until 1 A.M. to work them off. I sat through all of them. When Roosevelt was finally renominated there was the usual highly artificial uproar, with the delegates and alternates parading in the aisles. In the course of it a gang of New Yorkers trooped by, and among them was Herbert Bayard Swope.* When I caught sight of him I began to yell "Shame! Shame!" and Frank Kent, who was sitting with me in the press-stand, joined in. Swope is a blond and blushes easily. When he saw and heard us he grew radiant with the reddest blush of his whole career.

Roosevelt came to Philadelphia to accept the nomination *viva voce,* as he had accepted his first nomination at Chicago in 1932. He brought old Jack Garner with him. All the more earnest New Dealers had been strongly against renominating Garner, for everyone knew that he was an enemy of the New Deal, and was doing his best to wreck it behind the door, but Roosevelt decided to let him hang on. It must be said for him that in his own brief speech of acceptance, which followed Roosevelt's, he said nothing in favor of the Roosevelt theology, but contented himself with declaring that he was a good soldier, and ready to go withersoever his leader led. The acceptance speeches were made in Franklin Field, an immense amphitheatre. Just before they began there was a brisk shower of rain, and Henry Hyde and I covered our typewriters with newspapers. The press-stand, a temporary affair, was very shaky, and when the cere-monies got under way I found working at it impossible, for there was a man in the row ahead of me (not a newspaper man, but a ringer let in by the police) who stood up on his seat and kept jogging my desk. More-over, he cut off my vision of the speakers' platform, so that I couldn't see what was going on there. After jawing with him in vain, I appointed him my legman—on condition that he keep still. Thereafter, until the end of the show, he called off to me what was going on on the platform and in the field, and I got my work done in reasonable comfort. Many such ringers try to horn into the press-stand at national conventions, and they are usually aided by the local police and by the sergeants-at-arms and other such functionaries, nearly all of whom are local politicians. But the press-stands in the halls are so well policed by attachés of the Senate and House press-galleries, who know all authentic correspondents, that the invaders are quickly detected and thrown out. In Franklin Field, unhap-pily, there was no such policing. The most striking feature of the notifi-cation ceremony, next to the rain, was the meagreness of the whooping for Roosevelt. He was seldom interrupted, and when he finished the ap-plause lasted no more than a minute. I so reported in my dispatch to the *Sun,* printed June 27, but in the same issue Fred Essary had a piece saying

---

* Three years earlier President Roosevelt had named Swope, retired editor of the New York *World,* a delegate to the London Economic Conference.

that the reception of Roosevelt was one of record-breaking enthusiasm. Essary was an ardent New Dealer; moreover, he was always strongly in favor of any sitting President. He was a useful man at such grandiose affairs, for he had the knack of writing new leads of successive editions with great speed, but what he had to say seldom showed any sense, and not infrequently it was in sharp conflict with the palpable facts.

James Bone came from London to do both conventions for the Manchester *Guardian* and also to do some articles for the *Sun*. The latter were poor stuff, and Jim himself was something of a nuisance. At the Philadelphia convention he got tight one day, and began to urge me to ask the band leader to play some English march that he admired—I think it was Elgar's "Pomp and Circumstance." To put him off I told him that the band did not have the music. He then went to a music-store in Chestnut street and bought the full orchestral score. I tried to explain to him that what was needed was the parts, not the orchestral score, and that, moreover, a brass band was not an orchestra, but he was suffering from the form of *Biereifer* [beery enthusiasm] produced by Scotch whiskey, and so kept on plaguing me. In the end Patterson hauled him off, but not until I was at the point of bawling him out. Jim had relatively little to write, so he had plenty of time to loll in the press-stand, where he bothered the rest of us by making fatuous suggestions. Directly in front of the seats of the *Sunpapers* were those of the New York *Herald-Tribune*. They were occupied all day by the publisher thereof, Ogden Reid, by his wife, by his editor, Geoffrey Parsons, and by various other idling functionaries. Sometimes these functionaries were present in such numbers that there was no room left for the working members of the staff. One day Patterson discovered that one of the men thus crowded out was Leland Stowe, though he was assigned to do the running story from the hall. He was trying to do it in the *Herald-Tribune*'s tar-paper office under the stand, with occasional hasty dashes to the hall itself. This gross violation of the elementary newspaper principle that the man doing the story should have right of way outraged all of us, and we were delighted when Patterson invited Stowe to occupy one of the *Sun* seats. The Reids saw him at work there, but the fact apparently made no impression on them. Ogden, in truth, was more or less drunk all the time. In Cleveland I encountered Dr. Raymond Moley, the first member of the original Brain Trust to withdraw from it. He was now trying to operate a weekly called *Today* and was making heavy weather of it. This weekly, which was financed by Vincent Astor, was supposed to support the New Deal, but Moley told me that he no longer believed in it. I had breakfast with him and his sister. He was extremely cordial. What I had been writing about the New Deal in the *Evening Sun,* he said, pretty well coincided with his own views.

On July 12 I was back in Cleveland for the convention of the Townsendites, which began there on July 14, and when it was over I proceeded to Topeka, Kansas, for the Landon notification on July 23. On August 14 I returned to Cleveland again for the Coughlinite convention, which opened on August 15, and when it was over I joined Landon on his first campaign tour. The Townsend and Coughlin conventions were magnificent shows. Covering them was my own idea and I had no help, which made the work extremely hard, but it was also very amusing, and so I greatly enjoyed it. I had met Townsend a little while before, when he took the old Shearer house in the 900 block of north Charles street, Baltimore, and made it his national headquarters. I visited him there several times, and he came to Hollins street and put in a couple of evenings with my brother August and me. He was, at bottom, an innocent old boy, and quite honest, but the dizzy way in which money was rolling in on him had begun to upset him a bit, and he was even more upset by the riotous applause that greeted him every time he showed himself to his lieges. All sorts of racketeers had clustered about him, trying to grab shares of the swag. They ranged from cashiered Y.M.C.A. secretaries to former agents of the Anti-Saloon League, now thrown out of work by Repeal, and from local politicians in search of new issues and easy jobs to the most dubious sort of lobbyists and press-agents. One of his principal aides was a Methodist evangelist who had formerly gone about the country giving courses of illustrated lectures on the Bible; he now adapted his machinery to the whooping up of the Townsend Plan, and in the course of the next year or two got into the doctor to the extent of $30,000. Another was a former Y.M.C.A. and Red Cross worker who had taken to drink, and was now extraordinarily foul of speech and otherwise most offensive. A third was a San Francisco racketeer who had made a fortune as a bootlegger, then transferred to the narcotics traffic, and was now, for some reason unknown, devoting his time and money to promoting old-age pensions. A fourth was a press-agent who turned out, a little while later, to be a spy in the employ of Hearst, who apparently saw some possibility of turning the Townsend movement to his own uses. The politicians who had climbed aboard the doctor's wagon were of all parties and factions, but every one of them came from a region where the Townsendite revelation appeared to be the rage, and his one purpose was to round them up come election day. Most of these scoundrels were simultaneously trying to get money out of the doctor, but some of them—for example, Gomer Smith, of Oklahoma—had plenty of their own, and were willing to spend it to obtain his support. All the professional Utopians of the country flocked to his standard, some of them eager to swallow his new evangel and the rest trying to convert him to theirs.

At the top of the hierarchy of attendant wizards and visionaries was Gerald L. K. Smith, who had been chief of staff to Huey Long in Louisiana. When Huey was assassinated in September, 1935, Gerald cleared out at once, fearing that he might be killed next. He was now looking for a new crusade to join, and that of old Townsend seemed to be the most promising in sight. He was the loudest, gaudiest mob-orator I have ever heard. Put beside him, indeed, all the rest seemed pale and ineffectual. I came to terms with him at once, for such performers upon the vulgar spine and midriff have always interested me immensely, and we have remained friendly ever since. When the Townsend movement began to peter out he organized a show of his own, giving it the name of the Committee of One Million. This was in 1937 or 1938, and the million, of course, consisted of Gerald himself. He told me that he proposed to make New York his headquarters, "for that is where the real money is." All the other mob messiahs, he went on, had made the mistake of starting in the back country, where people were poor. He quickly rounded up a committee of well-heeled believers, and was presently launched upon a crusade against Communism. It went so well that he was invited to harangue a number of fashionable gatherings, one of them at the Piping Rock Club, the most doggy country club in the whole New York region. One night, at his invitation, I went to a radio station with him to hear his first attempt at radio crooning. It seemed to me to be a failure, for his oratory needed gestures, and at least half the fascination of it lay in looking at him. Soon afterward he moved from New York to Detroit, and there he quickly established himself as a specialist in the subversive activities of the C.I.O. The automobile manufacturers backed him liberally, and he became very prosperous.

There were 9000 delegates at the Townsend convention. Most of them were simple-minded elderly folk from the small towns and villages of the Middle West, but there were also some younger ones. I soon found, indeed, circulating among them, that a large part of the strength of the movement lay among persons who were not old themselves, but were burdened by the support of aged parents. One such convert that I encountered told me that he had to maintain not only his own father and mother, but also the father and mother of his wife. He said that the costs of discharging this filial duty kept him broke, and I could well believe him. The delegates viewed Townsend with a degree of trust and devotion far surpassing that which Jesus had from His disciples. They believed that he could actually get them pensions of $200 a month, and they were willing to follow him down any road which led, on his promise, to that end. They even followed him almost unanimously when he put the whole movement behind William Lemke, a North Dakota Congressman, who had nominated himself for the Presidency on what he called the Union party ticket. This Union party was a grotesque amalgam of all the crackpots, and Lemke was glad to add the Townsend old-age pension scheme to its platform, for Townsend promised confidently to deliver a million votes to it. But when the ballots were counted in November it turned out that Lemke had polled but 891,858 altogether, and so the Union party blew up, and Townsend had some painful wounds to lick. Many of his attendant zanies were strongly against this alliance with Lemke, especially Gomer Smith, who was hoping to get into Congress from Oklahoma as a Democrat.

This Smith was a strange fellow indeed. His swarthy face indicated that there was Indian blood in him, and he was, Indian-like, an orator of considerable horse-power, though much inferior to Gerald. He was a lawyer by trade, and represented both the Scripps-Howard newspapers in Oklahoma and a string of labor unions. One night, in the midst of his battle to save Townsend from Lemke, he asked me to come to his room in the Cleveland Hotel, saying that he had some confidential news of importance. When his message reached me I was entertaining a female customer who had dropped in to see me, and while I palavered with Gomer I parked her in an adjacent parlor. He turned out to be far gone in liquor, but was still able to talk fluently. Once the door was shut, he told me flatly that Townsend was a drug addict. The fact, he said, explained the influence of the San Francisco racketeer who called himself Edward Margett in the Townsend movement: it was Margett who supplied the old man with drugs. Why a registered physician should have to go to a narcotics pedlar for them he did not explain. When I refused to believe the story, he declared that he had seen the marks of the hypodermic needle on Townsend's arms. I listened to him for half an hour, and then withdrew. In the parlor I found that my female customer was in process of being ravished by another eminent Townsendite—this one a pious and elderly Methodist from Kansas, who had been an ardent Prohibitionist during all the thirteen dreadful years, and had only lately staged a vice crusade in his own town, where he was the local judge. I had introduced him to the lady, and she had been so much impressed by the fact that he was a judge that when I left her to listen to Smith, she accepted his invitation to have a drink. He poured out two whoppers, for Kansans love big drinks, and when she got hers down her faculties began to cloud at once. As I emerged from Gomer's den His Honor had her backed into a corner, and was preparing to pull off her clothes—the established Kansas technic in such cases. I commanded him to desist, denounced him as a lecher, and then escorted the lady downstairs and put her into a taxicab. She called up the next day to say that the whiskey she drank must have had knockout-drops in it, but on that point I had my doubts. In the same parlor, a couple of hours before, some of the correspondents had had to rebuke the dipsomaniacal Y.M.C.A. secretary for using language so obscene that the female reporters present almost blushed. After I got rid of my own visitor and was returning to my room I met Townsend in the corridor, and he asked me what I thought of his staff of master-minds. I told him that they were all palpable thieves—save one. "Which one?" he demanded. I replied that I had thrown in the exception simply to be fair. Later on he began to fire them—and nearly all of them entered suits against him for large but unintelligible damages. These suits kept him jumping for more than a year, and he told me in 1940 that they had cost him more than $200,000. It was not, to be sure, his money; it was the money of the trusting old folks.

Gerald's speech on June 15, though it came soon after the opening of the convention, was the climax of the week; everything that followed seemed banal by comparison. I described it at length in the *Sun* of the next morning. What it was about I do not recall, and probably never knew, but I'll never forget its stupendous effect upon that vast crowd of poor idiots. It not only thrilled them; it almost paralyzed them. Throughout my newspaper days I had been listening to mob orators, and, what is more, enjoying them, for nothing delights me more than the spectacle of simpletons being bamboozled, but never before had I heard anything even remotely comparable to that masterpiece. All the other correspondents at the press-table—many of them veterans of long years of political rhodomontade—agreed that it was incomparable. Indeed, it fetched them almost as effectively as it fetched the delegates. There is an unwritten law that "the press-stand has no opinion"—*i.e.*, that it must never show any sign of assent or dissent, or even of interest—but Gerald had not been going on more than a few minutes before that law was forgotten. Male and female, one and all, the correspondents forsook their typewriters, climbed to their shaky desks, and began to whoop and howl at every pause in the flow of red-hot words. Gerald had very little to say about the Townsend movement; he devoted all of his eloquence to the excoriation of Roosevelt. Of his argument I remember nothing save his declaration that when Henry Wallace undertook his famous slaughter of pigs in Iowa, "it caused the death by starvation of 200,000 little children in the Carolinas alone." This one set the old folks to howling in a really frantic manner. My report to the *Sun* dealt with the content of the speech very lightly, and was given over mainly to describing its manner and its effect. On July 27 I had an article on the editorial page of the *Evening Sun,* entitled "The Townsend Circus," in which I dealt with his singular gifts again. He liked my writings about him so much that he began to quote extracts from them in his circulars, and in fact continues to do so to this day. When I got back to Baltimore I tried to promote a Smith meeting at the Lyric, for the sole purpose of entertaining the town as it had never been entertained before.

Another figure at the Townsend convention was Charles E. Coughlin, the radio priest, who already had so large a following that he was beginning to alarm the politicians. He and Townsend were both operating upon the underprivileged, and naturally drew together, though they differed enormously both in their programmes and in their personalities. Coughlin was put up to speak on July 16, the day following Gerald's triumph, which he had witnessed. He undertook an imitation of Gerald's technic, pulling off his coat and rabat, rolling up his sleeves, working himself into a lather of sweat and howling in a deafening manner, but it was plainly only an imitation, and he did not lift the old folks as Gerald had done. One phrase of his speech, however, got a great deal more attention from the country than anything Gerald had said. It was his celebrated denunciation of Roosevelt as "the great betrayer and liar." In the early days of the New Deal he had been for it, but now he professed to believe that Roosevelt's achievements were lagging behind his promises. The word liar, applied to the President of the United States, shocked the plain people, and the newspapers were full of the speech during the days following. On July 19 I passed on to Patterson a report in Cleveland that Jim Farley had demanded that the Papal Delegate at Washington order Coughlin's bishop to silence him. Whether or not this was a fact I do not know, but on July 23 Coughlin issued an apology. His excuse was the lame one that he had had in mind, not the President, but only "Candidate Roosevelt." He added piously: "Whenever orders come forth from Rome curtailing my preaching social justice, I shall be only too happy to accede to the request and obey orders." During the months following efforts were made to induce his immediate superior, Bishop M. J. Gallagher of Detroit, to silence him, but Gallagher refused to do so, and he remained on the air until his money ran out.

When the Townsend convention ended I was worn out, for it had involved very heavy work. What went on in the hall was only half of the show; the grafters who were fighting for control of the old doctor and his flow of easy money played politics day and night, and it was a tough job to follow them. One day, as I recall, I was hard at it from 8 A.M. until after midnight. I covered the whole story alone, for though Frank Kent was in Cleveland he gave me no help. In such situations he never did, greatly to the ire of Patterson. I planned to go to Chicago by sleeper the night of July 19, which was the day the convention closed, take a room at the Blackstone Hotel, catch up on my lost sleep, and then leave by sleeper for Topeka on the night of July 20. Kent was to go with me, and Essary was to meet us in Chicago. Essary came in on July 21, and that night he and Kent and I left for Topeka.

The few hotels there were packed to the doors, but Arthur J. Carruth, Jr., editor of the *State Journal,* had offered to put us up at his house in the suburbs, and we accepted gratefully, though getting to and from the place was somewhat difficult. His wife and daughter were away for the Summer, and so there was plenty of room for us. Unhappily, Kansas was in the midst of a severe drought, so the city water supply was running low, and we had difficulty drawing enough of it for bathing. The heat in Topeka was really infernal. On July 24, the day after the Landon notification ceremony, the official temperature, for a brief time in the late afternoon, was actually 114 degrees. In Baltimore, with its high humidity, such heat would have killed hundreds, and maybe even thousands, but Kansas was so dry that it was bearable. Hamilton Owens came in during the day from Baltimore; he had been sent out by Patterson to have a look at Landon. {When the show was over Owens made a tour of Western Kansas to see the wind-belts of young trees that had been set out at great expense to the taxpayer by one of the camorras of New Deal visionaries at Washington. The device was plainly nonsensical, and in the end it failed miserably, but Owens came back professing to believe that it was destined to be a big success. His inclination toward the New Deal, in those days, was such that he was ready to believe in any of its projects, however wasteful and useless.} The town swarmed with newspaper correspondents, and both Landon and his wife gave press conferences.

Mencken loved a "carnival of buncombe." Here, in Cleveland, Ohio, he covers the Republican convention that nominated Governor Alf Landon for president in June, 1936.

Landon turned out to be a very pleasant fellow, and not without sense of humor, but I came away from him convinced that he was not smart enough to beat so adept a demagogue as Roosevelt, and that impression kept on gathering strength during the campaign.

The problem of victualling was a painful one in Topeka, for there were only a few places offering food fit to eat, and they were constantly crowded to the door by the politicians who had flocked in to hear Landon accept the nomination—and prepare his mind for giving them jobs, in the remote event that he were elected. But one night Nelson Antrim Crawford, editor of Senator Arthur Capper's *Household Magazine* and a contributor in my time to the *American Mercury,* gave me a dinner at the principal hotel, and it turned out to be excellent. The drink situation was also dismal, for the Kansas law forbade the sale of anything save 2.45% beer, and the stronger beer and hard liquors brought in by the Topeka bootleggers were dubious. Another hospitable Topekan was Dr. Karl A. Menninger, a psychiatrist who had sent a number of manuscripts to the *American Mercury* in my time, though I never, so far as I can recall, printed any of them. He had a large and prosperous private asylum in the outskirts of Topeka, and a farm ten or twelve miles out in the country. One night he invited a dozen of us correspondents to visit the farm, and we had a very pleasant evening. The place was given over to the propagation of rare trees, and I am sorry that the dark prevented me seeing more of it. The doctor had a supply of bottled beer, packed in tubs with ice, and his guests got down a tremendous amount of it.

The day after the notification ceremony Patterson wired me instructions to write my impressions of Landon for the *Sunday Sun* of July 26, and I did so at some length. I did the best I could for him, but it was not much, for his speech of acceptance had proved that he was hopeless as a campaign orator, and my brief meetings with him had convinced me that he lacked altogether the smartness needed to beat Roosevelt. "He is," I said, "respected and admired at home, but it would be an exaggeration to say that he boils the blood. Some of the men closest to him, and most responsible for his recent apotheosis, are the freest in pointing out his limitations. He is a bit slow, they say, in picking up facts, and has yet to explore certain areas of knowledge wherein a President is supposed to disport." I went on:

> He thinks clearly and talks plain English, but he never says anything that makes the head swim and the midriff leap. His speeches are plain recitals of what he conceives to be fact, and there is no more poetry in

them than you will find in a tax bill. If he ever took to hollering and waving his arms his neighbors would be as much surprised as if he stripped off his shirt.

His speeches will continue to be essays rather than orations. They will be made as plain as he can make them, and that will be very plain indeed, but there will be nothing in them to enchant movie fans, editorial writers and other such aesthetes.

This judgment turned out to be sound; it was, in fact, obvious. I had been hopeful up to the Spring of 1936 that the Republicans might unearth a demagogue capable of meeting Roosevelt on his own ground, and beating him, but when Landon was nominated my hopes vanished. His only chance of election lay in the possibility that the plain people had tired of Roosevelt, but that possibility was very remote, for the flow of New Deal money was still at high tide, and millions were getting shares of it. Virtually all the other correspondents at Topeka agreed with me— all, that is, save Roy Roberts, Duke Shoop and the rest of the Kansas City *Star* outfit. One of those I encountered was W. G. Clugston, Topeka correspondent of the Kansas City *Journal-Post,* who had contributed to the *American Mercury* in my time. He disliked Landon for some reason unknown to me, but he was a man if wide political experience and sound judgment, and so I listened to him. He predicted flatly that Landon would lose the whole cow country in November, including Kansas. The yokels, he said, were still full of hope and confidence that the New Deal wizardries would save them from all the great curses that beset them— drought, overproduction, and so on—and make them fat and happy. The only way to wean them from Roosevelt was to promise them enormously more than he was already giving them—and Landon's mind was too literal to permit him to indulge in any such poetry. This was my own opinion precisely.

After the show at Topeka was over I went to Atchison to visit my old friend, E. W. Howe, who was then 83 years old and beginning to fail; in fact, he died on October 3, 1937. I was a great admirer of Howe's, and had once edited a collection of his extraordinarily pungent apothegms for Knopf. In 1935, when Sara was at the Johns Hopkins for her last illness, he was also there, having cataracts removed from his eyes, and I well remembered his friendly sympathy, blind and helpless as he was. I traveled to Atchison by an accommodation train and found the journey comfortable enough, despite the record-breaking heat. Up the line some distance a man I had met in Topeka came aboard the train, and asked me how I was making out. "Very well," I answered. "I'd be sweating ten times as much at 90 degrees in Baltimore." "Stand up," he said, and I stood up—and discovered instantly that there was plenty of sweating going on where the dry air could not reach. My back and backside were streaming. I had dinner in Atchison with Howe and his niece Adelaide, and left for home that night. He lived in a vast and gloomy red brick house set in a grove elevated about thirty feet above the street. It had been built, he told me, by one of the more opulent pioneers of the town, and he had bought it very cheaply. There were no other guests, and we had a pleasant evening. Howe was full of shrewd judgments about all the political figures of the day. Roosevelt, he said, was a demagogue from snout to tail, and had no more conscience than a shyster lawyer. Landon was a well-meaning but bewildered fellow, and probably believed in the New Deal much more than Roosevelt. I did not dispute these characterizations, and I see no reason to question them now.

The Coughlin convention, which began at Cleveland on August 15, was less amusing than the Townsend convention, but of the same general order. I palavered with Coughlin as soon as I got in, and took an immediate dislike to him. He was an extremely shifty and nefarious fellow, and lied constantly at his daily press conferences—sometimes in an effort to cover up his frequent indiscretions, but often for no apparent reason at all. As I have recorded, he had been invited to make a speech at the Townsend convention, and had promised, in turn, to let Townsend and Gerald Smith make speeches at his, but when they got to town he tried to put them off with various transparent excuses. In the end, he scheduled them for the end of his very last session—and actually adjourned it before they went on, in order to be able to say that they had not been on the programme. Inasmuch as the last session had started at 9 A.M. and the delegates had been kept in their seats, without any time out for meals, until the evening, they were naturally worn out when Townsend and Smith arrived. Townsend made one of his usual dull speeches and was received coldly, but when Gerald cut loose he lifted the poor idiots to their feet almost instantly, and in a few minutes had them roaring. His speech was a duplicate of the masterpiece he had delivered at the Townsend convention, but somewhat shorter. While it was going on Coughlin watched him with envious eyes.

The Townsend delegates had been 100% Americans from the small towns of the Middle West; the Coughlin delegates were mainly foreign-born working folk from the steel and coal regions. Some of the speakers spoke such bad English that it was difficult to follow them. {One day

Jonathan Mitchell of the *New Republic,* who was sitting beside me in the press-stand, amused himself by compiling a list of the strange names in the programme-book. This list he handed to me, and I printed part of it in an article on Coughlin for the *Evening Sun* of August 24, by title "The Radio Priest." Among the names were Dziedzic, Szilagyi, Zwier, Kmelty, Ghyselinck, Mercansits, Dzygun and Wodjdylak.} Coughlin was on his feet nearly the whole length of the convention; the other speakers were allowed to speak only briefly. He had been doing most of his talking, for some years past, for the radio, and had developed a curious technic. Unable, because of the need for keeping to the mike, to make the usual gestures, he emphasized his points by wriggling and revolving his backside. Later in 1936, booked to make a speech at a baseball ground in New York, he devised a mike which was held in front of his mouth by a framework going around his shoulders, but I did not hear that speech, and do not know if the device worked. In Cleveland, on the Sunday following the adjournment of his convention, he held a meeting at the local baseball ground, and blew up in the midst of his speech. When he suddenly stopped, said "I can't go on. God bless you!", and was hurried away in an automobile, all sorts of wild rumors went about, and we reporters spent the next three or four hours trying to find out what had floored him. In the end it turned out that it was nothing more romantic than diarrhea.

While I was in Baltimore between the Democratic convention and the Townsend convention I had a telephone call one day from William M. Baskervill, editor of the *News*; he said he wanted to see me on a matter of business. I suggested meeting at Schellhase's restaurant, and we sat down there one evening. I had no idea what he wanted, but suspected that it had to do with either one of two subjects—first, my effort, instructed by Patterson, to try to buy the *News* from Hearst six months before, or, second, the effort of Edmund Coblentz and his feature editor, B. A. Bergman, to induce me to resume writing for the opposite-editorial page of the New York *American*. He surprised me by introducing something quite new. He said that Arthur Brisbane, who had been doing a daily column of comment for the Hearst papers for years past, was seriously and apparently mortally ill in Europe, and that Hearst expected him to die within six months. {He actually died on December 25, 1936.} Then Baskervill said that he had been instructed by Hearst, who had just left for Europe to visit the invalid, to ask me if I would consent to take over the column on Brisbane's death. He said that I would be offered "not less than $1,000 a week," and that I could expect a raise later on. He proposed a contract for five years. Under it I'd be expected to supply not only a daily column of comment on the news, but also an occasional editorial for the Sunday Hearst papers.

I refused, of course, for I was making more money than I needed, and had no desire to put on the galling harness of a daily columnist, especially for the Hearst papers. In the course of the ensuing conversation, which was very amicable, Baskervill told me that Hearst had been looking for a successor to Brisbane for some time. I reminded him that, in the event that I had accepted, my column would have differed enormously from Brisbane's—that my point of view was much more realistic than his, and I couldn't be expected to modify it in signed stuff. He replied that Hearst didn't care. He was not eager to maintain any particular point of view; all he wanted was a column that would attract attention. Hearst, said Baskervill, knew that I dissented sharply from some of his own ideas, but was willing to give me a reasonably free hand. The same offer, I gathered, had been made to various other men before I was approached, and no doubt it was made to still others afterward, but Hearst never found the man he was looking for. In the Spring of 1940, giving up the quest at last, he began to write a daily column of his own, under the title of "In the News." It was much better than Brisbane's column had been for a long while, for Hearst was an extremely competent writer. During the rest of 1940 and most of 1941 he devoted himself largely to arguing against Roosevelt's elaborate efforts to horn into the war, but when Roosevelt succeeded at last, on December 7, he made a flop like the one he had made in 1927, and two days later was supporting the Administration almost as vigorously and as innocently as John Owens had been supporting it in the *Sun*.

My first visit to Hearst with a proposal to buy the *News* (I saw him again in 1937) must have been made early in 1936, though I can't fix the date. It flowed out of a fear that Moe Annenberg, who had just bought the Philadelphia *Inquirer*, might be planning to set up a chain, in which case Baltimore would logically be his next port of call. The state of the *News* was known to be parlous, and the whole Hearst empire seemed to be breaking up. The New York *American*, always the old boy's chief pride, was merged with the tabloid *Mirror*. A year later, in 1939 the Chicago *Herald-Examiner* was merged with the evening Chicago *American*, and in the intervals various other Hearst papers were merged, sold or abandoned. Schmick figured in 1936 that the Baltimore *News* was losing close to $1,000,000 a year, for though its circulation was greater than that of the *Evening Sun,* it was getting much less advertising, and at lower rates. Hearst could never hope to get back his total investment in Baltimore—now nearly $20,000,000—by a sale of the *News,* and he was undoubtedly well aware of that fact, so it seemed a good time to tackle him. Patterson's first idea was for the *Sun* to make an offer for the *News,* and, if it were accepted, to put me in charge of the paper as editor, with Schmick or one of his assistants as business manager. Schmick believed that if it abandoned its costly effort to keep its circulation above that of the *Evening Sun,* and accepted frankly the inescapable but not uncomfortable position of the second paper of the town, its losses could be brought below $100,000 within a year, and converted into a modest profit thereafter.

But there were plain objections to the open purchase of the *News* by the *Sun.* For one thing, Walter Abell, who was then, as I have related, in violent eruption, might object, and even go into court in an effort to prevent the transaction. For another thing, buying the *News* would give the *Sun* a complete monopoly in Baltimore, unparallelled in any other American city of like size, and so open the way to a devastating attack by demagogues, and the possible entry of an entirely new paper—perhaps with Stern, Annenberg or some other even worse mountebank as its proprietor. When the situation was discussed at board meetings, Semmes, Morgan, Fenhagen and Cutler appeared to be doubtful that buying the *News* with *Sun* money would be a good idea, and so Patterson turned to the device of trying to buy it with other money. Where this other money was to come from was never clearly determined, but I assumed that most of it would be supplied by Harry Black, with a substantial contribution from Patterson, and maybe smaller ones from Schmick and others. There would have been no difficulty, in fact, in raising it, for every rich Baltimorean knew what Patterson had achieved with the *Sun,* and almost any of them would have been glad to back him in a new venture—that is, provided the *News* could be got at a reasonable price. Schmick figured that we could afford to pay $1,000,000 for it, and I was commissioned to see Hearst.

I visited him by appointment in his hotel suite the next time he was in New York, and got a very cordial reception. He said politely that he had long hoped to induce me to join his organization, and I replied with equal politeness that, if I ever left the *Sun,* I'd be delighted. I then proceeded to business without further ado. "I am here," I said, "to ask you if you will sell me the *News.*" His reply was "Heavens, no!", but this, in large part, was only rhetorical, and we went into the proposal at some length. Among other things, as I recall, I offered the stipulation that in case I took over the paper I would continue the Hearst Sunday magazine, the *American Weekly*—an important consideration, for losing Baltimore would make a considerable dent in the *Weekly*'s circulation, which was then advertised as the largest on earth. I also offered to continue some of the Hearst features, though without specifying which ones, and we discussed them in detail. Hearst never asked me who my backers were, and I did not offer to tell him. I asked him to promise, in case he ever changed his mind about selling it, to let me know in time for me to make another offer for it, and he promised. He then asked me to visit him some time at his estate at San Simeon in California, and I told him that I'd be delighted. We fell after that to talking of mutual friends in California, chiefly in the movies, and parted on the best of terms.

When, in 1937, the New York *American* was merged with the *Mirror,* and the Hearst empire was taken over by the banks and appeared to be in collapse, I tried to see him again, but he was in Europe, and I had to be content with his son, William Randolph, Jr. Young Bill was the only one of the Hearst boys who showed any talent for newspaper management—and he was surely no great shakes. But I had met him before and found him an amiable fellow, and when I now approached him with a request that he give me first chance at the *News* if it were ever offered for sale, he agreed very readily. This was on June 24, 1937, and it was the end of my attempt to buy the paper. If we had collared it, it was Patterson's plan to make me editor with a large degree of independence. I would have been free to adopt policies in opposition to those of the *Sunpapers,* and to wage editorial feuds with them. His idea was that this would keep alive the public impression that the *News* was quite independent, and that my competition might put some life into the two Owenses and their third-rate editorial writers.

To return, now, to 1936. When I got back from the Landon notification ceremony I found Patterson in a very uneasy state about the approaching campaign. My impressions of Landon, printed in the *Sunday Sun* of July 26, had been anything but encouraging, and Patterson was in fear that they had given aid and comfort to the New Dealers in the office. I shared that fear, but refused to accept any blame for the fact, for I had told the truth as I saw it, and if there was any coloring of my dispatch it was in favor of Landon. {On September 15 I was asked by Dorothy Russell, of the Republican National Committee's staff of press-agents, to give her a statement for publication in a campaign magazine called the *Trumpeter*. She said that she already had such statements from Booth Tarkington, George Ade, Will Irwin, Cornelia Otis Skinner and others. I sent her the following: "I am, and always have been a Democrat, but I shall vote for Landon this year. My reason is simple. I believe that the snake-charmers now operating at Washington have been disgracing the party and harassing the country long enough. They have some talent as mountebanks, and for a year or so they gave an amusing show, but such shows always wear out. What we need now is a reasonable amount of common sense and common decency in government. Landon, I believe, can supply enough for all practical purposes. Put him beside Roosevelt, and he looks like an honest horse-doctor beside Lydia Pinkham. I don't believe the Presidency requires genius. If it did, we'd have gone the way of Carthage and Gomorrah long ago. All the job needs is the sound, homely, enduring competence that one looks for in the better sort of college president, newspaper city editor, or saloon-keeper. Landon has it. The Hon. Mr. Roosevelt's gifts, rich as they are, all lie in other directions. He is a swell sorcerer, but who would employ a sorcerer to run even a cigar-store?" Whether or not this was ever printed in the *Trumpeter* I do not know.}

I proposed to vote for him [Landon] in November, but only as a means of voting against Roosevelt: he was obviously anything but the inspired and triumphant messiah the Republicans had been hoping for. Patterson's blast against the New Deal itchings of the *Evening Sun*, directed at Hamilton Owens on December 5, 1935, had produced little effect. There had been some reduction in the number of frankly New Deal editorials, but there had been little direct criticism of Roosevelt, and that little had been feeble and hollow. In the morning *Sun* the editorials of John Owens and his forward-lookers were tantalizingly vague, and Patterson now began to suspect that Owens would soon edge away from all pretense of supporting Landon and flop boldly to Roosevelt. The easy way out would have been to issue a positive order, setting forth the paper's position clearly, but that was the sort of remedy that Patterson always hesitated to resort to, and in the present case he was deterred by a lingering dread of John Owens, born of the battle with the archbishop in 1934. I urged him to come to a clear-cut decision, and then enforce it rigorously, but he preferred to wait. When the time approached for Landon to begin his campaign tours Patterson surprised me one day by saying that he was going to send John Owens on the first of them. Whether this was his own idea or Owens's I never found out. It seemed to me that, from Patterson's standpoint, this was a risky plan, for while there was a possibility that Landon would win Owens there was an even greater possibility that he would come home hopeless. I had been told off to make the same tour, so Owens and I boarded the Landon campaign train at Chicago on August 20, and remained with it for about a week. I saw Owens at all hours of the day and night, but was at great pains to avoid any discussion of the position of the *Sunpapers* in the campaign. So far as I can recall, the subject was not mentioned once, though we talked of the campaign itself at great length, and listened to Landon's speeches together.

Meanwhile, Patterson was at last seizing the bull by the horns in Baltimore. The *Evening Sun* editorial page had been again edging toward the New Deal, this time under cover of a discussion of Landon's obvious deficiencies. One day, coming suddenly to the end of his nearly four years of endurance, Patterson had it out, not with Hamilton Owens, who was hardly more than an echo of Black, but with Black himself. All I know of the row, of course, was what Patterson told me when I got back from the Landon tour. He said that he had said to Black that the covert support of the New Deal by the *Evening Sun* must come to an end at once, and forever; that Black was responsible for it and must take the blame for it; and that if he (Black) did not see that Hamilton Owens stopped it at once, he (Patterson) would ask him (Black) to keep away from the office. This was hot stuff, indeed, and though I rejoiced to see Patterson recovering his fire and asserting his authority at last, I was in some fear that his rough manner (as he described it) had offended Black, and would cause trouble in the office thereafter. But Black, as it turned out, took the whole episode in good part. On September 3 I wrote to Patterson: "Harry Black called me up yesterday. He said that he wanted it understood that, whatever his private ideas, he would go along with the paper. He said that if we hold a palaver during his absence and decide on a definite course he will go along 100%."

If any such palaver was held I was not present at it, and I heard nothing more of the matter until Patterson got back to Baltimore. Then he told me, with palpable relief, that John Owens's cogitations had at last borne fruit, and that the verdict reached was that the *Sunpapers* could not support Roosevelt. But neither, it appeared, could they support Landon—that is, unless and if he began to show more vigor than had been apparent in him so far in the campaign. In other words, they would straddle. This seemed to me to be a rather sorry compromise, but I had to admit that there was logic to it. My own dispatches from the Landon campaign tour had described the candidate's dreadful failure on the stump without any mincing of words, and I was convinced that he had ruined by his own incompetence any chance of winning that he had ever had.

At a board meeting on September 10, with Black absent, Patterson informed the directors of the programme decided upon. He made it plain to them that, by the *Sunpaper* tradition, they were being informed, not consulted—that they could influence the policy of the papers only by changing the president, and had no authority to interfere with his editorial decisions so long as he remained in office. They took this warning in good part, but when the editorial that John Owens had written for September 11 was read to them two of them, Morgan and Stemmes, made speeches of protest. Both, at that time, were inclined toward Roosevelt; it was not until his second term was half over that they began to lose confidence in him. Morgan's speech was really impassioned. He made all the usual arguments for the New Deal, and said that the *Sunpapers'* dissent from it grieved him sorely. Semmes was a good deal less vehement, but he, also, declared that the decision to oppose Roosevelt, was a blow to him. Patterson listened politely to these caveats, but undertook no rebuttal. George Cutler, a Republican, was delighted that Roosevelt was not to get the *Sunpapers'* support, but somewhat dashed by the fact that Landon was going on what amounted to probation. Fenhagen and I said nothing. The next day the Owens editorial was printed on the first page of the *Sun*.

What followed was in the same tone of old-fashioned ponderousness—a frank harking back to the *Sun*'s bow-wow style in the days of the Abells. John Owens was at his best in such heavy writing, but on this occasion, I should add, he was rather cloudy. The defect of Landon, it appeared, lay in the fact that he appeared to be "a merely frugal Roosevelt," with a programme of sure cures almost as long as Roosevelt's own, and no apparent enthusiasm for the "free competitive system at home and abroad" which was described as the center of the *Sunpapers'* system, though without any explanation of its precise nature. The editorial ended thus:

> If Governor Landon speaks in clear and bold terms, facing specific problems and taking his stand unequivocally on the side of true economic liberalism, the *Sun* will support him, no matter what his prospects will be. If he does not speak in clear terms the *Sun* intends to continue the fight for ideas that it believes to be sound and in the interest of the people, and will make the best of a situation in which it cannot advocate the election of either candidate.

Landon, of course, never came up to these demands, and so the *Sun-papers* continued on the fence until the end of the campaign, with the *Evening Sun,* purged at last, delivering occasional gingery blows at Roosevelt and his associated quacks. It was obvious by now that Landon hadn't the ghost of a chance of winning. I rejoined him in Chicago on September 11, and continued with him to Portland, Maine, and late in October I joined him again for the last days of his campaign, culminating in a final meeting at Madison Square Garden, New York, on October 29. On the trip into New England I took Gerald W. Johnson along, and in Portland let him cover the meeting, which was held at a baseball park in a dense fog. Johnson had been showing signs of disintegration for some time, and it was Patterson's idea that immediate contact with a news story might shake him up. The experiment failed dismally. I acted as leg man for him, and roved the foggy field digging up odd incidents of the meeting and delivering them to him in the press-stand. They made no impression on him whatsoever: as Hamilton Owens had said, he was allergic to facts. Nor could he make anything out of Landon's speech—a circumstance that was perhaps not surprising. At the end of the meeting he had less than half a column written, and it read far more like an editorial than a news story. I put it on the wire, and took him downtown for a couple of beers. Of the three Landon tours I remember only a few episodes. Landon's chief aide on all of them was my old friend Henry J. Allen of Kansas—now, with Repeal in effect, a careful and polished drinker. He got down a daily ration of Scotch, but I never saw him drunk. I had many pleasant palavers with him, for he had some humor and was full of pawky political sagacities. One evening, after a long day of platform speeches, he sent out word that Landon wanted to see me, and I went to the private car at the end of the train, taking along Henry M. Hyde, who was covering the tour for the *Evening Sun.* When we got to Landon's sitting-room he looked to be in a state of collapse. He greeted us cordially, but it was apparent at once that he was barely functioning. Allen, noticing this, motioned us out, and in his own quarters asked us to return in half an hour. "Alf," he said, "is all in. He has been hard at it since 6 o'clock this morning—making speeches and talking to politicians. But all he needs is half an hour of sleep. Once he has had it he'll be as good as new." When we returned we found that this was quite true. Alf had stripped off his coat and waistcoat and stretched out on his couch, and now he was not only wide awake, but very lively.

Hyde had been listening to the day's speeches and had been somewhat shocked by them, for in them Alf had promised the yokels everything on the New Deal programme and a great many additions of his own. "What I can't understand, Governor," said the serious and highly honorable Hyde, "is how you can promise those poor yaps so many things that you must know you can never give them. Put together everything you listed today, and the cost, as I figure it, runs to at least ten billions a year. How are you going to balance the budget?" Alf thought for a moment, smiled sadly, and then replied. "Mr. Hyde," he said, "I agree with you thoroughly. You are quite right when you say that very few of the articles on my farm programme are realizable at all, and that those that are would cost enough to bankrupt the country. But let me recall to your mind the fact that, unless I can round up the farm vote, my chances of being elected are reduced to precisely nothing. That is the only difference between us. You are not a candidate for the Presidency of the United States, I am." So we had a drink with Alf and Henry Allen, and retired to our stateroom, with Hyde still shaking his head.

Another evening Alf began questioning me about the once-famous Baltimore cuisine, and showed especial interest in terrapin à la Maryland. He said that he had been hearing of it all his life, but had never eaten it. I thereupon promised to give him a terrapin dinner in Baltimore at any time convenient to him after election day, win or lose. At the end of November I reminded him of this, and he finally fixed Sunday, December 13 as the day. The dinner was at the Southern Hotel in Baltimore, and all the other guests save one were Democrats. That one exception was Ogden L. Mills, who happened to be in Baltimore, and was brought by Frank R. Kent. Before dinner Alf and Mills came to my house in Hollins street, and we had a few preliminary drinks. I have mislaid the list of guests at the dinner, but I recall that it included Fenhagen, John Owens, Schmick and one or two others of the *Sun,* and several from Washington. Alf professed to be delighted with the terrapin, but I noticed that he declined a second helping, and later on I was told by one of his confidantes that he had found it hard going. He invited me to give him revenge by coming to Topeka for a dinner of fried rabbit. I asked Landon at my dinner if there had ever been a time during the campaign when he really believed he could be elected, and he answered yes. "It was," he said, "after the big meeting in Madison Square Garden on October 29. The New York Republican organization put on such a magnificent show that it fooled me. I said to myself: 'If New York City is for you, you have a good chance to win, and God knows it seems to be for you.'" He was not the first candidate to be fooled by the superb technic of the New York machine.

On July 3 I received a letter from Frank Kent enclosing a copy of another from Mark Sullivan. The Sullivan letter was dated June 29, two days after the adjournment of the Democratic National Convention at Philadelphia. It was addressed to Kent and was as follows:

> Here is something important which I think you folks on the *Sun* ought to do. The best newspaper writing about the conventions, the best I have seen in any newspaper this year, the best indeed that I have seen in many a year, is Mencken's account of the Democratic convention. I think I read three stories in all: I read particularly the last two, and it was the last two, especially the one in Sunday's *Sun*, that excited my enthusiasm and led to this suggestion.
>
> I think you folks on the *Sun* ought to be sure that these articles of Mencken's go before that Pulitzer jury which, as I recall, gives awards for the best newspaper writing of the year. If you carry out this suggestion, be sure to insist that the judges actually read Mencken's articles. Unless they actually read them they may take it for granted that these newspaper stories of Mencken's are like his ordinary writing which they used to see in the *Mercury* and elsewhere. And the fact is, these newspaper articles are straightaway accounts, with just enough of Mencken's humor and personality to give them flavor. As straightaway accounts of a public event I have never seen anything better done.

Kent was a member of the Pulitzer prize board. He called me up and told me of the Sullivan letter, and at my request sent me a copy of it. With it came this note of his own:

> Here is the letter I wanted to show you. I completely agree with it. I am told, however, that your contempt for the Pulitzer board, of which I am a lowly and inconspicuous member, is so profound that you would resent any such action and spurn the $1000 check.
>
> Perhaps they have been stupid about the drama and novels. I do not defend them, but on the newspaper end I think they have on the whole been pretty sound. Here is an instance where they could do properly what ought to be their main job—that is, the stimulation of good writing in newspapers. At any rate, I wanted you to see Mark's letter. What is your feeling about it? I am not sensitive about the board, so you need not hesitate for fear of wounding me.

I replied, of course, that it would be impossible for me to accept the Pulitzer prize if it were offered me, and asked Kent to say no more about it. The award in the class I fell into was given for "a distinguished example of a reporter's work during the year, the test being strict accuracy, terseness, and the preference being given to news stories prepared under the pressure of edition time, that redound to the credit of the profession of journalism." It went to Lauren D. Lyman of the New York *Times* "for his exclusive story revealing that the Lindberghs were leaving the United States to live in England"!

14

A Chapter Had Ended

1937–1939

The war that was to come in September, 1939, was already in plain prospect, and I printed several articles during 1937 on its probable issues as they were then apparent. On August 16, under the title of "The Wicked Wop," I discussed the operations of Mussolini in Abyssinia and Spain, and on November 1, under that of "The Mediterranean Beelzebub," the general situation of Italy. Both times I tried to refute the grotesquely false and poisonous English propaganda that was already flooding the United States—and fetching John Owens and the *Sun*. On October 4 I had my say about Japan, and once more argued that Americans were being hornswoggled by "news" emanating from London. Such caveats, of course, had no influence on Owens: he was, by the end of 1937, so thoroughly under the influence of the Manchester *Guardian* and the preposterous Hull that it was plain where he would carry the *Sun* when the war came at last. I also printed articles on Roosevelt's scheme to pack the Supreme Court, on his appointment of Hugo L. Black to its bench, on the treason trials going on in Russia, on the sit-down strikes in the Middle West, and on various new phases of the New Deal spending spree, with special reference to its cost to the taxpayer. Altogether, there were three articles on the Black appointment—"Nightshirt Into Ermine" on August 23, "The Pains of Disillusion" on September 6, and "Last Words on Hugo" on October 11. In the second of these I poked some gentle fun at Oswald Garrison Villard, who, as a lifelong and highly ingenuous Liberal, had received in the recent past some painful jolts—for example, the ousting of Glenn Frank from the presidency of the University of Wisconsin by the LaFollette machine, the butcheries in Russia, the increasing successes of Franco in Spain, and the sit-down strikes staged by John L. Lewis and his goons of the C.I.O. Among other things I said of Villard that I had "known and venerated" him for "close to one hundred years." It was characteristic of the man's lack of humor that he objected to this in a letter to John Owens, saying that I had actually known him for no more than twenty years. In the same article was the following characterization of Roosevelt:

> Of all the quacks that the Liberals have followed in my time Roosevelt II is probably the worst. His pretensions to high patriotic and altruistic purpose appear to be worth no more than the pledges he makes when he is running for office. He is the demagogue pure and simple, rounding up the boobs wherever he can find them, and on whatever pretext promises to work at the moment. The notion that he harbors a profound plan for the salvation of democracy and the reform of the government is apparently not an iota sounder than the notion that Stalin is actually a Communist.

This was the text of all my subsequent writing about Roosevelt, down to the time it became obvious that his war scare had fetched the boobs again, and any further attempt to discuss him rationally became impossible. At least half of my *Evening Sun* articles during 1937 were variations upon themes that were far from unfamiliar to my customers—for example, that reformers and do-gooders of all sorts are frauds, that professional labor-leaders are much less interested in the welfare of the workers than in the enhancement of their own puissance and importance, that government at all times and everywhere is the enemy of every industrious and well-disposed man, and that democracy is bound, soon or late, to succumb to its own dishonesty and incompetence. It was still generally believed, in 1937, that the Depression which began in 1930 would soon pass off, but I had begun to doubt it, and said so.

About the middle of January, 1938, Patterson asked me to come to his house one night, and there I found Owens. The two of them tackled me with a scheme that they had evidently been hatching for some time: whose it was, originally, I never found out. It was that I should take charge of the *Evening Sun* editorial page for three months, try to reorganize it and give it a new lease on life, make a careful study of the men working on it (Johnson, Wagner, Harriss, Beirne and Hobbs), and report upon them frankly at the end, with special attention to Wagner. Both argued that it was impossible to do anything with Hamilton Owens. So long as he was editor of the *Evening Sun* he would have to be given a considerable amount of discretion, and hard experience had proved that he would use it badly. The plan now was to transfer him to the *Sun,* where, despite his title of editor, he would work directly under John Owens's eye. In his room on the *Evening Sun* the only man available was Wagner, and him I was to investigate at length, in the hope that he would turn out to be good enough to succeed Hamilton Owens at the end of my three months' service. Gerald Johnson had been brought to the *Evening Sun* in 1926 with the idea that he would develop into a good second man for the editorial page, but for reasons that I have hitherto recounted it had been found on trial that he was quite incompetent for command. To his other disabilities was now added the fact that he had been gradually losing his hearing for four or five years past, and still refused to admit the fact frankly and employ a mechanical aid for it, so that anything properly describable as conversation with him was impossible. Thus Hamilton Owens had begun to rely on Wagner instead, and the question was whether Wagner had developed sufficiently to take over the management of the editorial page when Owens moved to the morning *Sun.*

I agreed to tackle the job—but only on condition that my taking over be postponed for a couple of weeks, to give me time for a trip to the West Indies that my brother August and I had planned. This was agreed to, and August and I left in my old favorite, the *Columbus,* on January 22. We visited Havana, Kingston, the Canal Zone and Cartagena in Colombia, and had a very pleasant and restful trip. Exactly when we got back I forget, but it must have been only a few days after February 1, for my last article on the editorial page of the *Evening Sun* appeared on January 31. It was a review of current politics, headed "Third Term," and its essence was in these sentences: "The White House's favorite and probably only genuine candidate for 1940 is the present gifted incumbent, the Hon. Mr. Roosevelt. He will unquestionably run again if he can, and the chances seem to be at least even that he can." After January 31 I was too busy with editing the *Evening Sun* editorial page to write any more articles for it; moreover, it seemed to me to be unwise to print any signed stuff of my own while I was in charge. Thus ended at long last (though I was unaware of it at the time) a series that had been running for more than 17 years, for when my three months as editor were over I found myself disinclined to go on under Wagner, and so Patterson transferred me to the opposite-editorial page of the *Sun,* and then, after a little while, to the editorial page. There I continued every Sunday until February 2, 1941, when I finally quit writing for the *Sunpapers*.

My first job as editor of the editorial page, of course, was to get rid of the rigid formula that Hamilton Owens had been following for years, and that I had protested against to Patterson at least a hundred times— two and a half columns of brief and mainly silly editorials, Frank Beirne's "The Rolling Road" filling out column three, then a signed article at the top of the two columns following, with clipped stuff under it, and two columns of letters to the editor in columns six and seven. For a few days the most I could do was to change the type in which the heads were set, but after that I began a series of experiments that soon had the whole office agog. I abolished the rule that there had to be a set amount of editorials every day, I introduced a large number of new heads, some of them running to four columns, I reformed the correspondence department by throwing out all the dull bores who had been polluting it for so long and by reducing a major part of its contents to brief paragraphs headed "Points From Letters" (an idea borrowed from the London *Times*), and I made free use of illustrations, many of them large and bold. Also, I resumed printing a quotation under the flagstaff [or masthead] every day— a custom prevailing on the *Evening Sun* in Stanley Reynolds's day as editor, but allowed to lapse under Hamilton Owens. These quotations I supplied myself. They came out of the immense stock that I was accumulating for my "New Dictionary of Quotations." They came from such rubrics as Democracy, Government, Speech (Free) and Press (Free), and all of them set forth views with which, as John Owens used to say, borrowing from the official English jargon, I associated myself. They were thus often strong stuff for Owens, and for the rest of the brethren, but he never made any complaint against them.

On February 10 I gave over six whole columns of the editorial pages to a mass of small dots—each supposed to represent a jobholder at the Federal trough. A brief editorial in the first column, headed by a hand pointing to the wilderness of dots, explained that their purpose was to give taxpayers a graphic representation of the vast army of parasites devouring their money. This somewhat obvious device got a great deal of notice in the other newspapers of the country, and was imitated later on. On March 4, the fifth anniversary of Roosevelt's first inauguration, I got more notice for the *Evening Sun* by printing an editorial which filled every inch of the editorial page save the space given over to the flagstaff. It was entitled "Five Years of the New Deal," and was anything but encomiastic in tone. Wagner, I gathered, was something of New Dealer, but when I put him to work gathering material for this blast he did a faithful and competent job, though most of the actual writing I had to do myself. The editorial gave a considerable shock to all the New Dealers in the office, especially those on the *Evening Sun*. When it came out I invited Gerald Johnson to undertake a counterblast, and this was published under his signature and with the title of "On the Profit Side" on March 8. It was feeble stuff, and took nothing from the effectiveness of the six-and-a-half column editorial—the longest ever printed in the *Sunpapers,* and in fact the longest, so far as I know, ever printed in America, at least in my time. At other times I printed other longish editorials, though never one as long as the monster of March 4. Some of them were illustrated with maps, portraits in half-tone or line drawings; one even included a one-column cartoon. I made early efforts to get some cartoons from Edmund Duffy, the cartoonist of the *Sun,* and despite his indolence managed to wangle three out of him. The first, printed on February 14, was three columns wide and exactly resembled those he was doing daily for the *Sun,* but in the course of my negotiations with him I discovered that he disliked being cribbed, cabined and confined to that space every day, and harbored a yearning to burst its bounds. The best drawings of Daumier, he told me, were often wide and shallow. So on March 22 I let him go to five columns, and on April 9 to seven, which is to say, to the whole width of the page. Paul Patterson and I had lunch at the Maryland Club on April 9, and when the *Evening Sun* came in it was plain to see that he was startled, to say the least, for in order to make room for the cartoon at the top of the editorial page I had to drop the flagstaff below it— another event unprecedented on the *Sunpapers.* The cartoon was one of the best ever done by Duffy, and if I had continued as editor I'd have put him to work drawing more of the same width—but deeper.

It took me only a few days to discover that there was little to be got out of the staff of the editorial page. The best man on it, and by long odds, was Wagner. He was then 34 years old, which is to say, he was in the full tide of his youthful energy. Unhappily, his practical newspaper experience had been very limited; indeed, he had never worked on the street as a reporter. His stock of information was not large, but he was a hard worker and knew how to work quickly under pressure, so I found him very useful—in fact, more useful than all the rest put together. His editorials were all superficial, but he was a handy man at writing heads, and after he got the hang of the new make-up he became a pretty good make-up man. His private politics I never inquired into, though there was evidence that he inclined toward New Deal ideas.

The rest of the gentlemen of the *Evening Sun* editorial staff ranged downward from third-rate. Clark S. Hobbs, who had run the column headed "Good Evening" until September 7, 1935, when it became unendurable and was abolished, was the son of a Methodist preacher, and showed it in both his mien and his ways of thought. He was one of the few teetotalers in the office, and in the days of Prohibition actually argued for it. He had a wide acquaintance in Baltimore, especially among clergymen and uplifters (two classes usually disdained and avoided by newspaper men), and that acquaintance could be made more or less useful to the editorial page. He was also a diligent digger up of facts, at least when properly directed.

Beirne and Harriss, who have appeared hitherto in this chronicle, turned out to be almost useless. Beirne, a very charming Virginian, ran an editorial page column headed "The Rolling Road" and was also expected to do a few editorials. "The Rolling Road" was made up of a short prose sketch, always dealing humorously with domestic matters and usually with suburban life, and a series of paragraphs commenting on the news of the day. The prose sketch was mildly amusing, and had a following, but the paragraphs were bad indeed, and I began to lay plans, as soon as I found my way about, to get rid of them. This was finally achieved by inducing an old *Sun* reporter turned syndicate manager, Frank Jay Markey by name, to attempt to syndicate the sketch. Markey, of course, could not market the paragraphs, so I had an excuse for ordering them dropped. Beirne was a willing worker during my three months as editor of the *Evening Sun*, but I got very little useful stuff out of him. Several times I put him to writing editorial page articles on financial subjects, with which he was supposed (on what ground I do not know) to have some acquaintance. It took him two or three days to produce a short article, and the job of copy-reading it was always onerous. His editorials were few and far between, and none of them showed any vigor. I was fond of Beirne, as everyone was, but it took me only a few days to see that he could not be fitted into any scheme to revive and improve the editorial page of the *Evening Sun*.

Harriss was another Southerner, and like Beirne, a very pleasant fellow. After three years on the city staff of the *Evening Sun* he had gone to Paris, and on his return in 1934 was added to the staff of the editorial page. I found that he was in charge of the book reviews which, for many years, had filled five columns of the editorial page every Saturday, and that this labor occupied at least four-fifths of his time. Books that came in for notice were entered upon a record, and then stored in a huge cabinet that took up half of one wall of the ante-room outside the editor's office. Harriss put in his time either reading and reviewing them, or negotiating with various other members of the staff for reviews. These reviews turned out, on examination, to be extremely bad, so I ordered them abolished at once, and substituted brief check-list notices on the order of those that used to appear in the advertising pages of the *American Mercury*. Unhappily, it was just as difficult to get competent check-list notices as competent longer reviews, and I decided to rid the *Evening Sun* of the book page altogether. It wasted nearly 12% of the total weekly space on the editorial page, and interested only a minute minority of readers, for Baltimore was and is one of the worst book towns on earth.

My chief headache, however, was not Hobbs, Beirne or Harriss, but Johnson. It was on my recommendation that he was brought to the *Evening Sun* from his native North Carolina in 1926, and for five or six years thereafter he did very good work. He had a style that was both graceful and pungent, and he had mastered the trick of writing quickly. Indeed, most of the short editorials that he did occupied him for no more than 15 minutes, and he could do three or four of a morning without strain. Unhappily, he was not only a Southerner, but also a Southern cracker, and as he passed into the forties he gradually accumulated the weaknesses that I have described, all of them apparently incurable. Long before 1938 Hamilton Owens had told me "Gerald has become the problem child of the office." More recently he had added "Gerald is a share-cropper." My own verdict, after a few days' experience with him, was that he was completely hopeless, and I actually began to suspect that he might be infested by hookworms or stricken by pellagra: in fact, I once proposed to Patterson, at least half seriously, that he be turned over to Dr. Maxson, the staff surgeon, for investigation. I found at once that it was simply impossible to get an idea into his head. He would listen politely, profess understanding in his high-pitched cracker voice—and then come back with a piece of copy which proved that he had comprehended nothing. His deafness, of course, had something to do with this, but there was at bottom an apparently incurable incapacity to take in facts. One morning, as I recall, he came into my office with an editorial that was competently written—but started off from a premiss that was so false as to be almost idiotic. I told him where he could ascertain the facts, and he departed with his copy to make repairs, but when he came back with it it started off with precisely the same insane premiss. After a week or two of such experiences I gave him no more assignments. Instead, I let him write whatever he pleased, and then picked out the little that was printable. That little chiefly had to do with themes drawn from his native North Carolina. He read its bad newspapers diligently, but apparently nothing else. As I have said, he wrote effectively, and so he earned at least a part of his keep. The rest of the time he sat at his desk with his feet on it, laboriously plowing through his North Carolina papers.

Under Hamilton Owens the work put into the editorial page had been reduced to a luxurious minimum. He held an editorial conference on his arrival at the office in the morning, usually at about 9 o'clock. Owens himself and all the others, like Johnson, had learned the trick of writing brief editorials at high speed, and the whole grist for the day was in the composing-room by 10.30. This system, of course, made for extremely superficial writing, but that was the only kind of writing that Owens really liked and understood. He believed that a long editorial was necessarily dull, and so it was rare for the *Evening Sun* to deal with any subject in a well-informed and intelligent manner. Most of the editorials, in fact, were mere paragraphs, and many of them hardly got beyond the estate of gags. This was the sort of thing that Harry Black appreciated, and Owens, always a fellow of policy, was eager to give him what he wanted. After the editorial page closed for the day little work was done by anyone. Johnson, to be sure, wrote a signed article once a week, but the rest had next to nothing to do, for I also wrote (before I took over the page) a weekly article, and Saturday, as I have said, was given over to book reviews, so only three days called for any thought, and on most of them the chief place was occupied by articles contributed by outsiders. The rest of the page was filled by "The Rolling Road," by little features which appeared day after day (for example, "Gob Humor," the copy of which was prepared by an office-boy named Mike!), by badly selected clippings from a very narrow range of papers, and by letters to the editor. The latter put no burden on whoever handled them, for the same correspondents were represented almost every day. Most of them were Jews of low mental visibility, and in the early part of 1938 virtually all of their letters were devoted to denouncing Hitler. This rubbish, of course, had driven all intelligent correspondents out of the letter column, for whenever one ventured in he was immediately beset by the Jews. It was, in fact, several years since the last had made the venture.

I had this beautiful scheme of editing without pain wrecked in two days, but it took me longer to devise and execute a better one. I abolished the daily editorial conference, and instructed the editorial writers (all, that is, save Johnson) to see me individually before setting to work on a given editorial. The ideas they offered were usually bad ones, and I tried to substitute better, but it was not always possible. When an idea was approved I saw to it that it was given thorough and careful treatment, and not merely dashed off according to the Owens pattern. This, of course, usually made it impossible to finish the job by 10.30, and so the gentlemen of the staff began to suffer the novelty of working in the afternoons, and what is more, working hard. Hobbs I sent out on assignments for signed articles that sometimes occupied him for days: once, indeed, an unusually refractory article occupied him for a week. The letters to the editor I took into my own hands on February 11, and in a few days I was rid of Hamilton Owens's whole stock company of palpitating nonentities, whether of the Old Testament or the New. Meanwhile, I tried to draw reprint from a much wider range of sources than he had ever tapped, and substituted, whenever possible, intelligent summarization for mere reprinting. Here I encountered serious difficulties, for it appeared at once that no one on the staff did much reading. Many papers that came into the office regularly—for example, the London *Times*—were seldom opened; in fact, large stocks of them, still in their wrappers, were always accumulating. In the end, I had to find most of the reprint myself, for whenever I put the heat on the others, and they essayed to bestir themselves, they came in with stuff not worth printing. I tried to avoid writing editorials as much as possible, but it turned out to be necessary almost every time anything serious was afoot. I could seldom get anything worth printing out of anyone save Wagner, and even Wagner never wrote an editorial of genuine force, for he had been trained too long in the Hamilton Owens school of whimsy. There was, of course, no time for writing at the office, so I had to do it at home in the evenings. Inasmuch as I always got to work by 9 A.M. and often kept going at high pressure until after 4 P.M., and in addition, had to work nearly every Sunday, I was pretty well worn out by the time my servitude terminated at the end of April. Indeed, I was actually ill, for a serious discomfort had developed in the region of the heart. My doctor, Benjamin M. Baker, Jr., discovered that it originated in the stomach and was caused by a spastic pylorus. He sent me to the Johns Hopkins Hospital on May 18 for an investigation. When it was over he put me on belladonna and ordered me to take a complete rest. In June I sailed for Bremen on the *Columbus* and spent the next month wandering about Germany.

I went to Germany in June, 1938, mainly because I was used up and needed a rest, but also because I wanted to see it again before the next war began, and especially parts of it that I had seen only briefly or not at all on my previous trips. Patterson had already left for Europe when I sailed, but he was in England, with a trip to France in the company of Jim Bone in the offing, and inasmuch as I never went outside Germany we never met. Before he sailed he gave me a letter of credentials as a *Sun* correspondent, and asked me to send home some correspondence for the *Sun,* but though I took the credentials, which might be useful if I decided to travel outside Germany, I refused to do any articles, for it was already apparent that the *Sun* was firmly committed to the English side, and anything I could possibly write would be pretty sure to lie beyond its principalia. On the *Columbus* I encountered Mrs. Walter Paepke, a granddaughter of my old friend Henry G. Hilken, and on our arrival at Bremen I put in a couple of pleasant days with her and her German relatives, including a charming Bonn professor whose name I forget. I then went to Berlin, and made my headquarters at the Bristol Hotel. I kept away from the American newspaper correspondents, {They were, as I knew, mainly dubs. They had proved it in World War I and they were to prove it again in World War II} and saw only a few German friends—for example, Otto J. Merkel, now an aircraft manufacturer; Dr. Georg Kartzke, a professor in the University of Berlin, and Friedrich Schönemann, also a professor there and formerly one of the Berlin correspondents of the *Sun.* Schönemann I disliked, but he was full of useful information. From Merkel I got a great deal more. I had known him since the last war, and he trusted me, so he talked to me freely. He had access to the highest army circles, and I gathered from him that the German General Staff regarded another great war as inevitable. The German army was not yet quite ready, but it was making fast progress, and if the war could be held off until 1940 it would face the music with confidence. Merkel told me that the best German professional opinion held that the Maginot line was mainly a delusion, and that the French would be disposed of almost as quickly as in 1870. This naturally surprised me, but I had confidence both in Merkel's information and in his good sense, so I accepted his word for it. He said that everyone expected the Russians to enter the war, soon or late, on the English-French side, and that it was believed they might do considerable damage during the first stages, if only because of the immense size of their air-fleet. "But it is not likely," he said, "that they will last. It may take some time to finish them, but in the long run they will not only be beaten but destroyed."

From Berlin I made excursions to East Prussia, to Saxony and to Oldenburg, travelling partly by train and partly by car. I also went to

Potsdam to call upon Mrs. Henry Wood, now a widow, and found her full of stories of the brutality of the Poles to some of her friends. These friends were *Junker* who had estates in what had formerly been Posen, but was now the Polish province of Poznan. They had been permitted to retain their property, but were horribly beset by excessive taxation and by stringent passport regulations. Only a few days before one of Mrs. Wood's intimates, a lady of an aristocratic family, had been kept standing in line at the Polish consulate in Berlin for three hours while the officials deliberated about giving her a passport to visit relatives in Posen. She was ill at the time, and made heavy weather of it. In the end the Poles told her curtly that she could have the passport, but that it would be good for but three days. Inasmuch as she was planning to stay four or five weeks, in the hope of recovering her health, she had to abandon the visit. I went to the Polish consulate myself to get a visa permitting me to cross the Polish Corridor into East Prussia, but found it surrounded by a large crowd of other applicants, chiefly Jews. The entrance to the office was through a yard, and the yard was separated from the street by high iron gates. These gates were locked, and the Pole on guard refused to let me through, so I never got into the consulate. The next day I learned that passengers on trains going through the Corridor without stop did not need visas. I accordingly bought a ticket for such a train leaving Berlin for Königsberg the next Sunday morning.

I had a reserved seat, but never got within two cars of it, for the train was packed. In fact, I never got a seat of any sort, save in the dining-car. I made lunch last as long as possible, and then stood up on one of the car platforms, guarding my bags. There was a toilet just inside the door, and I was unhappily entertained by the efforts of women to force their way to it through the crowd with panting and squawling children. Once a woman got into the place, locked the door, and then apparently sat down for a rest. After she had been within for half an hour other eager customers began beating on the door, and at the next stop the *Schaffner* [conductor] was found on the platform and brought in to get her out. He rattled the door handle and howled orders and objurgations, but the lady took another ten minutes. Germany, in those days, was buzzing with activity, and all trains were crowded. Not many soldiers were visible in the big towns, for most of the barracks were in smaller places, but on the country roads they were numerous, and the sky seemed to be filled with airships. It is a literal fact that, during a month in the country, I never looked aloft by daylight without seeing at least one, and sometimes there were dozens. Mrs. Wood's youngest son, Ernest Friedrich, told me at

Potsdam that a great many youngsters of his class and generation were in training as pilots. He said that the death-rate among these learners was high, but that there were always plenty of volunteers.

Every German that I encountered looked upon another war as inevitable. All hands believed that the Polish cancer would have to be cut out soon or late, and that the operation would bring in France and England, and probably also Russia. The Poles were carrying on in a highhanded and intolerable manner. Convinced that the support of England and France made them invulnerable, and that in case of war their army would be in Berlin in a few weeks, they devoted themselves to looting and oppressing their German subjects, and fresh outrages were reported by the newspapers every day. The Czechs were almost as tyrannical, but not quite. The Germans laid the doings of the Czechs to their politicians, and especially to the Jews among them, and there was little apparent enmity to the Czech people. But the Poles were hated in a bitter and all-out way, and it was plain that if a German army ever got into their territory they would be used very roughly. Their army, at that time, was being whooped up as invincible by the English, and the American newspapers were so reporting it. Large quantities of military supplies were pouring into Poland from England through the Baltic port of Gydnia. As for the Czechs, they were known to be armed to the teeth, for they had the great Skoda arms works and were being subsidized on a large scale by both England and France. Before leaving New York I had seen a propaganda film showing the Czech army: it appeared to have almost unlimited numbers of cannon and airships. I was thus surprised when Merkel told me that the chiefs of the new German army did not greatly fear it, or the Polish army. He said that they counted on capturing most of the *matériel* of both, and using it against France.

I got off the train at Marienburg and made it my headquarters for several days. It turned out to be a small and sleepy provincial town whose trade had been pretty well ruined by the setting up of the Polish Corridor. One day I went by *Bummelzug* [milk train] to Marienwerder, 23 miles to the southward, and tried to find the memorial to Eilhard Mencken in the old cathedral of the Prussian knights. He had died there as its archpresbyter in 1657, and by his will set up the Mencken family *Stipendium,* still in existence. There were plenty of tablets along the wall, but I could not find any that mentioned Eilhard. As I was examining them in the dim light a stranger addressed me in excellent English, introducing himself as a minor lay official of the cathedral and offering me help. When I told him what I was looking for he showed it to me at once. It was an ornate tablet fastened to one of the walls, probably fifteen feet above the floor. It seemed to be in a good state of preservation, though it had been there for nearly three centuries. I told the stranger that I'd like to have a photograph of it, and he gave me his card and said that he would see that scaffolding was erected and one was made. He promised to send it to me in Baltimore, along with the photographer's bill. But though I wrote to him after I got home I heard nothing from him, and the photograph never reached me.

Another day I hired an automobile in Marienburg and made a trip to the battlefield of Tannenberg, on the Polish border, 60 miles to the south. It was a lovely Summer day and a magnificent trip. My chauffeur was an old soldier, but he had not been in the battle, for his whole service had been on the Western front. At the end of the war he was deep in France—and started back for East Prussia on foot! He told me that he had got as far as Hesse before he found a train to carry him the rest of the way. But though he had not fought at Tannenberg, he knew the battlefield thoroughly, and it was pleasant indeed, and very instructive, to tour it under his guidance. After twenty-four years the lovely rolling country was once more smiling, with the fields full of men and women busy with the hay harvest, but when we got below Osterode we began to encounter old artillery emplacements, now grass grown, and other evidences of the battle. I put in an hour at the great war memorial near Hindenburg's field headquarters, begun as a monument to the soldiers who fell in the battle, but now, under Hitler, converted into a sort of shrine to Hindenburg, who is buried there. The thing is extraordinarily grim, harsh—and effective. In form, it is a high circle of colonnades, built of the local brick and showing the stark simplicity of an East Prussian church. Hindenburg's tomb is a small chamber opposite the entrance, set rather below than above the ground level. It is barely large enough to hold his coffin. To each side is a small stained glass window in the outer wall. These windows do not show the usual angels and armored knights, but only lines out of old German soldier songs. To the right they are from "Ich hatt' einen Kameraden [I had a comrade]"; to the left from "Morgenrot [The Dawn]." There was a line of pious pilgrims passing through; they were flocking to the place from all over Germany. In front of Hindenburg's tomb, with the sarcophagus visible through the simple iron gate, stood a sentry. I watched this sentry for perhaps ten minutes. He did not move, and in the somewhat dim light it was almost impossible to detect the blinking of his eyes. He was in field gray, armed and with his bayonet fixed. There is such a sentry there all the time, day and night.

I invited my chauffeur to have lunch with me, and we had an excellent meal in one of the restaurants maintained on the field by the German government. There was a complete absence of all the gimcrackery that one encounters at Gettysburg. Hot dogs were obtainable, and so were postcards, but they were sold in a group of shops and other such conveniences standing two or three hundred miles [feet?] from the memorial, and harmonious with it in architecture. As far as the eye could see—and it could see a long way, for the memorial is on a knoll in open country— there was not a sign of litter. I had a glass of beer with lunch, but my chauffeur asked for *Apfelsaft*—literally, apple juice—a charged cider that seemed to be very popular all over Germany. It was the preferred drink of teetotalers—and Hitler's own avoidance of the mug and the jug had made total abstinence fashionable, especially among the young. My chauffeur was still a reservist, and told me that he greatly enjoyed the annual manoeuvres. They gave him a chance, he said, to meet old comrades, and to relax for a couple of weeks in purely male society. The only objection to them, he said, was that the married men taking part in them were allowed only a mark and a half a day for the consolation of their wives. If that allowance were doubled, he said, there would be universal satisfaction. On our way back to Marienburg he insisted on driving ten miles out of our way to show me the region where the manoeuvres had been held in the Autumn of 1937, and especially the hillside where his own regiment had camped. But first we made another visit to the memorial and inspected the tablets lining the colonnade, some of them commemorating army corps, others divisions, others regiments, and yet others individual commanders. These tablets harmonized with one another and with the architecture of the memorial, and some of them were very beautiful. Driving back to Marienburg we encountered many trucks hauling sugar beets to the mills that dot East Prussia. We also saw a good many trucks hauling soldiers, for there were barracks in many of the towns along the Polish border. Ten miles from Marienburg we left the region of open farms and entered a forested area, mainly made up of large estates. "Are there any deer in the woods?" I asked the chauffeur. "There stand two," he answered, pointing, and sure enough I saw them not a hundred yards away, peeping out at us.

I came back to Berlin by sleeper, and had a comfortable trip in a luxurious German stateroom—something that our own railroads, in 1937, had just begun to imitate. A few days afterward I went to Leipzig, and there hired a car for a trip to the birthplace of my Grandfather Mencken—a little village called Laas, about half way between Leipzig and Dresden. There, in 1828, my great-grandfather operated a stock farm. When my car pulled up at the village inn the alarm went out and in a few minutes a little crowd had gathered. It was made up wholly of the very old or the very young, for all the able-bodied inhabitants were busy in the fields. Farm labor, I soon learned, had become almost unobtainable, for all the boys were going into the army at eighteen, and all the girls were flocking to Dresden, lured by its high wages. Thus the farmers who were left had to work very hard, and at this season they were at it from dawn to dark. I asked the assembled Laasians if the Mencken family was remembered in the neighborhood, but found that none of them had ever heard the name. Presently a little girl was sent to fetch the oldest woman in the village, for she was, so they told me, a walking register of its history. But when she hobbled in it turned out to be impossible to get anything out of her fading mind. Four or five times she recalled people who had gone to America, but when she was pressed it always turned out that they had gone there in 1874 or thereabout, and that their names were Schmidt, Scharnagle, Zimmerman or Kraus. I asked if there were any picture postcards obtainable, and the little girl who had fetched the crone said she knew a woman who had some. I gave her a mark and asked her to bring me a dozen. When she came back she had the dozen, but all of them were photographs of the same view. Laas, I gathered, was too small to attract the postcard publishers who then flooded all larger German places—and all Europe—with their wares. The Saxon dialect of these peasants was almost unintelligible to me, but my chauffeur, a Leipziger, both understood and spoke it, so he acted as interpreter when I ran aground. On my way back he told me that wages were high in Leipzig, but that the cost of living was going up, and so the people were poor, as they have always been in Saxony. He himself was half owner of the car he was driving, and hence a prosperous man. When we pulled up at the Atlantic Hotel he asked me hesitatingly if I knew it was a Jewish headquarters. I replied that I didn't, but added that it appeared to be a good hotel. He agreed that it was, but said that German patriots were beginning to avoid it.

I knew a number of persons in Leipzig, including several bookdealers and Dr. Otto Glauning, former librarian of the university, but I did not make my visit known to them, for I was eager to keep on my own as much as possible. When I got back to Berlin and went out to the Wien restaurant in the Kurfürstendamm for dinner I found out that there had been an anti-Jewish outbreak the night before. But, save for one or two smashed windows, I could see no evidence of violence. The mob had contented itself with chalking the names of the Jewish shopkeepers on their plate-glass windows. There was a law requiring every Jew to put out his right name, but it had been evaded. Now it was instructive to note that the real owner of Mlle. Félicie's hat shop was Jacob Goldfarb and that those of the Bon Marché perfume establishment upstairs were the Gebrüder Margolis. I dined at the Wien almost every night, for the cooking was superb, there was good beer, and the music by a small group of excellent performers was lovely. No jazz was permitted. After dinner I commonly took a taxicab for the Schloss at the other end of downtown Berlin, where there were concerts in the courtyard, open to the sky, by the Berlin Philharmonic Orchestra. There were lights, of course, for the musicians' stands, but the rest of the courtyard was in darkness save for a row of flambeaux around the four sides. The effect was very picturesque and romantic. A good seat cost a mark. Several nights I tried to get opera tickets, but always the house was sold out.

As I have said, I saw few persons besides Merkel. His position in the airplane industry gave him access to the highest circles of the army, and so he was full of interesting, and, what is more important, accurate information. One day he took me to the Aero Club for lunch, and there submitted to an hour of frank questioning. The only other man I saw more than once was Kartzke. Unlike Schönemann, who had joined the Nazi party in order to promote his university fortunes, Kartzke remained a Liberal, so what he had to say reflected the opinion of what remained of the opposition. The methods and manners of Hitler were thus very obnoxious to him, but it soon became apparent that, like many other Germans of his class, he had begun to see that the Hitlerian system was serving Germany well, and had come to be in favor of it, at least to that extent. The defeatism of the Weimar constitution era was now fast disappearing. Hitler, whatever his outrages, had found a way to restore hope and self-respect to the country, and, what is more, confidence. When I was there in 1922 the most that any intelligent German would venture upon was the hope that England and France might eventually come to see that the Treaty of Versailles was intolerably harsh, and show some voluntary disposition to ameliorate it. Nothing of the sort had appeared, and so hope gradually yielded to despair. But now hope was born again, and it was fast turning into assurance. Hitler had already taken Austria into the Reich, and it was plain to everyone that the Sudetenland over the artificial Czech border would come next. These rectifications of the Treaty of Versailles were no longer sought as boons; they were demanded—and in a little while Hitler would have the strength to enforce his demands.

By September, indeed, he would be strong enough to bring Chamberlain to Munich, and by the end of the year he would be more than half way toward building up an army far mightier than any the Keiser had imagined. This change of climate affected every German, and it affected Kartzke with the rest.

He told me that the roughing of Jews upset him, but that he had come to the conclusion that their own gigantic folly was to blame for it. In illustration thereof he told me a story. In the Weimar days he had made a visit to the United States, and on his return to Bremen rode to Berlin in a railroad compartment with four or five fellow voyagers. One of them was the daughter of a well-known Jewish pianist—as I recall it, Artur Schnabel. The talk fell upon anti-Semitism, and this lady ventured the view that it was definitely dead in Germany. "How, indeed," she asked, "could it ever revive? Think of all the Jews in key places—" and then she recited a long list of them, beginning with members of the Federal cabinet and ending with the *Polizeipräsident* [police commissioner] of Berlin. They appeared, indeed, to have the country firmly by the neck. Kartzke told me that the list greatly astonished him, for he was not actively interested in politics, and paid little attention to officeholders. More, it set him to thinking, and the more he thought the more he became convinced that the Jews were digging their own graves. In the long run, he said to himself, the Germans would never tolerate any such hegemony of a minority, and especially of a minority that had been lukewarm in World War I, and was now far too friendly with the French and English. He concluded, he told me, that on some day not too distant the Jews would come to grief in a melodramatic manner, and so he was not surprised when Hitler began to preach a *jihad* against them. In a day of bitter trouble they had tried to seize the state, though their loyalty was plainly questionable. Soon or late the German Michael would rise against them and put them down. Now that it had happened Kartzke was not surprised, though he still insisted that he was against the ill-usage of individual Jews, especially those who had not sought public office and power.

After my trip to Leipzig I made brief trips to Halle and Wittenberg, where the Menckens had been professors in the Eighteenth Century. On my way to Wittenberg I stopped off for a few hours at Braunschweig, and had lunch on its famous chicken and even more famous asparagus, then in full season. I'd like to have added its yet more famous *Leberwurst,* but there was no room for it in my recesses. The train ran along the foothills of the Harz mountains, and the landscape was lovely beyond description. Never in this world have I seen more smiling fields or more charming villages. After that I went to Karlsruhe for a glimpse of the Black Forest, and then worked back to Frankfort-am-Rhein and boarded a Rhine steamer for Koblenz. The weather everywhere had been glorious: it was in Koblenz that I encountered my first rain. One day I made a trip up the Moselle valley by the little train that runs to Treves, and was amazed to find a brewery facing the station at Berncastel. Unhappily, I could not drink the magnificent wines of the region, for the spastic pylorus that had floored me in May had not yet abated, and I was diligently taking the belladonna prescribed by Dr. Baker. I tried a bottle or two of Moselle, but found that it made for immediate acidity. Beer I stood better, and once I had got into the Rhine country I devoted myself to the excellent *Helles* of Dortmund—a bland brew with hardly any taste of hops. From Coblenz I proceeded to Köln, and there I took train for Northwestern Germany, for my time was running short and I was booked to sail from Bremen in the *Europa* on July 20.

But first I went to Oldenburg and there hired a car for a tour of the flat, marshy country in which the Mencken clan seems to have originated. I thus saw, for the first and last time, Jever, Aurich and various other towns in which long-dead Menckenii had lived, and made my second examination of Oldenburg—a dull provincial town, but full of odd delights for a visitor. The one remaining German relative that I had ever met, Fräulein Anna Mencke, had died a few years before. I tried to find her grave in the old St. Gertrud cemetery, where other Menckenii, including her brother, are buried, but failed. She was a very energetic old woman, and one of the grand ladies of the town, with a hand in all the official charities. She was the last of her line to live there. There must be Menckens or Menckes surviving in other parts of the province of Oldenburg, but I made no effort to find them. The province itself, though it is low-lying, is made picturesque by the frequent lakes and water-courses. Its peasants devote themselves to horse and cattle raising and appear to be prosperous, for they live in really immense houses, some of them five or six stories high at the peak of the roof. The roofs, at first glance, seem to be thatched, but the thatching is simply a protection against the cold of Winter, for under it are red tiles. I had now seen all of the places in Germany in which my people lived in the old days—Marienwerder, Potsdam, Leipzig, Halle, Wittenberg and the Oldenburg towns—and in nearly all had found memorials of them. I started for home feeling that a chapter had ended—that I'd probably never visit Germany again. I was already 58 years old, and my state of health was showing it; moreover, another great European war was certain, and it would be a long while before peaceful travel would again be possible.

Thus 1938 dragged on into 1939. The chief event of 1939, in my own life, was my illness in July—a sudden blow that served warning that, with sixty approaching, I was no longer the resilient and indomitable youngster that I had once been. On a hot day, happening to be walking down Baltimore street, I felt a numbness at the back of my head as I passed the Savings Bank of Baltimore, and it was soon followed by a tingling in the finger tips of my left hand and along the left side of my face. It was all very slight, but it was nevertheless something that plainly needed investigation, so I consulted Dr. Benjamin M. Baker, Jr., a very competent young Johns Hopkins internist who had been Sara's physician in her last illness. He ordered me to hospital at once, and I remained there for ten days. The diagnosis recorded on my chart was as follows: "Generalized arteriosclerosis; cerebral arteriosclerosis; cerebral thrombosis, due to arteriosclerosis obesity due to excess food; paresthenias of left face and left arm, due to thromboses of terminal branch of right Rolandic artery." All this, happily, was less formidable than it sounds. Baker told me that he could find no evidence that the thrombus (blood clot) had caused a hemorrhage, and hence the effects were not extensive. There was the aforesaid numbness along the left side of my upper lip and some tingling in my left fingers, but there was no suspension of either sensation or motion. This numbness and tingling gradually wore off, but there were brief returns of both for a long time afterward, and indeed I am still conscious of them occasionally (1942). No treatment save rest in bed was indicated. I was kept there rigidly for a week, and then permitted to sit up; on July 31 I returned home. Baker and his colleague seized the chance to investigate me thoroughly. What they found was simply that my arteries had begun to harden—in other words, that I was growing old at last, and that the end of my sojourn in this vale was looming into view. There was, they said, no imminent danger. I might live, indeed, for ten years, or even more. But the process that had started was irreversible, and nothing could be done to stay it. They cautioned me against violent exertion, but there was no need for that, for violent exertion was not one of my follies. They told me that it might be a good thing to reduce my weight a bit, but did not prescribe any diet, and said that a reasonable amount of alcohol would give me comfort without doing any appreciable harm. In a little while I was back in my routine, but I never felt really well. There was a persistent malaise, and I found that I tired much quicker than formerly. In April 1941 this malaise grew so bad that work became impossible, and I was sent to the Johns Hopkins again by Baker's associate, Dr. Charles W. Wainwright. The diagnosis this time was: "Obesity due to excess food; arteriorsclerosis, generalized; questionable arteriosclerotic heart disease." Wainwright put me on 2500 calories a day, and I lost a few pounds during the five days of my stay. There was no other treatment. While I was in the hospital I seized the chance to have the resident surgeon, Dr. Hogeboom, remove a couple of warts on my face that had been getting in my way, just as I had seized the chance, when I was at the Union Memorial Hospital in 1937, to have Dr. George G. Finney remove a couple of wens on my scalp. On my discharge Wainwright advised me to take a rest, and I went to Havana by sea. After ten days there I returned home, and found myself so fit for work that I quickly finished "Newspaper Days," which had been suspended by my illness.

This unpleasant episode had some influence upon my relations to the *Sunpapers,* as I shall record in due course, but it did not prevent me performing my usual grist of miscellaneous chores for them. The year 1939 was a busy one, and included the beginnings of another long bout with the Newspaper Guild. It opened, as I have said, with the vain discussion of Patterson's half-hearted effort to set up a sort of super-editorial department, and before it was over I had a hand in half a dozen other pieces of *Sun* business, some of them editorial and the rest not. Early in the year news came in that the *Nation* was planning to send a man to Baltimore to do an article on the *Sunpapers,* apparently for the purpose of recording changes in them since its publication of Oswald Garrison Villard's article, afterward reprinted in his "Newspapers and Newspaper Men." The person chosen for this job, it appeared, was one Willard R. Espy [Willard H. Espey]. Patterson asked me to report on him, but I had never heard of him and could find no one who knew him. When he arrived in Baltimore he turned out to be a young Jew of unpleasing personality and no apparent knowledge of newspapers. I saw him at Patterson's request, and answered such questions as he had to ask, but most of his inquiry was done among the leaders of the Guild, all of whom were specialists in the infamy of the *Sunpapers.* His article finally appeared on February 4, 1939. It was entitled "The Baltimore *Sun* Goes Down," was extremely unfriendly, and included a great many misstatements of fact. The essence of it was an attempt to depict me as the boss of the paper, and to lay to it all the crimes that pseudo-Liberals of the *Nation–New Republic* had been charging to me since their conversion, first, to Communism, and then to the New Deal. It began with a quotation from me on the subject of democracy (accurate enough), proceeded to describe me as "a bright-eyed, graying, broad-grinning little man, astonishingly Hooverish-looking," and then went on, idiotically, to allege that I was responsible for the *Sun*'s view of the late Spanish revolution, which was described as unfriendly to the so-called "Loyalists"! A little later on this wholly imaginary attitude was ascribed to fear of the Catholic Church!

All the fables circulating among the boss-haters of the office were revived and embellished—for example, that the *Sun* had lost 50,000 circulation during the battle with the archbishop, and that Patterson had borrowed $3,000,000 from the banks to buy A. S. Abell stock and was still in hock to them. The *Sunpapers'* course in labor affairs was depicted as bitterly anti-union, the firing of Drew Pearson in 1932 was laid to the intervention of bankers whose frenzied finance he had exposed, and much was made of the fact that John Owens and Frank Kent, who had denounced David J. Lewis for his part in the attempted purge of Senator Tydings in 1938, had supported him in 1916. One of the evident objects of the article was to cause ill-feeling in the office by greatly exaggerating my power and influence. To that end, John Owens was described as "a tired Liberal but a civilized gentleman," and it was alleged and hinted a dozen times that he was forced to follow my lead. "Mencken," said "Espy," "is pervasive on the *Sun*. He is a member of the board of directors. He has no editorial post, yet he sits in on every important editorial meeting." Even more artful was the attempt to exacerbate the vanity of Patterson. "Patterson not only is fond of Mencken but believes him to be a genius. Moreover, Mencken is a celebrity, and the publisher, like many another small-town-boy-who-made-good, to the tune of $85,000 a year, beams on celebrities. In the *Sun* office Mencken's pungent comments on the social scene live again a few days later on Patterson's lips." Finally, Frank Kent was described as one of the five persons—the others being Patterson, Black, John Owens and me—who were "behind the views of the *Sunpapers*," though in fact he has never been consulted once, nor even so much as informed of a decision, since his demotion from the managing editorship in 1921. This diatribe naturally made some pother in the office, and it is conceivable that its direct attempts upon Owens and Patterson fortified their resolution, when the war came, to keep the

Sunpapers' position at the opposite pole from my own, but on that point I have some doubt: in all probability they would have stood just as firm for England if I had been with them, not against them. No effort was made to dispute the misstatements in the article, nor was any other notice taken of it. Its malicious purpose was self-evident and it had little if any effect either inside the office or outside. Inside, everyone not insane knew that I was completely out of accord with most of the editorial policies of Owens, and outside it was known to all that the *Nation,* under Freda Kirchwey, had become mendacious, shrewish and idiotic.

The Al Capone episode was trivial but amusing. I was drawn into the business by Dr. Joseph Earle Moore, who was Capone's doctor. The gangster, during his incarceration in Alcatraz prison, had developed symptoms of paresis, the terminal stage of syphilis. The doctors there had undertaken to treat him with the new malaria cure, but his reactions were so alarming that they abandoned it, and when he was released it was plain that his mind had seriously deteriorated. His brothers (one of whom was a respectable provision dealer in Chicago) thereupon decided to bring him to Baltimore to consult Dr. Moore, who is head of the syphilis clinic at the Johns Hopkins. Moore, a humorless and somewhat timorous fellow, was perturbed by the prospect of having a patient so notorious and so certain to get attention from the newspapers, but the assurance of a substantial fee stilled his qualms, and he put down Capone for admission to the Johns Hopkins. Dr. Winford H. Smith, the director, made no objection, but the lay board of trustees, learning of the matter through the newspapers, raised a row. The presence of Capone, they argued, would drive other patients out of the hospital, for it was quite possible that his gangster enemies would pursue him there and try to kill him. So Moore transferred his booking to the Union Memorial Hospital, where much the same thing was repeated. This time it was the board of lady managers who made the uproar, led by Mrs. William A. Cochran, the wife of a rich but imbecile leader of the uplift in Baltimore. Now, however, the fiat of Dr. John M. T. Finney, head of the medical board of the hospital and the most distinguished living Baltimore surgeon, sufficed to still all objections, and Capone was admitted on November 16, 1939. He occupied a suite consisting of two rooms and a bath and costing $30 a day. One of the rooms was his own bedroom, with a cot for his wife. The other was headquarters for his old mother, who could barely speak English, and his three brothers, one of them the honest provision dealer aforesaid and the others gangsters like himself. In order to reassure the other patients on the floor the hospital asked J. Edgar Hoover, the head of the Federal Bureau of Investigation, if there were any likelihood that enemies would try to break in and murder the patient. Hoover reported that, to the best of his knowledge and belief, no such enterprise was afoot, so the excitement in the hospital gradually died away.

Moore, whom I had known for years, asked me to advise him about ways and means of preventing the New York tabloids and other such sensational newspapers making a Roman carnival of Al's stay in Baltimore. They had all sent photographers to town when the first news went out, and these photographers were now clamoring for shots at the patient. I suggested that he let them take one series of pictures if they would promise to bother him no more, and told him that they could be trusted to keep that promise, but he refused on the ground that Capone looked too terrible. I then explained to him how he could get rid of constant calls from reporters by issuing bulletins at frequent intervals, and he agreed to issue them. They were wordy documents that told next to nothing, and every time he had one in preparation he called me up to consult me about it. I was glad to help him, but this service got me some kidding in the *Sun* office, where I was called Capone's press-agent. As a matter of fact, I never saw him. His treatment was so rigorous that all visitors were forbidden, and after it was over he was moved from the hospital to a house in Mt. Washington, where his brothers guarded him day and night. His presence in peaceful Mt. Washington almost caused a panic there, and the man who had leased him the house was denounced violently.

As war came closer I wrote upon it almost every week—specifically, July 16 and 23, and August 13 and 27. My article of August 13 was an attempt to set forth the case for the Japs, and on August 27 I recorded my conviction that if, as I believed certain, the American people were induced to lay their lives, their fortunes and their sacred honor on the English, they would be backing a spavined horse. To quote:

> The British Empire is bound to disintegrate soon or late, if only because it is grounded upon a completely preposterous series of frauds and false assumptions. . . . Empires rise and empires fall, and when they fall their clients and hangers-on share their fate.

Once the war began Roosevelt launched instantly into that long series of gross violations of neutrality and other deliberate provocations which finally drove the Japs to make their attack upon Pearl Harbor on December 7, 1941. "How can any man pretending to be rational," I wrote so early as September 10, "accept seriously the current canoodlings of Roosevelt, Hull and company, or argue with a sober face that they ought to be given full faith and credit?" This article, to my astonishment, brought me a letter from Gerald W. Johnson, the most abject and trusting of all the New Dealers in the office. "For once," he wrote to me on September 10, "I am compelled to agree with you about Roosevelt. I have no objection to the direction his partisanship is taking, but that he is partisan there is no doubt, and I wish he would say so." Unhappily, the campaign of 1940 was still ahead, and it was too soon for him to throw off his false-face. On September 17 I raised my first alarm about the bogus war news that was already pouring out of England and France, and paid my tribute to Daniel De Luce, the young Associated Press correspondent. Thereafter, save for an article on the National Labor Relations Board, another on the gimme farmers, and two installments of selections from my note-books, I discussed the war on the editorial page of the *Sun* every Sunday. It was, of course, useless to try to get a calm hearing for the plain facts in the face of the hurricane of balderdash that was raging there. Not only were the actual editorials devoted passionately to supporting the consecrated English cause; it was also maintained in all the keys of the moral scale by Duffy's cartoons, by the letters in the correspondence column, by the reprints from other papers, and by a weekly article by Frederic C. Nelson, running next to mine. I was convinced from the start, indeed, that the United States would be cajoled and hustled into the war soon or late, and that arguing against it was a waste of time and labor, but in its earlier stages, at least, I enjoyed the job, and so I kept going from week to week, always resolving to shut down, but never actually doing it until the early days of 1941.

15

Leaving the Stage

1939–1941

The presidential campaign, of course, was the overshadowing event of the year. It had been obvious since 1938 that Roosevelt would seek a third term, and I believed that he would make adroit and unconscionable use of the war to further his chances, with long odds in his favor. All the other Democratic candidates, from Jack Garner down, had blown up, and there was no sign on the Republican side of a champion able to beat him. As I had frequently argued in my *Sun* articles, the only way to dispose of a demagogue, in a democratic country, is to find a worse demagogue, and no such prodigy was in sight. Nevertheless, it seemed worth while to take a look at the principal Republican aspirants, and this I did during December, 1939, and January, 1940. The first I tackled was Thomas E. Dewey, the New York district attorney. I had met him several times before, and on May 23, 1939, had had a political gabble with him at his home in New York.

Dewey, at that time, was in the midst of his war upon gangsters, and the house at 1142 Fifth avenue wherein he had an apartment was guarded day and night by detectives and uniformed police. When I wrote to him toward the end of 1939, saying that I'd like to have another session with him, he invited me to have lunch with him on December 16 at his office at 137 Centre street, and I had to pass through a barrage of guards to get at him. We lunched alone and somewhat meagrely, for it appeared that Dewey's own midday meal consisted only of an apple and a glass of milk. Before the food was brought in he retired to the wash-room and broke into loud and jubilant song. He was, in fact, an excellent baritone, and there was a time in his youth when he thought seriously of trying for an operatic career. He was a short, brisk, sturdy fellow with a bristling and extraordinarily black moustache, and his manner had already begun to show something of the fawning of the politician. We talked at length and I came away with a better impression of him than I had had in May.

I proposed to Dewey that he let me write an interview with him for publication in the *Sun,* but he refused for two reasons, first, that his plan of campaign involved taking up issues one by one, and according to a programme already formulated, and second, that if he allowed the *Sun* to quote him all the other papers would besiege him and he couldn't shake them off. His real reason, of course, was that he was playing for time, and didn't want to run any risk of making a mistake before the issues of the campaign became clarified. I wrote a piece about him for the *Sun,* but when I got back to Baltimore the next day and discussed it with Patterson and Moore the three of us decided not to print it. {The only thing interesting in it was this: that Dewey, though he had already set up a Brain Trust to collect facts, wrote his own speeches, and that he found writing a very laborious business. He told me that it took him 35 hours of working time to write a speech of 3500 words that he had made at a meeting of Pennsylvanians on December 16.}

The next candidate I inspected was Senator Arthur H. Vandenberg of Michigan. I had an hour or so with him at his office in the Senate Office Building, Washington, on December 21, 1939, and prepared a memorandum for Patterson the same night. The essential parts of it were as follows:

My former impression of him was reinforced, to wit, that he is an able man, well informed beyond the common and extremely frank for a politician, but that he is rather too cocky in manner to make a popular hero. His article, "The New Deal Must Be Salvaged," in the January *American Mercury* (out December 20), is the most candid statement of doctrine, and by long odds, that any candidate has made in this campaign. In it he says categorically that he believes in some of the devices of the New Deal, and that some of those he doesn't believe in are probably here to stay, and cannot be got rid of. Vandenberg told me that this article, which is extremely well written, was done on the typewriter by his own hand, and that he got no help from anyone. There are some good phrases in it. He said that he wished there were more, but that he had been unable to concoct them, and hoped kindly volunteers would come forward with contributions. This seemed a cue for offering one, which I did, and was thanked politely. It was a bad one.

I asked him how he proposed to balance the budget. He replied that it would probably be impossible for the first two years, though he hoped to diminish the deficit at once. He believes that unloading Roosevelt will encourage business enterprise enough to lift the national income from 60 to 80 billions—that is, in two years. This will raise the tax income enough to take care of half of the deficit, and reduce governmental expenses (chiefly by providing work for the unemployed) enough to dispose of the rest. "Roosevelt," he said, "has made the mistake of thinking that he could convert 60 billions into 80 by spending the difference." In addition, Vandenberg believes he can make a large reduction in the number of jobholders, and get rid of many useless boards and commissions.

He supported the Haugen-McNary farm bill, and still believes in it. He is convinced that the farmers need some sort of governmental assistance—but not necessarily in the form of subsidies, open or concealed. He believes that their primary difficulty is lack of intelligent organization: they plant without rational forethought, are at the mercy of their markets, and get caught in every squeeze.

Vandenberg believes that Roosevelt is eager to get into the war, and would not hesitate to employ a war scare to help him get a renomination. He said that when the special session of Congress began the White House and all its agents were convinced that the United States would be in the war very soon. There were all sorts of evidences of this—the calling of the War Resources committee, the proclamation of an emergency, the melodramatic closing of the White House itself, and many others.

Vandenberg believes that the Russian invasion of Finland may give Roosevelt another chance. He himself is in favor of sending the Russian ambassador home. He says that the Dies committee has demonstrated beyond the slightest doubt that the Russians have not kept the agreement they made when they were recognized—to refrain from political operations in the United States. He says this country is the only American republic that has ever recognized them.

Vandenberg said he rather hoped that Roosevelt would be renominated—but not, of course, on the war issue, for that would give him a walkover. "It would not settle anything," he said, "for a Republican to beat Garner, Farley or McNutt, or to be beaten by him. What we need is a square knockout of Roosevelt himself. He is the real and only issue."

Vandenberg, at the end of 1939, had seen more than eleven years of service in the Senate, and his record, taking one year with another, was excellent. But I left him convinced that he would not get the nomination in 1940—mainly because of the cocky air mentioned in my memorandum to Patterson. He was a smart fellow, but it was all too evident that he knew it. He could be agreeable, but the fawning of the politician was simply not in him. Moreover, his superior manner was accentuated by the way he combed his hair and tossed his head, and I could not imagine the plain people taking to him, though he had managed somehow to be reëlected to the Senate in 1935 and was to be reëlected again in 1941. The third candidate I called on was Senator Robert A. Taft of Ohio. I saw him, as I had seen Vandenberg, at his office in the Senate Office Building. This was on January 9. The next day I made the following report on him to Patterson:

He struck me as a far more lively and genial man face to face than he appears to be when he makes speeches. There is, in fact, a considerable humor to him, and he is quite alive to the absurdities of the present political situation. I had previously read a number of his speeches, put together in a pamphlet by the Republican National Committee. They turned out to be intelligent, but extremely dull.

Taft told me that he is not too optimistic, in case of a Republican victory, of an immediate reform. He told me that he believed it would take at least two years to make any appreciable progress toward balancing the budget. During the first year of Republican rule, of course, the country would be still operating on the budget prepared by Roosevelt. Taft said that he believed some reductions might be made during the second year, but not many. Even during the third year it would probably be necessary to carry over items from the New Deal.

Taft, like the other Republican candidates, shrinks from a realistic discussion of the farm question. He is apparently convinced that some sort of farm relief will become as permanent a part of the American system as the tariff set-up. He seems to be much more hopeful of diminishing the doles now going to the city proletarians. Like Dewey and Vandenberg, he argues that a Republican victory will be sufficient in itself to stimulate industry, and so reduce unemployment. He is not unaware of the fact that the country has accumulated an enormous gang of chronic unemployables, but he doesn't seem to have formulated any coherent scheme for dealing with them.

My net impression was that Taft is an honest fellow and not without information and ability, but that there is nothing really vigorous and effective in his personality. He would probably make as feeble a President as he has made a candidate.

Patterson passed on these memoranda to John Owens and Moore, but there was no discussion of them that I can recall, and they had no apparent influence upon the course of the *Sunpapers*. Owens, of course, found himself in a difficult, and indeed an almost impossible position, for he was supporting Roosevelt's war-mongering and yet arguing against a third term.

In the Spring of 1940 Patterson suddenly broke out with a violent crush on Willkie. Down to a few months before nothing had been heard of or about Willkie save that he was a small-town lawyer who had made a success in Wall Street, and argued for its malefactors very plausibly before Congressional investigating committees. His occasional speeches at banquets got very little attention, and no one thought of him as a serious figure in politics. But then, almost overnight, his name began to be heard, and it quickly appeared that some party or parties unknown were doing a vigorous job of pushing him into public notice. The identity of these parties remained mysterious, and after he got the Republican nomination on June 28 the question was copiously and feverishly discussed, and many Wall Street notables were mentioned, but it was always my private suspicion that he was his own chief motive power. Put up to speak at the annual dinner of the American Newspaper Publishers' Association in New York on May 3 he made a big hit with the assembled Barabbases, and large numbers of them returned home convinced that he was the Moses long sought to lead the Republic out of the New Deal wilderness. Patterson was one of these converts, and on his return to Baltimore he filled the office with his enthusiasm, but I don't think he made much impression on Owens and I am sure he made none on me. I could see very little in Willkie, either then or later on. He was a smooth fellow, but only too obviously, by my criteria, a fraud. Patterson urged me to look him up, along with Frank E. Gannett, and so complete my investigation of the Republican aspirants, but I hung back, for I was thoroughly convinced by this time that Roosevelt would be renominated and reëlected, and that the whole inquiry had thus become moot. Moreover, I was strongly against Gannett for two reasons, and did not want to meet him. The first reason was that he was a newspaper proprietor who had violated all my notions of professional fitness and decency by seeking public-office, and the second was that during the thirteen years of Prohibition his papers had supported it. At Patterson's urging I made several half-hearted attempts to arrange a session with him, but was relieved when his busy campaign travels forced one after the other to be abandoned. In the end I never met him at all, and have never met him, in fact, to this day.

Willkie I also evaded until a short while before the conventions. On May 23 I received the following letter from Irita Van Doren, editor of the literary supplement of the New York *Herald-Tribune* and an old acquaintance:

> For a long time we have talked of getting together for dinner and done nothing about it, and for almost as long a time I have wanted very much to have you meet a great friend of mine who is an admirer of yours— Wendell Willkie. After he read "Happy Days" he was so delighted that he has several times reminded me that I promised to introduce him to you.
>
> In view of all this can't we really bring off this dinner? I called up Wendell yesterday and find that he is on the move until the early part of June and would like nothing better than a chance to meet you. I do not know at what times you are apt to be in town, but will you have dinner with me some time during the first week or ten days of June? Just set your date. It would be grand to see you.

This was somewhat astonishing, but I was very fond of Irita, and so accepted. It was finally arranged that she and Willkie and I should have dinner at her house at 123 west 11th street on June 10th. When I got to New York a few days before this I was again astonished to learn that she and Willkie were reputed to be carrying on a love affair. That it had gone beyond the limits set by divine and human law did not appear, but it was said that Willkie was very much mashed on her, and that his wife was greatly upset. Irita, whom I had known for many years and who was a good friend of Sara's, was a very attractive woman, despite her 49 years. She had been married to another old acquaintance, Carl Van Doren, back in 1912, and they had three grown daughters, but in 1939 they had been divorced, and Irita was now living alone at the house in 11th street, which she owned. She was a small, slight, dark woman whose bushy hair had now turned iron gray, and there were few pleasanter companions for a dinner party. Once, in 1929 or thereabout, she had turned up in Baltimore on her way to visit Ellen Glasgow in Richmond, Va., and Sara and I had given her a dinner at the Marconi. I recall that it was somewhat wet, and that Sara and I, on depositing Irita aboard a sleeper for Richmond at midnight, wondered whether she'd be in shape for literary conversation when she reached Richmond early the next morning. But La Glasgow afterward reported that, despite her few hours of sleep, she turned up fresh and brisk, and put in a long day meeting the Richmond intelligentsia.

When I got to her house on June 10 Willkie was *non est*. He had been detained, she told me, somewhere in the wilds above New York City, where he had been campaigning all day. He appeared at 8:30 P.M. or thereabout, and after dinner we settled down for a palaver. He turned out to be a very charming fellow, and I got on with him pleasantly enough, but there was nothing in his talk to make me believe that he could beat Roosevelt if nominated. Indeed, it appeared on cross-examination that he was a good deal of a New Dealer, despite his Wall Street connections, and I came away with the suspicion that some of his more active backers were of the same kidney. The most conspicuous of these were young Oren Root, Jr., a grandson of old Elihu, and Russell Davenport, who had lately resigned as editor of *Fortune* to help manage the Willkie campaign. Willkie told me that he believed Roosevelt, if reëlected, would try to take the United States into the war, and that the majority of Americans were strongly against it, but his own position was by no means clear, for he professed to be against going to war and yet admitted that he was in favor of helping England. When I pointed out that this interference would get us into the war inevitably he had no answer that made sense. In brief, I concluded that, like John Owens on the *Sun* and his own associates in Wall Street, he was trying to carry water on two shoulders, and that if he were nominated by the Republicans and managed by some miracle to beat Roosevelt, the country would simply be swapping Tweedledum for Tweedledee. All this I reported to Patterson verbally: I made no written report. He tried to convince me that I was wrong—that Willkie was really a very superior fellow, and would make a strong candidate and a good President—but I remained of the same opinion still. During the two weeks following we discussed the business frequently and at great length, but both of us stood fast. After Willkie was nominated, on June 28, Patterson was much concerned about the reaction of John Owens, who had hitherto, it appeared, shown a considerable skepticism, though he and Willkie were in the same boat. Patterson wanted the *Sunpapers* to go into the campaign with all arms, but he had authority under the by-laws to order it, but he was still afraid of Owens, and so waited impatiently and uneasily. He was greatly relieved when Owens decided, in the end, that the *Sunpapers* should support Willkie. It was never done very heartily, but nevertheless it was done, and Patterson told me more than once how delighted he was that Owens had decided spontaneously without orders or urging. The whole episode amused me very much, for I was convinced from the start that Willkie could not conceivably beat Roosevelt.

I helped to cover the two national conventions, and enjoyed them as usual. I went to Philadelphia a week or so before the Republican convention was scheduled to meet, to look over the ground, and returned again on June 21, though the opening was not until June 24. The *Sunpaper* outfit had quarters at the Ritz Hotel in Broad street, directly opposite the Bellevue-Stratford, which was the headquarters hotel. Our rooms were comfortable enough, but the Ritz had gone downhill since the last time we were there, and its only decent eating accommodations were on the roof. The hotel, it appeared, was now mainly patronized by Jews, and on the night I got in there were no less than six Jewish weddings and other parties going on, and the elevators and corridors swarmed with the Chosen. Service on the roof being excessively slow, I ate there very seldom.

As usual, Patterson and I had a room together. One morning I was awakened by his heavy breathing and on turning out found that he was ill. Dr. Maxson, the staff surgeon, on being summoned from Baltimore, ordered him to return there at once, and the next day news came that he had pneumonia. This was disturbing indeed, and a few days later I went to Baltimore to see him. To my relief, but hardly to my astonishment, I found him virtually recovered: he had a high susceptibility to pneumonia, but an equally high capacity for throwing it off, and this time he was helped by the new drugs. On the last day of the convention he actually managed to get back to Philadelphia. Irita Van Doren was on hand from the start, hoping and agitating for the nomination of her admirer. He was at another hotel with his wife, who had apparently agreed to forgive and forget, like Frank Knox's wife in 1936, for the term of the campaign. All the other avowed candidates were also in town—something rather unusual at a national convention.

The war issue dominated the convention, though all the so-called leaders tried to keep it in the background, for it was full of dynamite. In my first dispatch to the *Sun*, dated June 21, was this:

> It might be said without paradox that Hitler will be the most important of all the politicoes gathered here next week, though he is not a delegate and is not likely to have any actual agents on the floor. For as the

statesmen begin to wander in from near and far, it becomes more and more apparent that the one hope of the Republicans, come November, is to oppose Roosevelt on his war course, and that no such opposition will be feasible if the war is still going on.

Thus the Republican wizards are full of care, and scratch their heads sadly. Their prayer is that the war will be over by November, with the United States still out of it, and that it will be therefore possible to denounce Roosevelt for scaring millions of people and wasting billions of dollars to no end.

But they are uneasily conscious that the war may last well beyond election day and that the question whether or not the United States is to get into it is largely to be determined by Roosevelt himself. Hence their painful pensiveness and the slow tempo of their deliberations.

The chairman of the resolutions committee was Alf M. Landon, by now converted by adversity into a very smart politician, with traces of pawky cynicism. In the end he and his associates delegated their job to a sub-committee consisting of Glenn Frank and George Wharton Pepper, and these wizards framed a war plank which denounced "involving this nation in foreign war," but declared for "the extension to all peoples fighting for liberty, or whose liberty is threatened, of such aid as shall not be in violation of international law or inconsistent with the requirements of our own national defense." The contradiction here, of course, was glaring, and since Roosevelt's speech at the University of Virginia on June 10, everyone knew that he was determined to get the United States into the war on the English side. But Alf and his wizards were on a hot spot, and such a straddle was the best they could do. Two eminent Republicans, Stimson and Knox, had already accepted places in the Roosevelt Cabinet and were before the Senate for confirmation, and both places were admittedly war jobs. There was some talk in Philadelphia of expelling these traitors from the party, but nothing came of it. Landon himself had been offered the Navy portfolio before Knox, but refused it. He reported that Roosevelt, on offering it to him in May, at the time the Battle of France was just beginning, had volunteered a promise, if he would take it, to abandon the attempt to get a third term. "The difference between Knox and me," said Alf, "was that Knox believed him." Alf also reported that when he called at the White House he found a huge war map of the Western front in the presidential office. Using a pointer, Roosevelt explained the strategic situation to him at length, and showed how the French could stop the Germans. "In an hour," he said, "Bill Bullitt will be calling up from Paris, and I'll instruct him to pass on what I have worked out to the French generals."

The most energetic candidate on the ground was Gannett, who had huge and expensive quarters in one of the hotels, with a busy staff of propagandists. They had hired three small elephants from a one-ring circus, and paraded them through the town day and night, swathed in Gannett banners. But the man who had the most votes was Taft, the favorite of what remained of the old-time professionals. If Dewey and Vandenberg had gone over to him after the second or third ballot he would have been nominated, but Dewey, who knew nothing about the ways of national conventions, cherished the delusion that he himself would win if he held out, and so he refused to deliver his delegates. As a result some of them began to desert to Willkie, who had the advantage that used to accrue, in the old-time days of public stews, to the newest girl in the parlor. Simultaneously, Vandenberg's small *bloc* of delegates became restless, and on the fifth ballot Willkie was nominated. The actual break was started on the fourth by Alf Landon, who was chairman of the Kansas delegation. He saw clearly, by that time, that Taft and Dewey would never get together, so he resolved to grab whatever could be got out of throwing the Kansas vote to the inevitable winner.

When Willkie was nominated some of the newspaper girls rushed off to find Mrs. Willkie, but the majority made tracks for the Taft headquarters to see Mrs. Taft, who had been working very ardently for her husband. They found her in tears, and full of indignation. In fact, she denounced them as "buzzards" and accused them of coming to gloat over her in her hour of defeat and dismay. When they came back, now bursting with indignation themselves, I could only ask them what they were if they were not buzzards.

Willkie's apparently easy victory surprised the country, and during the weeks following the convention it was discussed at great length, in and out of the newspapers. Among persons unfamiliar with the technic of politics there was a tendency to credit it to the fact that the Philadelphia gallery was overwhelmingly for him, but that fact, as I knew, was irrelevant, for I had seen too many noisy galleries fail to help their man— for example, the Tammany gallery in New York in 1924.

It was plain all through the convention that the delegates and alternates, and likewise the people in the gallery, were overwhelmingly against American entrance into the war. When, on the evening of June 25, the corpse of Herbert Hoover was put up to make a pep-talk, the loudest applause it got followed the declaration that "if we are to keep cool and not

Eminent journalists gather for the farewell dinner given for James Bone of the Manchester *Guardian*. Hamilton Street Club, Baltimore. November, 1940. *Top row (left to right):* J. Fred Essary, J. Harry Scharf, Newton Aiken, Edmund Duffy, Paul Patterson. *Middle row:* Philip M. Wagner, A. D. Emmart, Frederic Nelson, Paul Ward, Hulbert Footner, Maclean Patterson. *Bottom row:* Hamilton Owens, August Mencken, J. Edwin Murphy, Mulvaney (British vice-consul at Baltimore), James Bone, Gerald W. Johnson, H.L.M., John W. Owens.

stimulate war there must be an end to provocative speech by our officials," and when, the next day, one C. Whalen Brooks of Indiana arose to second the motion adopting the platform, he brought down the house by bellowing that "the blood of Americans belongs to America to the last drop, and should not be spilled in a foreign war." But all this, of course, had become moot by now, for every person of any political experience knew that Roosevelt would be nominated for a third term and most probably reëlected, and that he would take his reëlection as a mandate to continue and exaggerate the provocations that had already made the United States a belligerent in all save the name. Moreover, it was already obvious that nearly all his chief opponents would fall into line for him when the band began to play. On this point, with John Owens and the *Sun* frankly in mind, I had written in the *Sunday Sun* on February 4: "Most of the newspapers which now fulminate against his renomination will support him with loud gloats and yells if he is actually renominated, for he will undoubtedly whoop up a war scare to further his campaign, and nearly all of them are lathering to do their bits for what he calls 'religion and morality.'" He was still, to be sure, refusing coyly to announce his formal candidacy, but everyone knew that he wanted it, and that no other Democrat could get it without his permission. His itch, indeed, was plain to all, and there was patent logic in it, for if he went out of office in 1941 his record would show only the gigantic imbecility and failure of the New Deal, whereas if he took a third term and devoted it to getting the United States into the war he might, by good luck, lead it to victory, and so be sure of immortality, at least in the school-books. Thus I wrote in the *Sunday Sun* on March 3:

> If he has read history, which I assume he has, he must know that all the American Presidents who continue in high repute *post-mortem* were war Presidents—Washington, Jackson, Lincoln, Roosevelt I and Wilson. Jefferson, who was actually a far better man than any of them, has fallen so low that his fellow-Democrats have abandoned him to the Republicans, and Grover Cleveland, who was certainly better than at least three of the five, gets little more public veneration than Aaron Burr or John Wilkes Booth. The people do not estimate Presidents by the capacity they show for the job, but by the amount of blood they let.

Despite the fact that everyone knew that Roosevelt wanted and would get a renomination he continued his pretense of indifference up to the opening of the Chicago convention on July 15. Indeed, he kept up the imposture until after the convention actually named him, and then pretended to submit only as a sacrifice to patriotism. Because of its pervasive air of false pretenses the show was a poor one, as such things go, but even so it had its moments. One came on the night of July 16, when the Kelly-Nash-Nudelman machine of Chicago, which had packed the galleries and was running the hall, staged a Roosevelt demonstration with the aid of the loud-speaker system. The din was really appalling, and the steady yelling of "Roosevelt! Roosevelt!" by an unidentified but stentorian voice—later discovered to be that of the Chicago sewer commissioner, one Garry—almost deafened the delegates. The other bright spot came on the last night of the convention, when, on order from the White House, it nominated a Republican, Henry A. Wallace, for second place on the ticket. These orders were resented by a majority of the delegates, including nearly all of those from the South, and poor Wallace was booed a great deal more heartily than he was cheered. In the end he got but 575½ votes, which would have been too few to nominate him if the two-thirds rule had still been in effect. Before the result was announced, of course, a motion was made and carried to make the vote unanimous, but nevertheless the embarrassing figures became known. Old William B. Bankhead of Alabama, Speaker of the House of Representatives and key-noter of the convention, actually got 296 votes. After the uproar was over Mrs. Roosevelt, who had been present while it was on, was put up to make a short speech, and a little while later, beginning at 12:21 A.M., Roosevelt himself made his speech of acceptance by telephone from the White House. In it he let it be known that he had hoped to retire to Krum Elbow, but that he had submitted to the same draft which was already roping so many American boys for the war. The delegates to that *ja*-convention *à la* Hitler, still flattened by the operations of his steam-roller, snickered sadly at this. There was very little applause.

In his crooning he made a categorical promise—his tenth or twelfth—to keep the United States out of the war, but since his University of Virginia speech no one not insane had taken such promises seriously. The platform, prepared at the White House, made another. "The American people," it said, "are determined that war, raging in Europe, Asia and Africa, shall not come to America. We will not participate in foreign wars, and we will not send our army, naval or air forces to fight in foreign lands outside the Americas, except in case of attack." Most of the delegates were plainly in favor of this declaration, though everyone assumed that Roosevelt would be making renewed efforts to horn into the war as soon as election day was behind him; in fact, he did not wait for election day, for on September 3 he announced the transaction whereby the United States took over the defense of the British colonies in America and gave the sweating Motherland fifty destroyers to boot, on September 14 he got his Selective Service Act through Congress, and on September 27 he forced Japan into the arms of the Axis. By this time it had become evident that he had nothing to fear from Willkie, and would have his way at the polls. But at the Chicago convention, as at the Philadelphia convention, there was still applause for every speaker who whooped up staying out of the war. This whooping was heard at every session.

Henry M. Hyde and I traveled to Chicago together, and on the train met many fellow newspaper people and a number of politicoes. One of the latter was Senator Bennett C. Clark of Missouri, who, as usual, was far gone in liquor. He told us that he was implacably against Roosevelt and would remain so to the bitter end. "If there is no other vote cast against him," he declared, "there will always be my half one." Knowing politicians, Hyde and I laughed at this. In the end Missouri joined in making the vote for Roosevelt unanimous, but I should add that Clark was probably absent when this was done—and drunk again, for he was a very heavy boozer, like his father, Champ Clark, before him. On the train we encountered Doris Fleeson of the New York *Daily News*, a very smart newspaper woman and not without good looks. She, Clark, Hyde and I settled down at a table in the club-car for some drinks, with Hyde and I on one side and she and Clark on the other. Presently, Clark, growing oratorical, came down with his fat paw on her left knee, and finding it soft and shapely, began to squeeze it. Doris made signs to Hyde and me to come to her rescue, but we pretended not to notice. After a while Clark became so drunk that he had to be taken to bed, and Doris upbraided Hyde and me for so ungallantly letting her suffer. We told her that the show was too good to be spoiled, and that newspaper women should be tough. It was our rule, we said, to refrain from interference in such cases until we heard a bone crack.

Sitting in the almost incandescent press-stand in Chicago, trying to work in all that glare and uproar, I found myself reflecting lazily upon the significance of the show unrolling before me. It was obvious that Roosevelt would be reëlected and almost equally obvious that he would take the United States into the war. What then? It seemed to me, as I had been writing in the *Sunday Sun* for months past, that, notwithstanding his almost certain success in November, he would have a far from united country behind him, that fighting the war would present difficulties immensely more serious than those encountered by Wilson in the walk-over of 1917–18, that England would quickly contrive to saddle most of the cost on the United States, and that the total bill, even if luck ran with the Moral Powers, would be stupendous, and perhaps downright ruinous. Out of the ensuing alarms and turmoils, I became convinced, would issue grave constitutional changes at home, with something indistinguishable from totalitarianism in the not too remote distance. Indeed, as I left the hall after Roosevelt's telephoned croon of acceptance I found myself wondering if the United States would ever see another national convention. This one had gone through the traditional forms, but in substance it was actually no more democratic than one of the outpourings staged by

Hitler in Nurnberg or Berlin. Though most of the delegates were New Deal jobholders, probably a good half of them had been opposed to a third term, and many more than half were against the nomination of the preposterous Wallace, yet they had been flogged into line with the greatest ease, and even now were afraid to speak their minds. On my return to Baltimore I wrote four articles for the *Sunday Sun* on the situation confronting the country, and then prepared to go to Elwood, Ind., to hear Willkie's speech of acceptance. I believed by this time that his chances of election were virtually nothing, but Patterson was still fevered with enthusiasm for him, and so I resolved to have a look at him in action.

I had gone to Indianapolis several days before the notification ceremony at Elwood, and seized the chance to have a close look at rural Indiana. The first day I went out to Elwood by motor, and the next day I went to Rushville, where Willkie and his wife were staying with her relatives, and from Rushville proceeded again to Elwood. Altogether, I covered a couple of hundred miles by motor, and saw many small Indiana towns. Rushville was a charming village set in the midst of a lush farming country, and I was sorry that I had so little time to give to it. While I was there I took a walk and presently found myself at a place where a single railroad track crossed the main residence street. The railroad had been reduced to two strings of rust by bus and truck competition, but there was still a locomotive in service, and as I came to the crossing this locomotive, pulling a couple of freight-cars, was approaching. I noticed with a flash of pleasure that it was brushed by nodding hollyhocks as it slowly came on. Elwood was much less charming—a boom town that had long ago blown up. Its once busy factories were idle, and its stores and eating-houses looked shabby and forlorn. The best restaurant in it was run by a Greek, and the one meal I ate there was dreadful, indeed. During the rest of my two-days' stay I subsisted on hot-dogs and Coca-Cola. The weather was cruelly hot and I was very thirsty, but I distrusted the town water and the only iced tea I could find was undrinkable. When I got to town I found that the one small hotel was packed to the doors, but some radio brethren presently got me a room in the private house of a doctor's widow. The room was one that they had engaged for a female colleague, but the widow refused to let her occupy it, for the presence of a strange woman in a bedroom beside one full of strange men would be an invitation to sin, and, by the local theory, an assurance of it. The night was so infernally hot that I could not sleep, but I did get a bath in the morning. The widow, it appeared, lived alone, but her sister, an old-maid high-school teacher serving in Texas, was with her for the Summer. The two ladies, once they learned my name, were very polite, and after I got back to Baltimore I sent the sister a copy of "The American Language" as a souvenir of my visit.

I parked my bag and typewriter in the little Western Union office, and presently added my seersucker coat. Calloway Park, where the notification ceremony was to be held, was a mile from the center of town, and getting to and from it was difficult, for there were no taxicabs. I finally solved the problem by flagging police cars: the cops let me ride on my badge—every reporter had a gaudy badge—whenever they had room. The park was a grove in the last stages of desiccation, for there had been no rain for two months, and beyond it lay a couple of hundred acres of plowed and dusty fields, with room for 40,000 cars. The temperature in the press-stand was really infernal, for a bright sun was shining and the trees gave very little shade. My typewriter was so hot that I could barely use it, and the iron undertaker's chair in my place was even hotter: in fact, I had to put newspapers on it before I could sit down.

How I managed to get my dispatch written I do not know, for the discomforts of the press-stand were even worse than those of the press-stand at Chicago. But somehow I did it, and my story read smoothly enough. Barring acts of God and the public enemy, they always do. Looking back over my years in press-stands I can recall a dozen times when getting my work done came within an ace of finishing me. In Elwood, once Willkie had shut down, I walked back to the town, recovered my coat and bag from the Western Union office, and looked about for some means of getting to Indianapolis.

I began to realize, after this trip to Elwood, that my days of active reporting were nearing an end. Unlike poor Essary, I was still able to cover a story competently, but I was tiring more and more quickly, and it was obvious that a really exhausting job of work might easily floor me. My old colleague, Henry M. Hyde, then 74, was showing me that a certain conservation of energy would soon be necessary. In the Spring of 1940 Hyde had notified Patterson that he would be unable to cover more than one of the two national conventions, but after he had done Philadelphia it was not hard to induce him to tackle Chicago also. One day in Chicago, during the hurricane of rumors that preceded Roosevelt's order to the convention to nominate Wallace for second place, it occurred to Patterson that it might be a good idea to record all of the wild reports that came into the *Sun* bureau, and then print them seriatim next day. Instructions were thereupon issued to all of us to write down whatever we heard—and during the first two hours Hyde brought in more than all the rest of us put together. The roster, alas, was never printed, for Roosevelt issued his mandate for Wallace before the day was out, and the story thus became stale. Hyde, for years past, had been doing very hard work in Washington, but he was wise enough to take long and frequent holidays, and to make his working-day as short as possible. He would turn out early in the morning, but by 3 P.M. he would disappear for a quiet nap in his room, and after that he seldom returned to work. By 9 P.M. he was always in bed again.

Despite my rockiness, I decided to travel with Willkie on at least one or two of his campaign tours. Dewey L. Fleming had been with him since a couple of weeks before his nomination, and was doing excellent work, but Fleming needed a holiday. Moreover, Patterson wanted me to know Willkie better, in the hope that his magic would dispel my doubts about him. I joined him, first, in New York on October 8 and accompanied him on his tour of New England, ending at Albany, N.Y., on October 13. It was a headlong and onerous journey, and toward the end of it I picked up a respiratory infection that had already floored nearly everyone else on the campaign train, but I managed to get through the Albany meeting and was already half recovered when I reached home. I came nearest to blowing up in Boston on October 11. We had spent all morning covering a long route through lower Massachusetts by bus and motor, and when I reached Boston during the afternoon and took a room in a suburban hotel, whose name I forget, I had not only to write my story of the trip but also to do an editorial page article for the *Sunday Sun* of October 13. I felt wretched in the extreme, and more than once had to stop work and lie down. When the job was done I was in a state close to collapse, but after an hour's nap I felt much better, and late that night went aboard the campaign train for the next day's trip through Western Massachusetts.

I enjoyed such tours, though the work was hard and included listening to many dull and repetitious speeches, for they gave me a chance to see some of the back regions of the country and it was pleasant to eat, drink and work with so many newspaper colleagues, many of them old friends. Some of these last I seldom saw save during political campaigns. Almost every morning Willkie left his train early to tour by motor-car, and we correspondents trailed along in busses. Sometimes, because of bad police arrangements, we fell behind and missed several of his speeches, but that did not worry us, for the press association men, in an open car, were always directly behind him, and we could depend upon them for anything we missed. Like any other such candidate he made the same speech over and over again. His wife, who had rejoined him for the duration, had to listen to him all day long, and, what is worse, to pretend to be attentive. She turned out to be a small, good-looking woman with a sparkle of humor in her eye. As I got to know her I concluded that she took the whole show with her tongue in her cheek. Their son, a youth of eighteen or nineteen, was with them, and I had several friendly palavers with him. He seemed to be an honest fellow, but not brilliant. I saw nothing of Irita Van Doren in the campaign after her appearance at the Philadelphia convention.

Willkie and his wife and son occupied a private car at the end of the train. Now and then the candidate came into the correspondents' club-car to palaver with them, but not often. Twice, at his invitation, I had sessions with him in his car. He made a show of frankness, but I continued to be of the opinion that he was a rather smooth and somewhat devious fellow. I think he realized that his only chance of beating Roosevelt lay in fanning the popular resentment of Roosevelt's war-mongering, and this he tried to do in nearly all his speeches, but at the same time he inclined toward it himself, and was in fear some event of the war might suddenly inflame the war spirit. So he compromised by denouncing American participation in the slaughter in one breath, and howling against Hitler in the next. He tried to pump out of me my opinion of his chances, and I let him know that it was not optimistic. Already, on September 15, I had described his campaign train, in a *Sunday Sun* article, as a funeral train, and on September 22 I had argued that the campaign itself was in a state of collapse—that all that remained of it was "only sound and *pfui*, signifying nothing."

Covering the local meetings was uncomfortable physically, but full of entertainment and instruction. During the second tour, as we worked our way into New York, I went ashore in one of the Northern Jersey towns, and had my pocket neatly picked. The thieves took all my money save some loose change, but spared my watch. I was able to borrow enough money to get me to New York, and there I cashed a check at the Knopf office. The trips by bus were especially amusing, and I liked to watch the reactions of the crowds along the way, and the performance of the local politicians, all of them flustered by the contact with eminence. I also liked to listen to the local newspaper men who came aboard from time to time, for they knew a lot about the politics of their bailiwicks that was tart and illuminating. In Rhode Island I was astonished to discover large regions of waste land, some of it almost desert. I had always thought of that little State as densely packed with people, but I found that nearly all of them were concentrated in towns. On the bright

Autumn morning devoted to a tour of the State the candidatorial motor-cade sometimes ran on for four or five miles without encountering a single human being. The arrangements for handling the campaign train always interested me, and I liked to meet the railway men in charge of it, and the telegraph men who sent off the enormous output of the correspondents aboard. These telegraph men had the job of providing wires and operators enough to clear this flood in small and remote places. Usually they succeeded, but sometimes they failed. On my second trip with Willkie, as we traveled down from West Virginia toward Baltimore, there was a period of three or four hours when no wires were reachable, and a large part of my own story of the day was held up.

After leaving Willkie at Albany on October 13 I remained in Baltimore until October 27, when I went to Louisville, Ky., to rejoin him. I stuck to him after that until the final meeting of the campaign, at Madison Square Garden, New York, on the night of November 2. He spoke at the Fifth Regiment Armory in Baltimore on October 30, but though I was in the press-stand, I did not cover the meeting, which was turned over to the *Sun*'s local staff. At the Madison Square Garden meeting the press-stand was crowded, and I could get no seat for my telegraph operator. Thus, after writing a take of copy, I had to stand in the aisle while he sent it from my place. After Willkie had finished his speech and a demonstration was in progress, the police nabbed a man not ten feet from me, and hustled him out of the hall. In the confusion he had somehow worked his way up to the front. He was an oldish fellow in a long-tailed coat and wearing a moustache that looked artificial. He had a pistol in his hand and was apparently preparing to fire it, but the cops grabbed it instantly, and he was out of sight before anyone on the platform knew what was happening. The police, in fact, handled him with amazing speed and skill, and on my return to Baltimore I sent a letter to the police commissioner of New York commending the excellent work of the officer principally concerned, a brisk and handsome young sergeant named Edmund Unger. At the Baltimore meeting the cops were considerably less efficient, and I had a hard time getting off the Willkie train in Mt. Royal Station, and an even harder time getting into the hall.

During the rest of 1940 my contributions to the *Sunpapers* consisted mainly of signed articles for the editorial page of the *Sunday Sun,* and most of them were devoted to the war. In the Spring there had been two diversions—first, the effort of Howard Bruce to wrest one of the Maryland Senatorships from George L. Radcliffe, and second, the uproar over the appointment of Bertrand Russell to a professorship in the College of the City of New York. Bruce I had long distrusted and I was thus delighted to see Radcliffe give him a sound trouncing in the primary. He was a man of large wealth and spent a great deal of money on his campaign. His defeat pretty well eliminated him from Maryland politics, and soon afterward he resigned as Democratic national committeeman from Maryland, a post he had held since 1924. On my way to the Chicago convention I met him on the train and found him in an extremely low frame of mind. He had been itching for high public office—first the governorship and then the senatorship—for years, and had spent a fortune on his quest, but now, so he told me, he realized that it had all been in vain. "They simply don't want me," he said sadly. "I am done for." I tried to console him, but without much diligence, for I agreed with him that he was finished, and was glad of it. My two articles on the Russell case were devoted to rearguing an old doctrine of mine—that a public school is the mere creature of the state, and that the constituted authorities have a clear right to determine what shall be taught in it. Thus I could see no invasion of free speech in the effort to keep Russell out of the New York public school system. He had a right to expound his ideas—for example, his theory that adultery was a mild and venial offence—as much as he pleased, but not at the expense of the Catholics and Jews who constituted a majority of New York's taxpayers, and subscribed (at least in theory) to the Seventh Commandment.

As I have sufficiently indicated in this record, I had long since abandoned the high hopes for the *Sunpapers* which seemed reasonable enough in the 1920's. Like all human institutions, they depended for their character upon concrete men, and the men available, with the single exception of Swanson, were simply not equal to the task of making them genuinely distinguished. Patterson had great ability, but it issued from a cultural background that was rather drab, and so he was not equal to the task of formulating and enforcing a really enlightened editorial policy. His interest in the editorial pages was always very slight and seldom more than intermittent: he gave his chief attention to the news department, or to such cony-catching features as the comic section. In that direction his judgment was sound—if usually very sordid—and he showed plenty of energy, but it was hard to interest him in opinion. He never read a book of any authority or distinction, and among magazines his favorites were the *Saturday Evening Post* and *Time*. His opposition to the New Deal was instinctive rather than logical: he saw it as an old-line Republican might have seen it, and never distinguished between the measures that had been forced on it by the unhappy state of the nation and those that represented only the wild yearnings and hallucinations of its tin-pot messiahs. During the years between 1933 and 1939 its operations had become so manifold and so gigantic that it was a sheer impossibility to follow them—that is, in the sense that governmental acts had been followed in the days before Roosevelt came in. Patterson made frequent efforts to whip up the Washington bureau, but they were always in vain. It would cover a given enterprise of the messiahs for a week or two, but then the story would get beyond it, and it would have to turn to something else.

In the campaign of 1940 Patterson was not incommoded by the New Deal piety of Edwin F. A. Morgan and John E. Semmes. By this time both of them had discovered that Roosevelt was a fraud. But the course of the *Sunpapers* was nevertheless lacking in force and directness, for they had fallen into the same trap that closed upon Willkie. That is to say, they denounced Roosevelt in one column for wasting the hard-earned money of the American people, and praised him in the next for imperilling their very lives. No more shining example of putting property rights above human rights could have been imagined—and this time it happened to be only too real. The result, of course, was that the two editorial pages became completely ridiculous, and indeed almost imbecilic.

Thus I closed 1940 in an unhappy frame of mind. Roosevelt had broken the anti-third-term tradition, it was obvious that he would lead the United States into the war as quickly as possible, and the *Sunpapers* were in a state of complete intellectual collapse. I thus turned to other concerns. My "Happy Days," published at the beginning of the year, was very well received, and by May 13 had sold 9912 copies. I had begun work as soon as it was out on its successor, "Newspaper Days," but some time in April I fell down the third-floor stairway in Hollins street, and was so badly bruised that I could not go on. This injury was not serious, but it left me with a sore elbow and shoulder for more than a year. On November 17 I was flabbergasted by the sudden and unexpected death of my friend Raymond Pearl, professor of biology at the Johns Hopkins. We had been on intimate terms since he came to Baltimore in

1918, and I always saw him at least once a week. His death left a great vacancy, and it has not been filled.

The long-forecast and inevitable end of my years of service in the editorial department of the *Sunpapers* came on January 16, 1941. It would have come two months earlier if it had not been for the collapse and desperate illness of William E. Moore, which greatly concerned and upset Patterson, and raised problems that needed long and earnest discussion. I had a hand in that discussion, and so postponed my own discontents. But in January I made up my mind that I could no longer endure the nauseous atmosphere of the *Sunday Sun* editorial page, and told Patterson that I wanted to be relieved at once. In fact, I told him that I was ready to clear out of the *Sunpapers* altogether. He protested against this and asked for a palaver at my house. We had it on the evening of January 16. It took me, as I recall, exactly an hour to say my say, and he listened without interruption. It seemed to me that it would have been unjust to both of us for me to waste any time on mere politeness, so I told him the plain truth as I saw it. He had made a great success of the *Sunpapers* as a corporation operated for profit, but he had failed completely to give them the high and independent character we had dreamed of in 1920, and it was now obvious that he would never do so thereafter. I told him that I did not question his motives, or even his judgment, but that I simply could not go on as I had been going for so many years. I was resolved, I said, to quit writing for the editorial page of the *Sun,* at once and forever. I was resolved, further, to undertake no more writing for its news pages. Yet further, I refused to take any more responsibility, whether direct or indirect, for its editorial conduct, and would not undertake to offer him any more advice on the subject. He protested that this was making a sorry end to our old and intimate association, but I convinced him that my decision had been reached only after long reflection and was irrevocable, so he made no attempt to dissuade me.

He said, however, that he hoped my withdrawal from the editorial department would not involve my quitting the *Sunpapers* altogether, and argued at some length that there was no reason why it should. After all, I had by no means confined myself since 1920 to editorial affairs; on the contrary, I had devoted more than half of my time to business matters. Several such matters were still pending, and some of them were important. About one of them, the struggle with the Newspaper Guild, I knew

H.L.M. in the winter of his years, c. 1945. Unidentified charcoal drawing.

more than anyone else in the office. Why shouldn't I go on representing the papers in Guild negotiations, which would probably be resumed in the very near future? Why, indeed, shouldn't I take a more active interest in other labor difficulties? I had managed to throw off the Guild in 1938, and there was every likelihood that I'd be able to lend a useful hand in other such enterprises. Above all, I was still needed on the board of directors, where I was the only member, save Patterson himself, who was a professional newspaper man, and familiar from long contact with all the problems of the office, upstairs and down. I was tempted to say no to all this, and clear out at once, but on reflection I concluded that there was something in it. In view of the state of the Guild negotiations my abandoning them would be something akin to desertion in the face of the enemy. Moreover, they interested me very much, and I was really eager to go on with them. More, I was not innocent of a certain amount of curiosity about the future editorial course of the papers with John Owens as commander in chief and Patterson tagging along. It would be, at worst, an excellent show, and as the chickens that had been set loose since 1934 came home to roost it might be instructive, especially from a ringside seat. So I finally consented, but with the understanding, of course, that my responsibility for editorial affairs was definitely and finally ended, and that I would not consider any proposal that I resume it save in the unlikely event that there was a complete reversal of policy, satisfactory to me in every detail.

Along with this, I insisted that there be a reduction in my compensation, and suggested one of $5,000 a year. My theory was that my Sunday articles, at a moderate estimate, had been worth $100 apiece; in truth, Patterson well knew that, for years past, I might have got at least twice as much for them from other papers. He objected to any reduction at all, on the polite ground that I had been grossly underpaid for years before 1936, and that the *Sunpapers* would still be in my debt if I went on drawing full salary without doing anything at all. But I insisted that there must be some reduction, and after a long discussion we postponed a decision for a couple of days, when we compromised on one of $3,000 a year. In the course of that discussion Patterson made plain enough his present attitude toward the papers. For years past, he said, we had been working hard to pile up profits for a motley of worthless stockholders—for example, the innumerable Abells, and Van Lear Black's vixenish wife and trashy children. Why shouldn't we now grab what we could for ourselves? Who deserved it better? I was tempted to make the priggish reply that I had never looked on the *Sunpapers* from that standpoint—that struggling to get something resembling character into them had been a game with me rather than a business enterprise, and that my alleged underpayment had always been with my free consent. But it seemed too late in the day to be raising such ghosts, so I agreed to the truce we had patched up. It seemed to me to be highly unlikely that it would last long, but while it endured I was willing to give it a fair trial. So we had another drink, and called it a day.

I had said nothing to John Owens about my decision; in fact, I had not been in his office for months, and had had little communication with him on office business. Nor had I consulted Harry Black, whose state of mind, by this time, was such that it was difficult to carry on any sensible discussion with him. All his talk was made up of the endless repetition of banal phrases. He would frame one out of nothing, and then keep on reiterating it until his talk became maddening. Patterson, of course, told him of our meeting, and on January 17 he sent me the following note:

> This afternoon Patterson told me of the talk you and he had last night. You don't know how happy I am that you and he came to an understanding that relieves your mind and enables the company to receive the invaluable help you so often give it. All I can say is that you are a fine human being—they don't come better. With every best wish.

I gathered from this that Patterson's account of our discussion had been very vague, to say the least—and perhaps deliberately misleading. He was plainly not eager to take Black into his full confidence, and I could hardly blame him. I replied to Black's note as follows on January 18:

> Thanks very much for your note. It seemed to me that a situation was developing that would be increasingly embarrassing to all hands, and so there was nothing to do save clear out and hope for happier times. On the matter of my pay hereafter I am still at odds with Paul, and I may need your help. He is trying to make me accept a valuation on my Sunday pieces that goes even beyond his effort to break poor Cutler's heart over A. S. Abell stock. We must look to this.
>
> I appreciate your note very much. It is like you.

My last contribution to the editorial page of the *Sunday Sun* was printed on February 2. It was entitled "Progress of the Great Crusade." It was devoted to Roosevelt's constantly more furious and disingenuous efforts to carry the United States into the war, and embodied a sort of final summing-up of my position. The essential parts of it were as follows:

Win or lose, the United States is doomed to suffer some appalling headaches during the next dozen years. If the cause of humanity triumphs we will have the bills to pay, and if Beelzebub gets the better of it we'll have the damages. In either case half of the human race will hate us very earnestly, and the rest will hold us in a kind of esteem hard to distinguish from contempt.

While the issue is pending, it is instructive to contemplate the manner in which the nation was roped—an almost perfect example of classical demagogy. First scare 'em with a bugaboo, and then leap to save 'em from it: such has been the program since the days of the Greeks, and never has it been carried out with greater impudence or larger success than by the Hon. Mr. Roosevelt. His technique from first to last was impeccable. To be sure, he got some valuable help from fortuitous and perhaps unexpected events—for example, the failure of all of England's former allies and the consequent desperate concentration of English propaganda upon the United States, and, again, the shabby feebleness of the Hon. Mr. Willkie's opposition in the third-term campaign. But allowing everything to these aids, it must be plain that the Hon. Mr. Roosevelt's virtuosity was magnificent, and that he well deserved his victory at the polls.

The country, I fear, deserved it no less, for in giving him that victory it emblazoned on the record its pathetic lack of common sense. Here was a demagogue who had been fooling it over and over for eight years—and yet it fell for him again. Here was a bugaboo that had been worn to tatters twenty-three years ago—and yet it shivered and quaked once more. In the annals of demagogy, brilliant though they are, there is probably no triumph more impressive than these. The whole science, indeed, had a face-lifting, a rejuvenation, almost a resurrection. It acquired a new dimension. It became double-entry.

Was this unparalleled feat a surprise? I can only say that it was not so to me: I predicted it formally, in fact, at the beginning of the third-term campaign. The credulity of the American people, whether in peace or in war, has always been grossly underestimated even by those who charge it against them. Fomented by demagogues on the one side and pedagogues on the other, it has become almost infinite. . . .

My relations with Patterson, save for one unpleasant episode, hereinafter to be described, continued peaceful during 1941, but certainly not harmonious. I was at pains to make no editorial suggestions if it could be avoided, but I could not conceal my low opinion of the course of the *Sunpapers*. As the year wore on, and American participation in the war became more and more certain, John Owens began to rant and moan in a really appalling manner. The editorial page, by this time, could no longer hold him, and he began to break out with his chants upon Page 1 of the *Sun:* for a while he appeared there five days a week. Simultaneously, his evangelistic style grew more and more impassioned, and many of his editorials had banal refrains which gave them almost the effect of hymns. He raged and roared against Hitler, against the so-called isolationists, and (with an occasional cut-back to his crusade for "competitive capitalism") against labor's effort to get a fair share of the "defense" swag. All the old principles of "Liberalism" went out of the window along with all the principles set forth in the White Paper, and he began to demand that every opponent of the Roosevelt war-mongering, however honest and innocent, be slapped down. By October he had abandoned all pretense of "defense" and was openly howling for war.

On November 20, Thanksgiving Day, he summed up as follows:

> Above all nations, we Americans have cause to give thanks.
>
> At the end of the last war we failed, as did all other nations. We, like the others, sought ease. We enshrined materialism. We denied responsibility for the preservation of law and order in the world, responsibility for the slow, uphill task of establishing justice between the nations of the world. . . .
>
> We begin to restore our character. When the Scourge descended upon the earth, our first thought was to stand aloof. We soon found that our hearts would not permit us to stand aloof, whatever temptations our minds, trained in materialism, whispered to us. We felt the terrible impact of evil upon good. Not upon perfection, but upon good— that good which embodies the long struggle of men to chasten and correct themselves and to establish the moral law.
>
> And when the shadow of the Scourge spread so far that it reached our own land, we found in ourselves the power to acknowledge it and to face it. We found the strength to put aside the counsels of those who told us that it was not the Scourge in truth; that in any event its shadow did not reach to our shores; that even if its shadow did reach to our shores we could deal with it, barter with it and remain fat. . . .
>
> Of this we are sure:
>
> We shall pour out our sympathy and our aid, in ever-enlarging measure, to all peoples who lie under the Scourge.

We shall train our youth and shall pile up war armaments that we may be prepared to meet the Scourge in the manner of men.

We shall discipline and direct the vain and selfish at home, and yet we shall preserve their essential rights against their destructive folly.

We shall seek humbly in the tomorrow not to fail in our duty to the family of nations as we failed on that awful yesterday of 1920.

For all of this, which we cherish deep in our hearts, we offer thanks to the God of our fathers!

Seventeen days later came Pearl Harbor. . . . I must confess that this fever of rhetoric delighted my malicious mind, even while it made me blush for the *Sun*. I got a good many quiet laughs, too, out of the compositions of the other Peter the Hermits of the staff, most of whom, if they were less impassioned, were even more ignorant than Owens.

I did the best I could for the *Sunpapers* against the Guild,* and with an easy conscience, for it was dominated by highly dubious persons athirst for power, and its concern for the welfare of working newspaper men and women was always less than its yearning to afflict publishers. It drove many weak newspapers out of existence, and I am half convinced that if the amount of money it got for its members in increased pay were set off against their losses during strikes and by reason of suspensions and consolidations the latter would at least equal the former. In so far as it promoted security of tenure and actually increased salaries I was for it, and had long advocated these ends in the *Sun* office. The tendency there, as in every other newspaper office, was to overpay the men at the top and underpay those at the bottom. Against this I began to protest so early as 1920, and I never let up. If the Guild accomplished no other useful purpose, it at least forced Patterson, Black and Schmick to give serious consideration to this matter. The Guild failed in its effort to organize the editorial department in 1938, but the threat it offered was largely responsible for the decision to go to the five-day week in 1939. Again, in 1940 and 1941, it undoubtedly had some influence on the detection and clearing out of hidden sweatshops. General increases in pay had begun in the editorial rooms long before it was heard of, but they were certainly

---

* In 1938 the *Sunpapers* appointed Mencken chair of a committee representing management in negotiations with the American Newspaper Guild. Afterward he devoted considerable time to the task, as his manuscript memoirs make abundantly clear.

not impeded by its constant allegation that the scale on the *Sunpapers* was less than on like papers elsewhere.

Most of my *Sun* business toward the end of 1941 had to do with plans to meet the apparently inevitable drop in revenues in 1942. Patterson gave both papers the most careful scrutiny that they had had for years, seeking to discover features that might be safely abandoned. I was in favor of most of the cuts that were made—for example, the abandonment of the daily half-column report of real-estate transactions. These transactions were reported also, and in greater detail, in the *Daily Record,* a paper read by all real-estate men and all lawyers. In the days when the *Sun* began printing them, far back in the era of the Abells, there was no *Daily Record,* but for many years it had been absurd for us to try to compete with it in its own special field. I was also strongly in favor of abandoning the daily society column in the morning paper, for it was extraordinarily formal, prissy and idiotic. In large part it was made up of banal paragraphs recording that this or that nonentity was giving a luncheon or preparing to marry off a daughter. There could be no longer any pretense that it recorded the doings of the town *noblesse* and was thus fascinating to the lowly. Baltimore society, in fact, had been under invasion for years by all sorts of new people, and most of those whose names appeared frequently were of dubious position and no importance whatsoever. But Patterson clung to the society column, largely, I suspect, because he had a certain inclination toward fashionable life himself. One of the other recurrent discussions at the end of 1941 had to do with the cafeteria, which was operating at a loss of about $6,000, less the $100 a month charged against it as rent. The space it occupied was worth much more, and was badly needed for other purposes. The cafeteria was a great convenience to the employés of the papers, but there was little indication that they appreciated the fact. Indeed, the only comments that came from them were complaints. I was in favor of abandoning it, but Patterson and Black inclined toward going on with it a bit longer. By this time it had become plain that all efforts to promote the security and comfort of the employés were in vain. Their gratitude, even for such things as free insurance, was seldom apparent, and the labor agitators who operated upon them preached that all things of the sort were simply manifestations of a vicious paternalism.

My position in the office at the end of 1941 was comfortable enough, for I had at last managed to throw off all responsibility for its editorial course, and with it all concern, for I have never been one to mourn over the inevitable and irremediable. As the *Sunpapers* plunged, under John Owens's evangelical leadership and with the consent of Patterson, into worse and worse absurdities, I could only rejoice quietly that I had never entrusted too many of my private eggs to their frail basket. There was plenty of ground for suspecting that Patterson, in his more reflective moments, was becoming increasingly uncertain and uneasy, and not infrequently he showed signs of wanting to discuss the editorial situation with me, but I always evaded the subject, for going into it would have led almost certainly to recrimination, and recrimination seems to me to be vain. He had made his bed, and now he was lying in it. My belief was that he had missed one of the greatest opportunities ever presented to an American newspaper man, and that belief I could not conceal, but it was not, after all, my funeral, and so I did not labor the thought, even *in petto* [in private]. His merits have been sufficiently set forth in this chronicle. He was an excellent manager, and knew how to stick through thick and thin to a coherent purpose. In all my days of journalism I have never known his superior—within his limits. But those limits, unhappily, were narrow. There was tenacity in him, but not much boldness, and his thinking went on in very conventional patterns. Ideas always alarmed him, for they were not his habitual provender. He read nothing, and knew intimately very few men who were worth knowing. Whenever fate forced him to venture into the unknown he proceeded timorously, and needed constant support. Over many years a large part of that support had come from me, if only because I was the one man in the office who was not wholly dependent upon it, either for money or for position, and could thus afford to take chances; but now, at the end, we were too far apart to work together to any effect, and so I withdrew myself from his confidence as much as possible. Once a principal actor in the exhilarating but far from profound or important drama of the *Sunpapers,* I now retired to a stage-box, and became a spectator of the show which no longer really engrossed me. There were still plenty of ways in which I could be useful. To questions of personnel I could contribute something, for I usually had intimate knowledge of the men under discussion, and there were always ways for me to be helpful in labor matters, for I occupied a ground midway between that of Patterson himself, who could see nothing save treason and pillage in the demands of the unions, and that of the New Dealers who stood behind them, supporting them in their most preposterous extravagances. But even in this field I confined myself as much as possible to Newspaper Guild affairs, and kept out of other labor squabbles whenever I could decently do so. For the rest, I enjoyed my seat in the stage-box, and no less my occasional visits to the dressing-rooms. The show, in large part, had descended to farce, but nevertheless it still had its moments. Soon or late, I was convinced, I would have to put on my hat and clear out altogether, but that time was not quite yet, and the state of my health supplied the consoling if not cheering prospect that I'd be wafted to bliss eternal before I really had to make the decision.

Looking back over my long years on the *Sunpapers*, I found little to regret. After all, I had had a pleasant time, and my labors, such as they were, had at least sustained me well enough, and left me free to devote a large part of my energy to other enterprises. The game was brisk and amusing while it lasted, but now it was nearing its foredoomed end, and there was nothing to be done about it. Whether anyone will be interested enough, twenty-five years after my death, to read this record I do not know, and at the moment the chances against it seem to me to be very large, but of one thing I am sure: that if I am remembered that long it will be for other and quite different enterprises, and not for my long and vain effort to change the apparently inevitable destiny of the Baltimore *Sunpapers*.

An Editorial Memorandum

1919

INTRODUCTION

Although my knowledge of the Chinese theatre is extremely limited I am under the impression, an impression perhaps entirely erroneous, that the scenes presented therein are always explained to the audience in advance. That if, for instance, the back of a bench is supposed to be a wall, the audience is so informed before the action of the play gets under way, thereby eliminating all possibility of misapprehension.

Now, despite the fact that I am not a Chinaman I none the less deem it wise to take a leaf out of the book of the Chinese theatre and hence now and here, before going any further, I shall endeavor to explain exactly what my ideas are and what my purpose is in writing that which is to follow. Observation, study and thought all convince me that though the *Sun* essentially is first-rate, it lacks something and the something that it lacks is character. Each and every ingredient necessary to make a character for the *Sun* is present, but character is not present.

The reason character is not present is because what the character of the *Sun* (and I speak only of the *Sun* of after July, 1914) should be

Regarding authorship of this important essay in the history of American journalism, Mencken explains that "as the document stands the first section, headed 'Introduction' is [Harry] Black's but nearly all the rest is mine, though Black made a number of changes and interpolations, for example, the quotation from Lowell under 'The Question of Policy.'" For background see Harold A. Williams, *The Baltimore Sun, 1837–1987* (Baltimore and London: Johns Hopkins University Press, 1987), 165–68. [Eds.]

has never been carefully, painstakingly and closely worked up and worked out.

To attain something it is necessary first to decide what the something is that you wish to attain. To attain the aeroplane, for example, it was first necessary for man to decide that he desired to fly. Had man not made up his mind that he wanted to fly, the aeroplane would never have been invented. In the same way, the *Sun* will lack character until we decide we wish character for it and wish for it some particular kind of character.

Now as I have been using the word character so freely and so frequently I think, or rather know, I should define what I mean by character and I can best do this I believe by asking a question.

In the newspaper field today does the *Sun* unmistakably stand out as did the old New York *Sun,* or as did the London *Times* when it was earning its famous appellation of "the thunderer"?

Obviously the answer to my question is no!

The *Sun* is a good newspaper and it is an honest newspaper. I believe, because should the necessity ever arise I know I could prove, that a very great deal more can reasonably and dispassionately be said for the *Sun* than for any other American newspaper. Refreshingly little can be justly said against it—99 percent less, in fact, than can be said against, say, the New York *Times.* None the less you know and I know and everybody else knows that the *Sun* is not nearly as conspicuous in the newspaper field as is the New York *Times,* which, in its turn, is not nearly so conspicuous as were the London *Times* and New York *Sun* of the days that are no more.

To illustrate, from an entirely different angle, the point I am trying to make, you may say that any institution's character is that which causes the institution noticeably, notably and nationally to stand out from its fellows.

The foreign policy of England has character. What is that policy? Fundamentally, it is the ancient Roman policy of "Civis Romanus sum," which translated into rough American means "Don't monkey with a British subject!" If you start any foolishness with any British subject, whether of high or low degree, there is going to be hell to pay and if necessary the entire resources and forces of the British Empire will come to the bat to raise the hell and see to it that you do the paying. "Civis Romanus sum" is the simple, fundamental, easily understood and well known thing that supplies character (or shall I use character and individuality as two words with the same meaning?) to British foreign policy.

What is the fundamental, simple, easily understood and well known (and I ask you especially to note "well known") thing that makes the *Sun* stand out, *i.e.*, that gives it character from Maine to Texas and from the Atlantic to the Pacific?

Nothing, just as yet!

There is not a single thing which has been calculated to give the *Sun* individuality—that is, individuality which at once is specific, famous, pronounced and nation-wide. That is our lack and to this lack I am asking you to direct your thoughts.

To make the *Sun* a nationally distinctive newspaper and a newspaper of national distinction, just as were the New York *Sun* and London *Times*, is the goal I have in mind for us to reach. Not to make the *Sun*, mark you, like the old New York *Sun* or London *Times*, but to make it equal them in degree but not in kind.

This goal can be reached when the paper has character and to that end I present a study and analysis of the *Sun*'s whole situation as it appears to me.

THE PRESENT SITUATION OF THE *SUN*

Two facts are immediately apparent when the present situation of the paper is considered. The first is that it is now in good, and probably secure, financial position—that, with due prudence and economy, it can buy and pay for whatever it needs in the way of editorial and business skill and mechanical equipment. The second is that it occupies a peculiarly favourable position editorially, both locally and nationally, and that it thus faces an exceptionally fine opportunity very materially to increase its importance and influence.

The local situation, I believe, is better than ever before. True enough, the purchase of the *American* by Mr. Munsey has set up stronger competition than that afforded by General Agnus, but at the same time it likewise has cut off the threat of competition that might well have been very much more dangerous than that of Mr. Munsey. From past experience it is safe to assume that both the *News* and the *American* will be ably conducted editorially and that they will make vigorous bids for circulation, but in the last analysis they always must suffer from the fact that they are controlled by a man who is not a Baltimorean, and cannot take quick advantage of local conditions, and who is beside hampered by political ideas and political ambitions that must necessarily influence him constantly. His Baltimore staff will have a free hand up to a certain point, but not beyond. It will never be permitted to go directly counter to the Munsey politics—and the Munsey politics are fundamentally opposed, in more than one way, to the fundamental politics of Maryland. This outsidedness or foreignness will ever constitute a weak link in the *News* and *American* chain, and if we are alert we will take advantage of it.

The national situation offers ever greater opportunities to the *Sun*. First and foremost, it now faces four years in opposition, with perfect freedom to deal with the Administration honestly and realistically, absolutely no obligation to any person or party in power, and no commitment to the private political aspirations of anyone. The slate is clean. Secondly, it occupies geographically an unique position, for it can get into the capitol of the United States with the full news of the day earlier than any other first-class outside newspaper and further, it is not handicapped by those local obligations which press upon all the newspapers of Washington. The Washington papers are severely damaged by the character of their patronage. The great majority of their readers are Government employés, and in all national matters they must consider the Government employés before they consider the country. This makes their politics not infrequently dishonest and frequently puerile and in great part explains their very obvious lack of influence in the nation at large. The *Sun* has always profited by this fact. From the earliest days it has enjoyed considerable circulation in Washington and, now and then, no little influence. Even when it was a party organ and its policies were thus discounted by the majority of its Washington readers, who commonly belonged to the opposite party, it was nevertheless read, if only because of its news service. Hereafter it should cultivate this field more diligently, more studiously and more carefully. No matter how much circulation and influence the *Sun* obtains in Maryland, it will always remain a local newspaper. But if, by presenting the full news of the day earlier than any New York paper can do it and better than any Washington paper can do it, it can compel every important man in Washington to read it daily, then it will attain to national importance, and exert an influence upon national affairs out of all proportion to its size and the nature of its principal circulation.

THE QUESTION OF POLICY

Obviously, it must have a consistent and vigorous policy to attain any such influence, and that policy must be free from any suspicion of loyalty to private interest or to rigid formulae. The *Sun* must convince by means of sound information, unquestionable honesty and unshakable common sense. It must be alert to new ideas and hospitable to them. It must be absolutely free and when I write of freedom I think of the lines of James Russell Lowell:

> To honour the man
> Who is ready to sink
> Half his present repute
> For the freedom to think.
> And when he has thought,
> Be his cause strong or weak,
> Will risk t'other half
> For the freedom to speak;
> Caring not for what vengeance
> The mob has in store,
> Be that mob the upper
> Ten thousand or lower.

All this at once bars out any steady fidelity to either of the great political parties as such. It may, at times, support the policies of either one of them with all of its resources, but the *Sun* cannot allow itself to be forced to accept policies ready-made, or to vacillate over them as the two great political parties often vacillate. In the old days it did both things and was very seriously damaged thereby; in fact, its decline was as much due to party loyalty in a time of party disintegration as to any other one cause. Even more lately, it has borrowed some of the weaknesses of party when what it needed was strength—for instance, in the early days of the Prohibition fight. If the *Sun* would make its influence felt, it ever must be most vigorous at the precise and very time that politicians are most cautious: and most independent at the precise and very time when politicians are most severely hampered by party loyalties. In other words, the *Sun* must march ahead of the thought of the two great political parties and not trail behind either of them. In the long run, so it seems to me, it is safer and better to be wrong on such terms than to be right on the old terms.

Such independence, of course, does not presuppose any doctrinaire denial of the importance and continued strength or even of the value of political parties. They are decaying now in the United States only because the two of them that have been historically important have been converted into mere job-seeking machines, and thus have lost all the enthusiasm for ideas that once enlivened and justified them. On many capital issues it is difficult to distinguish between them. On other issues, one party takes one side because the other party has previously taken the other side. They tend to become mobs following a few ambitious and daring men and not infrequently these men are mere opportunists, whose doctrines and acts are tremendously at variance. On the overwhelmingly important question of national economy neither party stood for and offered an intelligible programme. On the question of Prohibition, and the larger underlying question of personal liberty, both parties temporized. On the question of international relations there is today no clear alignment and no straightforward, comprehensible and honest statement of ideas. Thus it is that the two parties nationally have come to be little more than names—names as empty and hollow as a drum. The defeat of one party at the last election and the victory of another had no ponderable effect upon the question of national economy, none upon the question of personal liberty and little, if any, upon the question of international relations. Which one of the issues raised in the late campaign was settled, save only from the standpoint of officeholders? But in local affairs the two parties yet show a certain real differentiation, and this is particularly true in Maryland. Here we have an important and a living issue in the question of the Negro and his part in politics, and the two parties are still clearly separated upon it. On this question the *Sun* can take but one position. As between the black man and the white man, it must be in favour of the white man. Thus the *Sun* will find itself in the Democratic camp so long as the Democrats view this issue as they do now. In the course of time, needless to say, the Negro question may leap the gap between the two parties as Prohibition already has leapt it, but, in my judgment, that time will not be soon. Until it comes, the *Sun* will remain a Democratic paper in city and state affairs—perfectly free to oppose men and even measures, but logically committed to the underlying principle of the Democratic party in the State.

But beyond this it would be hazardous to go, for on the higher level of national affairs issues promptly become obscured and there is no clear body of Democratic ideas that one may lay hold of and support intelligently. Party loyalty on this level soon converts itself into fidelity, not to ideas but to mere men, and support of such men is made difficult and often extremely embarrassing by the devices circumstances compel them to adopt in order to maintain their hold upon their parties and the masses. It would be hard to imagine, by way of example, anything more vexatious than the straits of a newspaper which sought to support

Roosevelt throughout his career, save it be the straits of a newspaper which seeks to support Harding throughout his term. Such loyalties, in truth, are slaveries—and they constitute all that is left of the old party loyalties. A great newspaper should stand clear of them. As a necessary function of its independence it should be free to make its own mistakes. More important still, it should generally resist this tendency to convert the old conflict of ideas into a conflict of mere men, for the governmental theory of the United States rests firmly upon the doctrine that the latter is undesirable and evil, and that theory has been amply borne out by experience. What is needed primarily is a careful and unsentimental separation of genuine national issues from all merely superficial and transient issues. What is needed secondarily is a prompt and vigorous statement of preferences and a support of them that goes beyond eloquence and enthusiasm—a support which is securely grounded upon complete information, absolute independence of judgment and a persistent and intelligent concern for the national welfare. To political parties the national welfare must always be less important than the party welfare and to great popular leaders it must always be less important than their own success. But to a great national newspaper it must be the object of first and sole concern, above and beyond all questions of party personality. To such a newspaper its loyalties are its greatest weaknesses. It must get rid of them in order to acquire something infinitely more valuable and useful and that is its reputation for having special and early information, for presenting it honestly and fairly and for interpreting it with the utmost independence that is humanly possible.

Thus we come to two propositions. The first is that the *Sun,* despite its commitment to the Democratic party in the State, must stand free, and obviously free, of all party entanglements nationally if ever it is to exert an influence at once useful and powerful. The second is that the two great political parties have made such a muddle and such a mess of all the issues before the people that they now offer but meagre materials for the formulation of an effective and vigorous general policy. Some of these issues have been reduced to puerility; others have been obscured by identification with transient personalities; yet others are not really issues at all, but mere phrases. Out of this muddle and mess nothing useful is recoverable. The politics of the future will seek new and more fundamental issues. If the *Sun* can determine them before the generality of the people determine them, it will lead to that extent. If it can force their consideration before the popular demand for it arises, it will be powerful to that extent.

FUNDAMENTAL AMERICAN IDEAS

Under the whole complex of American politics, national and international, there are two main ideas. The first is that the American people, as a people, shall be independent; the second is that, as individuals, they shall be free. These ideas, remember, when they were first stated, were novel in the world, at least as anything more than mere words. No nation in Europe in the latter Eighteenth Century was really independent. They were all members of larger groups of nations, and each lay under obligations that materially conditioned its independence. And no people of Europe was genuinely free; upon every one lay the burden of dynasty, of a state church, and of harsh and irrational laws. The two aims of the founders of the American Republic were, first, to set up a state that should stand aside from the political entanglements which harassed Europe, and secondly, to take off the fetters of the citizen, and make him free to choose his own rulers, to worship God in his own way, and to think his own thoughts and carry on his chosen avocations and seek his private joy and recreation without any more interference from the state than was necessary for maintaining the most elemental public order. These aims may have been mistaken, but, mistaken or not, they were honestly held and when the Republic was established an honest effort was made to realize them. To this very day they enter into the texture of our national thought and even when they are abandoned they are abandoned on the theory that abandoning them in little will help to secure them in gross. No American of any influence has ever seriously proposed to set them aside, formally and forever.

Nevertheless, the fortunes of life in a somewhat imperfect world have sometimes caused them to be set aside, though always, as I have just pointed out, on the theory that yielding an inch might save a mile. The old independence of the United States, as a nation lying wholly outside the orbits of all other nations, has vanished, and no doubt for all time. Increasing rapidity of communications and the great growth of international trade have made a sheer physical impossibility of such a state as Washington dreamed of. There still remains an acrimonious difference of opinion as to what part precisely America should play in the new international politics, but there is no longer any serious contention that she should hold herself entirely aloof. Therefore questions of foreign alliances and of foreign enterprises will hereafter constantly arise, and out of them must grow vexatious domestic issues. In every such dispute the *Sun* must have an opinion and take a hand. But here there is little room to establish a fixed policy. Every new situation will present a new problem, and the consideration of what is right in principle will always be conditioned by a regard for what is feasible in practise. All we can hope to do is to advocate a steady leaning, in so far as it is possible, toward the original American idea, now so much modified by events—that is, toward a politics that will put American interests first and foremost (and pray recall, just here, that American interests were, at one time, put first and foremost in China through an unconventional and unselfish refusal of the Boxer Indemnity) and avoid all exploitation of the moral and material resources of the country by other Powers.

Yet even in this field there is some room for something permanent, and that is a constant, rigorous and cold examination of all foreign bids for American support. The foreign news that comes to the United States is still colored in the interest of this nation or that, or in the interests of this band of schemers or that. The Associated Press and the United Press still depend quite largely for their European news upon exchange arrangements with the great European news agencies, and all these agencies are controlled by foreign governments. Furthermore, there is a constant and deliberate effort to influence the American people at closer quarters. The propaganda carried on by Irish Republicans and the French propaganda carried on by Frank H. Simonds are specimens of what we face. It should be the aim of the *Sun* to scrutinize all tainted news with the utmost care; to make every endeavor to detect and counteract it. We must try, as we go on towards becoming a great national newspaper, to find news sources of our own. We must join other papers of like mind in destroying the abuses, often gross abuses, which now exist. First of all, we must use our membership in the two great press associations and our growing power as an independent newspaper to subject their news to diligent review, and to take prompt and forceful measures against them when they go astray. To get fair and accurate news is by no means as difficult an enterprise as they pretend. The Associated Press, in particular, is open to grave criticism, both in the domestic field and in the foreign field. (In this general connection, note the last paragraph of C. G. Miller's "Pittsburgh Press" in the *Nation* of Jan. 5, 1921.) If, as has been argued, its management is worn out and incompetent, then our influence should be used to bring about a change.

The second of the two basic American ideas remains to be considered. It differs from the first basic idea in the fact that no external pressure forces us to abandon it, or even to modify it. If, in times of public turmoil and peril, it has been abandoned, then the loss has ever been greater than the gain. That loss today mounts up to a staggering total. The American citizen, once the freest man in the world, is now rapidly becoming the least free. (An unusual sidelight on this topic is to be had from S. M. Bouton's "What is the Reason" in the *Atlantic Monthly* of January, 1921.) In many fields the American citizen has no more rights than the Russian subject had in the days before the Revolution. A multitude of absurd and oppressive laws burden him and the number of laws is steadily and surely being augmented. All sorts of utopian ideas, economical, political and ethical, are precipitated into statutes without sensible consideration and efforts are made to enforce them against the will and against the consciences of large numbers of people. As a logical and a natural consequence, the land is overrun with stupid and often dishonest police, uniformed and ununiformed, and there is much persecution. Assuredly no well-disposed American can comfortably contemplate the fact that scores of his fellow citizens are in prison today as the victims of bureaucratic stupidity and malignancy and that thousands are habitually deprived of their rights of free speech, free assemblage and even free suffrage. This sinister thing rolls up like an evil snowball. One crime makes another. As they gain in power, the bureaucrats gain in enterprise and daring. No man of active, original and courageous mind, unless he be rich or of established position, is any too safe in the United States today. The desire for draconian laws has passed beyond the stage of interference with private acts; it now seeks to challenge even secret thoughts. And this enterprise, instead of being checked by a judiciary jealous of the common rights of man, is actually fostered by a judiciary that seems to have forgotten the elemental principles of justice and rules of law.

Here is an opportunity for a great newspaper that seeks to lead rather than to follow in politics, for the harsh observation of a Spaniard concerning us is a practical one that, "Not until a large and aggressive body of American citizens has formed the habit of loudly and immediately repudiating every abuse internal and external of governmental authority and every instance of mob intolerance will Americans as a nation show that 'decent respect for the opinions of mankind' necessary to reconquer the confidence of the only body of foreign opinion whose confidence is worth having." Here is an issue that needs only intelligent and persistent exploitation to arrest the attention of the whole country. It is fundamental and of high importance. It passes beyond any issue based upon transient abuses and transient remedies. It gets right down to the basic and real idea in the American view of the world and it seems to revive and vitalize that idea to the good of all of us. The American people still believe it to be a sound idea. Despite the efforts made to cause them to lose sight of it, they still show constantly that they have not forgotten it. Boldly to advocate it and to advocate it without compromise would be to appeal tremendously to their imaginations, and to enlist their ready and hearty support. Beside it all other political ideas are things of a day. If the nation holds fast to it, then all smaller problems may be faced with assurance and solved with decorum. But if ever it is permanently abandoned then the entire democratic process is doomed and even the least of political differences will lead inevitably to chaos.

A newspaper cannot hope to establish that issue—the primary, simple, easily comprehensible issue of fairness, justice and freedom—by mere argument and expostulation. The thing must be put into dramatic form. It must show the people what is going on, and not infrequently what is going on is going on in secret. It must devote itself to news gathering in new fields and against new difficulties. It must oppose to the last drop of its ink every effort to color the news. It must see clearly that the evil of injustice lies not in the importance of the victim, but lies in the lethargy of the spectators—that when a Mooney case* passes without indignant challenge the damage to all that is essentially American, to all justice and honesty and fair dealing among free men, is as great as the damage that would arise if a foreign invasion went unchallenged. And, demanding fairness to all men, it must itself be unquestionably fair. It cannot protest when striking steel-workers are deprived of the right of free assemblage and remain quiet when violent legislation impairs the inviolability of contract. It cannot denounce one man for robbing the government and stand by silent when another man is robbed by the government.

The programme seems vast, but in reality it is not so vast as it seems. It is actually quite simple. In such matters it is not necessary to fight alone. Immediately the issue is joined support will come from all directions. The generality of men, perhaps, are not fighters and they are seldom eager to make any sacrifice for the sake of fairness, justice and freedom, but fairness, justice and freedom are nevertheless words which arouse their enthusiasm, and they love a good fight for its own sake and, as a rule, are always ready to help the aggressor. But what would most

---

* The radical labor leader Tom Mooney had been imprisoned for his supposed role in the bombing of a pro-war parade in San Francisco in 1916. He was pardoned in 1939.

help to establish such an issue would be the general weakness of all the existing issues. Some of the existing issues merely array phrase against phrase. Others are outworn and decrepit. Nearly all that show any life whatsoever are just functions of the larger issue. In every case where Americans battle wholeheartedly for an idea, it is an idea which is rooted in the master idea of them all—the idea that it is wiser and better in this world to treat all men decently and squarely, and to trust to their good will and common sense for peace and order, rather than to their fears. This is the idea that has been damaged in the United States by the progress of events since the Civil War. It is in danger today of becoming extinct. To revive it is an enterprise that offers not only a great deal of interesting, pioneering work, but also promises a great and lasting benefit to the common weal.

The question of detailed and specific ways and means is not gone into here. All that is attempted is a rough survey and general outline of a broad scheme—a scheme to get around obvious political difficulties, to lift the *Sun* above the average level of newspapers and to make it count for more in American life and in American thought than it has counted for in the past. What is suggested is not Liberalism, at any rate in the usual sense of the word. Liberalism, as practically met with, is always a scheme of specific reforms, and far too often they are quite visionary reforms. The thing advocated here is simply a renewed fidelity to the idea which lies at the bottom of all other modern political ideas—the renaissance of a principle that is fundamental, of first importance and beyond logical challenge. Should it enlist the interest of those to whom it is presented, the details will work themselves out. Had man not made up his mind that he wanted to fly the aeroplane would never have been invented. The next four years will present an unexampled opportunity to a newspaper that sets itself free from the old formulae and tries honestly to get at the primary problems of the country. The *Sun* faces them in opposition, with its hands free and a clean slate to write upon. The opportunity is too tempting to lose.

THE *EVENING SUN*

The *Evening Sun* has not been mentioned, but it does not lie outside this inquiry. It cannot enter Washington on terms as favourable as those which confront the morning edition, and hence it will not have the same chance to exert an influence upon national affairs. But in its narrower field it faces an opportunity almost as fine. There is injustice in Baltimore as well as in the steel-works of Pennsylvania. There is room in Baltimore, as well as in America, for a newspaper ever alert, ever vigorous and ever absolutely independent. It is started on the right road. It can lend valuable aid to the *Sun* and it can get valuable aid from the *Sun*.

APPENDIX B

Gridiron Club Speech

(December 8, 1934)

Mr. President, Mr. Wright, and Fellow Subjects of the Reich:—

Put up this evening to speak for the Rotten Rich, I find myself under considerable embarrassment, mainly of a pecuniary nature. The fact is that we millionaire newspaper reporters have gone downhill like the rest of you, and I question that the net liquid assets of the Gridiron Club at this minute would be enough to make a pint of alphabet soup. The only thing we have left is liberty to doubt what we are told, and that isn't worth much any more, for what we are told is often incomprehensible and hence unanswerable, and even when we can understand it we are told the exact contrary the next day.

But this is not the time to complain, and indeed there is nothing to complain of. For if the flow of ideas is somewhat confusing, it must still be admitted that the show that goes with it is a very good one. Here we come upon one of the really sound and salient merits of the American republic. It is the most amusing country ever heard of in history. Amusing and good-humored. It tackles all of its most horrible problems in the manner of a young fellow necking a new girl, and even its wars produce quite as many comedians as heroes.

When I sit down with a European, which is very often, I am always struck by his solemnity. And when I go to Europe, which is more seldom, I am depressed by the general gloom. The people over there take politics very seriously and indeed tragically, though even the World War seems to have left many of them more or less alive, and more or less able to eat, drink and curse the government. But in this country we take it more lightly. Every American is born with full confidence that it will probably get well, even if you pick it. No matter how wildly he kicks up, he knows that the judge is likely to be lenient in the morning. And if, by any mischance, he finds himself in the hoosegow or even the deathhouse, he knows that he has an inalienable constitutional right to bust out.

I often hear people speculating about how long the New Deal will last. As I go about the country preaching in the Sunday-schools and visiting what we Baltimorons call the kaifs, I am asked the question constantly. I always answer by advising everyone who asks it to trust in Providence, which has always fooled us in the past. Or in the Constitution, which is still to be found in the National Museum, stuffed with excelsior and waiting for the Judgment Day. No doubt the bankers are there too, but what they are waiting for I don't know. I could name some other inmates, but refrain on advice of counsel. Which recalls that a learned judge called me up the other day to say that he had found an article of the Bill of Rights that was still in working order. I put his wild talk down to insomnia, the old curse of the judiciary, but he actually read it to me. It was Article III, reading as follows: "No soldier shall, in time of peace, be quartered in any house without the consent of the owner." Certainly this is something. Small oaks from little acorns grow. Some of these days the Constitution may stage a come-back.

But probably not yet. We are still on a honeymoon, and that honeymoon, for all I know, may last a geological epoch. There seems to be a high mortality in the Brain Trust, but its brains apparently renew themselves like the lost claws of a Chesapeake crab. Their functions, also, are not altogether dissimilar. Maybe we are in the darkness before the dawn. Maybe we are out on a limb. Maybe we are still going up. Maybe we have been up, and are now coming down. Maybe we don't know where we are, or how we got there, or how we are ever going to get back.

Some time ago, while Congress was in session, I had the pleasure of showing my pastor over Washington. I took him to the White House, and then down to the Capitol. He listened while both houses jawed away, and he peeped into the dreadful refrigerator of the Supreme Court. Then he said to me: "My boy, you cherish a chimera if you ever hope to see the smart fellows who now run this great republic turned out. They are ace high at the White House, and they carry the two Houses of Congress in their two vest pockets. I wouldn't go so far as to say that they influence the courts, but nevertheless you may be sure that the judges have heard of them, and know that they pack a wallop. The overwhelming majority of the American people are with them. Rid your mind of any notion that you will ever see them on their way. They will stick until the last galoot's ashore, and then go on sticking until the shore itself sinks beneath the waves of the sea, and is resolved into its primordial hydrogen, ptomaines and manganese. When you lift an impious hand at such colossi you make yourself ridiculous. You'll be 10,000 years old before they let go their hold and fade away."

The pastor's words made a powerful impression on me, and for a couple of weeks I kept off politics and devoted myself to writing about moral science. To this day I often think of them. But maybe I should add something. They were uttered a little less than three years ago, in the forepart of the year 1932, and the camorra that the pastor referred to was not the Brain Trust but the Anti-Saloon League.

NOTE

It is impossible to verify the entire text of President Roosevelt's reply to Mencken's remarks, which was neither taped nor transcribed. Among papers at the Franklin D. Roosevelt Library in Hyde Park, New York, however, are five typed pages labeled "Suggestions," to which the president added a number of comments in his own hand. An additional page of notes in his hand accompanies three typed pages of excerpts from Mencken's books, in which two passages are quoted from each of the following sources: *Prejudices: Sixth Series; Prejudices: Third Series; Notes on Democracy; Prejudices: Fifth Series;* and *Making a President,* and one from *In Defense of Women.* (*See* Notes, Speech to the Gridiron Club, Speech File 1582, Franklin D. Roosevelt Library.)

The first three paragraphs on page 1 of "Suggestions" read as follows:

I felicitate the preceding speaker, Mr. Henry L. Mencken, on the temperateness of his remarks and criticisms. I had really expected more fireworks, in the inimitable Mencken style. When he deals so gently with the achi[e]vements and misachievements of the present Administration I opine that we must be pretty good, after all.

But why is Mr. Mencken here tonight as the "opposition speaker"? My understanding of Gridiron dinners has been that there are only two unreported speakers—one a spokesman for the Administration temporarily in power, the other a critic thereof. Thus, through the years, the Gridiron Club has heard Republicans and Democrats and there has been much mirth as the oratorical rapiers flashed.

Has the Republican party reached such a paucity of talent that no one branded G.O.P. could be conscripted tonight to do his stuff? How is Mr. Mencken branded? I never regarded hi[m] as either a Democrat or a Republican. After following his writings I'd rather list him as a follower of that famous old Irishman who landed on our shores some years ago and announced, as he got off the boat, "I don't know what sort of government you've got over here, but whatever it is I'm agin it."

Later in his talk, the president turned Mencken's own commentary upon American journalists against him. According to Carl Bode's *Mencken* (Carbondale: Southern Illinois University Press, 1969), the president read, without first identifying the source, from *Prejudices: Sixth Series:* "Most of the evils that continue to beset American journalism today, in truth, are not due to the rascality of the owners nor even to the Kiwanian bombast of business managers, but simply and solely to the stupidity, cowardice and Philistinism of the working newspaper men." (Further quotation followed, and, at the end of his speech, the president remarked that such commentary had been written by none other than his "old friend Henry Mencken.")

EPILOGUE

Mencken's farewell to the *Sunpapers* in 1941 proved premature. During those seven years before he ascended the stage again, a variety of tasks filled his days. In fact, the productivity of his seventh decade—with the completion of the *Days* trilogy, the appearance of *A New Dictionary of Quotations,* and the publication of the two supplements to *The American Language*—gave him considerable satisfaction. Moreover, in addition to the writing consigned to time-lock, he published several magazine pieces that rank with his finest writing.

Mencken was quite conscious of his own mortality—and the country's morbidity. He still railed, at times, about the idiocy of the contemporary scene. On other occasions he assumed a very different role in which he felt eminently comfortable: the American elegist who looked back gratefully upon a better day. In the collected edition of the *Days* trilogy, Mencken talked about what his native land had lost and what, he hoped, his art could preserve:

> As the shadows close in we can at least recall that there was a time when people could spend weeks, months and even years without being badgered, bilked or alarmed. . . . The human race . . . had a better time in the days when I was a boy, and also in the days when I was a young newspaper reporter, and some of that better time even slopped over into the first half of the space between the two World Wars. I enjoyed myself immensely, and all I try to do here is to convey some of my joy to the nobility and gentry of this once great and happy Republic, now only a dismal burlesque of its former self.[1]

A half century before, this role would have seemed unthinkable—Mencken as Prospero waving his wand.

But there was still, as there had always been, the lure of the newspaper. Mencken managed to resist in 1944 when Paul Patterson invited him to attend the presidential conventions as a spectator. "I don't think that would be fair to the paper," Mencken explained to Henry Hyde. "Moreover it would be almost impossible for me to sit beside the battle and not barge in."[2] Four years later, though, Mencken returned to his old stand and covered the three presidential conventions in Philadelphia.[3] As always, this gaudy spectacle, the American political animal in the flesh, gave him a great deal of fun.

Beginning in August 1948, Mencken wrote sixteen more columns for the *Sun*. His final piece, which ran on November 9, discussed something far more important than the follies of democracy's electoral system. Blacks and whites had been arrested for playing tennis together in Baltimore's city-owned Druid Hill Park. Appalled by such bigotry, Mencken announced that "it is astounding to find so much of the spirit of the Georgia Cracker surviving in the Maryland Free State." He declared that "it is high time that all such relics of Ku Kluxry be wiped out in Maryland."[4] It is appropriate that this final column dealt, as had so much of his previous writing, with civil liberty.

Exactly two weeks later, Mencken suffered a stroke that robbed him of his ability to read and write. In December 1949, he resigned from the board of directors of the A. S. Abell Company; the next year, the Saturday Night Club disbanded. The shadows had finally engulfed this man of huge gifts and extraordinary energy, and Mencken endured more than seven years of what Dr. Carl Bode has so appropriately called "nighttime at Hollins Street."[5] On January 29, 1956, about twenty weeks past his seventy-fifth birthday, Mencken died in his sleep of a coronary occlusion.

Once more, he tried to manage his affairs from the grave; he was as punctilious about commentary on his passing as he had been about the disposition of his papers. For decades the story has circulated that Mencken left a colorful command: "Don't overplay it." Actually, his instructions, written on June 1, 1943 and then locked away, were considerably more prosaic: "Save in the event that the circumstances of my death make necessary a news story, it is my earnest request to my old colleagues of the *Sunpapers* that they print only a very brief announcement of it, with no attempt at a biographical sketch, no portrait, and no editorial."[6] Mencken perhaps suspected that his request could not be honored. On Monday, January 30, 1956, the *Sun* ran a photograph and three stories on the front page, plus additional stories and a page of photographs inside; the *Evening Sun* offered a lengthy retrospective and an editorial. The *Sun*'s editorial applauded the author—Mencken was a "superb technician" who was a "model for a whole generation of aspiring young writers"—as well as the man: "To many outsiders who had been scourged by his pen, he was the embodiment of evil . . . but to those of his colleagues who knew that his battle was waged against sham and hypocrisy and not against individuals as such, he was simple, compassionate and even humble."[7] Perhaps the most eloquent obituary by any of Mencken's former journalistic colleagues was written by Gerald Johnson, whom Mencken had published in the *Mercury* and brought to the *Sunpapers* three decades before. On February 11, Johnson used the *Saturday Review of Literature* to give thanks for the good times and to celebrate this writer and his extraordinary vitality. Mencken "caused a zest for life to be renewed in other men," Johnson remarked in a poignant trope that Mencken would have appreciated; "[he] touched the dull fabric of our days and gave it a silken sheen."[8]

NOTES

1. Mencken, "Author's Note," in *The Days of H. L. Mencken: Happy Days, Newspaper Days, Heathen Days* (New York: Knopf, 1947), vi.

2. Mencken to Henry Hyde, June 15, 1944, in "Documents Relating to the Baltimore *Sunpapers*," box 9 (Enoch Pratt Free Library).

3. These columns are collected in Joseph Goulden, *Mencken's Last Campaign: H. L. Mencken on the 1948 Election* (Washington, D.C.: New Republic Book Company, 1976).

4. Mencken, "Equal Rights in Parks: Mencken Calls Tennis Order Silly, Nefarious," Baltimore *Sun*, November 9, 1948.

5. Carl Bode, *Mencken* (Carbondale: Southern Illinois University Press, 1969), Chapter 18.

6. This letter is now housed at the Enoch Pratt Free Library.

7. "Henry Louis Mencken," Baltimore *Sun*, January 30, 1956, editorial page.

8. Gerald W. Johnson, "H. L. Mencken, 1880–1956," *Saturday Review of Literature* 39:12–13 (February 11, 1956); reprinted in Johnson, *America-Watching* (Baltimore: Stemmer House, 1976), 199–202.

ACKNOWLEDGMENTS

A number of able and generous people have helped with the preparation of this volume. Mrs. Averil Kadis, director of public relations at the Enoch Pratt Free Library in Baltimore, has proven, as is her wont, most knowledgeable and gracious from the inception of this project. Dr. Robert J. Brugger, history editor of the Johns Hopkins University Press, is wise and patient and highly skilled; a fine writer himself, he has offered invaluable counsel at every stage of this project. Jeanne Pinault copy-edited the manuscript; the final text is better for her punctilious queries and suggestions. John Innes of Baltimore, a specialist in the German language, generously translated Mencken's numerous German terms into English.

A variety of authors and newspaper people in Baltimore, all possessing long and thorough familiarity with Mencken's canon, generously examined the editorial apparatus and offered eminently useful suggestions. More than once, they saved us from error. We thus are grateful to Harold A. Williams, James H. Bready, Charles A. Fecher, Frederick N. Rasmussen, and Arthur J. Gutman. We also owe debts, in various ways, to William Manchester, Russell Baker, Gwinn Owens, Philip Wagner, Richard Hart, and Olga Owens.

Dr. Edward C. Papenfuse kindly provided information about the meeting of the Gridiron Club in Washington, D. C., on December 8, 1934. Marion Elizabeth Rodgers generously tracked down the source for the epigraph to the Introduction. Tina Entzminger, Anne Coletta, Chris Drennen, and Sara Clemence provided valuable help with proofreading.

For many decades, Mencken had a warm relationship with the Enoch Pratt Free Library and was justifiably grateful for the skill of its employees. The editors are similarly grateful to those at the library who have contributed information about a variety of subjects. John Sondheim, head of special collections, provided assistance throughout the project. We are thankful to the members of the Humanities Department—Neil Jordahl (head), Faye Houston, Wilbur McGill, Charlotte Gettes, and Thomas Himmel—as well as to Shirley Viviano, Eleanor Swidan, Michael Donnelly, and Ralph Clayton. This volume has benefited a good deal from their skill, diligence, and generosity.

Books are rarely the product of authors laboring in the proverbial ivory tower; inevitably, families sacrifice a good deal during the process. We are grateful for the help and advice given by Ann Henley, busy with a Sara Haardt book of her own as this one was in progress, and we particularly appreciate the patience and editorial assistance of Carol Fitzpatrick. She was writing yet another of her own books while this one was in progress, and she maintained her good humor in the face of production deadlines, a lively toddler, and a husband who was paying more attention to Mencken's Baltimore than to his own.

INDEX

Index

Library of Congress Cataloging-in-Publication Data

Mencken, H. L. (Henry Louis), 1880–1956.
   Thirty-five years of newspaper work / H. L. Mencken ; edited and with an introduc-
tion by Fred Hobson, Vincent Fitzpatrick, Bradford Jacobs.
     p.   cm.
   ISBN 0-8018-4791-5
   1. Mencken, H. L. (Henry Louis), 1880–1956—Knowledge—Communications.
2. Authors, American—20th century—Biography.   3. Journalists—United States—
Biography.   I. Hobson, Fred C., 1943–   .   II. Fitzpatrick, Vincent.   III. Jacobs,
Bradford.   IV. Title.
PS3525.E43Z475 1994
818'.5209—dc20
[B]   94-2077